BALTIC INDEPENDENCE
AND RUSSIAN EMPIRE

BALTIC
INDEPENDENCE
AND
RUSSIAN
EMPIRE

Walter C. Clemens, Jr.
Professor of Political Science
Boston University

ST. MARTIN'S PRESS
NEW YORK

All rights reserved. For information, write:
Scholarly and Reference Division,
St. Martin's Press, Inc.,
175 Fifth Avenue, New York, NY 10010
First published in the United States of America in 1991
Printed in the United States
ISBN 0-312-04806-8

Library of Congress Cataloging-in-Publication Data
Clemens, Walter C.
Baltic independence and Russian empire / Walter C. Clemens, Jr.
    p. cm.
Includes index.
ISBN 0-312-04806-8
1. Baltic States — History — Autonomy and independence movements.
2. Soviet Union — History — Autonomy and independence movements.
3. Soviet Union — History — 1953- I. Title.
DK502.7C54 1991 947'.4085 — dc20   90-40681
                                              CIP

why would they say Hades

Kalevipoeg's strength is broken. Nonetheless he can still fight the devils and block with his legless body the Gate to Hades. A spell is cast that conjures Kalevipoeg's hand so he cannot remove it from the rocky face. Kalevipoeg shakes and rends the walls so that they tremble. A peal of thunder shudders the vaults of the underworld. In vain: Kalevipoeg is forged to the rocks and cannot pull away.

But one day an age will dawn when....
A bright flame bursts forth to free
His hand from the vise of stone—
Then Kalev's son will return home
To bring happiness to his children
and build Estonia's life anew.

— *Kalevipoeg*

For Rose Elizabeth, Olivia Ellen, Nastenka, Tõnis, and Pui Lam

Contents

Acknowledgments

interesting spelling

The author is indebted to many kind and knowledgeable persons in the Baltic, in Russia, and in North America who have shared their knowledge and viewpoints with him. They include Viacheslav Ivanov and other editors of *Sovetskaia Estoniia*; Priit Järve, Tiiu Pohl, and other scholars at the Estonian Academy of Sciences; various scholars and political activists from different organizations cited in the text who spoke with the author during visits to the Baltic and Russia in January 1988, March 1989, and March 1990. The 1989 visit was sponsored by the Institute for World Economic and International Relations in Moscow; the second, by the Estonian Academy of Sciences. Järve and Pohl also critiqued portions of the manuscript.

Stimulation, critiques, and moral support came also from Karl Deutsch, Dov Ronen, Benjamin Schwartz, and other participants in the Ethnic Claims and the State seminars at the Center for International Affairs, Harvard University, in 1989; from Alexander J. Motyl and the Columbia University Nationalities and Siberian Studies Program; from Uri Ra'anan, Igor Lukes, and Ladislaw Bittman at Boston University.

Rein Taagepera, University of California at Irvine, and Toivo U. Raun, Indiana University, provided detailed critiques of the manuscript as it evolved. Taagepera shared his files as well as his own writings on Estonia with me, even faxing comments on various queries. Mari-Ann Rikken and Jaak Juhansoo of the Estonian American National Council provided valuable documents and suggestions. Tönu Parming, University of Toronto, also made useful comments and sent drafts of his own writings. The editors of *Kodumaa* in Tallinn sent back copies of *Homeland* difficult to obtain elsewhere.

This book depends primarily upon primary and secondary sources in English, Russian, and German. Many but by no means all relevant Baltic documents and secondary works have been translated into these languages. Many Baltic materials are simply not available in Western — or any — libraries, because glasnost has unleashed a flood of periodical literature throughout the

Baltic and Russian empire generally. These problems have been partially alleviated by the generosity and diligence of many Balts, representing a variety of political standpoints, who have discussed parts of this book with the author, contributed critiques, and even translated some relevant documents. Most assistance has come from Estonians, the focus of the study, but valuable discussions have also been conducted with Latvians and Lithuanians.

The compilers of the *Current Digest of the Soviet Press*, the Foreign Broadcast Information Service, Daily Report, and Radio Liberty's Report on the USSR have created a body of information without which this study would have been impossible.

A number of Boston University students have also helped with the research: Andrei V. Bell, Lisa Ferrari, Lisa Masiello, Mark Jacobson, and Isabelle Turci.

Boston University's Graduate School provided funds for travel to the USSR. Joseph Nye and the Harvard Center for Science and International Affairs contributed an intellectual milieu in which hard thinking, seasoned by many disciplines and viewpoints, could prosper.

None of the expert and generous persons who have offered comments and suggestions is likely to be entirely satisfied with the book that has emerged. But their efforts have helped to make it more factually accurate and more balanced in its judgments.

Earlier versions of some chapters have been published in the Christian Science Monitor, *National Interest*, the *New York Times*, the *Wall Street Journal, World Monitor*, and in Uri Ra'anan, ed., *The Soviet Empire: The Challenge of National and Democratic Movements* (Lexington Books, 1990).

Simon Winder at St. Martin's Press and Macmillan offered strong encouragement and practical assistance. Lisa Goldberg prepared the manuscript for publication. Mark Jacobson did the index.

My wife, Lai-Lin Ho Clemens, has nurtured me and the project in countless ways.

All humanity is indebted to those Balts and Russians whose courage, persistence, and long-range vision have inspired this study. They have demonstrated that, against tough odds, the human condition can be improved. The book is dedicated to the grandchild of two such Russians, Valery and Milana Riabskii; my own grandchildren; and to their peers, a Russian-Estonian boy and my niece in Hong Kong, with the hope that they can live in a free and humane world.

Glossary

CC: Central Committee

CoCom: Coordinating Committee on Multilateral Export Controls

Comecon: Council of Mutual Economic Assistance

CP: Communist Party

CPSU: Communist Party of the Soviet Union

CPE: Communist Party of Estonia

CPL: Communist Party of Latvia

CPSU: Communist Party of the Soviet Union

CSCE: Conference on Security and Cooperation in Europe

ENIP: Estonian National Independence Party

GATT: General Agreement on Tariffs and Trade

Glasnost: Giving voice, expressing the truth, at least within current limits of CPSU tolerance

GNP: gross national product

IME: Self-Managing Estonia

Intermovement: "International" political organization in Estonia

Interdependence: Mutual vulnerability and mutual sensitivity

IRG: Interregional Group in USSR Congress of People's Deputies

Kto kovo?: Leninist conception that politics is a zero-sum contest

LCP: Lithuanian Communist Party

Maapäev: Estonian National Council elected in 1917

MVD: Ministry of Internal Affairs

NATO: North Atlantic Treaty Organization

Nomenklatura: List of persons eligible for ranking jobs in the Soviet system

Perestroika: M. S. Gorbachev's plan to restructure the economy and other aspects of Soviet life

PFE: Popular Front of Estonia

PFL: Popular Front of Latvia

Realpolitik: Political realism, power politics

RSFSR: Russian Soviet Federative Socialist Republic

Sajudis: Lithuanian Movement for Restructuring

Samizdat: "Self-publishing"; unofficial carbon copies; reproduction by mimeographing, xeroxing, photocopying, etc.

SSR: Soviet Socialist Republic

TVD: Theater of Military Operations for Soviet Armed Forces

Value-claiming: Acting or negotiating to obtain unilateral gains

Value-creating: Acting or negotiating to generate joint gains

WTO: Warsaw Treaty Organization or Warsaw Pact

Zero-sum relations: Relationships in which the gains of one side equal the losses of the other

Note: Transliterations from the Russian follow a simplified version of the Library of Congress system except for familiar names such as Trotsky and words such as glasnost. An attempt has been made to restore Baltic names and words to their original spelling when taken from Russian-language texts. Some diacritical markings in Baltic words have, with regrets, been omitted.

Introduction

O my fatherland, my people!
What is there that could be done
so that everything would sooner,
sooner be just as it should?

This verse, from "A Song of Impatience," by Estonian poet August Sang, was written in 1953 but published only in 1962.[1] Sang made his artistic debut in the 1930s, when Estonia — like Latvia and Lithuania — was an independent republic. He endured the subsequent Stalinist terror in silence and then reemerged in the 1960s. His career paralleled that of his people. Like them, Sang was also tied to the culture of Western Europe and Russia. He translated not just Goethe, Molière, Heine, and Brecht but also Russian poet Nikolai Nekrasov. *Who is that?*

The Baltic and other nations of the USSR became like the stallion Gulsary in the short story by Kirghiz writer Chinghiz Aitmatov, *Farewell Gulsary!* Nurtured by a free, passionate, and knowledgeable trainer, Tanabai, Gulsary thrived. When he was appropriated by the greedy, stupid, and vain Communist chairman of a collective farm, the stallion balked. When he broke powerful chains and tried to run home to Tanabai, the chairman had Gulsary castrated. Years later, when Tanabai again met Gulsary, both were broken in spirit and body. *odd moment of central Asian resistance*

Gulsary's story provides a powerful metaphor for the fate that befell not only the Kirghiz but most nations of the USSR — including the Russians. Indeed, a Soviet review of Aitmatov's work compares it with novels and verses mourning the destruction of Russian culture, for example, the "village poet" Valentin Rasputin's *Farewell to Matëra*, a community whose name evokes an image of "Mother."[2]

In the last decade of the millennium the Soviet empire collapses. In the late 1980s many Russians joined Balts and other peoples subject to the USSR in seeking liberation from empire. In 1990 Boris Yeltsin, President of the Russian Republic, pushed for radical economic reform within Russia, pressuring "all-Union" institutions to adapt or be left behind. World chess champion Gary Kasparov chose to play with a Soviet Russian flag at his side rather than that of the USSR. Novelist Aleksandr Solzhenitsyn urged that Russia and the other two Slavic republics stay together, unburdening themselves of the other border republics. In the Ukraine, however, tens of thousands marched through Kiev, calling for greater independence. "Mother Moscow: We want to be orphans," declared one of their banners. Millions of other Ukrainian residents preferred close ties with Moscow. How even "Russia" would look at the end of the decade was unclear, because many of the peoples within its borders — Yakuts and others — also wanted control over their own destinies.

Why then does this book address "Baltic independence and *Russian* empire?" First, because Balts have been subject to Russian emperors and commissars for most of the last three centuries, excluding parts of the eighteenth century and the years 1918-1940. Second, because few Russians actively tried to divest Russia of these imperial responsibilities until the late 1980s. Third, because the Soviet empire has been built upon Russian hegemony. Even when directed by a Georgian, the empire operated mainly through Russians who headed all-Union enterprises or stood immediately behind "first" party secretaries in each republic. It used and extended the domain of the Russian language and culture, even while promising to respect local cultures. Fourth, Russia's empire was not just a legal apparatus but a living organism, represented by Russian soldiers and settlers who made up a large fraction of the population in the Baltic and many other republics.

In the 1980s the movement for Baltic independence became a battering ram against the Russian empire. Balts' demands and actions encouraged other Soviet subjects to rise up against Moscow. The Baltic way provided an example of nonviolent resistance that could be emulated not only within the USSR but wherever one set of humans wants to throw off the yoke of another.

Many of the same complaints that Balts made against the Kremlin articulated grievances felt by other Soviet subjects including Russians. By 1990 the term "Kremlin" symbolized the rule of all-Union institutions over Russia and the other republics. It represented those who tried to preserve the Union, such as Soviet President Mikhail S. Gorbachev, as against Russian President Boris Yeltsin and the leaders of most other republics within the erstwhile union. In 1990 Balts found an ally in the Russian president against all-Union Russians in the Kremlin.

So much happened in little more than a decade! In the 1970s it appeared to one astute observer that the Estonians, Latvians, and Lithuanians were on the way to physical and cultural extinction. The Baltic nations perceived this danger, but did nothing to prevent it. "Faced with this fate, the Baltic nationalities seem not even able to react by forming a Baltic bloc. Each becomes weaker still by isolating itself in its particularism and the things which separate it historically from the other nations in the region." Although they are the most modern, the most Western, and the least sovietized of all nations in the USSR, "none of this can impede the Baltic peoples from advancing toward the annihilation of their nations." [3]

By the late 1980s this forecast seemed far off target. Why? This book explores the factors—in the Baltic, in the Soviet Union as a whole, and worldwide—that shaped the turnaround. It studies the roots and organizational framework of Baltic reformers; their goals and methods; the responses of authorities in Moscow to Baltic demands. Finally, it surveys alternative models that might accommodate the claims and counterclaims, the felt needs of the conflicting parties.

The "Balts" on which this book focuses are the Estonians, Latvians, and Lithuanians—peoples whose independent states became Union Republics of the Soviet Union in 1940. Other nations also live on the shores of the Baltic—Germans, Danes, Swedes, Poles, Finns, as well as Russians and smaller peoples such as the Karelians, first cousins of Finns and Estonians. The "Baltic" on which we concentrate is known to Russians as *Pribaltika*, the region next to the Baltic Sea.

The book's underlying hypothesis is that exploitative, zero-sum policies can net short-term gains (at least for some segments of the exploiting society), but that they tend to backfire over time, creating greater burdens than profits for the exploiter. Put another way, the optimal way to pursue national objectives is by creating values with other partners—not by claiming values in a one-sided way. [4] Value-creating strategies are difficult to conceive and to work out. They depend ultimately upon reciprocity, although a large power such as

Russia can initiate them far easier than can smaller ones such as the Baltic countries.

This hypothesis helps explain why empires become too costly for metropoles to sustain. Ancient empires could and did endure longer than modern. The time period in which exploitation can pay has shrunk in our age of rapid communication and global interdependence. Real influence and prosperity depend increasingly upon quick and efficient communication, on coordination of complementary assets, on adaptation to new opportunities and challenges. Any diversion of resources to repression or deception detracts from optimal performance.

Modern alliances and empires resemble businesses, where "competitive advantage grows fundamentally out of the value a firm is able to create for its buyers." [5] United States leadership in the West has been accepted because it helped generate values for other system members; Soviet leadership in the East has collapsed because it took rather than created values for Moscow's vassals.

For Russians as for Balts, and probably for all nations, there was a profound truth in the "mutual aid" thesis developed by Pëtr Kropotkin to rebut the simplistic idea that evolution is the survival of the fittest. Kropotkin found that, in the human as in the animal kingdom, the groups in which individual struggle was reduced to its narrowest limits, and the practice of mutual aid had attained the greatest development, were the most prosperous "and the most open to further progress. The mutual protection which is obtained in this case, the possibility of attaining old age and of accumulating experience, the higher intellectual development, and the further growth of sociable habits, secure the maintenance of the species, its extension, and its further progressive evolution. The unsociable species, on the contrary, are doomed to decay." [6]

Kropotkin's thesis helps to explain why the Russian empire, still expanding in the 1970s, ran out of steam and contracted in the late 1980s. Moscow had depleted all assets that could be marshalled easily for "extensive development" and was finally compelled to depend upon the quality rather than the quantity of its productive assets. The ultimate source of failure was ideological and moral rather than material: The Kremlin leadership had failed to cultivate a sentiment of mutual aid and value-creating between itself and its subjects — Russians and border peoples. Communists (abroad as well as in Russia) were wounded, even crippled by their dedication to the mutual distrust of zero-sum *what?*

politics, by their acceptance of Lenin's axiom, *Kto kovo?*, "Who will do in whom?" This world view was probably useful when the Bolsheviks struggled against tsarism; it was a liability when coping with the demands of the late twentieth century.[7]

value—claiming id

The peoples located between Russia and Western Europe also disregarded Kropotkin to their peril. Value-claiming rather than mutual aid has often been the rule for their policymakers, both at home and abroad. "Beggar thy neighbor" has been practiced more than "help one another." Mutual distrust has often weakened them as they faced threats from both sides, as in the 1930s. Each has often sought to save itself even if its neighbors were devoured. To be sure, Western Europeans and Americans often behaved in similar fashion until they were sobered by Hitler and Stalin. Only since the late 1940s have the Western nations and Japan managed to subdue distrust and zero-sum competition with cooperation and trade. This spiritual revolution underlay their material transformation. *(not present)*

If the West followed the narrow precepts of Social Darwinism, it too might have imploded or exploded. In this century, however, Western societies have come to balance the imperatives of individual freedom with those of communal welfare. Adam Smith and John Locke, tempered by the Fabians, Henry Ford, and John Maynard Keynes, have won out over Marx and Lenin. *I don't get too excited*

As the trajectory of Soviet power ebbed in the late 1970s and the 1980s, the life force of Balts—bubbling below the surface even in earlier times— emerged and became stronger. The small Baltic peoples, none larger than a few million souls, acquired new hope and determination that their genes and their cultures would flourish in the same lands where their ancestors had lived for millennia.

As the three Baltic nations mounted active campaigns to control their own destinies, mutual aid became a reality in the Baltic. Increasingly, Estonians, Latvians, and Lithuanians cooperated with one another and with other dissident forces in Russia and other border lands. Steadfast and persistent against a Leviathan, their efforts in the late 1980s-early 1990s became a near-perfect model for nonviolent resistance and nonviolent assertion of national self-determination against alien rule.

Still, Kropotkin's message might go unheeded. First, the Kremlin might attempt to reassert its hegemony by force—a formula for short-term victory and long-term backlash. Second, if the Baltic republics became independent, the Kremlin and the Balts might pursue mutual gain or they could try to sever all ties in a fury of national self-righteousness. Within each republic, nationalist reformers might drop their common stance and pursue zero-sum politics among themselves and/or with the Russian and other settlers. Some might call for deportation of non-Balts.

While President Gorbachev's glasnost campaigns stimulated strife among Russians and other nations of the USSR, they also contributed to a new willingness to admit past mistakes. Ethnic slurs could deepen or open wounds, but frank communication was probably essential to ethnic understanding and to problem-solving. Even Baltic Communists came to recognize that Soviet Russian dominion, executed mainly by local Communists, had done more harm than good for the Baltic peoples. As Vaino Väljas, First Secretary of the Estonian Communist Party put it in May 1989: "As a result of the nationalities policy during [Stalin's] personality cult and stagnation [of the Brezhnev years], the potential for development arising from Soviet society's national diversity is to a very considerable extent unrealized. The critical situation stemming from this in a number of regions attests that the future fate of the USSR as a multinational society largely depends on how far its national state structure can ensure coordination between the interests of sovereign republics and their peoples and ensure their real interest in the Union of Soviet Socialist Republics."

Väljas also warned the Estonian Party's Central Committee: "Leftist errors on the nationalities question and the repudiation of people's desires for sovereignty have always undermined the Estonian Communists' prestige." [8]

An even more radical nostra culpa was uttered by Lithuanian Communist leaders in early 1990.[9] Latvian Communists were slower to make such admissions, but the Latvian public had long blamed them and Moscow for abuses and misguided policies of all kinds.

Indeed, it was my first visit to the Baltic—to Riga, capital of Latvia, in early 1959—that alerted me to the profound tension between occupiers and occupied in that part of the world. The trip occurred shortly after Soviet authorities lifted the ban on travel by foreigners to the Baltic capitals. Then an exchange student at Moscow State University, I had been accustomed to intensive surveillance. But this did not prepare me for what happened in Riga.

There, four to five tails accompanied me most of the time, even peering through binoculars from an adjoining building into my hotel room. I gathered that the Soviets were trying to hide something. If they wished to intimidate, they succeeded, and I did not speak to any Latvians except for elementary necessities.

During that 1958-1959 school year the American students' basketball team at Moscow University needed reinforcements. Our "firemen" were all from the Baltic. Their aggressive style against Russians won us a certain notoriety. The Russians called us *kanadskie khokeiisti* — "Canadian hockey players." The only student in Moscow who openly said he wanted to defect was a Balt.

Another revealing incident occurred when I sat next to two Estonians at breakfast in a Yalta hotel in 1969. Noticing that we had only spoons, I asked the Russian waitress to bring us knives and forks. "If we did that," the Estonians said, "she would call us Fascists."

Imagine my surprise then when, visiting Tallinn, Estonia in 1988, I read a candid essay about Estonian-Russian conflicts in the Russian-language newspaper of the Estonian Communist Party (ECP) and government, *Sovetskaia Estoniia*.[10] My surprise was still greater when, having phoned the newspaper asking to talk with the article's author, he and an editor showed up at my hotel and embarked on a broad-ranging discussion that went on for a few hours. The surprise continued the following day when the paper sent a car to the hotel so that four Boston University students and I could visit its offices and meet with the staff. Openness, however, had limits, and the entire editorial staff told one of the students he erred in thinking that there had been any Estonian guerrilla opposition to Soviet rule after 1945, even though the realities of partisan warfare in the Baltic are well established.[1]

By 1989 a new kind of surprise arose: a new capacity in the Soviet regime to tolerate sharp challenges on many fronts — democratic critiques of Gorbachev's accumulated powers, demands by striking miners for free trade unions, nationalist calls for "sovereignty" and even "independence" in the Baltic and elsewhere. Instead of trying to hide this kind of thing from me when I visited the Institute of World Economics and International Relations (IMEMO) in Moscow, the Institute arranged for me to make another trip to Estonia, accompanied by Boris Messiia, where he and I were taken by Tiiu

Pohl, of the Estonian Academy of Sciences, to meet leaders and thinkers of the new Estonia.

In 1990 the pace of change throughout the Baltic and all of East Central Europe quickened, some of which I observed in new visits to the Baltic and Russia.

The determination of President Gorbachev and his supporters to restructure Soviet life presented opportunity as well as danger to the Balts and others long subject to Soviet rule. The evolution of the Soviet "nationality question" would shape and be shaped by the entire fabric of East-West relations.

The future of Estonia, Latvia, and Lithuania of course was linked to that of the entire Russian empire — overseas, in Eastern Europe, and within official Soviet borders. The precedents of other imperial systems — Athenian, Roman, Ottoman, Austro-Hungarian, Tsarist, British, et al. — suggested alternative courses for the evolution and devolution of empire.

In the late 1980s many Balts wondered to what realistic model they could aspire. Many concluded: Less than Hungary would be too little; to be like Finland would be too much. As Hungary itself became more like Finland, however, new possibilities arose. As the Third Rome shrank and a new Europe arose, other visions could be entertained.

What approach might permit all sides — the Balts, the Russians, the former East bloc and West Europeans — to create values together instead of claiming them against one another? How might they best enhance their security, economic, cultural, and other objectives? Perhaps an Austrian model would serve the interests of all parties. A chain of lightly armed, nonaligned nations between Russia and the West could provide a transmission belt through which trade could flow and ideas be exchanged, breathing new life into a region that has endured a long stagnation. It could satisfy the security interests of all parties at a time when the scientific-technological and information revolutions have altered the nature of power, influence, and well being.

Soviet rule in Eastern Europe and in every border republic has rested on coercion. In our age of escalating interdependencies, continued coercion is inefficient and, over time, untenable. Russia's deepest needs are security, prosperity, and cultural vitality, none of which requires a feudal empire.

Russian nationalists want to hold on to empire, but at some point they may not be able to contain the forces of liberation. They must weigh the costs and losses entailed in repression with the likely gains from permitting freedom and prosperity to return to the lands between Russia and Western Europe. Past Soviet regimes have welcomed neutrality and nonalignment in countries they could not dominate and that might otherwise drift westward. Sweden, Austria, and Switzerland are among the neutral and prosperous nations that some Soviets — even Russians — see as models for their own evolution.

For Russia to be accepted in what President Gorbachev called "our common European home," Moscow could do no better than to foster a zone of free states between Russia and the European Community. Such a step would ease divisions between the "First" and "Second" Worlds, helping them pool strengths and experiences to cope with the waves of environmental and other problems that threaten civilization and even human survival.

The United States never recognized Moscow's 1940 annexation of the Baltic. It kept alive the idea that there are "captive nations" within and beyond Soviet borders. The United States and other Western countries will continue to need a thoughtful, skillful, and humane blend of firmness and conciliation as the Soviet empire contracts. The West can play only a supporting role as Baltic and other peoples seek national self-determination, but Western diplomacy can draw from a wide range of legal, moral, economic, political, military, and other assets. Washington and its partners could underscore the advantages to all sides that could flow from creating a zone of neutral, lightly armed states in the Baltic and other parts of East Central Europe.

NOTES

1. Translation of *Laul Cärsitusest* in George Kurman, "Estonian Literature," in Tönu Parming and Elmar Järvesoo, eds., *A Case Study of a Soviet Republic: The Estonian SSR* (Boulder, Colo.: Westview, 1978), pp. 247-80, at p. 255.
2. Aleksandr Kvatov in his review essay, "The Moral Inquietude of a Humanist," in a collection of Aitmatov's works, *Rannie zhuravli* [and others] (Leningrad: Lenizdat, 1982), pp. 471-79, at p. 478.
3. Hélène Carrère d'Encausse, *Decline of an Empire: The Soviet Socialist Republics in Revolt* (New York: Harper, 1981; first published in France in 1978 under the title *L'Empire éclaté*), p. 268.

4. Value-claiming and value-creating are analyzed by David A. Lax and James K. Sebenius in *The Manager as Negotiator: Bargaining for Cooperation and Competitive Gain* (New York: Free Press, 1986). The dichotomy is easier to uphold in theory than to identify in practice, where elements of both approaches often overlap. The two poles probably stem in part from contradictory interpretations of Darwinism. Rugged individualists say that evolution is shaped by the struggle of the fittest.

5. See Michael E. Porter, *Competitive Advantage: Creating and Sustaining Superior Performance* (New York: Free Press, 1985), p. xvi.

6. Pëtr Kropotkin, *Mutual Aid* (London, 1902; Boston: Extending Horizon Books, 1955), pp. 293ff.

7. See the analysis of Soviet achievements and failures, and underlying reasons for them, in Walter C. Clemens, Jr., *Can Russia Change? The USSR Confronts Global Interdependence* (Boston: Unwin Hyman, 1990), chap. 1.

8. Speech by Väljas to 14th Estonian Communist Party Central Committee plenum, 4 May 1989 in *Sovetskaia Estoniia*, 5 May 1989, pp. 1-3.

9. See, for example, the program adopted by the Communist Party of Lithuania (*Sovetskaia Litva*, 5 January 1990, pp. 1, 2) and many speeches at its December 1989 congress.

10. L. Sher, "Intelligentnost' i internatsionalizm," *Sovetskaia Estoniia*, 6 January 1988, p. 2.

11. See Romuald J. Misiunas and Rein Taagepera, *The Baltic States: Years of Dependence, 1940-1980* (Berkeley: University of California Press, 1983), pp. 81-91, 99-100, 276-80.

1

Independence versus Empire: Why and How

Why were the Baltic republics the first in the USSR to apply real pressure on Moscow for more independence? How did they pursue their struggle? Why did the Kremlin relax its grip? What was at stake for the USSR in the changes taking place? Did these developments support or challenge theories advanced about nationalism, imperialism, bargaining, social change? The answers to such questions are complex. The evidence to begin answering them is marshalled in the chapters that follow. In this chapter we abstract from the historical detail to underscore what appear as the main trends.

How Did the Last Become the First?

Many factors combined to create a powerful synergy for liberation:

1. Estonia, Latvia, and Lithuania were the last independent nations to become Soviet Socialist Republics, in 1940. Habits of compliance with Kremlin diktat had a shorter history among these peoples than elsewhere in the Russian empire. To be sure, Balts had been subjugated by a variety of foreign rulers for many centuries. But they challenged alien rule in the nineteenth century and then cast it off during a generation of independence, 1918-1940.

2. Unlike any other nationalities of the USSR, the three Baltic peoples already had the experience of liberating themselves from Russian dominion and maintaining their independence for more than two decades. The other border peoples experienced at most a few years of independence after 1917.

3. The Baltic nations were the only peoples of the USSR to have a living memory of independent statehood. Moldavians and Karelians were joined to

the USSR in Union Republics in 1940, but neither people had been independent and many persons from each group had already lived under Soviet rule.

4. The Balts closely observed the liberation processes in East Central Europe in the 1980s. Many Ukrainians and Belorussians also gained inspiration from these developments, but local nationalism in their republics was countervailed by extensive Russification, especially in their eastern regions.[1]

In the 1970s-1980s the Baltic peoples maintained the highest educational and living standards in the USSR. Culture, science, agriculture, and industry proceeded from strong foundations laid in earlier centuries and were brought to new heights during independence and even under Soviet rule.

But why were the richest of Soviet republics most anxious to leave the Union?

5. The tiny populations of the Baltic republics — especially the Latvians and Estonians — feared that the time was now or never to save their gene pool and culture from assimilation with outsiders. No other titular peoples of a Soviet Union Republic were so threatened by extinction. Gorbachev's forbearance created a window of opportunity that might later close.

6. Of all Soviet peoples, the Balts were the most westernized and enjoyed the most active ties with Western countries, especially Finland and Sweden. All Baltic countries had windows on the world.

7. Balts compared themselves not with other Soviet peoples but with Westerners. Estonians and Latvians recalled that Finnish living standards were slightly above theirs in 1939, but had now become much higher.

Having been independent and relatively prosperous within living memory, many Balts had little doubt that they could survive and prosper in free economic competition. Like Czechs and Hungarians, they felt that, liberated from alien controls, their countries could do well in world trade.

8. The Kremlin had long permitted the Baltic republics a certain degree of autonomy. Experiments in management, technology, and culture could be carried out there without necessarily affecting or stimulating other Soviet peoples. Gorbachev hoped in 1988-1989 that Baltic innovations and enterprise might nudge the whole USSR toward a meaningful perestroika. Having given Balts the reins, it became hard to pull them up short.

not well. ant rutated.

9. The 1980s saw a shift toward market economies and pluralistic politics in most countries. History and circumstances made the Balts, of all nations in the USSR, the most likely to climb on the global bandwagon.

10. Balts saw little need for a Big Brother to guard against aggressive neighbors as do some of the southern peoples of the USSR looking out toward Turkey and China, although Lithuania in 1990 encountered territorial challenges from Belorussia and internal minorities. || *hulo*

11. Russian dominion of the Baltic had less legitimacy than in other border lands. The Kremlin in 1989 conceded that Stalin's deals with Hitler to divide Eastern Europe were illegal and immoral. This admission left little legitimacy for Soviet claims to the Baltic, claims that most other governments have never recognized. Moscow could let the Balts depart without undercutting the legal basis for Moscow's authority in other border lands. Dominoes might still fall, of course, regardless of legalisms.

12. The patient, nonviolent approach to liberation by the Baltic peoples was much less threatening to the Kremlin than the violent words and deeds resounding in the Transcaucasus and Central Asia. The Balts implemented principles of the kind endorsed by Gandhi and Martin Luther King, Jr. in what some Balts called their "Singing Revolution." || *violence in the transcaucasus*   )

Balts were not dogmatic pacifists. In 1918-1920 they fought against Soviet Russia and won. In 1941-1953 they fought — more from despair than from hope — and lost. They saw their neighbors' peaceful revolutions crushed by tanks in 1953, 1956, and 1968. But they also saw how "Socialism with a Human Face" in Czechoslovakia and Poland's Solidarity movement either delayed or forestalled armed intervention for many months, in part by avoiding direct challenges to Russian hegemony.

Moscow's responses to East European independence movements became slower and less violent from 1953 to the 1980s.[3] By the late 1980s Gorbachev's policies rested more on persuasion than coercion. This created an opportunity for peaceful change. There were no Baltic disputes so deeply rooted as those in Nagorno-Karabakh or Abkhazia. *than why didn't they succeed in*

The violent ethnic strife in other Soviet border lands presented both *value* potential dangers and advantages for the Balts. This strife tempted Kremlin *building* hardliners to demand a crackdown on all dissident forces within the empire, but it also engaged Moscow's energies so that the more orderly independence movements in the Baltic could proceed with less resistance than if they alone challenged Russia's rule over nearly 150 million non-Russians.

Why did the Singing Revolution work? Because the burdens of empire, linked to economic ills, weakened Russia's imperial will and capacity. Because Balts proceeded in a firm, steady path that offered no direct threat and perhaps some advantage to Soviet interests. Because the West dangled a carrot of trade before the Kremlin while simultaneously refusing to recognize Moscow's annexation of the Baltic.

Baltic Independence and Social Theory

How did the processes of Baltic independence support or challenge leading theories about social change, nationalism, revolution, and bargaining?

1. Baltic developments gave no backing for the idea that nationalism erodes and disappears as a people reaches economic maturity. The Balts had probably the highest living standards in the USSR in the 1980s, but were among the most nationalistic of its peoples. Many Balts living abroad—even born abroad—notwithstanding their virtually world-class living standards, tenaciously supported the independence of their native lands and maintained their Old World languages and other values.

2. Balts showed that small peoples can maintain their culture despite heavy foreign colonization and global trends toward homogenization. They demonstrated that a small people can hold out for a long time and then reassert national self-determination. Balts overcame the debilitating effects of slavery. Enserfed for many centuries, they quickly threw off the habits of submission.[4] Subjected to haphazard Russification in the late nineteenth century and again in the Soviet period, they maintained their own languages and cultures.

National awakening among the Baltic peoples in the nineteenth century was the more remarkable because the roots of their cultures had been poorly nourished compared to those of their neighbors. Thousands of folk melodies and lyrics went back many hundreds of years, but there was as yet little literature in Baltic languages. Still, Balts glorified whatever existed and quickly produced more. Estonia's national epic, *Kalevipoeg,* compiled in mid-century, depicted a clumsy Hercules who accidentally cuts off his own legs. Whatever his other attributes, he steadfastly guards the gates of hell.[5]

Baltic national consciousness did not require artificial stimulation by skillful leaders seeking support for themselves or for other objectives. Rather, the idea of nationhood was an end in itself for most Estonians, Latvians, and Lithuanians regardless of their place in society. Their experience upheld the image that a "nation is a soul, a spiritual principle....The existence of a nation is a plebiscite of every day." [6]

3. Each Baltic nationalism sought to preserve a culture that had taken shape in the same territory over thousands of years. The underlying force may have included a territorial imperative and biological drive to preserve and promulgate the gene pool. Keeping alive Baltic languages and cultures was both an end and a tool of national survival. Even though their genes had long mixed with their neighbors', and their cultures had long been influenced by many sources, Balts wore their identity as a badge of pride. They wished to maintain their way of life and basic values. Why did they persist while other peoples surrendered to assimilation? Smaller peoples, such as the Karelians, were even more inundated by a sea of Russians and had less independent political tradition to sustain them. Although the odds were difficult, Balts had cause to hope that their stock and culture might endure. *use log*

4. National self-assertion in the Baltic was fueled also by a sense of relative deprivation and by rising expectations, both political and economic. From the mid-1950s through the late 1960s, Soviet consumers got more and better goods almost every year. Political and cultural restraints were eased, although many setbacks also took place. For Balts, however, these gains were mixed, because demographic and environmental challenges became more severe. Gains in consumer goods slowed markedly in the late 1960s and halted altogether at times in the late 1970s and early 1980s — what Gorbachev's people called the "stagnation" years.[7] Political dissent became more vocal in the Baltic during the decade before Gorbachev, but often met sharp repression. From 1985 through 1990 perestroika brought steady decreases in consumer goods available to Soviet buyers, even as glasnost permitted a dramatic rise in political and artistic freedom. Demographic and environmental perils did not stop and were debated more openly, adding to pressures for change.

But similar patterns prevailed for most other Soviet citizens. What made the Balts more independence-minded than others? "What is" and "what will be" (if present trends continued) looked especially bad to Balts relative to what could be if they regained independence.

5. Nationalism is often directed against external threats, real or imagined. For centuries Balts felt threatened by Germans, Scandinavians, Poles, and Russians. In the 1970s and 1980s their hostility focused on Russians — those in Moscow and those who, in their midst, were taking up apartments and other consumer goods and displacing Baltic languages and culture. The alien foe was much more visible than in most parts of the USSR.

Outsiders also contributed to Balts' self-image. German Baltophile scholars helped enshrine the Latvian and Estonian folk heritage in the nineteenth century, while Russification helped Balts see themselves as different from Germans. Many Balts of the late twentieth century measured their potential against the West and North and felt themselves superior to the East.

Baltic liberation was more positive than negative. Despite external oppression, the Balts' focus has been to develop their own potential rather than to wreak vengeance. In 1990 they showed almost no drive to conquer or dominate others.

6. Baltic national sentiments have been shaped since the early and mid-nineteenth century by cultural figures and intellectuals leading broadly based, popular movements — not by the bourgeoisie seeking ever larger markets, as Stalin and the Karl Deutsch school of political science expected.[9] The small burgher groupings of the nineteenth century sought to avoid antagonizing the Germans, Poles, or Russians who then dominated economic life. National consciousness was stirred rather by intellectuals and rural school teachers. In the late twentieth century Baltic nationalism was sparked by dissident intellectuals and also, in Lithuania, by priests. The Soviet *nomenklatura* — the Communist equivalent of "high bourgeois circles" — opposed change and supported Russian rule.

7. In line with Deutsch's expectations, Baltic national consciousness grew as communications radiated the symbols and rewards of a growing interdependence.[10] The processes of modernization contributed to this consciousness: The growth of rural schools meant more literacy. The expansion of railroads uniting port cities and interior stations permitted ideas to travel along with commerce. Expanding communication networks made it possible to hold song festivals that joined not just single parishes or counties but an entire country.

In the 1980s Lithuanians, Latvians, and Estonians maintained telephone contact with relatives in Europe and North America. Election results in 1989-1991 were faxed around the world.

8. Historian Hans Kohn distinguished two early forms of nationalism: English and French.[11] Have Baltic nationalists behaved with a Lockean regard for human rights or like Rousseauian collectivists indifferent to minority concerns? They have teetered between these poles, aspiring to the former but feeling pushed toward the latter.

Estonia prided itself on exemplary treatment of its national minorities in the 1920s, but Baltic events have not been conducive to absolute regard for minority rights. To begin with, Balts had little experience with democracy before trying to implement it in the 1920s. Each Baltic republic, like many countries, became authoritarian by the 1930s — Lithuania in 1926, Estonia and Latvia in 1934. From 1940 until the late 1980s, Baltic nationalists experienced persecution.

Even in the era of glasnost Balts felt themselves embattled minorities within the total Soviet context. Most Balts perceived the Kremlin and Russian settlers as adversaries rather than partners. Baltic nationalists were impatient with one another — exchanging epithets such as "collaborationist" and "reckless and naive." They found it simpler to cope with a distant foe — the Kremlin — than with disagreements among themselves and with large populations of alien settlers.

In the late 1980s Russians and other outsiders formed resistance movements to local self-assertion in Estonia, Latvia, and Lithuania. Some Jews reported anti-Semitism among Latvians. In Lithuania many Poles joined Russians in fearing majority rule.

9. National reawakening throughout the Baltic in the 1980s was not a substitute for religion or some other ideology, for it occurred in tandem with a resurgence of traditional culture and religion. Baltic nationalism did not fill a void left by the collapse of Communist ideology, which few Balts ever accepted. The established churches — especially in Lithuania but also in contemporary Latvia and Estonia — both supported and benefited from a stronger national consciousness.

Still, Sir Isaiah Berlin's thesis probably fits the Baltic under perestroika. He argued that nationalism feeds on anomie and alienation amid the breakdown of old moral and religious values.] It gains explosive power from the combination of unhealed mental wounds, however caused, with the image of the nation as a society of the living, the dead and those yet unborn." [12] Anomie —expressed in alcoholism, crime, divorce—were rising in the Baltics in the 1980s, perhaps at higher rates than the Soviet average. But a sense of belonging to a resurgent nation could restore meaning to an otherwise difficult existence.

10. Balts may be richer and more independent minded than other Soviet citizens, thanks in part to their acceptance of western Christianity with its emphasis on individual responsibility and, in its Protestant varieties, on Bible-reading.

Baltic developments gave some support to Max Weber's thesis that Protestantism is conducive to a work ethic, savings, and other virtues useful to the development of capitalism. Protestant Latvia and Estonia industrialized earlier than Catholic Lithuania. All three Baltic republics reached higher levels of economic development than other parts of the Russian Empire/USSR dominated by the otherworldly outlooks of Orthodox Christianity and Islam. But many Lithuanians in the 1980s toiled with a Protestant-like work ethic and achieved living standards rivaling if not exceeding those of Latvia and Estonia—thanks in part to more attention to private gardening and, perhaps, to fewer immigrants in their populations.

Weber, like social psychologist David McClelland in recent decades, pointed out the linkage between world view and economic behavior. [13] But their approach leaves many questions unresolved. Weber focused on the role of Calvinist belief in predestination, an anxiety that did not belong to the Lutheran theology. Also, many of the erstwhile pagans seemed not to take religion too seriously. In the nineteenth century many Estonians converted to the "faith of the tsar" in the hope of getting more land.

Protestant missionaries spurred literacy in Estonia and Latvia. Many Estonians and Latvians had some reading ability by the late 1700s. By the 1980s Estonia probably produced more books per capita than any other country save Iceland (another Protestant outpost). But Catholic as well as Lutheran church leaders in the Baltic learned the spirit of the Enlightenment at Dorpat and Vilnius universities. In the nineteenth century they founded schools based on the principles of central European pedagogy. Their efforts interacted positively with those of Baltic Germans and Polish nobles who, closely associated with

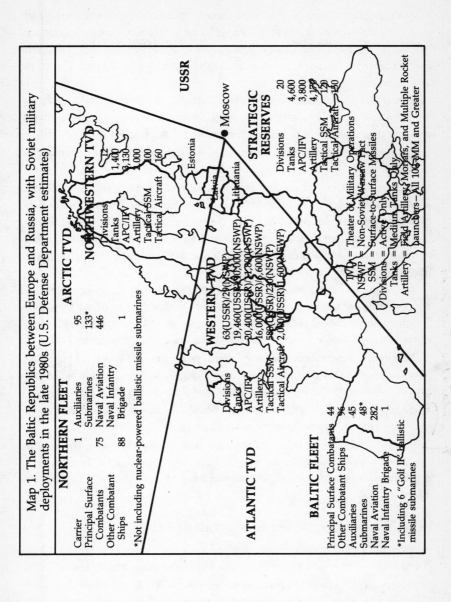

Map 1. The Baltic Republics between Europe and Russia, with Soviet military deployments in the late 1980s (U.S. Defense Department estimates)

NORTHERN FLEET

Carrier	1
Auxiliaries	95
Principal Surface Combatants	75
Submarines	133*
Other Combatant Ships	88
Naval Aviation	446
	Brigade	1

*Not including nuclear-powered ballistic missile submarines

ARCTIC TVD

NORTHWESTERN TVD

Divisions	12
Tanks	1,400
APC/IFV	3,130
Artillery	1,000
Tactical SSM	100
Tactical Aircraft	160

USSR

Estonia

Latvia

Lithuania

● Moscow

STRATEGIC RESERVES

Divisions	20
Tanks	4,600
APC/IFV	3,800
Artillery	4,170
Tactical SSM	120
Tactical Aircraft	150

WESTERN TVD

Divisions	63(USSR)/20(NSWP)
Tanks	19,460(USSR)/14,000(NSWP)
APC/IFV	20,400(USSR)/13,380(NSWP)
Artillery	16,000(USSR)/5,600(NSWP)
Tactical SSM	580(USSR)/230(NSWP)
Tactical Aircraft	2,000(USSR)/1,600(NSWP)

TVD = Theater of Military Operations
NSWP = Non-Soviet Warsaw Pact
SSM = Surface-to-Surface Missiles
Divisions = Active Only
Tanks = Medium Tanks Only
Artillery = Field Artillery, Mortars, and Multiple Rocket Launchers—All 100 MM and Greater

ATLANTIC TVD

BALTIC FLEET

Principal Surface Combatants	44
Other Combatant Ships	96
Auxiliaries	45
Submarines	48*
Naval Aviation	282
Naval Infantry Brigade	1

*Including 6 "Golf II" ballistic missile submarines

broader European trends, promoted new agricultural methods, crops and technologies as well as new forms of communication and mobilization. Lithuania lagged behind Estonia and Latvia in these respects, but the entire Baltic region was much more dynamic than adjoining Belorussian, Ukranian and Russian parts of the tsarist empire.[14]

Whatever the reasons, most Balts — Catholic, Protestant, and secular — believed in the late 1980s that they were far more industrious, skilled, and cultured than Russians and most other peoples of the USSR.

11. The processes of Baltic liberation showed the value of four approaches to policy:

Support for international law and organization. Nonrecognition of Baltic annexation by the United States and most Western governments, derided as moralism-legalism by some, has helped sustain Baltic morale. The Helsinki meetings on European security and cooperation since 1975 gave Balts another moral-legal leg on which to justify their demands. They got additional support from the European Parliament.

The West and the Balts have benefited from the fact that most Western governments did not base their Baltic policies on acceptance of the view that "might makes right." At least in this case, devotion to legal and moral norms, upheld through long periods of detente as well as confrontation, paid off.

Nonviolent resistance and nonviolent programs of reform. These approaches worked in the late 1980s and 1990, even though they were not carefully articulated and propagated as national liberation strategies.

Neutralization. The 1955 Austrian model looked again to be a way to reconcile great power differences in ways useful to all parties.

Value-creating. The Baltic experience shows that, even in difficult circumstances, political actors can best enhance their objectives if they develop strategies aimed at creating values rather than just claiming them from other actors.

Why Moscow Opposed Independence

Why did the Kremlin want to maintain its empire? What interests were at stake in preserving Moscow's control over the Baltic and other border lands?

1. *Personal power and political survival.* As Gorbachev told the Lithuanians in early 1990, his own regime was at risk if nationalist movements

in the republics became too strong. Even if his opponents were indifferent to empire, they would hold him responsible for its disintegration. By 1990 this Soviet "Teflon president" was losing his ability to transform setbacks into victories.

2. *Strategic positions.* Soviet military deployments — naval, ground, and air — have been extensive along the Baltic. To renounce them would be to surrender forward positions useful to bully Europe and to defend the USSR. Pulling these forces back to Russia, however, would not necessarily weaken Soviet foreign policy if the Kremlin no longer hoped to intimidate Europeans and no longer feared some kind of Teutonic push to the east. The ambitions and power of a reunited Germany, however, posed major questions at the onset of the 1990s.

3. *Legitimacy and morale.* Communist ideology was openly renounced by many East Europeans and Soviets in 1988-1990, leaving its future in doubt. The dismantling of Communism in the Baltic or other erstwhile Union Republics could give communism a virtual coup de grace. Communist bureaucrats and true believers, some of whom still existed in Russia, stood to lose face, fortune, and faith.

4. *Institutional interests.* Not just the Soviet military but many all-Union ministries were accustomed to working their will in the Baltic without interference by the locals. Muscovites' operating styles would be upset if the center could not dictate and take what it wanted from the Baltic (such as computers, paid for in rubles at prices set in Moscow).

If self-management and market economies flourished in the Baltic, this could put pressure on Soviet institutions to change their ways drastically. Soviet reformers might welcome such a demonstration effect; diehards would not.

5. *Holding the line.* The Kremlin's operational code dictated: "Avoid giving a meter lest others ask for a kilometer." If the Balts become independent, similar claims by other border peoples and other territorial adjustments will be the more difficult to resist. A domino effect could strip away other border lands and even unleash demands for absolute autonomy by ethnic minorities enclaved within the Russian Republic.

But another part of the operational code advised: "Take one step back to go two forward." Letting go of extraneous concerns might permit the Kremlin to focus on essentials.

The balance sheet. How serious were these various military, political, and economic concerns? Whether an interest is "vital" depends heavily upon intentions and perceptions. Whether a movement gets a positive or negative sign depends on judgment. If the bases of power and influence no longer rested upon arms and territory but upon mastering the scientific-technological revolution, as Gorbachev's "new thinking" stated, the Soviet state could *gain* from cutting its imperial burdens and replacing them with cooperative arrangements freely arising from shared interdependence and from exchanges based on comparative advantage.

A wise security policy aims at protecting and enhancing a people's deepest values and way of life. From this standpoint, the Soviet system has been a failure. At least fifty million of its subjects have died unnaturally and unnecessarily since 1917 due to the purges, famines, relocations, and other policies shaped by the whims and blunders of dictators produced by that system.

Stalin was a product of the Soviet system, but he gave it a cast that shaped Soviet life for generations after his death. The system spared no Soviet peoples. Indeed, Slavs—Belorussians, Ukrainians, and Russians—perished at rates comparable to the most ravaged Soviet nationalities. Balts and other smaller nationalities were brought closer to extinction, however, because they have been few in number and subject not just to physical but linguistic and cultural repression.

Russians would be well advised to discard an unprofitable empire and to seek a place in an evolving world based upon free choice—economic, political, cultural. We must all grope to find ways to maintain our own identities while creating values with others. A large country such as Russia will always be a weighty factor in world affairs. If the Kremlin should revert to its old ways—the knout, bayonet, or tank—the West must respond with firmness. But the West should demonstrate its willingness to welcome Balts, Russians, and other peoples of the erstwhile Soviet Union into a world of mutual gain rather than exploitation.

NOTES

1. See Alexander J. Motyl, *Will the Non-Russians Rebel? State, Ethnicity, and Stability in the USSR* (Ithaca, N.Y.: Cornell University Press, 1987).
2. Unlike Latvia and Estonia, Lithuania was once a large and powerful state. Its comparatively small population dominated a large expanse. Lithuanians, like Poles, have shown a zeal for conquest and for armed struggle, even when the odds are unfavorable. They behaved with honor in 1939, refusing Hitler's blandishments. They were more active than Latvians or Estonians in partisan resistance after 1944.
3. The trend was toward ever slower reaction, involving less and less bloodshed. Moscow immediately sent tanks to suppress East Germany's 1953 *Aufstand*; it waited weeks before moving against Hungary in 1956; it delayed eight months before occupying Czechoslovakia in 1968; in Poland the Kremlin did not use its own forces against Solidarity but waited sixteen months until a local general did the job.
4. Balts, like African slaves, were taught submission by Christian missionaries, but they were able to throw off the psychological fetters of slavery much more readily than Caribbean or American blacks. Unlike Africans, transported to another world, Balts remained in their native lands and kept their native tongues. Even those shipped to Soviet gulags retained more contact with their native land than Africans sent to Haiti or Alabama.
5. Written down in the mid-nineteenth century by Friedrich Reinhold Kreutzwald, working from an outline by Friedrich Faehlmann, *Kalevipoeg* could be a metaphor for the politics of the late twentieth century.
6. See Ernest Renan, "The Meaning of Nationality" (1887), in Hans Kohn, ed., *Nationalism: Its Meaning and History*, rev. ed. (New York: D. Van Nostrand, 1965), reading no. 11.
7. Laurie Kurtzweg, "Trends in Soviet Gross National Product," in Joint Economic Committee, Congress of the United States, *Gorbachev's Economic Plans*, 2 vols. (Washington: U.S. Government Printing Office, 1987), 1, pp. 126-65; also Gregory Grossman, "Roots of Gorbachev's Problems: Private Income and Outlay in the Late 1970s," ibid., 1, pp. 213-29.
8. On repression in the early 1980s, see Rein Taagepera, *Softening Without Liberalization in the Soviet Union: The Case of Jüri Kukk* (Lanham, Md.: University Press of America, 1984).
9. See J. V. Stalin, "Marxism and the National Question" (1913); in Josef V. Stalin, *Marxism and the National-Colonial Question* (San Francisco: Proletarian Press, 1975); and see Karl W. Deutsch, *Nationalism and Its Alternatives* (New York: Knopf, 1969), chap. 1.
10. Deutsch, *Nationalism and Its Alternatives*; see also Karl W. Deutsch and William J. Foltz, eds., *Nation-Building* (New York: Atherton, 1966).
11. Kohn, *Nationalism: Its Meaning and History*, pp. 16-18.
12. Isaiah Berlin, "Nationalism: Past Neglect and Present Power," *Partisan Review*, 46, 3 (1979), 337-58, at p. 356.
13. For a bibliography, see Lawrence E. Harrison, *Underdevelopment As a State of Mind* (Lanham, Md.: Madison, 1985), pp. 179-83; also Walter C. Clemens, Jr., "Perestroika Needs a Work Ethic to Work," *Wall Street Journal*, 5 December 1989, p. A22.
14. Edward C. Thaden, "Baltic National Movements During the Nineteenth Century," *Journal of Baltic Studies*, 16, 4 (Winter 1985) pp. 411-21, at p. 414.

2
The Baltic:
A Bridge Between East
and West

Just Another Faraway Land? Why Is the Baltic Important?

Estonia, Latvia, and Lithuania occupy a vital crossroads at the intersections of Northern, Central, and Eastern Europe. They are part of a region whose waters the Vikings once plowed with their rugged longboats; many of whose pagan peoples the Teutonic knights chastened into Christianity; and whose reaches the vast Hanseatic League regarded for several centuries as its own private fish-and-amber preserve.[1]

Estonia occupies an area about equal to that of New Hampshire and Vermont combined with Latvia half again as large Lithuania's area is larger than the combination of New Hampshire, Vermont, Massachusetts, and Rhode Island.

Estonians, Latvians, and Lithuanians can all look westward across the Baltic toward Sweden; to the north, Estonians also face Helsinki across the Gulf of Finland. The Baltic Sea stretches roughly a thousand miles and varies from 50 to 200 miles in width. It slants obliquely north-northeast from Denmark and Germany through the Gulf of Bothnia to the point where Finland and Sweden meet This tideless ocean, called by Germans the *Ostsee*, measures more than three times the size of the Adriatic, but it is less than one-fifth the size of the Mediterranean.) *why is it to delew?*

Estonia's capital, Tallinn (formerly Reval), guards the southern entrance to the Gulf of Finland, the main waterway leading to the port that Peter the Great

(Tsar Peter I) made Russia's "window on the West" early in the eighteenth century. Soviet Russia lost control of the Baltic provinces in 1918, however, and Leningrad Party chief Andrei Zhdavov warned (November 26, 1936) that the USSR might need to use force against "small neighbors" to preempt their dreams of "great adventures." [2] Four years later he became Stalin's viceroy directing sovietization of Estonia.

Russia again lost the *Pribaltika* in 1941 but reestablished its three Soviet republics there in 1944. That year the Kremlin also compelled Finland to lease to the USSR a naval base at Porkkala, west of Helsinki. These arrangements gave Russia a pincer to dominate both the northern and southern approaches to Leningrad. But N. S. Khrushchev returned the base to Finland in 1955-1956 in his quest for detente. || *why "but"*

Did the Baltic lose its strategic importance in the nuclear-missile age? Soviet military planners in the mid-1970s placed the Baltic in their Northwestern Theater of Military Operations (TVD). This expanse included the northwestern districts of the USSR and Soviet Baltic republics; NATO members Norway, Denmark, and Iceland; and neutral countries Finland and Sweden. Forty-five million peopled live in this TVD in the mid-1970s, about half outside the USSR. "To its north," Soviet planners noted, "lies the North Arctic Ocean, where air and space routes connecting the USA and USSR constitute the shortest ranges for intercontinental ballistic missiles and strategic aircraft." [3]

Major naval forces of the Warsaw Pact were deployed in the Northwestern TVD. "This area," Soviet strategists said, "will provide favorable conditions for Warsaw Pact naval forces to get access to the northern and central Atlantic Ocean, which is under NATO control and influence. This action will isolate Norway and Denmark and provide suitable opportunities for the Northern and Baltic Fleets of the Soviet Navy, as well as for Poland and the German Democratic Republic, to accomplish missions for the purpose of destroying the main groupings of NATO forces operating in the Western TVD." [4]

Has Gorbachevian "new thinking" made naval bases and operations irrelevant? Despite Moscow's efforts to allay Western anxieties about Kremlin intentions, Soviet submarines have penetrated deep into the territorial waters of neutral Sweden for decades. Intrusions reached record levels in 1988 and continued at a brisk pace in 1989-1990. Sweden lies between Norway and the

Kola Peninsula, home to the largest Soviet submarine fleet. The Soviets updated intelligence and probably hoped to bully Sweden into permitting transit to Norway in time of war. Despite reservations about NATO, Norway stockpiled U.S. weapons and Oslo welcomed American Marine reserves who practiced weekend landings on its rocky coasts. Meanwhile, the Kremlin stepped up calls for naval disarmament and reduced the number of Soviet military ships patrolling the high seas.[5]

In the 1990s the Baltic countries provide a window on the West for many Soviet citizens in ways that might not have entirely displeased Russia's first major modernizer, Peter the Great. Estonians watch not just *Dallas* but the world news on Finnish television; Lithuanians keep abreast of every twist in the struggle to rebuild Poland; Latvians expand their ties with Sweden and Canada and recall those they once had with Tobago.

In the years before Washington recognized Soviet Russia, the Baltic capitals were America's window on the East. Until 1933 the U.S. State Department posted Soviet watchers such as George F. Kennan to Riga, Tallinn, and Kaunas to keep abreast of Soviet affairs. Kennan found Riga to be a minor edition of imperial St. Petersburg.[6]

The Baltic lands have long been a meeting place and battle field between Germans, Scandinavians, and Finns from the west and north and Slavs from the east and south. Varangian traders, passing through the Baltic on their way to Constantinople, were invited by the Slavs, according to the chronicle, to establish "order" in Novgorod in 862. The Balts in those times were sometimes compelled to pay tribute to the Vikings or to the princes of the incipient Russian state.

Any Western leader who thought of the Baltic or other East Central European lands as "faraway" countries involved in quarrels "between people of whom we know nothing" should have seen the film *Alexander Nevsky*. Commissioned by Stalin in the late 1930s, the film reminded Russians of their primordial conflicts — and occasional triumphs — over invaders from the north and west. Alexander, Prince of Novgorod and Vladimir, vanquished the Swedes on the River Neva in 1240. Two years later he turned back the Livonian Knights (with their Estonian conscripts) on the ice of Lake Peipsi (Peipus) separating Estonia and Russia, a suggestion — propagandized in Sergei Eisenstein's film — that Russian mass and morale could defeat a mechanized Germanic blitzkrieg.

Any notion that the Baltic is irrelevant to the West could be dispelled even for riders in the London tube in 1989, where a clever ad explained how — centuries ago — English ale shipped to the Baltic had to be placed under special seal lest thirsty sailors sample their precious cargo. London and Novgorod, along with Bruges and Bergen, were the major foreign trading posts for the Hanseantic League of Germanic city-states in the fourteenth and fifteenth centuries. Baltic towns such as Riga, Reval (modern Tallinn), and Dorpat (Tartu) took part in the League. To this day Tallinn retains medieval guild houses looking like those of northern Germany. For Kennan in the 1920s Tallinn was a "northern replica of the German Lübeck — surrounded, incongruously but not unattractively, by purely Russian suburbs." [7]

Baltic Variations

All three Baltic peoples have lived in their present environs for thousands of years. From about 1500 B.C. to the time of Christ there was a slow transition from nomadic hunting and fishing to agriculture. By about 500 B.C. two distinct cultural and ethnic groups had formed. North of the Daugava (Düna, Russian Dvina) River were the Balto-Finns; to the south were the ancestors of the Latvians and Lithuanians. By A.D. 500 the Latvians had expanded beyond the Daugava close to the present border of Estonia.[8] Of living languages, Lithuanian and Latvian (Lettish) are probably the closest to Proto-Indo-European.[9] Estonian, like Finnish and Karelian, belongs to the Finno-Ugric language family.

Lithuania

Balts have known times of glory. While Britain and France wasted themselves in deadly battles, and while Russia labored under the "Mongol yoke," Lithuania became Europe's largest state in the fourteenth century. Lithuania then expanded from the Baltic to the Black Sea, absorbing much of Belorussia and the Ukraine. Lithuania allied with Poland in 1386. Together they resisted Ivan the Terrible's western campaigns (the indecisive "Livonian wars") for twenty-five years.

With the collapse of the Mongol empire, Moscow gradually regained the eastern Slavic lands from Lithuania and Poland. Threatened by Russian expansion, Lithuania merged with Poland in 1569. When Poland was partitioned in the eighteenth century, Lithuania disappeared as a national unit and passed to Russia.

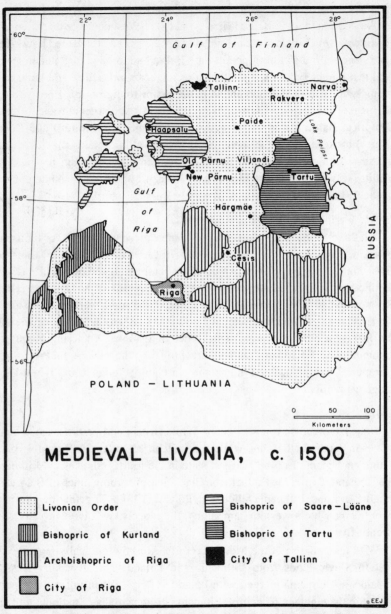

MEDIEVAL LIVONIA, c. 1500

Legend:
- Livonian Order
- Bishopric of Kurland
- Archbishopric of Riga
- City of Riga
- Bishopric of Saare–Lääne
- Bishopric of Tartu
- City of Tallinn

From Toivo U. Raun, *Estonia and the Estonians* (Stanford, CA: Hoover Institution Press, 1987). Used by permission of the publisher.

Estonia and Latvia

Estonia (*Eesti* in Estonian, *Estland* in German) did not acquire a national self-consciousness until the nineteenth century, but the roots of Estonian identity extend far into the pre-Christian era. In the A.D. first century Tacitus wrote of "Aesti" living on the Baltic coast. Estonia became an important transit station for Varangian trade through Russia to Byzantium in the ninth and tenth centuries. Kiev's Prince Yaroslav established a Russian foothold near Tartu, A.D. 1030-1061, but Estonian tribes were basically independent until the German conquest in the early thirteenth century. When the Varangian trade route to the south fell into disuse, Estonians traded and plundered along the Baltic. The Estonian fort at Tallinn was noted by an Arab cartographer in A.D. 1154.[10]

The well-equipped Livonian Knights (a Germanic order founded in 1201) subjected Latvians and Estonians, county by county, in the early thirteenth century. Stopped at Lake Peipsi by Nevsky in 1242, the knights settled and colonized "Livonia" (German *Livland*) — what is now Estonia and part of Latvia — for more than three centuries. They brought serfdom, Christianity, and waves of other Germans to the Baltic shores. The Germans — knights, bishops, and towns — often clashed with each other in civil war. In the fourteenth century still another group joined the fray, the landed German nobility (from the earlier vassaldom). What peace existed was also shattered by occasional peasant uprisings.

Martin Luther's challenge to authority also reached the Baltic, pitting more liberal towns against more conservative land owners. For enserfed peasants it brought the first seeds of a cultural revolution: Bible-reading Protestants published religious texts in Latvian and Estonian in the sixteenth century. Gradually, literacy increased among Latvian and Estonian peasants.[11]

Weakened by religious and other controversies from within, German hegemony in the Baltic met ever stronger challenges from without. Old Livonia dissolved in 1561 and was divided between Sweden and Poland. Sweden took what is now the north of Estonia while the King of Poland obtained suzerainty over southern regions of Livonia including Courland (the west of modern Latvia).

Peter the Great established Russian dominion over the Baltic in the Great Northern War that killed up to three-fourths of the population of what is now

Latvia and Estonia from fighting, pestilence and famine.[12] Sweden ceded Livonia (Estonia and northern Latvia) to Russia, while Courland remained under Poland. From his window on the West in St. Petersburg he dispatched the African-born general, Hannibal (Pushkin's maternal grandfather), to Tallinn as governor.

The Dukes of Courland, operating under Polish suzerainty, experienced a few decades of glory. Jutting into the Baltic just northeast of Lithuania, Courland joined the triangular slave trade of European imperialists in the seventeenth century. Courland's ships sailed even to west Africa and the Caribbean, and left settlements at the Gambia River and on Tobago.[13] Despite advances from Sweden and Russia, Poland retained suzerainty over Courland until 1795, when the territory passed to Russia in the third partition of Poland, along with Lithuania (see Map 2).

Thus, by 1795 all three Baltic peoples had come under Russian rule. Their national consciousness was long impeded by many factors. Lithuanians had early come under Polish dominion. The lands where Estonians and Latvians lived rarely formed distinct political entities but were long divided into Estland, Livonia, and Courland, all ruled by foreigners, whose languages — German, Polish, Russian — set them off from the peasant masses.

Imperial Russian rule over today's Latvia and Estonia relied upon the German elite already molded into the service of the German and Swedish administrations that it superseded. At the request of the German landowners, Russia abrogated Swedish reform laws and stripped Estonian and Latvian peasants of all human rights and personal freedom. By 1777 they had become "not persons, but slaves, merchandise and objects which are sold and bartered against horses, dogs, pipe-bowls, etc." [14] Lithuanian peasants also lost their rights and were bound to the soil as serfs. St. Petersburg did not displace the German merchants who dominated the ports of Riga and Tallinn or the landed aristocracy, the "Baltic barons," who kept Latvian and Estonian peasants as serfs until emancipation in 1816-1819. Indeed, German remained the official language until replaced by Russian in 1885. There were many peasant revolts against the despotism of Baltic German landlords and the more distant Russians, but they were quickly crushed.

Almost no literature existed in Estonian or Latvian until the eighteenth century except for popular sayings and religious texts.[15] But religion did not link Estonian or Latvian nationalists, because the established church served German interests. Estonians and Latvians could not enter the clergy except with great difficulty. Estonians borrowed cultural traditions from neighboring Finland.

Weak links between the peasants and the town markets also impeded the development of Baltic nationalism. Tied to the land and unable to gain access to higher education or crafts in the towns, the sole route for Estonians to education and a broader social outlook was the rural school.[16]

As industrialization came to Latvia and Estonia in the nineteenth century, Riga and Tallinn became two of imperial Russia's most active ports. Control of commerce and agriculture remained in German hands. The Latvian and Estonian bourgeoisie was small but growing. Still, many of its members did not want to alienate the Germans or Russians. Professionals in Riga took a more active role in mobilizing national sentiment than their counterparts in Estonia. The small but growing number of Estonian merchants played a slim role in the national awakening, contrary to the theories of Joseph Stalin and modern integrationists.[17]

Romantics and revolutionaries have exaggerated the degree to which Baltic peoples had a national (*Volk*) or class consciousness. Before the nineteenth century the vast majority of the population had a peasant mentality, one narrowly concerned with daily local problems. They did not see themselves as "Latvians" or "Estonians" but as "the people of the country" who spoke "the language of the country." When modernizing influences developed in the nineteenth century, they shattered peasant societies into haves and have-nots — those who stayed on the land and those who went to towns or abroad, especially Russia, in quest of education and work.[18]

But how did national self-consciousness first arise in the Baltic? Why did the Latvians and Estonians, enserfed by foreigners for more than half a millennium, quickly throw off serf mentality and press for national self-determination? How did they move from a series of dispersed rural communities to an integrated national life balanced between farm and city?

Cultural factors constitute the matrix from which political and economic behavior flows. Western forms of Christianity and education have played major roles in the Baltic. Roman Catholic, Lutheran, and Moravian Brethren influences there helped to create a theology of individual responsibility and freedom relative to the world views inculcated elsewhere by Russian Orthodoxy and Islam.

After an abortive attempt in the thirteenth century, a second royal effort, beginning in 1386, to introduce Roman Catholicism gradually took hold in Lithuania. The Church often backed efforts to assert the national greatness against foreigners. (Emblematic of this role in the late twentieth century, the longest lived samizdat publication in the Soviet Union has been the *Chronicle of the Catholic Church in Lithuania*.)

Christianity was received differently by Estonians and Latvians because it was imposed on them by outsiders. When the long-dominant Baltic Germans accepted Lutheranism in the sixteenth century, however, this started a qualitative shift in the mentality of Estonian and Latvian peasants. The Lutherans, followed by Moravian pietists, promoted literacy so that Baltic peoples could read the Bible. Baltic Germans translated both Testaments into the local languages. Religious texts and finally complete Bibles were published in Estonian and Latvian. Results were not uniform, but by the late eighteenth century about two-thirds of adult peasants in central Estonia could read, at least at a primitive level—far more than in Russia.[19]

For Protestant Estonia and Latvia, literacy preceded and facilitated industrialization, urbanization, and lower birth rates—a modernization syndrome that has continued for more than a century.[20] Catholic Lithuania has ranked lower in urbanization than Protestant/secular Baltic areas, and has sustained births at levels that clearly maintain the nation's identity.

The Latvians and Estonians seemed more attracted to the German than to the French Enlightenment—to order, rather than to flamboyant gesture.[21] German influences probably contributed to the disciplined way in which they worked for independence in the 1980s—much less alarming to Moscow than the emotional and often violent disturbances in other parts of the empire.

Despite many barriers, national consciousness slowly came alive in the mid-nineteenth century. It was facilitated by agrarian and bourgeois reforms that permitted Estonians and Latvians to enter a number of urban trades and to pursue (for a few) higher education; and by the spread of rural schools and literacy. Song festivals brought together choirs, which sprang up in every parish, stirring patriotic sentiments. They formed channels bridging the gaps among dispersed agrarian settlements. In Estonia and Latvia the song festivals brought word that a nation lived and needed to throw off foreign oppression. Nearly a century later the cassette tape player did the same for Khomeini's revolution in Iran.

Even after Estonian consciousness began to stir, there was no definite center from which it could radiate. When railroads began to link Tallinn, Tartu, Võru and Viljandi in the nineteenth century, however, cultural and political ideas began to travel along with commerce. But in the 1850s the idea of Estonian national awareness received only minor support from the few Estonian students at Tartu University.[22]

Estonia's national spirit got a boost from publication of the epic poem, *Kalevipoeg*, in 1857; Latvia's, from the epic *Lacplesis* (The Bear Slayer), published in 1888.

In the 1860s Tartu became the recognized Estonian cultural center. At the beginning of the 1870s two patriotic organizations arose, the Society of Estonian Literati and the Estonian Alexander School movement. Just as Baltic popular fronts in the late 1980s claimed to be endorsing the Kremlin's program of perestroika, so the movement in the 1870s for secondary schools in Estonia and Latvia had called itself the Alexander School, after the "tsar liberator."

Estonians and Latvians in the late 1980s formed Citizens' Committees to support independence; in the late 1870s-early 1880s they had formed networks of correspondents and contributors. The Estonian patriotic newspaper *Sakala*, founded 1878, gained a dominant position in the Alexander movement and sponsored agitation against the German landlords. The work was carried forward in the main by rural Estonian schoolteachers, who gradually replaced German pastors in the 1860s and 1870s, and ignited considerable support among the peasantry.

In the mid-1880s, as national consciousness fanned out from a few intellectuals to the peasants and then to urbanized Balts, tsarist authorities started a campaign of open Russification throughout the Baltic. For example, in 1893 the name Yurev was given to the town that Germans and Swedes had long known as Dorpat. Not until Estonia's independence in 1918 was it officially called Tartu.

Russification campaigns helped Estonians and Latvians to see both Germans and Russians as "others." Baltic national consciousness originated in part as class hatred toward foreign oppressors.[23] Russians tried but failed to repress Estonian and Latvian cultural revivals.

Following the Polish uprising of 1863, which spread to Lithuania, Russian authorities forbade the Lithuanian language to appear in print. Between 1864 and 1904 all Lithuanian literature was smuggled from East Prussia. A strong national and Social Democratic movement grew up in Lithuania during the late nineteenth and early twentieth centuries. The Social Democratic party reconstituted in Lithuania in 1989-1990 looked proudly back to earlier struggle against Russian empire.

Balts played active roles in the 1905 revolution against the tsarist regime and later suffered bloody reprisals.

As Russia weakened in 1917-1918, the Baltic remained a bridge between East and West—a major element in the negotiations between Lenin's Bolsheviks and Imperial Germany. One day after it seized power on November 7, 1917, the Bolshevik regime issued its Decree on Peace denouncing subjugation of any nation "by force within the boundaries of a certain State" and calling for an end to secret diplomacy and war. The December 15, 1917, armistice between Soviet Russia and Germany dealt with borders, commerce, and shipping from the Baltic to the Black Sea.[24]

Germany's Field Marshal Erich von Ludendorff wanted not an "Austrian solution" but a "German solution" for Poland, Courland, and Lithuania—a personal union with the German Crown. The Germans tried to hold the Bolsheviks to their word and grant independence to Poland, Lithuania, Courland, and portions of Estonia and Livonia. Soviet negotiators countered on January 12, 1918, proposing plebiscites for Estonia and Livonia and for the areas occupied by Germany. The scheme would be conditioned on a Russian commitment "not to exercise direct or indirect pressure on these territories to accept a particular form of government" and a pledge by Germany and Austria-Hungary not "to annex the territories of the former Russian Empire now occupied by their armies."[25]

Pressed by Germany, Lenin on January 20, 1918, advised peace at any price. The Bolsheviks should be fighting a revolutionary war, he said, to liberate Poland, Lithuania, and Courland. Indeed, the Socialist Republic was "doing everything possible to give self-determination to Finland, the Ukraine, etc." But the security of the Socialist Republic took precedence over the "right of self-determination of a few nations (Poland, Lithuania, Courland)." Therefore, Russia should accept a "humiliating" peace with Germany.[26]

Unable to get his comrades' backing for this course, and unwilling to support a revolutionary offensive, Lenin on January 22 agreed to try out Leon Trotsky's "no peace, no war" policy toward Germany. As Lenin put it, "We will only risk losing Estonia or Livonia, and for the sake of a good peace with Trotsky, Livonia and Estonia are worth losing." [27]

Trotsky's approach failed as the Germans advanced, compelling the Bolsheviks to accept an even more humiliating peace than was available to them in January. The March 3 Brest-Litovsk treaty included many provisions regarding the Baltic. Article VI called for the withdrawal of Russian troops and Red Guards from Estonia and Livonia and their occupation by "a German police force until security is ensured by proper national institutions and until public order has been established." Russia pledged "to liberate at once all arrested or deported inhabitants of Estonia and Livonia" and ensure their safe return. Russia would also withdraw from Finland and the Aaland Islands and halt agitation there.

A supplementary treaty signed in Berlin on August 27 required Russia to renounce sovereignty over Estonia and Livonia and any claims arising from their former union with Russia. But the treaty also protected Russia's commercial and trade interests. It provided that Estonia, Livonia, Courland, and Lithuania would charge no transit fees for Russian goods. They would keep charges for railroad and river traffic to a minimum. All parties would protect the property of Russians in the Baltic and of Balts in Russia. Lake Peipus (Peipsi) waters would not be diverted so as to lower the water level; fish stocks there would be maintained; Narva River waters would be made available to supply electricity to St. Petersburg. [28]

After the German Reich collapsed, the Soviet government repudiated the Brest-Litovsk treaty on November 13, 1918, and called on the "working people of Russia, Livonia, Estonia, Courland, Lithuania, the Ukraine, the Crimea, and the Caucasus" to join in a revolutionary union with the liberated peoples of Germany and Austria-Hungary. [29] But all the border lands proved more nationalist than proletarian.

The fall of the Russian and German empires in 1917-1918 permitted Latvia, Estonia, and Lithuania to declare themselves independent republics, as detailed in the next chapter. German and then Soviet troops were expelled and peace treaties were signed with Moscow in 1920. In 1918 most of Courland became part of Latvia, but a strip of its southern coast went to Lithuania. A generation of independence began.

The evolution of Estonia, Latvia, and Lithuania underscored the staying power and influence of Western Christianity, of territorial roots, of a growing communications infrastructure, and of pressure from outsiders. Still, the Balts did not so much unite against outsiders as for themselves. Their nations were not engineered by a crafty merchant class or by political demagogues. Their unity took shape in the nineteenth century, as in the late twentieth, around "Singing Revolutions."

NOTES

1. See Douglas Chandler, "Flying Around the Baltic," *National Geographic*, 73, 6 (June 1938), pp. 767ff. Good coverage of the Baltic republics also appeared in the *Geographic* February 1921 and December 1939.

2. Zhdanov is quoted in Max Beloff, *The Foreign Policy of Soviet Russia, 1929-1941* (2 vols.; London and New York: Oxford University Press, 1952), 2, 78.

3. Ghulam Dastagir Wardak, comp., *The Voroshilov Lectures: Materials from the Soviet General Staff Academy* (Washington, D.C.: National Defense University Press, 1989), 1, 116-17. For relevant background, see also V. Stanley Vardys and Romuald J. Misiunas, eds., *The Baltic States in Peace and War, 1917-1945* (University Park: Pennsylvania State University Press, 1978); Toivo Miljan, "East vs. West: Political and Military Strategy and the Baltic Littoral," *Journal of Baltic Studies*, 12, 3 (Fall 1981), pp. 209-33; Gary L. Guertner, "Nuclear Strategy in the Nordic Region," ibid., 16, 1 (Spring 1985), pp. 6-17; Rein Taagepera, "Inclusion of the Baltic Republics in the Nordic Nuclear-Free Zone," ibid., 16, 1 (Spring 1985), pp. 33-51.

4. Wardak, *Voroshilov Lectures*, 1, pp. 117-18.

5. Moscow also pulled back aging planes and ships from Vietnam. How much these moves were due to economy considerations and how much to Gorbachev's "new thinking" was unclear. Some of Moscow's policies aimed at increasing pressures on Washington to depart its Philippine bases.

6. George F. Kennan, *Memoirs (1925-1950)* (New York: Bantam, 1969), pp. 25-30.

7. Kennan, *Memoirs*, p. 25.

8. Toivo U. Raun, *Estonia and the Estonians* (Stanford, Calif.: Hoover Institution, 1987), p. 8.

9. A third major Baltic language, Old Prussian, became a dead language in the seventeenth century.

10. The modern Estonian name Tallinn comes from *taani linn*, "Danish castle," stemming from the rebuilding and expansion of the old Estonian fortress by the Danes, who were called in by the Germans in 1219-1220 to put down Estonian resistance.

11. It is difficult to know how deeply and widely literacy penetrated. See Andrejs Plakans, "The Latvians," in Edward C. Thaden, ed., *Russification in the Baltic Provinces and Finland, 1855-1914* (Princeton, NJ: Princeton University Press, 1981), p. 212; also Toivo U. Raun, "The Estonians," ibid., p. 293.

12. See Tönu Parming, "Roots of Nationality Differences," in Edward Allworth, ed., *Nationality Group Survival in Multi-Ethnic States: Shifting Patterns in the Baltic Region* (New York: Praeger, 1977), pp. 24-57, at p. 38.

13. At least 2,000 Courlanders settled on Tobago in the years 1654-1658, sending back valuable spices and tobacco to Europe. Challenged by Sweden and the Dutch United Provinces, the position of the Duke of Courland weakened at home and abroad. See Douglas Archibald, *Tobago: "Melancholy Isle," 1498-1771* (Port-of-Spain: Westindiana Ltd., 1987), pp. 28-35.

14. Lutheran clergyman A. W. Hupel, quoted in William J. H. Hough, III, "The Annexation of the Baltic States and Its Effect on the Development of Law Prohibiting Forcible Seizure of Territory," *New York Law School Journal of International and Comparative Law*, 6, 2 (Winter 1985), p. 354, n. 180.

15. An Estonian grammar was published in 1637, but the literary language did not take its present shape until the late nineteenth-early twentieth century.

16. Miroslav Hroch, *Social Preconditions of National Revival in Europe: A Comparative Analysis of the Social Composition of Patriotic Groups among the Smaller European Nations* (Cambridge: Cambridge University Press, 1985), p. 82.

17. Note areas of agreement between Josef Stalin, "Marxism and the National Question" (1913) and Karl W. Deutsch, *Nationalism and Its Alternatives* (New York: Knopf, 1969), chap. 1.

18. See Andrejs Plakans, "The Latvians," in Thaden, ed., *Russification 1855-1914*, pp. 210-14; and Toivo U. Raun, "The Estonians," ibid., pp. 292-93.

19. See Toivo U. Raun, *Estonia and the Estonians*, pp. 54-55.

20. In the 1980s Estonians claimed to produce more books per capita than any other people except Icelanders (who are also Lutherans).

21. See Robert von Dassanowsky-Harris, "The Philosophy and Fate of Baltic Self-Determination," *East European Quarterly*, 20, 4 (January 1987), pp. 493-504.

22. The university had been founded in 1632 by Gustavus II, suppressed in 1656, reopened in 1690-1710, again suppressed, and reopened in 1802.

23. Hroch, *Social Preconditions of National Revival*, chap. 11, p. 84.

24. John W. Wheeler-Bennett, *The Forgotten Peace: Brest-Litovsk, March 1918* (New York: Morrow, 1939), pp. 381-83.

25. Wheeler-Bennett, *Forgotten Peace*, pp. 108, 128, 161.

26. Ibid., pp. 390-91.

27. Ibid., p. 193.

28. None of the former Russian provinces was represented. By implication, Germany spoke for them. See Wheeler-Bennett, *Forgotten Peace*, pp. 429-31.

29. Ibid., pp. 448-49.

3
Winning Independence

Lenin's party proclaimed the right of every people to national self-determination, but did not yield it willingly to the peoples of the former tsarist empire. All three Baltic peoples declared their autonomy or independence from Russia in 1917-1918, but then had to fight for it. Not until 1920 did the Soviet Republic, stalemated, acknowledge the Baltic republics' statehood. When Russia became more powerful, it occupied and annexed these same republics in 1940. Stalin's regime then conducted a campaign not only to russify but to sovietize the region.

Who Has the Right to National Self-Determination?

Lenin had long championed the right of national self-determination, but once the Bolsheviks took power in November 1917, and beheld the disintegration of the Russian empire, Stalin sharply modified Communist doctrine. Newly appointed Commissar of Nationalities, Stalin in December 1917-January 1918 wrote that the Soviet government could not permit national self-determination to serve as a cloak for counterrevolution. The Council of People's Commissars would recognize the independence of any republic but only "upon the demand of the working population of such an area." The principle of self-determination should be denied the bourgeoisie.[1]

The Bolshevik program on the national question was authentically Marxist in that it embraced two mutually contradictory principles: the self-determination of nations, and the centralized state. One way out of this impasse was to strip words of their meaning. Lenin assigned different meanings to words depending on the needs of the moment and modified them depending on the audience.[2]

Lenin continued to denounce Russian "chauvinism," which he imputed to Stalin and some leftists on the national question. But he injected a flexible double standard into the Communist Party program in March 1919: The Bolsheviks would champion the "full equality of nations" and the "right to political secession" — especially for colonies. But the Russian Communists took "the historical-class point of view" in defining "who is the carrier of the nation's will to separation." In other words, the party of the proletariat would have the last word in the transition from bourgeois to Soviet democracy.[3] Lenin's flexibility permitted the steamroller of Russian chauvinism, now dressed as "proletarian internationalism," to guide Soviet policy for decades to come. By 1922 Lenin wanted to stop Stalin's coercive, centralizing policies, but it was too late.[4]

Bolshevik

Soviet Russia tried by subversion, political action, and military force to keep the Baltic states and all other breakaways from the old empire within its grasp. Lenin's government exploited Party organizations established in the border lands under the Provisional Government and those Russian troops that obeyed the new regime. With these arms the Bolsheviks dissolved the Belorussian Rada, invaded the Ukraine, suppressed Muslim governments of Kokand, Crimea, the Alash Orda, and Bashkir republic, and eventually established Communist regimes in the Transcaucasus.[5] They tried but failed to rein in the Baltic republics and Finland.

Shortly after Germany's armistice with the Entente, on November 30, 1918, the Soviet authorities established the Council of Workers' and Peasants' Defense to mobilize the Soviet war effort on all fronts. It was headed by Lenin, Trotsky, Stalin and representatives of the Commissariats of Communication, Provisions, and the Extraordinary Commission for the Supply of the Red Army. All provincial Soviet institutions were instructed to obey the Council's directives. Thus, the Council's writ extended beyond the Russian Republic to the Ukraine and any other borderlands where Communists exercised power at that time.[6]

The Council's authority grew quickly, particularly in the Ukraine. In May 1919 the Soviet Government ordered unification of all the Red armies and railroad networks on the territories of the Ukraine, Latvia, Lithuania, Belorussia, and the Russian Republic under the Council of Workers' and Peasants' Defense.[7] Estonia, it is clear, was already beyond even the fictional scope of

FINLAND

GULF OF FINLAND

BALTIC

SEA

Paldiski · Tallinn

HIIUMAA

Kohtla-Järve · Narva

ESTONIA

·Kautla

Lake Peipsi

SAAREMAA

Pärnu · Viljandi

Kilingi-Nõmme

Tartu

Emajõgi

RUSSIA (RSFSR)

GULF OF RIGA

LIVONIA

Petseri · Pskov

Haanja

Ruusmäe

· Vent spils

Valmiera

KURZEME (COURLAND)

Cēsis

ABRENE

Rīga

LATVIA

Augspils

Jūrmala

Ogre

Madona

Liepāja

Dobele ·

LATGALE

· Jelgava

Plaviņas

Daugava

Žagarē

Rēzekne

Mažeikiai

Venta

Akmenē

Šiauliai

Daugavpils

Minija

Panevēžys

Zarasai

Lake Drukštai

Klaipēda

Nevėžis

LITHUANIA

Jurbarkas

Kēdainiai

Sovetsk (Tilsit)

Nemunas

· Jonava

KALININGRAD OBLAST (RSFSR)

Šešupe

Kaunas

Žiežmariai

BELORUSSIA

Elektrēnai · · Vilnius

Trakai

EAST PRUSSIA

Skardupiai

Pirčiupis

Suwałki

Varēna

0   100 KM

POLAND

· Minsk

- - - - 1938 borders
· · · · · June 1940 border of Lithuania
— · — Post-1945 borders

▨ Lithuania's gains in 1939 and 1940
☰ Estonia's and Latvia's losses in 1945

From Georg von Rauch, *The Baltic States: The Years of Independence*. Copyright
© 1974 by C. Hurst and Co. Used by permission of the University of California Press.

Soviet power. On June 1, 1919, the Soviet government issued a decree "On the Unification of the Soviet Republics of Russia, the Ukraine, Latvia, Lithuania, and Belorussia in the Struggle Against World Imperialism." This decree deprived the non-Russian republics of their commissariats of war, national economy, railroads, finance, and labor in favor of the corresponding Russian Republic commissariats. Thus, the origins of the USSR (formed 1922-1924) lay not in agreements between the RSFSR and individual, theoretically independent republics, but in decrees by the Russian government.[8]

Declaring Independence

Cultural nationalism and economic pragmatism were more powerful than political nationalism as Estonia moved toward independence. In late 1917-early 1918 most Estonian leaders would have settled for autonomy (rather than independence) within a federated, democratic Russian state. They demanded sovereignty only when Soviet Russia regressed into social chaos and imperial German armies approached Tallinn. The Estonian peasant was mobilized to fight for statehood not on the basis of a lofty ideology of political nationalism, but on the pragmatic need for land reform.[9]

Estonians in late 1917 considered a variety of alternative political futures: a non-Bolshevik Russian federation, a Scandinavian alliance, a Finnish-Estonian union, and an independent Estonia. They opted for independence only when the other options proved unattainable.

Russia's Provisional Government restored to Finland its constitution in March 1917. But Estonia was the only national region granted autonomy by the Provisional Government. This occurred in April 1917 after a massive demonstration by Estonians in Petrograd. The decree provided for the administrative union of Estland and northern Livland, marking the birth of the political entity of Estonia in the twentieth century. It also provided for a provincial assembly (*Maapäev*) based on universal and indirect suffrage. This assembly — in English, the Estonian National Council — was elected in July 1917 and took office in Tallinn.

Following the Bolshevik coup in Petrograd, the Maapäev on November 28, 1917, declared itself the supreme power in Estonia. But this organ was soon displaced — literally within minutes of its declaration — by a Bolshevik coup in Tallinn, backed by Communists in the Russian forces that remained. In

1917 — as in 1990 — there were more than 100,000 Russian troops in Estonia, few of them Estonians. Their presence created a shadow on Estonian politics even when they did not intervene directly. *(embeat?)*

When Imperial Germany responded to Trotsky's "no war, no peace" by resuming its eastward march in early 1918, most Estonian Bolsheviks retreated to Soviet Russia. With German occupation imminent, in Tallinn the Committee of Elders of Maapäev on February 24, 1918, declared Estonia an "independent and democratic republic" within its "historical and ethnographic borders." Konstantin Päts became prime minister of Estonia's Provisional Government. Almost unopposed, Germany then occupied Estonia from late February until mid-November 1918.[10] In May 1918, however, Estonian representatives abroad secured de facto recognition by Britain, France, and Italy of the Estonian National Council as the supreme power in Estonia. On November 11, 1918, the day of Germany's armistice with the Entente, the Estonian Provisional Government resumed its activities.

In 1917-1918, as in 1988-1990 (as Rein Taagepera has suggested to the author), Estonia was the first Baltic republic to declare its independence. Lithuania came next, followed by Estonia with another, more assertive statement, and then by Latvia.

On February 16, 1918 a Lithuanian Council elected by a National Council, which had convened in Vilnius the previous September, proclaimed Lithuania an independent nation — while it was occupied by Germans. Berlin had earlier hoped to use the Council for its own needs, and refused to recognize any Lithuanian state not tied to Germany. After November 1918 the Council proceeded to organize its own administration and army. In 1919 it managed to repulse a Soviet invasion and push a German-White Russian army into Latvia.

Latvia, split between German and Russian armies since 1915, followed suit only after Germany's armistice with the West. On November 18, 1918, the Council of Representatives from all Latvian political parties except the Bolsheviks met in Riga and proclaimed Latvia a sovereign and independent state. But the Latvian Rifles formed in the Russian army divided loyalties between a crystallizing national movement and the Bolsheviks. Many of them sided with the invading Red Army in 1919, compelling the Latvian nationalists to accept aid from Germans and White Russians, who wanted to set up a puppet regime. Estonian aid proved useful in defeating the Germans, White Russians, and Red Russians.

Fighting for Independence

Trying to bring Estonia into the Communist mold of enforced unity, Soviet forces marched into northern and southern Estonia on November 28, 1918, igniting what Estonians call their War of Independence.[11] The Estonians were poorly prepared and equipped. The retreating Germans had left little equipment. Estonia turned to Britain and Finland for supplies.

Meeting little organized opposition, the Soviet armies quickly occupied all but the western third of the country. On January 2, 1919 they stood only forty kilometers from Tallinn. But Estonian resistance began to firm. A Communist uprising in Tallinn on December 17, 1918 was suppressed. The post of commander-in-chief of Estonian forces was created on December 23 and filled by Colonel Johannes Laidoner, who occupied this position from 1918-1920, 1924-1925, and 1934-1940, by which time he was a lieutenant general, although a less modest country would by then have made him a general or marshal. A Soviet naval attack on Tallinn was foiled by a British squadron. While an appreciable minority of Estonians favored the Bolsheviks — particularly in Tallinn and other cities — the wide majority rallied to the cause of national statehood. By March 1919, Estonian territory was cleared of Soviet forces although hostilities continued at the frontiers.

Fighting on Estonian and Latvian soil came to involve many actors:

- Estonian and Latvian nationalists, backed by most of the local population and by the Entente
- Estonian and Latvian Communists — civilians working from within as well as soldiers and professional politicians working with or for Soviet Russia
- The Red Army
- The Latvian Rifles, a unit of the Red Army
- White Russian armies under several commanders
- The British navy, British and French advisers
- Finnish volunteers
- Polish forces

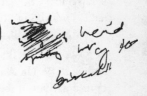

There was even a *Landeswehr* force of Baltic Germans and an "Iron Division" of German mercenaries. Both tried to retain German influence in the Baltic, but feigned cooperation at times with the Entente, with the Russian Whites, and even with Latvian nationalists.

The Estonian nationalists drove back the Russians in January 1919. They also moved against the Latvian Rifles and stopped them from wiping out the Latvian nationalists.

The Red Army launched a broad counterattack from February through May 1919. Despite the war, an Estonian Constituent Assembly met in Tallinn on April 23, 1919. It passed a provisional constitution on June 4.

In May 1919 Estonian forces combined with some White Russians drove back the Red Army. On June 14 their offensive carried into Russian territory and, by previous agreement, Laidoner relinquished command of Russian forces to General Nikolai Yudenich, who reorganized them as the Northwest Army.

In May Estonian troops helped to destroy Red forces in northern Latvia; in June the Estonians moved further south into Latvia to oppose the Baltic German forces that had occupied Riga and displaced the national Latvian government. On July 3, pressured by the Entente, the Estonians concluded an armistice with the Germans that required the Germans to leave Riga but permitted them to proceed to the Jelgava district of Courland.

In Lithuania, meanwhile, the Red Army seized Vilnius in January 1919, compelling the Lithuanian Council to retreat to Kovno (Kaunas). In April 1919, Poland captured Vilnius but lost it in a Soviet counterattack in July 1920.

Talk, Talk; Fight, Fight

But the Soviet Republic in 1919-1920 had other priorities far more pressing than retaking the Baltic states. Lenin wanted to avoid war with Japanese forces occupying the Soviet Far East and he feared a combined blow of Whites, Poles, and Balts striking Soviet Russia from the Crimea to the Baltic.

White armies were still operating from Estonia and Latvia when Moscow proposed peace talks to all three Baltic countries and Finland in August-September 1919. On August 26, however, the Entente brought together in Riga representatives of the Estonian, Latvian, and Lithuanian armies, plus those of General Yudenich and Colonel Pavel Bermondt-Avalov, commander of a

White army in Latvia. The British and French demanded that the Balts back the main offensive of Yudenich's Northwest Army by attacking Red forces on their respective fronts.

Backed by a British fleet and armed with some British tanks, the Northwest Army advanced on Petrograd in October while Estonian forces approached Pskov in the south. Stopped at the gates of Petrograd in November, Yudenich's army retreated into Estonia and was quickly disbanded and disarmed by the Estonians, who now treated the White Russians as a threat to their own security, because Yudenich would not recognize Baltic independence.

The anti-Soviet cause was hurt when Colonel Bermondt-Avalov, whose army included many Germans as well as White Russians, chose the moment of Yudenich's offensive to attack the Latvians in Riga. Bermondt's force was checked after the arrival of two Estonian armored trains in Riga helped spur Latvian resistance. More than one White leader believed in the slogan of General Anton Denikin: "Russia shall be great, united, undivided." [12] Russians — White or Red — meant trouble for the Balts.

Although some White forces had been routed, the Soviet Republic still faced severe threats on many sides in late 1919-1920. The Kremlin wanted to show the Baltic peoples the possibilities of peace and the dangers of war, luring them away from what Lenin saw as their many-sided dependence on the Entente — even for food. On December 2, 1919, Lenin asserted that Britain, France, and the United States had used every device to press "Estland,"(his word) Finland, Latvia, Lithuania, and Poland against Soviet Russia. A little more aid to Finland or Estland might have given Petrograd to Yudenich, said Lenin. But the Entente policy had failed. [13]

What Lenin ignored, of course, was the fact that Soviet Russian forces had attacked the Baltic states as soon as Imperial Germany surrendered to the Entente. It was Soviet and White Russian pressure that drove the Balts into the arms of the West. He ignored also that most Western and Finnish aid was not free. It was loaned, generating enormous debts for the young Baltic republics.

Both Soviet Russia and the Estonian government fine-tuned their diplomacy with battlefield operations and what Soviets would later call the "correlation of forces." Probably trying to head off the coordinated attack orchestrated by the Entente in Riga, the Soviets on August 31, 1919 proposed peace talks to the "Reval Government" (Estonia). The Soviet foreign commissar, Georgii V. Chicherin, offered to recognize Estonian independence on the basis of agreed borders and a demilitarized zone between Estonian and Soviet forces. Estonia agreed and proposed that talks begin September 10 in Pskov.[14] The Soviet Foreign Commissariat accepted the Estonian proposal on September 6 and announced in *Izvestiia*, September 13, that it had also proposed peace talks to Lithuania, Latvia, and Finland—claiming to have chosen a moment when the armies of General Aleksandr Kolchak and other Whites had been repulsed.

Estonian diplomats meeting with Soviets sought to delay further negotiations until their neighbors were included, a condition that the Soviets rejected on September 18, saying that this requirement was not specified when Estonia first agreed to talk.[15]

Estonia now became a conduit for combined Baltic diplomacy. On October 4 the foreign ministers of Estonia, Latvia, and Lithuania sent a joint message by telegram to the Soviet Foreign Commissariat: Their "independent republics" agreed to commence "preliminary negotiations" with Soviet Russia in Tartu not later than October 25. Chicherin immediately replied to Estonia, saying that Russia was ready to begin the expanded negotiations as early as October 12, preferably on Russian soil or in Reval (Tallinn) but also in Tartu if Estonia could guarantee secure communications. The exchange of hostages sought by Estonia should be considered with all other questions. On October 9 Chicherin protested to Finland its continued support for White Guards attacking Russia from Finnish soil.

Estonia replied on October 25 that Lithuania was ready to negotiate with the Bolsheviks only about the conditions of an armistice and that Latvia was engaged fighting the German-White Russian forces. Estonia, however, was ready to negotiate with Soviet Russia alone and would soon suggest another date.[16] Chicherin immediately wired Lithuania accepting its demand that initial negotiations concern only an armistice. By radio he informed Estonia that Russia was ready to negotiate separately with the Reval Government, but he asked sarcastically how Reval's peaceful declarations jibed with Estonian attacks on Soviet forces in the Petrograd and Pskov regions.[17]

On October 30, 1919, Chicherin appealed to the workers and peasants of England, France, and Estonia, asking them not to support attacks on Soviet Russia. Chicherin denounced the hypocrisy of Estonian negotiators who said they wanted peace, and were only interrupting negotiations — not halting them — even as Estonia backed the Yudenich push on Petrograd. The Estonian soldiers captured with Yudenich, Chicherin asserted, thought that they were fighting Germans in Latvia, not Russians in their own territory. Workers of England, France, and Estonia were urged to condemn these imperialist machinations.[18] (That Estonian troops would confuse Petrograd's geography with Riga's was, of course, implausible.)

On November 8 Estonia informed Soviet Russia that the Baltic countries would soon meet in Tartu to clarify the questions of peace with Soviet Russia, including an exchange of hostages (*zalozhnikov*). Estonia invited Soviet representatives to Tartu on November 17.

Chicherin replied two days later that Russia was willing to discuss the exchange and would send Maxim Litvinov and three other representatives to Tartu on November 16. On November 19 Litvinov concluded treaties with each Baltic republic on the exchange of hostages and other persons in whom the other side had a "legitimate (*zakonnyi*) interest."

Resuming talks with Soviet Russia in Tartu on December 5, Estonia announced that it would negotiate now without the other Baltic countries. Latvia wished to take part in the negotiations, but its delegates had not yet arrived; Estonia's other neighbors did not plan to take part, at least for the present. For Soviet Russia L.B. Krasin lamented the blood that had flowed since Estonia broke off the September negotiations. He cited Estonian, Latvian, and British reports indicating that the Baltic countries and the Entente had not given up their machinations to destroy Soviet Russia. Krasin's government wanted to ensure that the talks did not serve as a smokescreen for "military maneuvers."[19] Krasin's speech, like many Soviet statements addressed to the Baltic, was published in *Izvestiia*. The Soviets tried to talk to the masses, at home and abroad, at the same time that they addressed diplomats from the bourgeois world.

While the diplomats met, the Red Army in November drove back Yudenich and continued a broad advance all the way from Lake Peipsi to the Gulf of Finland. The Soviets launched a major drive on December 7, 1919, to break through to the Tallinn-Narva railway line and cut off the city of Narva. The attack, if successful, would influence the Estonian-Soviet peace negotiations that had begun in Tartu on December 5. On December 8 the Soviets proposed that the eastern half of Estonia's southeastern corner — the Viru district and the whole Petseri district — go to Russia. On December 14-16 the Reds took a major bridgehead on the Narva River and were stopped just three kilometers short of the Tallinn-Narva railway.

But on December 18 Chicherin's secret instructions to the Soviet delegation laid out a strategy of concessions, backed by the threat of renewed Soviet attack. Finnish volunteers backed by Latvian units passing through Estonia were gathering on Russia's Karelian border. Hence, Chicherin wrote, Estonians apparently suspected that the Tartu negotiations were a "cover [*maskirovka*]" for a Soviet attack on Narva to deflect Yudenich from Petrograd. "The logic of mutual fears and measures occasioned by them may lead to a new clash, undesirable for us...." Therefore the Soviet delegation should remove the Estonian fears and show that Russia was ready for peace. It should propose an armistice; far-reaching territorial concessions by Russia; a decision in principle on a basic peace treaty, details to be negotiated. Soviet diplomats should also warn that, "the negotiations had reached a critical moment. We keenly want their success, and we would not like to cause for Narva those sufferings that would result from an attack" that would be forced on us if Estonia failed to give the requested "guarantees." In conclusion, Chicherin told his comrades that Soviet military forces were ready to be thrown into the northwest front, but Soviet diplomacy "must try to avoid a new military crisis."[20]

Chief Soviet negotiator Adolf Joffe reported to Chicherin on December 22 that the Estonians rejected Soviet border proposals but that they agreed to "our guarantees." The Estonians were becoming more disposed to negotiate.

What happened was that the Soviets initially demanded the entire oil shale area near Narva for Soviet Russia, even though its population was ninety-five percent Estonian. By 1989-1990, when the area was heavily Russian populated, some Russians called for the area to become an "autonomous oblast" of the RSFSR. In 1919-1920, however, the Estonian delegation proposed borders that preserved what was demographically Estonian and historically "Estland."

Joffe added that an English naval captain in the Estonian delegation indicated that London wanted to explore peace talks with Russia on the condition that Soviet Russia disarmed its Baltic fleet. England would stop assisting anti-Soviet groups and lift its naval blockade, maintaining only a control to prevent military contraband from reaching Russia. England would deliver food to Petrograd in exchange for raw materials.

After these talks were encouraged by Chicherin, Joffe reported that the captain inquired whether Russia might make a separate peace with England without the Baltic republics, an English delegation visiting Petrograd on an English ship. The captain also asked if he could send some hats for English prisoners in Russia.[21] Joffe responded positively to all the English queries.

The Soviet diplomats withdrew their more extensive territorial demands, but on December 24 the Soviet delegation began to demand a ten kilometer demilitarized zone on both sides of the Narva River. Anticipating another Soviet offensive, the Estonians brought up fresh troops from the south. The Red Army launched a major attack along the Narva front on December 28 but was checked two days later. The Soviet delegation withdrew its demilitarization demand and an armistice was signed on December 31.[22]

Thirteen months of fighting had cost Estonia 3,588 dead and 13,775 wounded and heavy debts to Finland, Britain, France, and the United States.[23]

Soviet Russia's armistice with Estonia was followed by negotiations with Latvia in January 1920. Latvia's delegation at first rejected a Soviet proposal to neutralize the portion of Latgale from which Soviet troops had been driven, and to hold a plebiscite there. The area, Latvia asserted, belonged to Latvia. An armistice agreement reached on January 31 provided for severe limits on the number of troops permitted on each side of the Latgalian front, to be verified by mixed inspection teams. Latvia also agreed not to permit Polish, Estonian, or Lithuanian forces to attack Russia from its territory and to intern within forty-eight hours any White armies on its territory. Soviet Russia agreed not carry on propaganda or to support organizations in Latvia opposed to its political or social structure. Parts of the accord would remain secret until publicized by Latvia.[24]

On January 13, 1920, Chicherin wrote to the Soviet negotiators still meeting with Estonians in Tartu, noting that the first country to conclude peace with Soviet Russia would get the best terms. He suspected that Poland was goading the Baltic states to resume fighting with Russia so that Warsaw could reach an accord with the Soviets behind the backs of its neighbors. Chicherin observed that the Estonians were extremely demanding of Russia. He wondered if they had been inspired by conniving Poles or the Entente.

Chicherin said that the Communist Party's Politburo (where final authority obviously rested) agreed to transfer 15 million rubles of gold to Estonia, but refused to consider giving movable property or steamships to Estonia. If the Estonians wanted more, this would prove that they were not sincere about peace.

Chicherin noted that the Latvians, in their own bilateral talks with Russia, had become more cooperative. They would not permit the demilitarization of Latgale or a plebiscite there, but they assured the Soviets that the leftist tendencies among the Latgalians would impact on the country's parliament and facilitate better relations with Soviet Russia in the future. The Latvians told the Soviets that their port, Riga, was in better condition than Estonia's, Reval. The Latvians insisted, for the present, that many of their undertakings with Russia be kept secret until they chose to announce them. Chicherin hoped for a secret accord on trade rights eventually to be given Russia.[25]

Chicherin's hope that Warsaw might negotiate proved wrong. The Pilsudski regime wanted to regain Poland's borders of 1772 (before the first partition). The Polish army pushed deep into the Ukraine in April 1920. The Red Army drove back the Poles, reaching the gates of Warsaw in August, only to be repulsed. The Soviets meekly accepted an armistice in October, followed by the March 1921 Riga Treaty that left many Belorussians and Ukrainians under Polish rule.

The Tartu Treaty and "Peaceful Coexistence"

Estonia became the first European country to sign a peace treaty with Soviet Russia and received, as Chicherin predicted, the best terms. Still threatened on many fronts, Soviet diplomats no longer tried to drive hard bargains with Estonia. In the Tartu Peace Treaty of February 2, 1920, Soviet Russia recognized Estonia's independence.[26] Foreign Commissar G.V. Chicherin called the new relationship a "touchstone of the possibility of our peaceful coexistence with bourgeois states," a relationship Soviet diplomacy should protect.[27] This treaty became also the touchstone for Estonian nationalists in the late 1980s-1990, and they called on Moscow to respect the obligations it undertook at Tartu in 1920.

The treaty declared an end to the war between Russia and Estonia. Having proclaimed the right of all peoples to free self-determination including com-

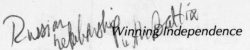

plete separation from the state to which they belong, Russia recognized "unconditionally the independence and autonomy [*samostoiatel'nost'*] of the Estonian state and freely renounces forever any rights of sovereignty held by Russia over the Estonian people and territory" arising from the past legal order or international accords.

Russia transferred to Estonia borderlands in the north and southeast populated heavily by Russians but occupied by Estonia in 1920. These lands added about five percent to the Estonian territory that combined the tsarist provinces of Estland and northern Livland. When Stalin's forces later retook Estonia, much of these territories was transferred back to the Russian republic. They became bones of contention when Estonia sought independence in 1990.

In 1920 the parties agreed to respect what might today be called an "Austrian solution": If Estonia's neutralization were recognized internationally, Russia would recognize and guarantee it. Both countries agreed to take part in and observe any international accord neutralizing the Gulf of Finland.

Estonia also pledged to demilitarize a belt of territory and waters from Narva to Lake Peipsi (Chudskoe, Peipus) and extending southwest from Lake Pihkva (Pskov). And Russia agreed to demilitarize an area east of that line up to the Velikaia River west of Pskov. But these commitments bound the parties only until January 1, 1922. On lakes Peipsi and Pihkva, however, both sides pledged not to have warships, with no time limit indicated.

Each party agreed not to permit its territory to serve as a base for armed aggression against the other. Each would disband guerrilla bands and prohibit recruitment on its territory for armies hostile to the other side or transit by such armies. A rapid timetable was provided for demobilization of irregulars, to be implemented under on-site inspection by mixed commissions with access to a telegraphic hot line (*Houghes'i aparaat* in Estonian) linking the inspectors with Tallinn and either Petrograd or Moscow.

Neither side would make any claims for war losses or expenditures, but Russia agreed to pay Estonia fifteen million in gold rubles and to turn over all Russian state properties — from port facilities and forts to library archives in Tartu — to Estonia. Non-Estonians in Estonia could claim Russian citizenship, but were in this case obliged to depart Estonia within a year and could take their property with them. The same rights applied to Estonians in Russia. By implication, if non-Estonians remained in Estonia, they became Estonian citizens, although some Russian Whites seem to have lived in Estonia in the 1920s-1930s on "Nansen" passports for stateless persons.

Russia even agreed to a kind of most-favored-nation clause: any rights that it gave to other succession states would be automatically extended to Estonia and its citizens.

Diplomatic relations would be established under a separate agreement.

The two countries recognized their mutual economic dependence. Their treaty provided also for an end to "war in economic and financial relations." The parties pledged to negotiate a trade treaty with most-favored-nation treatment and with special provisions for storage facilities at Estonian ports and duty free transit to Russia at low rates.

Using language similar to the August 27, 1918, German-Soviet treaty (noted in the previous chapter), Estonia and Russia agreed not to raise or lower the water levels of lakes Peipsi and Pihkva by more than a foot except by agreement or to deplete fish stocks there.

Estonia agreed to provide electricity to Russia. And Russia agreed to provide Estonia with concessions to build a railroad to Moscow and to exploit specified forests from Petrograd to Pskov to Arkhangelsk.

Estonia and Russia agreed to facilitate commercial shipping by means of lighthouses and other signals and by sweeping mines from the Baltic Sea.

Contrary to the Politburo's earlier expressed wish, a supplementary agreement listed Russian ships in Estonian ports that became Estonian property and the stocks of Estonian firms presently in the Russian People's Bank that would be returned to Estonia. One of them was the Dvigatel factory — in 1990 a military plant in Tallinn where many Russians worked.[28]

Russia's anxiety to solidify its relations with Estonia was seen in the fact that it ratified the Tartu Treaty just two days after it was signed. The Soviets concluded also a trade treaty with Estonia on March 31, 1920. Its success was seen in the fact that already in 1920 many goods passed through Estonia to Russia — the equivalent of 4,000 wagons of goods weighing 45,000 tons, over half of them agricultural machines and equipment.[29]

On July 12 Russia concluded a treaty with Lithuania similar to that signed with Estonia in February. The resolution of the Lithuania's borders with Poland and Latvia, however, was left to negotiations with those two countries.

Russia made a number of concessions related to properties evacuated from Lithuania in 1914-1917 and stated that these could not be "precedents" for a third party—a violation, it would seem, of Russia's obligations to Estonia regarding other succession states. But Russia paid Lithuania only three million gold rubles.[30]

A similar treaty with Latvia was signed August 11, 1920. As the threats to Russia's security dwindled, Moscow's terms became less generous. The pressure eased considerably when Poland agreed on August 6 to begin peace talks with Moscow.[31] On August 13 Russia signed an armistice with Finland.[32]

Unlike Russia's treaties with Estonia and Lithuania, the Latvian accord said nothing about that country's possible neutralization. Also, it permitted Russian armed forces to retain a unit known as the Latvian Rifles.

As with Estonia and Lithuania, Russia offered to negotiate a huge logging concession with Latvia, but pledged no gold ruble payments. Unlike the other two treaties, this one pledged the parties to seek agreement of other states in an "international peace fund" from which war damage would be restored. It also looked forward to economic cooperation with the other two Baltic republics.[33]

Having commenced negotiations with Finland in June, Russia signed a peace treaty with that country at Tartu on October 14, 1920. Finland, however—at least in Soviet eyes—invaded Russia again the next year, trying to recover Karelian territory, but was repulsed.

Indeed, Soviet Russia soon had problems with each Baltic republic. On July 10, 1920, Chicherin complained to the Estonian Minister of Foreign Affairs that Polish agents, Russian Whites, and anti-Soviet Ukrainians had established recruiting bureaus in several Estonian cities — at specified addresses — in violation of the Tartu Treaty, thereby creating a "bad [*tiazheloe*] impression" on the Russian government. Chicherin expressed the "firm certainty" that the Estonian government would stop these operations and report on the results of its efforts.[34]

On February 26, 1921, Chicherin complained that Latvia's representative in Moscow was abusing his diplomatic privileges to feed allegedly false information to the Latvian Telegraphic Agency, which reported an "armed uprising" in Moscow on February 25 and a few days earlier had told of inhumane conditions in Soviet prisons.[35]

Chicherin also worried in February 1921 that an international force might appear in Vilnius. Moscow wanted the city's status to be worked out between Lithuania and Poland, not by the League of Nations, whose authority the Soviet Republic denied.[36]

Open warfare between Soviet Russia and its western and northern neighbors halted in 1920-1921, but left traumatic memories on all sides. All parties needed cooperation with one another for trade and security. But distrust founded on past experience made such cooperation difficult. The history of 1917-1921 left both Communists and non-Communists with ample material for mutual recrimination for decades to come.

Despite Chicherin's plea that the 1920 Tartu treaty become a model of "peaceful coexistence," Soviet power continued to probe for weaknesses in the Baltic. The Communist Party of Estonia belonged to the Comintern and Party front organizations took an active part in Estonian elections. When Estonian Communist Viktor Kingissepp was executed for treason in 1922, the USSR renamed the border town of Iamburg (near Narva) for him. Estonian Communist leaders in exile, supported by Grigorii Zinoviev and other Comintern leaders, backed a coup d'état against Estonia's "bourgeois" government in late 1924. The Red Army partially mobilized along the Estonian border during the coup, but then returned to its normal status. After the abortive uprising and Estonian government crackdown, the Communist Party of Estonia never regained its precoup electoral strength and became a minor political actor for the rest of the interwar years.

NOTES

1. Quoted in Richard Pipes, *The Formation of the Soviet Union: Communism and Nationalism, 1917-1923*, rev. ed.(New York: Atheneum, 1968), p. 109.
2. Mikhail Heller and Aleksandr M. Nekrich, *Utopia in Power: The History of the Soviet Union from 1917 to the Present* (New York: Summit, 1986), pp. 76-77.
3. Party program quoted in Heller and Nekrich, *Utopia*, p. 110.
4. See Pipes, *Formation of the Soviet Union*, pp. 282-93.
5. Ibid.

6. Ibid., pp. 251-52.
7. Ibid., p. 253.
8. Ibid., p. 253.
9. Introduction to Tönu Parming and Elmar Järvesoo, eds., *A Case Study of a Soviet Republic: The Estonian SSR* (Boulder, Colo.: Westview, 1978), p. 8.
10. Toivo U. Raun, *Estonia and the Estonians* (Stanford, Calif.: Hoover Institution, 1987), pp. 104-5.
11. *Estonian War of Independence, 1918-1920*, reprint of a summary prepared by the Estonian National Historical Committee in 1938-1939 (Baltimore, Md.: Esto, Inc., 1988).
12. Donald W. Treadgold, *Twentieth Century Russia*, 7th ed. (Boulder, Colo.: Westview, 1990), pp. 164-65.
13. Political Report to the Central Committee on December 2, 1919, in V. I. Lenin, *Polnoe Sobranie Sochinenii*, 5th ed. (Moscow: Politizdat, 1963), 39, pp. 342-63, cited points at 347-49.
14. Soviet proposal and Estonian reply in *Dokumenty vneshnei politiki SSSR* [hereafter *DVP*](Moscow: Politizdat, 1958), 2, pp. 242-43.
15. *DVP*, 2, pp. 247-48.
16. See exchanges ibid., 2, pp. 254-56.
17. Ibid., 2, pp. 266-68.
18. Ibid., 2, pp. 268-72; also *Izvestiia*, 1, 1 November 1919.
19. *DVP*, 2, pp. 299-305; *Izvestiia*, 10 December 1919.
20. *DVP*, 2, pp. 310-11.
21. Ibid., 2, pp. 313-15.
22. *Estonian War of Independence*, p. 43.
23. Ibid., p. 45.
24. See notes on discussions held January 11 and 13, 1920, and the treaty of January 30 and supplementary agreement of February 1 in *DVP*, 2, pp. 320-22; 333-38.
25. *DVP*, 2, pp. 323-25.
26. Text republished in Estonian and Russian in Tallinn by Valgus, 1989: *Rahuleping Eesti ja Venemaa Vahel. Mirnyi dogovor mezhdu Rossiei i Estoniei*. Russian text *DVP*, 2, pp. 339-52 and supplementary February 12, 1920, accord at pp. 353-54. The map at p. 341 shows the demilitarized zone for Estonia but not for Russia!
27. Letter of G. V. Chicherin to the Soviet representative in Estonia, March 22, 1920, from Soviet archives, quoted in A. A. Gromyko and B. N. Ponomarev, eds., *Istoriia vneshnei politiki SSSR 1917-1975*, 2 vols. (Moscow: Nauka, 1976), 2, p. 114.
28. *DVP*, 2, pp. 353-54.
29. *Istoriia vneshnei politiki SSSR*, 1, p. 114.
30. Ibid., pp. 28-42. The accompanying map and text, however, show Vilnius and surrounding districts as part of Lithuania. They were later taken by Poland.
31. See Soviet announcement on August 12, 1920, ibid., pp. 119-21.
32. Ibid., pp. 124-29.
33. Ibid., pp. 101-16.
34. *DVP* (1959), 3, pp. 26-27.
35. Ibid., pp. 545-46.
36. Telegram to Russia's representative in Lithuania on 27 February 1921, ibid., pp. 546-47.

4
From Independence to Stalinism

Soviet recognition of the Baltic republics' independence lasted two decades. In 1940 they were forcibly incorporated into the USSR, becoming more like colonies than sovereign Union Republics or junior partners of a hegemonic power.

Interwar Symbiosis: Antagonistic and Unstable Between Russia and Germany

Newly independent and untested economically or politically, the three Baltic nations could seek security through a variety of approaches. Basically, they could deal with the other states alone or together. They could pursue neutrality or various shades of alignment. They could lean toward Moscow, toward Berlin, or toward the League of Nations. They could align with one or both principal League supporters, France or Britain. There was even a possibility of forming a Greater Baltic Union with Scandinavia, Finland, and Poland.

Solidarity among the Baltic states was difficult to sustain for many reasons, beginning with the special situation of Lithuania, which had ongoing problems with Poland and Germany (over Memel/Klaipeda) but no common border with the USSR (until Belorussia expanded at Poland's expense in 1939). Estonia and Latvia, on the other hand, bordered Russia, but not Germany.

Weimar Germany, for its part, wanted to prevent Polish hegemony in the Baltic and to protect the interests of Baltic Germans, mainly in Estonia and Latvia. Berlin cleared up the financial claims of all three Baltic states and signed trade treaties with them — at the same time that it courted Soviet Russia and, after the mid-1920s, the League of Nations.[1]

Rather than practice mutually beneficent symbiosis, the peoples of East Central Europe and the Baltic failed to nourish the individual and collective strengths that might have put off larger predators. Thus, Poland and Lithuania — having become free countries for the first time since the eighteenth century — came to blows over Vilnius. Immediately after Marshal Pilsudski stopped fighting Russia in October 1920, Poland seized Vilnius. Lithuania severed diplomatic ties with Poland until 1938, just before both countries were again partitioned and swallowed by their larger neighbors.

Following the Riga Treaty with Russia in 1921, Poland looked for allies against Soviet Russia and against Lithuania. Warsaw tried to organize a Baltic bloc including Finland, Estonia, and Latvia, buttressed perhaps by Romania. The foreign ministers of Finland, Estonia, and Latvia met with Poland in Warsaw from March 13 to 17, 1922, and signed a treaty of mutual assistance. This pact — which never went into effect — provided that in case of an unprovoked attack upon any of the signatories, the other parties would observe a benevolent attitude toward the country attacked and agree immediately upon measures to be taken.[2] Paris approved this orientation and a French commentator underscored that the Warsaw Treaty embodied no aggressive intentions. It was for defense against Russia, and perhaps against Germany. It would be an antidote to "the Bolshevik contagion" and a pledge of security.[3]

The Kremlin considered the Warsaw Treaty to be an anti-Soviet bloc sponsored by the Entente. Moscow feared that the pact could be used to justify aggression against Soviet Russia in spite of its formally defensive character. Indeed, Helsinki declined to ratify the Warsaw Treaty from anxiety that it might pull Finland into a Polish war with Russia.[4]

To counter the Warsaw Treaty orientation, Moscow persuaded Estonia, Latvia, and Poland to meet in Riga. Finland was also invited, but chose not to attend. On March 30 the conferees signed a Riga Protocol declaring their support for arms limitation in all countries; for demilitarized frontier zones cleared of raiding parties; for a mutual guarantee of the peace treaties between Russia and the other three signatories; for de jure recognition of Soviet Russia; and for a coordinated line at the forthcoming Genoa Economic Conference.[5]

Both Soviet and Western historians have underscored the advantages that the Riga Protocol provided to Moscow.[6] But Polish Foreign Minister Skirmundt said in April that the Polish delegation to Riga had exceeded its powers.[7] At the subsequent Genoa Conference Poland did not support Soviet positions and Skirmundt denied that the Riga Protocol produced any obligations for Warsaw. He said that to demilitarize borders would be to establish "foreign control" in violation of "national sovereignty." [8]

The Genoa Conference in April 1922 worsened Russia's relations with France, Britain, and Poland. Not only did it not produce a plan for economic reconstruction or disarmament, but it revealed the reluctance of Poland and other countries to ban the White armies that, Chicherin said, still operated against Russia from bases in Finland, Poland, Romania, and Yugoslavia.[9]

Unable to strike a deal with Paris and London at Genoa, Moscow signed the Rapallo Treaty with Germany.[10] The Kremlin also permitted clandestine German military training and production on Soviet soil — a harbinger of more extensive collaboration with Hitler in 1939-1941.[11]

Following Genoa and Rapallo, however, the Kremlin invited Estonia, Latvia, Poland, Finland, and Romania to the Moscow Conference on the Reduction of Armaments in late 1922. Most of these states met twice in Tallinn and once in Warsaw, August through October, to develop a common front. Romania ultimately refused to attend the Moscow conference, which finally convened in December. Lithuania, invited only on November 23, hastened to accept.

This meeting turned out to be another arms control conference that aggravated distrust. Poland followed France's slogan, "security first, disarmament later." Indeed, Russia's neighbors generally agreed that "material disarmament" depended on "moral disarmament." So long as distrust prevailed, nations would keep their arms. Maxim Litvinov, on the other hand, contended that material disarmament could generate trust. Poland argued that Litvinov was asking Russia's neighbors to match cuts that the Kremlin already planned to make in its own bloated Red Army. Litvinov, in turn, accused the other conferees of exaggerating the size of their forces so that any cuts would be imaginary.

As Litvinov spoke, *Izvestiia* (December 2, 1922) published a table showing that the Red Army outnumbered those of the other conferees (plus Romania) taken together. But the table also indicated that the other countries had a higher density of troops relative to overall population, to borders, and to overall territory, and higher defense expenditures in relation to the general budget. Romania and Poland, for example, had over 800 soldiers per 1,000 square kilometers of territory; Estonia and Latvia, over 300; Finland had 88, but Russia only 44. Since the Red Army had to fend off potential foes in Western Europe as well as Japan, its existing numbers were meager.

Mutual suspicion and enmity increased, making arms agreements impossible to attain. Russia's neighbors refused to cut their arms significantly, saying that their forces already approximated the lowest levels that small states could consider. When the conference ended, however, the Soviets announced a large cut in their forces—the very reduction that Poland had anticipated.[12]

Pravda (December 12, 1922) blamed Poland for breaking up the conference and said that "the poor Baltic countries" must have felt let down and deceived by Warsaw. "Russia...could easily have reached an agreement with them [the Baltic states] on the reciprocal reduction of armaments. In the final analysis, it is not so important for Russia whether the Estonian army consists of ten or of 15,000 soldiers." A "compromise" (*kompromis*) would have been possible had the Balts broken from Poland, but for this they had "not enough daring." *Izvestiia* (December 8, 1922) charged that Russia's neighbors wanted large armies to cope with an "internal foe"—their own peoples.

Neither the major powers nor Russia's neighbors did much to derail the "unholy alliance" that bound the two pariahs of Europe.

Economic Progress and Domestic Instability in the Baltic

Land reform in all three Baltic countries created the basis for a flourishing agriculture in the interwar years, with significant exports, particularly to England and Germany. Industrialization marched at a quick pace in Estonia and Latvia, but proceeded on a smaller scale in Lithuania.[13]

The Baltic countries, like most of Europe, suffered considerable political instability for much of the interwar period. In Lithuania an authoritarian presidential regime, similar to Pisudski's in Poland, emerged under Antanas Smetona in 1926. Smetona tried to fashion his regime on the fascist Italian model, but the pressures of the late 1930s induced him to permit coalition governments of national unity.

I always think, cumemakra

Estonia had twenty-one short-lived coalition cabinets, from 1919 to 1933, when a new constitution gave sweeping powers to the president, Konstantin Päts. Political parties were abolished in 1934, but a more democratic constitution came into force in 1938, at the very time that Austria and the Sudetenland were passing into the Third Reich.

In 1933 Latvian Prime Minister Karlis Ulmanis dissolved all parties and governed without a legislature. He combined the offices of president and prime minister. Championing "a strong and Latvian Latvia," he enlarged the state sector of the economy at the expense of the German minority.

Political authoritarianism, however, did not prevent significant cultural advance in each Baltic republic. Schools multiplied and universities were maintained, for the first time making higher education available in the native language.

As war clouds gathered in the late 1930s, the three Baltic countries tried to maintain their neutrality. But they did little to maintain a common cause against Russia or Germany. Lithuania and Poland threatened each other; Finland wanted no part of a southern alliance. An Estonian-Latvian defensive alliance in 1923 was supplemented in 1934 by a Baltic Entente including Lithuania, but it achieved little. Lithuania and Latvia saw the greater danger in Germany; Estonia, in the USSR.

All three Baltic republics signed nonaggression or neutrality treaties with Moscow — Lithuania in 1926, Latvia and Estonia in 1932. They also signed such pacts with Berlin — Lithuania when it ceded Klaipeda to Germany in March 1939; Latvia and Estonia in June 1939. They adopted neutrality laws patterned on the 1939 Swedish model in December 1938-January 1939.

Britain since 1919 had supported the Baltic countries, but appeared weak and irresolute by 1939. Still, one reason for the failure of the Anglo-French military mission to Moscow in the summer of 1939 was probably the unwillingness of London and Paris to grant Stalin a free hand in the Baltic.

When Germany took Klaipeda (Memel) in March 1939 it also stepped up economic pressure on Lithuania. Berlin offered the Kaunas government a military alliance against Poland, but Lithuania declined, even though Hitler proffered Vilnius as the prize.

Partition and Annexation of the Baltic

Alarmed by Hitler, the USSR joined the League of Nations in 1934 and led a campaign to forge a system of collective security. When the 1938 Munich accord demonstrated the futility of this approach, the Kremlin turned toward Germany. For much of the next year Moscow juggled two sets of negotiations, one with Paris and London, the other with Berlin. Probably Stalin wished to keep both tracks open to see which proved more useful. Certainly he played one against the other, pressing each for greater concessions in the Baltic.[14]

Hitler's *Mein Kampf* had called for establishing *Lebensraum*, "living space," for Germans. National Socialists, he said, should push German migration toward the East, toward "Russia and her border States."[15]

Stalin opted for the German alignment over the Anglo-French. Stalin perceived German intentions, but hoped to thwart or exploit them for his own objectives. Foreign ministers Joachim von Ribbentrop and V. M. Molotov signed a Treaty of Nonaggression on August 23, 1939. Its Secret Additional Protocol specified that "in the event of a territorial and political rearrangement in the areas belonging to the Baltic States (Finland, Estonia, Latvia, Lithuania) the northern boundary of Lithuania shall represent the boundary of the spheres of influence of Germany and the USSR. In this connection the interest of Lithuania in the Vilna area is recognized by each party." Poland was split into spheres of influence; Russia's interest in Bessarabia was also recognized.[16] Further negotiations led to a protocol, signed on September 28, 1939, that shifted Lithuania to Moscow's sphere in exchange for the Kremlin's conceding to Germany the province of Lublin and other parts of Poland earlier allotted to the USSR.[17]

Estonia became Moscow's first Baltic target. On September 19, one day after a Polish submarine's escape from internment in the Tallinn harbor, Molotov summoned the Estonian ambassador and informed him that since the Estonian government could not protect its coast, the Soviet Baltic Fleet would undertake this task. On September 25 Molotov demanded the immediate conclusion of a Soviet-Estonian military alliance providing for Soviet military bases on Estonian territory. The Estonian government agreed to this pact on September 28, along with a protocol specifying that 25,000 Soviet troops would be stationed in Estonia. The Red Army rushed in the same day.[18]

Latvia and Lithuania experienced similar treatment, but without pretexts such as the Polish submarine. Latvia signed a mutual assistance pact with Moscow on October 5 and Lithuania on October 10 (the latter getting Vilnius as part of the bargain).

Finland, however, refused Soviet demands, whereupon the Red Army attacked on November 30. On December 14, by unanimous vote the League of Nations Council expelled the USSR from the organization. Finland and three other Council members (China, Greece, Yugoslavia) abstained. Earlier, the League Assembly in record time condemned Soviet aggression and asked League members to aid Finland. Of thirty-nine states present for the Assembly vote, nine abstained on the resolution — the three Baltic republics, the three Scandinavian countries, Bulgaria, China, and Switzerland — each of which had its own fish to fry.

The "Winter War" ended on March 12, 1940, with Helsinki ceding the Karelian isthmus to the USSR and leasing to Moscow the Hango Peninsula for thirty years.[19]

Not appeased by their abstentions in Geneva, the Kremlin turned again on the three Baltic countries.[20] On May 25, 1940, Molotov began a series of accusations charging Lithuania with violating the 1939 mutual assistance pact. Despite desperate attempts by Lithuanian authorities to mollify the Kremlin, Molotov presented an ultimatum just before midnight on June 14: The Lithuanian interior and security ministers must be handed over to judicial authorities and a government formed in Lithuania "capable" of upholding the 1939 treaty. Soviet troops must be allowed to occupy the "most important centers" of Lithuania. Moscow demanded an answer the next morning.

The Lithuanians capitulated and the Red Army poured in. Moscow insisted on appointing the new prime minister and other key officials. Initially a popular front coalition was established including Populists and Social Democrats. Communists, however, took over the key interior ministry and state security department.

That same month — June 1940 — Latvia and Estonia faced the same Soviet tactics. They too were chided for having taken part in the Baltic Entente (periodic consultations by the three foreign ministers according to a 1934 agreement) and for having supported publication of a journal, the *Révue Baltique* published in English, French, and German but not Russian. Both *excellent breakdown of communist takeover of Poland*

republics capitulated, although their legitimate presidents had to be coerced by Soviet-organized demonstrations and other pressures to approve the new people's governments that started to function on June 22, 1940, precisely one year before Germany attacked Russia.

The USSR appointed high-ranking emissaries for each Baltic state — Vladimir Dekanozov for Lithuania, Andrei Vyshinskii for Latvia, and Leningrad Party leader Andrei Zhdanov for Estonia. Soviet citizens arrived from the USSR to take up leading positions, many of them Communists of Baltic extraction. In Estonia they were called "Yestonians" (for their Russian accents) and dominated political life for years.

Moscow imposed the same pattern simultaneously in all three Baltic states: First, the Communist Party was legalized in each country and the former ruling parties banned, thus creating one-party systems.[21] Second, by July many non-Communists had been purged from Baltic governments and the majority of all cabinet offices were held by Communists. Third, two waves of mass arrests (July 11-12 and 18-19) removed thousands of noncompliant elites from the political life of each Baltic nation. Fourth, with all non-Communists eliminated from the ballots, elections were held on July 14 in which over 90 percent of all votes went to the sole official slates of the Working People's Leagues. If results were not up to Soviet expectations, they were doctored. Fifth, the newly elected People's Diets met on July 21 and by acclamation voted to become Soviet Republics and to seek admission into the USSR — an issue not mentioned at all in the electoral campaigns or League platforms. Sixth, the accession requests were rubber-stamped by the USSR Supreme Soviet in August. Similar steps had sovietized the Ukraine and other border republics some two decades before; elements of this approach were utilized after World War II in Eastern Europe and elsewhere, as in Afghanistan in 1978-1979.

Many thousands of Balts were deported to Russian work camps in June 1941, during the week before Hitler's invasion. The precise numbers cannot be known without full access to Soviet archives, but preliminary data published in 1987 report that on just the night of June 14, 1941, more than 12,000 Estonians, 15,000 Latvians, and 34,000 Lithuanians were deported.[22] Another source estimates that in the initial Soviet occupation of 1940-1941 some 60,000 Estonians, 34,000 Latvians, and 75,000 Lithuanians were killed or

deportations

deported.[23] Even if the actual numbers were only half these, the result was tantamount to a Baltic holocaust, especially of elites and middle classes.

The indigenous Communist parties in all three Baltic republics had been tiny, sectarian, and clandestine. (In all of Eastern Europe only Czechoslovakia permitted the Communist Party to operate openly and legally). Soviet data put Communist Party memberships in June 1940 at 1,500 in Lithuania; less than 1,000 in Latvia; and only 133 in Estonia. In 1940-1941 they were backed by some "fellow travelers" (mainly intellectuals and ethnic minorities); by crypto-Communists who had posed as members of other parties; and by the Yestonian-type émigrés from the USSR.[24] Their main bulwark, however, was the USSR's overwhelming might and determination to seize and sovietize the Baltic. This might permitted Molotov to issue his diktats and the Red Army and Navy to surround and then occupy the region.

The Kremlin's subjugation of the Baltic flouted a series of international legal obligations in treaties between Moscow and the three Baltic republics: the peace and good-neighbor principles of the 1920 peace treaties; the renunciation of war "protocol" sponsored by Maxim Litvinov in 1929; the nonaggression and peaceful conciliation treaties signed between 1926 and 1932; the 1933 convention on aggression (concluded not only with the Baltic but with other states) specifying that no political, military, economic or other claim might serve as a justification for armed invasion; and the 1939 mutual assistance treaties with their promise "never to infringe upon the sovereign rights of these states, with particular pertinence to their political structure and social and economic organization." [25]

Moscow also stretched its 1939 territorial understandings with Berlin to take in Bukovina as well as Bessarabia; to occupy the strip of Lithuanian territory that was eventually supposed to go to Germany; and to eliminate the independent existence of the Baltic republics. The Ribbentrop-Molotov game rules did not provide that acknowledgment of a sphere of influence meant an automatic right to incorporate the subject territory, as shown in German-Soviet negotiations on Poland, where a special accord was needed to eliminate the "independent Polish rump state."

Despite repeated pressures from Stalin and the joint struggle against Hitler after 1941, the British and United States governments never recognized the incorporation of the Baltic republics into the USSR.[26] Even Hitler's regime never granted de jure recognition of Baltic incorporation. Ratification of a third German-Soviet border protocol, signed January 10, 1941 never took place (even though Moscow paid Berlin 7.5 million gold dollars to keep the "Lithuanian strip").

Since few states recognized Soviet annexation of the Baltic states, their international legal right to be treated as sovereign nations appeared to be unconditional.[27] It did not depend upon renunciation of the Molotov-Ribbentrop pact or on some local referendum or even on the approval of the USSR Supreme Soviet.

Sovietization

Occupied by Germany for much of World War II, the Baltic republics were "liberated" again by the Red Army in 1944.[28] Baltic partisans waged guerrilla warfare against Soviet occupiers for several years, but were effectively repressed by the late 1940s-early 1950s.

The essence of those times and their significance for Estonian life today was summed up by Communist Party First Secretary Vaino Väljas in 1989:

"The real experience of socialism came to Estonia with Stalinist deformations and crimes. The 1940 transformations were accompanied by violence and lawlessness camouflaged by noble slogans, by the restriction of democratic freedoms, and by unjustified brutality in the struggle against 'class enemies.' The ideas of socialism were irretrievably compromised by the deportations of June 14, 1941.

"Unfortunately, everything continued in the same vein even after the liberation of Soviet Estonia from the fascist occupiers. The long-awaited land reform was followed by forced collectivization, which was prefaced by the exile of about 20,000 people to Siberia.

"A blow to national cadres was struck by the 1950 Eighth Estonian Communist Party (Bolshevik) Central Committee plenum, after which over 90 percent of Estonian-born leadership personnel were dismissed from their posts and many well-known cultural figures were repressed." [29]

Demographic Change under Soviet and Nazi Rule

All three Baltic republics were depopulated during and after World War II, these losses later countered by an influx of immigrants, especially to Estonia and Latvia. Balts therefore remember not only their ancestors who perished under foreign rule, but those who were never born, because their potential fathers and mothers died unnaturally. Such thoughts provoked despair but also anger. As one Estonian scholar put it in 1989, "We can forgive, but never forget."

As noted earlier, an accurate picture of demographic change in the Baltic must await publication of data from Soviet archives. Preliminary Western estimates indicate that the three Baltic states lost about 20 percent of their populations under Soviet, Nazi, and then Soviet rule, 1940-1945. The biggest sources of loss were politically motivated flight and territorial changes. Discounting these factors, Estonia, Latvia, and Lithuania lost about 9 percent of their populations during the war—about the same as the USSR as a whole, but less than Yugoslavia (12 percent) and Poland (20 percent). Depopulation stemmed from many factors: Resettlement of Germans and nominal Swedes in 1939-1940; politically motivated flight by Balts, Jews, and others to neighboring Finland, Poland, and also, after June 1941, to Russia; Soviet deportations and executions that occurred in 1940-1941 and in 1944-1945. Still other deaths occurred when thousands of Balts were mobilized for military service in the Red Army and later the German. Many died also in partisan warfare.[30]

The postwar years were also a time of enormous population loss for all three Baltic peoples. Estonia lost about 100,000 natives due to deportations, executions, and guerrilla warfare; Latvia, at least 150,000; and Lithuania (where guerrilla activity was more widespread), about 450,000. In the decade 1945-1955 births compensated for less than half of these.[31]

Another case study reports even heavier losses for Estonia in nearly every category and estimates that fewer than 780,000 persons remained from a prewar population of 1,133,900.[32] One demand of Estonian demonstrators on August 23, 1987, was that Soviet authorities publish the actual dimensions of depopulation rather than understated "admissions that as many as 20,000 Estonians were deported" in 1940-1944, reiterated by Väljas even in 1989. Still, some Estonian demographers with access to Soviet archives said in 1990 that the Western estimates summarized here exaggerate Baltic population losses after 1945. Even if deflated by half, they would still be severe.

In Estonia and Latvia birth rates were low and demographic losses were made up by migration from Russia and other parts of the USSR; Lithuania, less industrialized, attracted fewer migrants and had higher birth rates than most of the western USSR.

Colonial or Hegemonic System?

Gradually, Soviet totalitarian controls had a severe impact on each nation's psychology. By 1953, throughout the Baltic, resistance to Soviet domination had wilted and Moscow's Soviet hegemony had come to be considered "more than a momentary and superficial occupation. In this sense, it had become 'legitimate'....The habit of mentally challenging every Soviet rule slowly shifted into the less strainful habit of submission. A significant change of attitude seems to have taken place — from struggle against a foreign 'occupation' to working for one's own interest within a framework of foreign 'rule.'" [33]

Tsarist Russia had treated its Baltic provinces as virtual colonies. Following the logic of one political scientist, the Baltic republics should have qualified by the 1940s to be treated not as colonies but as satellites or client states in a hegemonic system dominated by Russia.[34] Despite the fact that the Baltic republics had industrialized and known independence between the world wars, and despite the powers nominally reserved to the Union Republics by the 1936 Soviet Constitution, the Kremlin treated Estonia, Latvia, and Lithuania more like colonies than quasi-independent states. It killed or deported suspected oppositionists; decided how the local economy would be organized and what it would produce for the USSR; and proceeded with an intensive campaign of Russification that included not only language training and indoctrination but waves of non-Baltic immigrants who tried to make Russian not just the lingua franca but the dominant tongue.

To compare this system (or that established in Poland or other "East European" countries after 1945)[35] with British hegemony in the Middle East or that of the United States in Latin America is highly misleading. Even in Nicaragua, occupied intermittently by U.S. Marines, Washington sought in the 1930s and 1980s to establish a system of law and order based on free elections. Yankee influence on Latin economies, even in Guatemala, fell far short of Moscow's control of the Baltic and other Union Republics. In short, Communist Russia, no less than tsarist, treated the Baltic republics more as colonies than as independent clients.

If interesting that he felt the need to clarify.

NOTES

1. See John Hiden, *The Baltic States and Weimar Ostpolitik* (Cambridge and New York: Cambridge University Press, 1987); also essays by Alexander Dallin and Edgar Anderson, in Stanley Vardys and Romuald J. Misiunas, eds., *The Baltic States in Peace and War, 1917-1945* (University Park: Pennsylvania State University Press, 1978); and Royal Institute of International Affairs, *The Baltic States* (Westport, Conn.: Greenwood Press, 1970; first published, 1938).
2. *Materialy genuezskoi konferentsii* (Moscow: NKID, 1922), p. 49.
3. Jacques de Coussange, "La Finlande, les États baltes et la Pologne," *Journal des Débats* (Paris), No. 1467 (7 April 1922), pp. 546-47.
4. *Materialy genuezskoi konferentsii*, pp. 39-40; *Survey of International Affairs, 1920-1923*, Royal Institute of International Affairs (London and New York: Oxford University Press, 1923-), pp. 241-42.
5. *Materialy genuezskoi konferentsii*, pp. 52-53.
6. See I. F. Ivashin, *Ocherki istorii vneshnei politiki SSSR* (Moscow: Gospolizdat, 1958), pp. 97-98; Albert N. Tarulis, *Soviet Policy Toward the Baltic States, 1918-1940* (Notre Dame, Ind.: Notre Dame University Press, 1959), pp. 66-67.
7. Skirmundt in London, reported by *L'Europe Nouvelle* (Paris), No. 14 (14 April 1922), p. 435. His statement led the journal to print the Riga Protocol only with *"tout réserve."*
8. *Materialy genuezkoi konferentsii*, pp. 262-63.
9. Ibid., pp. 261-63, 270-78.
10. For a study based on German as well as Soviet archives, see A. Akhtamzian, *Rapall'skaia politika* (Moscow: Mezhdunarodnyie otnosheniia, 1974).
11. See Raymond L. Garthoff, *Soviet Military Policy: A Historical Analysis* (New York: Praeger, 1966), p. 13 and n. 31.
12. *Conférence de Moscou pour la limitation des armaments* (Moscow: NKID, 1923). Latvian archives on preliminary meetings of the Baltic states and Poland in Tallinn are quoted in *Istoriia vneshnei politiki SSSR*, 1, p. 179.
13. For a summary, see Romuald J. Misiunas and Rein Taagepera, *The Baltic States: Years of Dependence, 1940-1980* (Berkeley, Calif.: University of California Press, 1983), pp. 10ff. For detailed analysis, see Georg von Rauch, *The Baltic States: the Years of Independence, 1917-1940* (Berkeley, Calif.: University of California Press, 1974).
14. See Alexander Shtromas, *The Soviet Method of Conquest of the Baltic States: Lessons for the West* (Washington, D.C.: Washington Institute for Values in Public Policy, 1986), pp. 4-7.
15. Quoted in John W. Wheeler-Bennett, *The Forgotten Peace: Brest-Litovsk, March 1918* (New York: William Morrow, 1939), pp. xv-xvi.
16. Text in Raymond J. Sontag and James S. Beddie, eds., *Nazi-Soviet Relations 1939-1941: Documents from the Archives of the German Foreign Office* (Washington, D.C.: U.S. Department of State, 1948), pp. 76-78.
17. See also William J. H. Hough, III, "The Annexation of the Baltic States and Its Effect on the Development of Law Prohibiting Forcible Seizure of Territory," *New York Law School Journal of International and Comparative Law*, 6, 2 (Winter 1985).
18. A speech on 1 January 1940 by General I. Laidoner, commander of Estonian forces, to the general staff laid out the hard choices facing the country. It was printed with the secret protocol of the August 23, 1939, Soviet-German treaty and historical analyses by E. Laasi

and K. Arjakas in the Tallinn monthly *Raduga*, 12 (1988), pp. 78-94. Laidoner was removed to the USSR on 19 July 1940, where he died in prison on 13 March 1953.

19. Eino Jutikkala with Kauko Pirinen, *A History of Finland* (New York: Dorset, 1988), chap. 11.

20. Soviet legal undertakings with Estonia and other countries, 1920-1940, and Soviet actions against Estonia are analyzed and documented with many appendices in A. Köörna et al., comps., *1940 god v Estonii: Dokumenty i materialy* (Tallinn: Olion, 1989). See also Shtromas, *The Soviet Method of Conquest*, which distills recent secondary works as well as primary sources. For a Finnish analysis that treats the Balts not just as passive objects but as subjects, their policies responding to domestic compulsions, see Seppo Myllyniemi, *Die baltische Krise 1938-1941* (Stuttgart: Deutsche Verlags-Anstalt, 1977) (Finnish original, 1977).

21. In Estonia Communist political prisoners had been released in a general amnesty in 1938.

22. See Toomas Ilves, "Press Publishes Figures on Deportations and Partisan Warfare," *Radio Free Europe Research*, 13, 3 (22 January 1988), p. 5.

23. *Mass Deportations of Population from the Soviet Occupied Baltic States* (Stockholm: Estonian Information Centre and Latvian National Foundation, 1981), p. 28. The booklet reprints at p. 32 part of a decree of the People's Commissariat for State Security of the Lithuanian SSR on deportations from Lithuania dated 25 April 1941, but referring back to an NKVD order of 11 October 1939.

24. Shtromas, *Soviet Method*, pp. 26-27.

25. For analysis, see Hough, "Annexation of the Baltic States."

26. For more detail, see chap. 15, "Implications for the West."

27. Sweden transferred Baltic assets to Moscow in the 1940s, but stated in 1977 that it had not decided whether to recognize the incorporation as de facto or de jure. Australia and New Zealand in the 1974 recognized Moscow's Baltic claims as de jure, but Australia soon reverted to nonrecognition. China and Yugoslavia have strongly contested Soviet Baltic claims. See Hough, "Annexation of the Baltic States," pp. 429, 443; Shtromas, *Soviet Method*, p. 44.

28. Moscow's revived cabaret, "The Bat," tells the story of a provincial Balt who was enlisted for menial work by the Nazis and then jailed for this for twenty years. Later, in quiet retirement, he is sought out for a pension by the punctilious West Germans, a step that angers his Soviet neighbors and ruins what is left of his life. The laughter of the 1989 Muscovites was bitter. See Francis X. Clines in *The New York Times*, 16 August 1989, p. A4.

29. V. Väljas, "On the Political Situation in the Republic and Party Organizations' Work to Rally Working People and Social Forces to Resolve the Tasks of Restructuring" (speech to the 14th CPE CC plenum, 4 May 1988), *Sovetskaia Estoniia*, 5 May 1989, pp. 1-3, and Foreign Broadcast Information Service, *Daily Report: Soviet Union* (Washington, D.C.) 17 May 1989, pp. 61-74, at p. 62.

30. Misiunas and Taagepera, *The Baltic States*, pp. 72, 272-76.

31. Ibid., pp. 124-25. The number deported or killed in 1944-1952 has been put at 124,000 Estonians, 136,000 Latvians, and 245,000 Lithuanians—*Mass Deportations*, p. 28.

32. Orders of magnitude are similar to those in *Mass Deportations*, but Tönu Parming estimates the following losses. From resettlement of Germans, Swedes, and others: about 26,000; Soviet executions: 2,000; deportations by Soviet authorities: 19,000 in 1941, 30,000 in 1944, and 80,000 in 1949 when agriculture was collectivized; evacuation to Russia in 1941: 33,000 (many of whom later returned); executions by German authorities in 1941-1944: 6,000; men

mobilized into the Red Army in 1941, most of whom probably died in service: 33,000; men who died in German military units: 25,000; politically motivated flight westward: 117,000; residents of territory transferred in 1945 from Estonia to the Russian Republic, 71,500. Still others died fighting with German units or as partisans. Tönu Parming, "Roots of Nationality Differences," in Edward Allworth, ed., *Nationality Group Survival in Multi-Ethnic States: Shifting Support Patterns in the Soviet Baltic Region* (New York: Praeger, 1977), pp. 34-35; also Parming, "Population Changes and Processes," in Parming and Järvesoo, *A Case Study*, pp. 21-74, at pp. 24-28. When Soviet archives open, these estimates can be sharpened.

33. Misiunas and Taagepera, *Baltic States*, p. 124.
34. James R. Kurth, "Economic Change and State Development," in Jan F. Triska, ed., *Dominant Powers and Subordinate States: The United States in Latin America and the Soviet Union in Eastern Europe* (Durham, N.C.: Duke University Press, 1986), pp. 84-101.
35. The Czech-born writer Milan Kundera has sharply protested (in *Cross Currents*) the problem in referring to the region as Eastern Europe: "I am always shocked by the perfidious vocabulary that has transformed Central Europe into the East. Central Europe represents the destiny of the West, in concentrated form." While Bulgaria and Romania are geographically and culturally distant from the West, the Baltic peoples have been closer, both geographically and culturally, to the West than to Russia, despite the nominal sway of St. Petersburg and later of Moscow.

5
Gorbachev's Inheritance: Thaw and Stagnation, 1953-1985

Many Balts despaired of shaping their own lives for the better in the late 1940s-early 1950s, but the post-Stalin "Thaw" permitted some to dream of a freer, more prosperous life. Small gains fueled rising expectations.

The thrust of Soviet policy after 1953 was toward destalinization in internal and foreign affairs. In nationality affairs, however, Party leader Nikita Khrushchev and then Leonid Brezhnev continued the push toward Russification. Still, official admission that Stalin had erred in many ways and that there are many roads to socialism opened the door to criticism of Stalin's nationality policies. If Yugoslavia had the right to go its own way, as Khrushchev affirmed in 1955, why could not the border peoples of the USSR? Even though free speech and access to the media were still limited, the decline of terror and greater toleration of conflicting opinion led to direct criticism of Soviet nationality policies, as in the *Chornovil Papers*.[1] Few if any nationalist dissidents were shot, although many were sent to labor camps or psychiatric wards, where some died slowly.

Destalinization and other changes in Soviet society put the country's former wardens in jeopardy. Estonian poet August Sang compared them with clerics threatened by Galileo:

> *Those who till then seemed to stand securely*
> *suddenly grew fearful that they'd fall.*
> *Trembling church-fathers felt that surely*
> *this would wreck their good, old-fashioned world.*[2]

Estonian Party leader Vaino Väljas in 1989 summed up some negative developments of the 1960s and later: "With the sixties much of the industry of the Estonian SSR was placed under all-Union jurisdiction. Enterprises whose raw materials and manpower were imported and whose output was exported began to be constructed in Estonia. The result was uncontrolled migration. In less than fifty years many millions of people have passed through Estonia, where fewer than 1 million Estonians live. In a single generation the proportion of Estonians in their motherland's population declined from 92 to 60 percent. As a result of the extensive development of the economy, there has been a steady decline in the number of Estonian workers in base sectors of industry, and this is having a far-reaching negative influence on the formation of national worker cadres and the national technical intelligentsia, and also on the national composition of the republican party organization.

"This development led to difficulties in...the social sphere and in solving the problems of housing and of satisfying consumer demands, and also to very serious ecological problems [especially] in northeast Estonia.

"In light of these circumstances," Väljas noted, it was "natural that most Estonians' perception of socialism has been influenced by these negative phenomena."[3]

N. S. Khrushchev had endeavored to submerge national differences in the myth that the USSR was becoming a Communist "state of the entire people." At the 1961 Party Congress he put forward three propositions that became ideological dogmas for more than a decade: (1) Each national culture of the USSR was "flowering" under Soviet rule; (2) Lenin's policies were achieving a "coming together" [*sblizhenie*] of nations within the USSR; (3) the march was underway toward "fusion" [*sliianie*] of these nations.

At the height of the Brezhnev period many speakers at the 1976 CPSU Congress reiterated the first two points but were silent on the third. "Fusion" was then a contested point among Soviet Communists, especially among minority nations: Many doubted that it was necessary, desirable, or feasible. Even those who yearned for *sliianie* doubted it could be achieved quickly.

Despite doubts of this kind, the USSR Constitution adopted in 1977 sought to achieve even greater national union than had been written into the 1936 Constitution with its 1944 amendments.[4] To be sure, the right to secession was still guaranteed the Union Republics. But the Constitution declared that there existed a "Soviet people" and that the "state of the entire people" was led by the Communist Party. Article 3 declared that the organization and action of this state had to conform to "democratic centralism." Given all the pressures toward unity, what remained of federalism? Whereas the 1936 constitution elaborated the powers of each republic, the 1977 document spelled out only the powers of the central government. Indeed, Article 73, par. 12 left to this center "the solution of other problems of federal importance." The Union Republics could not be sure even that they retained the powers which through precedent and praxis had come to be theirs.[5]

The 1977 USSR Constitution affirmed that the USSR is a "single union multinational state" and the Soviet economy a "single national-economic complex." There was even talk of "the single Soviet culture" and Soviet "all-national pride." Soviet writers claimed that all nations of the USSR were united by "the indivisibility of their historical destinies." The Russian language was viewed as an important integrating factor, "the language of inter-nationality communication" for "the Soviet people," a "qualitatively new historical community of people" that had evolved organically in the process of building socialism." [6]

In presenting the 1977 Constitution Brezhnev acknowledged that the option of suppressing the Union Republics had been considered but rejected as premature. Instead, the scope of the republics was reduced in 1977. Still, preserving a federal constitution meant maintaining the legal framework in which national consciousness could develop.[7]

From the standpoint of ethnicity, Soviet society was portrayed as a monolith. Still, Brezhnev and other Party leaders recognized that there were "questions," "problems," and even "contradictions" in relations among the country's nationalities. The Latvian First Secretary warned readers of *Kommunist* as early as 1978 that some Latvians wanted no more large enterprises in their republic because of the resulting influx of non-Latvians.[8] In the decade before Gorbachev, *sliianie* remained the Kremlin's official long-term goal, but the Politburo treated *sblizhenie* as the more realistic near-term target.

In the Baltic republics passive resistance to Russification and sovietization gained some momentum after Stalin's death, but remained beneath the surface until the mid-1970s. Still, the degree of Baltic, and especially Estonian, particularism is shown by various measures: the low percentage of native Balts in the Communist Party; low levels of reported knowledge of Russian in Estonia; the high percentage of religious believers in the Baltic. The comparative affluence and low infant mortality rates of Balts also set them off from most other Soviet citizens. Before analyzing these statistics, however, we must focus on the small percentage of Balts in the total Soviet population.

Ethnic balance is crucial to understanding Baltic particularities. The indigenous population, according to the 1989 census, made up at most 80 percent of Lithuania's population; 61.5 percent of Estonia's; and only 52.0 percent of Latvia's. Estonians and Latvians thus had real cause to worry about physical and cultural extinction because their numbers were so low, both absolutely and relative to others in their midst.[9] Estonia, the least populous Union Republic, had only 963,000 natives living with about 602,000 non-Estonians.[10] In some industrial regions bordering the Russian Republic there were very few Estonian natives.

The influence of Russians and other outsiders in the Baltic was probably even greater than these percentages suggested, because many Communist officials with Baltic names were born outside the Baltic and imported with the Red Army in the 1940s. For example, the Communist Party of Estonia's Second Secretary between 1953 and 1964, Lentsman, was born in the Crimea of Estonian Communist parents who fled Estonia when it became independent in 1918.[11] Karl Vaino, First Secretary until summer 1988, came to Estonia in the late 1940s and hardly learned Estonian at all.

From these proportions, however, analysts drew plausible but mutually contradictory conclusions. When Latvians seemed passive, some said this was because they were intimidated by the hostile majority; when they were active, this was because they were desperate; at the other extreme, Lithuanians were sometimes said to be confident with little need to take risks; later, their risk-taking was attributed to confidence. If Estonians were bold, some analysts explained that Estonians were anxious not to become a minority in their own land and wanted to use their slim majority before it was too late; if Estonians proceeded in a more measured pace, some commentaries averred that Estonians were neither so desperate as Latvians nor so self-assured as Lithuanians.

With this broad picture in mind, let us review the ways that Balts stood out from other Soviet nationalities.

Some indicators of Baltic particularism

Party membership. In the early 1970s the three Baltic republics had only 40 to 49 Communist Party members per 1,000 inhabitants, compared with 74 in the Russian Republic and 80 in the Georgian. Moldavia and some Central Asian republics, however, had even less representation than the Baltic. Since this percentage included non-Balts living in the Baltic, however, it overstated Communist Party membership among native Balts. The influence of Balts in the Party's central organs was also limited by their small populations. Of total Communist Party members in the mid-1970s, only 0.32 percent were Estonians; 0.42, Latvians; 0.68 Lithuanians — compared with 60.63 Russians and 16.02 Ukrainians. By the same demographic logic the delegates from each Baltic republic made up less than 1 percent of those attending the CPSU congresses in 1952 and 1961. Estonia, the country's least populous republic, sent only 0.05 percent of the delegates at both congresses.[12]

Self-reported knowledge of Russian. The national exclusiveness of the Estonians was shown also by the fact that they were the only major nationality of the USSR to report a decrease (-15.4 percent) in the proportion of persons claiming a good knowledge of the Russian language in the period 1970-1979. This alleged decline did not correspond with reality but probably arose from anti-Russian, anti-Soviet sentiments. Most Central Asian republics, starting of course from a lower base, claimed increases of more than 100 percent. In Latvia there was a reported gain of 26.3 percent and in Lithuania of 55.3 percent.[13]

Religion. In the 1970s a Soviet source estimated that at least half of Lithuanians were practicing Catholics. A Lutheran study estimated that there were 450,000 Lutherans in Estonia — one-third of the entire (mixed) population — and that about one-fifth of native Latvians were Lutherans. In each Baltic republic there were other believers — Orthodox Christians, Jews, and others.[14]

Wealth. Underlying these other trends, in 1970 the annual income of Baltic collective farmers was in the stratosphere compared to those of other republics: nearly twice the national average in Estonia and about 50 percent higher in Latvia and Lithuania.[15] Lithuania's real wealth was probably higher than these official statistics suggested, because private plots played a larger role there than in the other Baltic republics.

Quality of Life. Perhaps the best single quality of life indicator is infant mortality. In 1975 the average number of deaths in the first year per 1,000 births for the entire USSR was 30.6, up from a low of 22.9 reached in 1971. In 1975 Estonia had the lowest infant mortality in the USSR, 18.2. Lithuania and Latvia were also low, 19.6 and 20.3, compared with 23.7 in the RSFSR and 80.8 in Tadzhikistan.[16]

The Baltic republics in 1988 had infant mortality rates approaching the U.S. average of just under 10 deaths in the first year per 1,000 births. Estonia's rate was 12.4 per 1,000; Lithuania, 11.5; and Latvia the lowest, 11.0 — compared with an all-Union average of 24.7 and a RSFSR average of 18.9 and 53.3 in Turkmenia.[17] That the Baltic republics could maintain such low rates in the face of severe environmental deterioration and economic chaos was by no means assured.

Fertility and Population Trends. Population increases in the Baltic were among the lowest for any Union Republic in the decade 1979-1988. In Latvia the population increased by only 6 percent; in Estonia and Belorussia, by 7 percent; but the Ukraine was even lower, 4 percent. By comparison, Kazakhstan increased by 13 percent; and other Central Asian republics by 22 to 34 percent, averaging out to 9 percent growth for the entire USSR.[18]

The entire USSR population had grown from 209 million in 1959 to 287 million in 1989. The Baltic region (*Pribaltika*) grew from 6.6 to 8.8 million in those years. Lithuania, from 2.7 to 3.7; Latvia, from 2.1 to 2.7; Estonia, from 1.2 to 1.57 million. The Kaliningrad oblast' of the RSFSR, also listed in Soviet statistics on *Pribaltika*, grew from 611,000 to 871,000. It included, however, virtually no Balts.

In those three decades the Baltic's rural population declined from 3.3 to 2.6 million. Lithuania's went from 1.7 to 1.2 million; Latvia's, from 919,000 to 774,000; Estonia's, from 521,000 to 446,000; Kaliningrad's, from 216,000 to 182,000.[19]

The natural rate of population increase (births over deaths) in the 1979-1988 decade ranged from 5.3 to 5.15 percent in Lithuania; 1.2 to 3.3 percent in Latvia; 2.7 to 4.1 percent in Estonia. Russia's rate, 5.6 to 5.3 percent, was slightly higher than Lithuania's. But the Central Asian republics had percentage rates ranging from 25 to the mid-30s (Tadzhikistan). While the Latvian and Estonian rates were extremely low, they increased in every year of the decade except 1985, when they plummeted.[20]

These numbers reflected the fact that Estonia and Latvia, with the RSFSR, were the most urbanized Union Republics — 71-74 percent in 1988.[21] Latvia, Russia, and Estonia also led in divorces, followed by the Ukraine and then Lithuania.[22]

Endogamy. Lithuanians and Estonians were among the least inclined of Union Republic nationalities to marry other nationals. Of Lithuanian men living in Lithuania, 92 percent married other Lithuanians in 1978, rising to 94 percent in 1988. Comparable numbers for Estonians: 90 percent in 1978 and 91 percent in 1988; for Latvians, 79.9 and 80.3 percent; for Russians in the RSFSR, 91 and 90 percent; for Russians in Estonia, less than 75 percent, and Russians in Latvia, under 50 percent. Of Jews living in the RSFSR, only 41 percent married other Jews in 1978, declining to 27 percent in 1988; for Tatars in the RSFSR, the numbers were 70 and 62 percent. Of Uzbeks in Uzbekistan, by contrast, over 95 percent married other Uzbeks.[23]

Relative Deprivation and Survival

Despite what appeared to many other Soviets as a privileged position within the Union, many Balts expressed increasing discontent in the 1970s. While they had many grievances, their most basic concern was survival, physical and cultural.

Writing during the Brezhnev period, Estonian poet Jaan Kaplinski accused "honored judges," presumably the Soviet leadership, of being a cancer that "doesn't know better than to grow at the expense of the living tissue of nature." Kaplinski claimed to speak "for those who are no more [and for] annihilated species and forgotten people [and] for tongues which are not spoken any more." He also wanted to speak for "those burned to ashes in Auschwitz" and for "sea birds who perished in oil spills" and for "barn swallows who have no place in your brave new world."[24]

Along with demographic and other objective considerations, however, a host of subjective grievances drove Baltic nationalism. More than a decade before the popular fronts took shape and Baltic Communist officials started to play the nationalist card, Baltic dissidents and émigrés demanded self-determination for their republics. Encouraged by the 1975 Helsinki Final Act and the subsequent Conference on Security and Cooperation in Europe (CSCE) "Helsinki Process," they demanded sovereignty and demilitarization of their republics. Years before perestroika they sent appeals to the Helsinki conferees even though this brought down repression from the Brezhnev-Andropov-Chernenko regimes.

Baltic dissidents asked the Helsinki security conferees not to recognize Soviet annexation of the three Baltic republics. They drew attention to the extreme militarization of the region; the militaristic education of Soviet children; nuclear accidents in the Baltic area and adjoining regions of the USSR; and inadequate preparations against them. They called for revocation of the Molotov-Ribbentrop pact and the establishment of a Nordic nuclear-free zone.

Dated Christmas Day 1983, a samizdat document entitled "A Declaration from Estonia to All Those Taking Part in the Stockholm Conference on Security Building Measures and Disarmament in Europe and to Peace Organizations in All Countries on the Baltic Sea," enumerated the various treaties with Estonia broken by the USSR and summarized the steps by which Moscow had incorporated the Baltic republics. The document called for the release by Soviet authorities of human rights advocates, including four signers of a Baltic appeal dated October 10, 1981, urging creation of a nuclear-free zone along the Baltic Sea. The December 25, 1983, document also called for acceptance of the recommendation of the European Parliament in January 1983 that the issue of decolonization of Estonia, Latvia, and Lithuania be put on the agenda of future sessions of the CSCE.[25]

Soviet propaganda paid little attention to Balts' attempts to bring their views to the attention of the Helsinki Conference in 1975 and to follow-up meetings in Belgrade in 1978 and Madrid in 1980. The convocation of a Baltic World Conference in Stockholm on January 16, 1984, helped to spur the Kremlin to mount a counteroffensive. In the year before Gorbachev became Party leader Soviet media launched a vigorous campaign against such appeals and other manifestations of Baltic nationalism.[26]

The Weight of Soviet Nationality Problems in 1985

The USSR's nationality problems became more acute during the decade or so of "stagnation" before Gorbachev's 1985 ascent to power, ensuring that the new regime would face complicated challenges on this front as well as in economics and other domains, most of them aggravated by unresolved nationality issues. To make matters worse, Gorbachev did not treat these issues with the necessary tact and urgency. Instead, he permitted them to fester and even made things worse by occasional Russian chauvinist slips of the tongue. As glasnost permitted the non-Russians to voice their grievances, Gorbachev gradually absorbed the gravity of the situation. Like his predecessors, he then blamed today's problems on the past.

By 1989 Gorbachev came to criticize the Brezhnev regime for its aim "of fusing all nations," because this "led in practice to a situation in which the objective and generally healthy tendency toward convergence and inter-nationalization was set up against the growth of national self-awareness." Looking back further in time, Gorbachev said that "today we are also reaping the fruits of lawless actions committed in previous decades – the expulsion of whole peoples from their land and the neglect of the national interests of numerically small nations." [27] While Gorbachev's comments referred to many peoples of the USSR, they could certainly be applied to the Balts.

This heritage made it difficult for Gorbachev, after he grasped the severity of the problems, to promote interethnic harmony. Throughout the USSR most ethnic groups – not just those associated with Union Republics but also Tatars, Jews, Germans, and others – were becoming more conscious of their cultural and other distinctiveness. Kindred concentrations outside the group's home area, even outside Soviet borders, tended to encourage minority claims against Moscow. Most believed that they were "deprived" by the existing system – if not relative to other Soviet nations, then relative to Western Europe or some other standard. Most felt that their group lacked representation and influence at the center: Either the group was too small to count or it was underrepresented relative to its objective importance. Some ethnic groupings lacked cohesion and confidence; others were well organized and self-assured. [28]

Looking more closely at the many factors driving the rising tide of nationalism throughout the USSR, some were common to most non-Russians;

some were unique to the "Soviet West" (the Baltic, Belorussia, the Ukraine, Moldavia); some applied with especially great force in the Baltic.

Factors shaping the lives of most non-Russian peoples of the USSR

1. Global trends toward national self-expression in many other countries, from Sri Lanka to Namibia;

2. A long history of Russian oppression – for the Baltic, extending back nearly three centuries; for others, including Ukrainians and some descendants of the great khans, even longer;

3. Failure of the Soviet system to deliver economically, combined with a belief that one's own people could do better without Muscovite plans and directives; memories (or at least fantasies) of a local prosperity and idyllic life before collectivization and nationalization of the means of production;

4. Discrediting of local Communist leaders by their kowtowing to Moscow;

5. Repeated attempts, mobilized in Moscow, to rewrite local history and to downgrade local culture/language relative to Russian;

6. The role of Russian and local Communists in destroying local monuments and persecuting the churches and believers;

7. Environmental disruption brought on by commands and controls from the center;

8. An end to terror and the beginnings of freer opportunities for expression, if only through samizdat mimeograph and photocopying.

Many of these factors also contributed to the growth of Great Russia nationalism, except that Russians blamed the destruction of their culture on Communists (including the partly Asiatic Lenin, the Georgian Stalin, and the many Jews among the Old Bolsheviks) rather than on Russians, and felt that much of their wealth was being unfairly shifted to non-Russians who lived better than they.[29]

Other factors shaping the Soviet West[30]

1. Proximity to political and economic experiments conducted in Eastern Europe – efforts that failed in 1956 and 1968 but that showed a potential for significant change in 1980-1982; and to which the Kremlin responded with ever greater hesitation and less force, relying in Poland upon a local remedy (martial law) that did not stanch the organized opposition of Solidarity;

2. Proximity to Finland and Sweden where participants in the "Helsinki process" (1975-), including the USSR, affirmed their devotion to human rights and East-West trade and cultural exchange;

3. Historical ties with Western countries and culture; knowledge of Polish, German, and Scandinavian languages;

4. Awareness of their assets and importance to the rest of the USSR — the sheer size of the Ukraine with its "black earth" zone and heavy industry;[31] the high tech and other economic activities of the Baltic.

Additional forces driving Baltic consciousness

All these factors were present in the Baltic, multiplied and aggravated by historical memories and current grievances.[32] Among the forces impelling their demands for independence were:

1. Resentment against the Stalinist takeover and deportations of the 1940s;

2. Discontent, especially among Latvians and Estonians, over the immigration that threatened to make them minorities in their own lands;

3. Environmental alarms throughout the Baltic, reinforced by Chernobyl and other catastrophes throughout the USSR;

4. Access of Estonians to Finnish television and the ability to understand Finnish; access of Lithuanians to Polish sources and the ability of many Lithuanians to understand Polish;

5. Cultural reawakening and a growing determination not to be extinguished or trampled by others more numerous but with no greater claim to a good life.

Thus, nationality questions formed part and parcel of the complex and troubled situation confronting Gorbachev when he took on the Party leadership from the septuagenarians who passed away 1982-1985.[33]

A typical Baltic perspective was expressed by a Latvian delegate to the USSR Supreme Soviet in 1989: "We are experiencing a social revolution in which the class that has to be toppled is the contemporary mutation of the Russian feudal aristocracy — the directors and administrators. In this [revolution] there are those who need liberating: we [Latvians] and the latter."[34]

NOTES

1. Vyacheslav Chornovil, *The Chornovil Papers* (New York: McGraw-Hill, 1968). Chornovil's tract was sent in 1966 to the Supreme Procurator of the Ukrainian SSR. See also Ivan Dzyuba, *Internationalism or Russification?* (New York: Monad, 1974), written in 1965 and sent to the heads of the Ukrainian Communist Party and government.
2. Sang's "Galilei," translated and excerpted in George Kurman, "Estonian Literature," in Tönu Parming and Elmar Järvesoo, eds., *A Case Study of a Soviet Republic: The Estonian SSR* (Boulder, Colo.: Westview, 1978), pp. 247-80, at p. 255.
3. Väljas in *Sovetskaia Estoniia*, 5 May 1989.
4. These amendments empowered the Union Republics to have their own national military formations and foreign ministries. The amendments helped legitimize Stalin's request for United Nations membership for all Soviet republics. The Ukraine and Belorussia won UN seats but have not so far conducted an independent foreign policy. No republic military formations were established, although they were demanded by the Baltic popular fronts in the late 1980s. Union Republic foreign ministries, however, became more active on many planes in the late 1980s.
5. Hélène Carrère d'Encausse, *Decline of an Empire: The Soviet Socialist Republics in Revolt* (New York: Harper, 1981), pp. 129-30.
6. *Razvitoi sotsializm* (Moscow: Politizdat, 1978), p. 260, cited by Roman Solchanyk, "Poland and the Soviet West," in S. Enders Wimbush, *Soviet Nationalities in Strategic Perspective* (New York: St. Martin's Press, 1985), pp. 158-80, at p. 159.
7. Carrère d'Encausse, *Decline*, p. 270.
8. Solchanyk, "Poland and the Soviet West," pp. 159-60.
9. Estonia's native population had made up 64.7 percent of the republic's inhabitants according to the 1979 census. Before the 1989 figures were published, many analysts put the native population as low as 60 percent, with only 40 to 50 percent in Tallinn. Russians in 1979 made up 27.9 percent of Estonia's population; in 1989, 30.3 percent. Ukrainians increased from 2.5 percent in 1979 to 3.1 percent in 1989. Other groups in Estonia's 1979 population included Belorussians (1.6 percent); Finns (1.2); Jews (0.03). See also Ann Sheehy, "Russian Share of Soviet Population Down to 50.8 Percent," in *Report on the USSR* (Radio Liberty), October 20, 1989, pp. 1-5; also *Rahva Hääl*, September 19, 1989, data supplied by Toivo U. Raun and Rein Taagepera.
10. The total of natives, said demographer Arvo Kuddo in March 1990, is inflated by thousands of Russians who for various motives listed themselves as Estonian in the 1989 census, even though they could not then speak Estonian.
11. Carrère d'Encausse, *Decline*, p. 146.
12. Ibid., pp. 134, 136.
13. Ibid., p. 170.
14. Ibid., p. 224.
15. Ibid., p. 118.
16. Based on preliminary results of the 1989 census and other data as presented in the yearbook of the USSR State Committee on Statistics (Gosudarstvennyi komitet SSSR po statistiki): *Naselenie SSSR 1988: Statisticheskii ezhegodnik* (Moscow: Finansy i statistika, 1989), pp. 474-77.
17. Ibid. In Karakalpak Autonomous Region next to the Aral Sea infant mortality was at least 60 per 1,000 births. In the District of Columbia, with the highest rate in the United States,

it was 21.1. See Esther B. Fein, "In Soviet Asia Backwater, Infancy's a Rite of Survival," *The New York Times*, 14 August 1989, pp. Al, A6.

18. *Naselenie SSSR*, p. 3.
19. Ibid., p. 22.
20. Ibid., pp. 58-72.
21. Ibid., p. 3.
22. Ibid., pp. 117-23.
23. Calculated from tables in *Naselenie SSSR*, pp. 204-321. See also the 1969-70 studies analyzed in Rasma Karklins, *Ethnic Relations in the USSR: The Perspective from Below* (Boston: Unwin Hyman, 1986), pp. 156-57.
24. A translation by Hellar Grabbi (1973) quoted in Kurman, "Estonian Literature," p. 254.
25. The Christmas Day 1983 document was from an unofficial Estonian organization for a "Neutral and Nuclear-Free Balticum." See Z. A., "Baltic Lobbying at Stockholm," in Vojtech Mastny, ed., *Soviet/East European Survey, 1984-1985. Selected Research and Analysis from Radio Free Europe/Radio Liberty* (Durham, N.C.: Duke University Press, 1986), pp. 342-43.
26. Ibid., p. 342.
27. M. S. Gorbachev, speech on central television, text in *Pravda*, 2 July 1989, p. 1.
28. For a list of such variables, see Edward Allworth, "Flexible Defenses of Nationality," in Edward Allworth, ed., *Nationality Group Survival in Multi-Ethnic States: Shifting Support Patterns in the Soviet Baltic Region* (New York: Praeger, 1977), pp. 1-23, at p. 3.
29. Some Russian nationalists responded by condemning the center for ill-advised policies; others condemned the periphery for exploiting the center; some were unhappy with both center and periphery. See John B. Dunlop, *The Faces of Contemporary Russian Nationalism* (Princeton, N.J.: Princeton University Press, 1983).
30. See Ralph S. Clem, ed., *The Soviet West: Interplay between Nationality and Social Organization* (New York: Praeger, 1975).
31. For a case study focusing on the Ukraine, see Alexander J. Motyl, *Will the Non-Russians Rebel? State, Ethnicity, and Stability in the USSR* (Ithaca, N.Y.: Cornell University Press, 1987).
32. See also the longer analysis, "Why Were the Last First?" in chap. 1, above.
33. For more on this inheritance, see Walter C. Clemens, Jr., *Can Russia Change? The USSR Confronts Global Interdependence* (Boston: Unwin Hyman, 1990).
34. Edvins Inkens quoted in John Lloyd, "A Visionary and a Fixer for the Baltic," *Financial Times*, 8 May 1989, an article about Anatolijs Gorbunovs, president of the Latvian Supreme Soviet.

6
Perestroika and Glasnost in the Baltic

Baltic nationalism emerged stronger in the first years after M. S. Gorbachev became CPSU General Secretary in April 1985. Economic reconstruction (perestroika), Gorbachev reasoned, required more glasnost — giving "voice" to problems and complaints about how the Soviet system operates. His policies stimulated and permitted "voices" and demands that went much further than mere suggestions for economic reform. Glasnost legitimized a wide range of demands for greater self-expression and self-determination. Gorbachev's calls to liquidate the "blank spots" of history and to "humanize international relations" extended the space in which Baltic and other nationalists could operate openly.[1]

Gorbachev soon faced two dilemmas: First, to unleash the energies of the Soviet peoples and make them more effective it would probably be necessary to give them more freedom. If they wielded more freedom, however, the traditional bases of Moscow's rule could be jeopardized.

Second, to suppress the truth about Moscow's historic treatment of Baltic and other ethnic groups induced resentment and distrust in authority; to admit the unpleasant historical truths risked inflaming nationalist sentiments, among Russians as well as minority groups.

Having permitted several genies to escape, Gorbachev tried (with little success) to control them, but did not try to stuff them back into Stalinist bottles.

In both domains — economic reconstruction and opening the historical record — Balts took the lead in the last half of the 1980s.[2] In each arena their words and actions challenged Russian imperium. In 1985-1987 Latvian reformists often broke new ground. For example, Latvians staged the first "calendar" demonstrations in June 1987, recalling the mass deportations to the USSR in 1941. From late 1987 until early 1989 Estonians often occupied the avant-garde, their acts of national self-assertion preceding Lithuania's by an average of three-and-a-half months and Latvia's by five months.[3] Indeed, this chapter and the next focus on Estonia, where national heritage, independence movements, and a popular front emerged in this period. By mid-1989, however, Lithuanians moved most boldly as the Lithuanian Communist Party, striving to beat the popular front at the polls, became the first republican Party organization to split from the CPSU. Also, Lithuania's Komsomol — Communist Youth Organization — became autonomous in June 1989. On March 11, 1990, Lithuania's parliament was the first of any Union Republic to declare the republic independent from the USSR. In 1990 Estonians, followed by Latvians, moved in the same direction as Lithuanians but by different routes.

Glasnost: Control or Spur to Nationalism?

Utilizing the new freedoms, and following Latvia's June 1987 example, thousands of people demonstrated in all three Baltic republics that year on August 23, anniversary of the Molotov-Ribbentrop pact, and on November 7, anniversary of the Bolshevik Revolution.

In Tallinn about 2,000 (some estimated more than 5,000) gathered in front of the Town Hall on August 23 — probably fewer than in Riga but more than in Vilnius that day. The Estonian group had received grudging permission from authorities to meet at Tallinn's Hirvepark (Deer Park). They marched from the Town Hall to Harjumäe, a nearby hilltop where stands a monument to Linda, wife of folk hero Kalev, whose own monuments were destroyed long ago by Soviet authorities. From Harjumäe the demonstrators moved to Hirvepark, where speakers called for an examination of Stalin's crimes against the Estonian people and for publication of the 1939 pact.[4]

Most of the speakers were former political prisoners. One of them, Raivo Raave, asked

> *Will pain unify our people*
> *with wires in their flesh and bones?*
> *....*
> *Who will dispel strangers....*

He replied:
It is time to come out
to fan the flames that will wipe the curse from your people
Estonia....
Estonia
strengthen your weakening knees...
your limp hands
Estonia
tell those who are timid
don't be afraid be bold
solidarity is like a blessed signet ring
what you let happen will happen

Slogans seen at the demonstration included: "Bring the Stalinist executioners to trial!" "The right of self-determination for the Baltic states!" "Support peace!" "No to fascism!" "No!" with a U.S. rocket crossed out. A wreath asserted: "The face of our fatherland is still beautiful, when it is wiped clean of all that is false."

Not all the speakers were Estonian nationalists. Platon Afanaseev from Moscow told the audience that he spoke in behalf of the Comintern's Military Group that worked underground in Tallinn against the "Fascist government" in 1942-1943. He denounced the Estonians who cooperated then with the Nazi SS and Gestapo. Whistled down, he complained: "You heard one side, now listen to the other side, that's democracy!" [5]

Organizer Tiit Madisson declared that "there was never a Fascist government in Estonia but rather a Fascist occupation," — a view endorsed by most of the crowd.

Local authorities did not break up these assemblies, but the official press in all three Baltic republics presented a jaundiced view of the demonstrations.

Bowing to political necessity or enlightenment, the Party's press in Estonia came to see some popular politics in a more positive way. This shift was seen in the coverage given by *Rahva Hääl* (*Voice of the People*, the Estonian language daily of the Estonian Communist Party and government) to a demonstration at the city of Pärnu on November 7, 1987. Some two thousand protestors demanded restoration of a monument to Estonians killed in the

1918-1920 struggle for independence. The monument had been razed by the Red Army in 1946 and Estonian soldiers' graves destroyed in 1956. The demonstrators were invited to discuss their grievances with local Party officials in two days of crowded meetings. Instead of condemning the demonstrators, *Rahva Hääl* (November 11) called the event an experiment in "democracy," describing the exchanges between protestors and Party leaders in virtually the same language already used in samizdat accounts.[6]

The year 1987 also saw an escalation of violence between immigrant and Estonian youths. Samizdat reports told of big gang fights between Russians and Estonians in Keila. Reportedly Russians beat up an Estonian; Estonians then attacked Russians, killing one. This led some Russians to adopt a slogan, "Kill 70 Estonians by the 70th Anniversary of the October Revolution." Although details of these encounters did not appear in the official press, the Russian-language Komsomol paper *Molodozh' Estonii* (November 20, 1987) noted that Russian youth had been told not to congregate at school after hours "in order to avoid conflicts." [7]

Concurrent with these events, graves of Soviet soldiers (presumably non-Estonians) in Tartu were destroyed. The Estonian-language paper *Edasi* [*Forward*] (November 22) then complained that some critics were blaming the anti-Soviet vandalism on its editorial policies. It shot back: "In the event that the destruction of tombstones causes the halting of democratization under the aegis of vigilance, then it will clearly be the conservatives...fearing reform who will benefit from what took place." *Edasi* also noted that no one had been bothered by the destruction of other graves not belonging to Soviet soldiers.[8]

The shocker came when a special commission from Moscow probing this apparent "nationalist provocation" discovered that the vandals were not Estonian "nationalist hooligans," but the sons of Soviet officers at the local garrison and students at the Russian-language trade school. This discovery, reported in two samizdat accounts, was not announced in the official press, perhaps because it would embarrass opponents of glasnost.[9]

Party authorities decided it was time for more glasnost on ethnic difficulties within Estonia. In November 1987 an article by historian Evald Laasi opened the public discussion of Stalin's crimes. In December, as detailed below, authorities permitted establishment of the Estonian Heritage Society. In

January 1988 the Stalinist CPE Ideology Secretary Rein Ristlaan was replaced by Indrek Toome, who established a dialogue with the reformists.[10]

The Estonian Communist Party (CPE) Central Committee and Estonian Council of Ministers had two organs, newspapers published six days a week in the Estonian and Russian languages — *Rahva Hääl* and *Sovetskaia Estoniia*.[11] At a time when society as a whole and the Party itself were both splintering, the content of the publications increasingly diverged as each sought to address — and appeal to — its own readership. The trend was toward two nationalistic versions of communism: *Rahva Hääl* gravitated toward fusing Estonian nationalism with Soviet patriotism or at least with Estonian communism, while *Sovetskaia Estoniia* sought to protect Russian interests in the Baltic border lands, using a variety of conservative and liberal tactics.

Beginning on December 9, 1987, *Sovetskaia Estoniia* ran a series of articles and printed many letters to the editor on ethnic problems. The headline on December 9 explained the aim: "A sober and objective view on problems of relations between nationalities [*mezhnatsional'nykh otnoshenii*] permits one to deliver oneself from the usual stereotypes and to break down prejudice." [12] The articles and letters presented the respective claims of Estonian and non-Estonian residents in Estonia. Russians and other non-Estonians explained why they were unwilling or unable to learn Estonian; why their presence in the republic was a positive factor; and why recent immigrants should have the latest housing. Estonians explained their concern to protect their culture, environment, and way of life.[13]

Follow-on letters and articles were published in *Sovetskaia Estoniia* on December 10, 18, and 27, 1987, and on January 6, 1988, and sporadically thereafter. Some gave prominence to Estonian views, some to Russian. One contributor lamented: "Most of us Russians care little about Estonians and what they think, even though we share the same habitat with them." A letter writer put the matter from another perspective: "I do not know Estonian. I am not interested in Estonian culture, dances or films. Estonians — they are basically Westernized." He and others conveyed a basic disdain for Estonians, even on the part of Russians who had lived in Estonia for decades.

The editors published such views but criticized them, calling on Russian-speakers to learn more about the Estonian-speaking natives and their way of life. "No wonder you do not appreciate their culture," *Sovetskaia Estoniia*, chided Russians, "if you do not bother to learn their language."

Some Russians replied that they wanted to learn Estonian, but that good texts or suitable classes were not available; that television programs on Estonian culture appeared late in the afternoon when they were still at work or commuting.

One Russian official conceded that after World War II Soviet authorities made a "cavalry attack" to force Estonians to learn Russian. Despite disclaimers such as those cited in the previous chapter, most Estonians in the 1980s understood Russian while few immigrants had even tried to learn Estonian. Street names were posted in Russian as well as Estonian. But what hurt Estonians even more was the heavy propaganda content of many name changes. Thus, Cathedral Boulevard in Tallinn became Gagarin Boulevard.

Another side of this battered coin is what Estonians thought of Russians, also revealed under glasnost. "This tram works so poorly because Russians can't do anything right." This was the comment overheard by the chief editor of the Estonian Telegraph Agency as he rode to work one morning in 1987. "In fact," he observed, "the tram was made in Czechoslovakia and operated mainly by native Estonians, so the complaint was wide of the mark. Still, where such feelings exist, there must be a reason." Russians, he said, should try to understand the reasons for Estonian hostility towards them.[14]

This editor, Leivy Sher, happened to be Jewish, one of the few Jews remaining in Estonia. His article, "Culture and Internationalism," argued that Estonian culture has long been influenced by many cultures — Germanic, Polish, Scandinavian, others — as well as by Russian. He suggested that Estonians and Russians alike should drop their chauvinism and see Estonia as part of world culture. His message brought little comfort, however, to Estonians who saw their genes and language threatened with extinction.

An Estonian scientist, interviewed by *Sovetskaia Estoniia* the same day that its first roundtable on ethnic issues appeared, reported on his impressions from a recent trip to the United States. Americans, Professor U. K. Nigul declared, "understand that Russians, like other peoples, want only peace, and that the Intermediate-range Missile Treaty between the two countries" is a step toward peace.[15] When even a distinguished Estonian cyberneticist refers to the people of his country as "Russians," how could Estonians meditate philosophically on "world culture"? If Nigul actually said "Soviets" and was misquoted by *Sovetskaia Estoniia* that would not diminish the hurt to Estonian sensitivities.

Gorbachev himself, visiting Kiev in 1985, asserted that there was no difference between "Russia" and the "Soviet Union." This viewpoint, broadcast on Soviet television, was not repeated publicly by Gorbachev. On the contrary, he underscored that every Soviet nationality has its own language and history.[16] Still, the harm was done: even the great reformer might be, at bottom, a Russian chauvinist.

Of four editors and journalists I met at *Sovetskaia Estonii*a in 1988, all carried "Russian" nationality in their passports, even though one was half-Estonian and the others had substantial Ukrainian or Belorussian origins.

Indeed, T. Kallas, head of the Estonian Writers' Union, complained in *Pravda* (Moscow, January 4, 1988) that Russians did not take Estonian culture seriously. Even after the local publishing house set up a branch to publish Estonian writers in Russian translation, the publication of local poets and novelists often became no more than promises of "later." Instead the Russian branch published an enormous edition of some ephemeral thing such as *Memoirs of the Procurator*.

Still, Kallas continued, progress had been made since the time when, if an Estonian writer complained that the local stores lacked mustard, he could be accused of "localism" or even "anti-Soviet" attitudes. Encouraged by the success of Russian writers in helping to thwart diversion of Siberian rivers, Estonian writers and other ecologically minded persons had succeeded in stopping "champions of bureaucratic interests" from further developing phosphate deposits in northeastern Estonia, where environmental quality was already low. "Internationalism is a two-way street," Kallas concluded, suggesting that Russians could also learn something useful from Estonian folklore on the need to husband natural resources. Despite the difficulties, Kallas said, Estonia was experiencing a cultural rebirth.[17]

In March 1989 I asked at *Sovetskaia Estoniia* whether the candor campaign had worked. "It has not touched the hearts of all people," replied deputy editor Viacheslav Ivanov. "But it has clarified some issues for some people. So we continue to run such articles and to print strong points of view in the letters column."

Communications between Estonians and Russians living in Estonia did not become more cordial in the first years of glasnost. Each group kept to its own kind, inhabiting different locales. Indeed, some industrial centers were populated almost exclusively by Russians. In 1988-1989 calls went out for them to secede from Estonian jurisdiction and become autonomous or part of the Russian Republic. Intermarriage between Estonians and Russians remained a rarity. Most Estonians continued to attend Estonian-language schools while most Russians went to Russian-language institutions, where facilities were poor for learning Estonian despite some effort to improve them in 1989. Young Estonians could talk to Russians but preferred not to; few Russians could manage anything beyond the most primitive Estonian. Some might appreciate the melodies of the folk songs dear to Estonians but few Russians could comprehend or enjoy their lyrics.

Other nationalities—Ukrainians, Belorussians, Moldavians, and others—joined Balts in 1989 in seeking constitutional changes to elevate the status of their languages. These changes were resisted by Russian and other immigrants to each republic, seeing a threat to their own status and privileges. Demonstrations and other forms of counterattack by monolingual "internationalists" became common. As argued in chapter 10, the outsiders faced a severe existential plight as they wondered whether to join or resist local independence movements.

A backlash arose in Russia itself. "Internationalism as a one-way street" seemed to be the main idea behind *Edinstvo* [Unity], a new association formed by Russian writers in 1989. Their goal was to support the "unification and friendship of the peoples in the name of strengthening the authority of our multinational socialist Fatherland." They wanted to support development of the languages of the peoples of Russia [*sic*], the drive to support the spiritual unity of Russians, development of collaboration by using the mass media, interaction with Russian-speakers abroad, and giving every assistance to the study of the history of the Russian language and literature. Special attention would be given to the problems of youth.[18]

Carrying this tendency still further, a faction of the Writers' Union in Leningrad in 1989 sought to establish a separate organization that excluded Jews, an action that badly divided the RSFSR Writers' Union.[19]

On balance it seemed that the new freedoms did more to aggravate ethnic tensions, in the Baltic and throughout the USSR, than to quell them in the late

1980s. Bringing "us versus them" feelings into the open was probably a necessary first step toward coping with them, but the near-term consequences were destabilizing. If serious ethnic incidents occurred in the Baltic (such as the pogroms in the Caucasus and Uzbekistan in 1989), long-term solutions would be even harder to construct and implement.

From Repression to Qualified Tolerance

Estonians in the late 1980s experienced a new, more permissive regime, coupled intermittently with repressive tactics common in earlier times. Was this a contradiction? Did a monolithic central authority send out both gentle and tough cops? Were individual political leaders (in Moscow as well as the Baltic) of two minds? Were these leaders internally divided into liberals and hardliners? Centralized directives became less likely as centrifugal forces gained throughout the USSR. But the bottom line for nationalist and other reformers was that dissent might still be punished.

To be sure, beginning in late 1987 Communist publications — in Russia as well as in Estonia — extended some glasnost to interethnic problems and to Baltic demands for self-determination. This did not mean, however, that every Estonian viewpoint could be printed or would be fairly portrayed in the official media. Sharp criticisms of Soviet practices and calls for Estonian independence were muted or distorted in the republic as well as the central press in the late 1980s. As we shall see later in this chapter, new groups with heavy Communist participation — the Popular Front of Estonia and Intermovement — acquired a loud voice in 1988-1989, but radical independence groups seldom got their views across on television or the major newspapers.

Indeed, police treatment of the radicals was quite rough in 1987-1988. Their apartments were entered and searched; sometimes they were beaten; a fair number were expelled from the USSR. On February 2, 1988, a demonstration in Tartu commemorating the 1920 peace treaty with Soviet Russia was dispersed by security forces with dogs and riot gear. Dozens of persons were injured and arrested. On February 24, 1988, authorities in Tallinn used buses equipped with loudspeakers and sirens to drown out speeches at a demonstration to recall Estonian independence in 1918. On March 11 several activists among the supporters of Estonian independence were forcibly removed from a train by uniformed and plainclothes police to prevent their attendance at a human rights seminar in Moscow. Conscientious objectors of various religious faiths continued to be arrested and tried for draft evasion. In November Soviet authorities refused permission to a U.S. Congressional delegation concerned with the "Helsinki process" to visit Estonia.[20]

It was *against and despite* continued repression that non-Party political and social organizations took root in Estonia in the late 1980s. Challenges to established authority used tactics similar to those pioneered in the nonviolent resistance campaigns of Gandhi and Martin Luther King, Jr.; closer to home, they resembled techniques developed by defenders of Alexander Dubcek's regime in August-September 1968 and by Poland's Solidarity movement throughout the 1980s.

Organizational Responses to Change: The Spectrum of Estonian Nationalist Movements

In the late 1980s Estonians created a wide spectrum of political movements, contributing to patterns soon followed in the other Baltic republics and elsewhere in the USSR. Those that purported to advance Estonian interests, or those of Estonia combined with other Soviet peoples, are discussed in this chapter. The Intermovement and interests of non-Estonians in the republic are analyzed in a later chapter.

The Estonian Heritage Society (EHS)

Culture, rooted in the history of an imagined community, is a touchstone of national sentiment. Kremlin policies threatened not just the national cultures of the border lands but of Russia. Russian nationalists took a cue from the border lands.

During Khrushchev's tenure, Russian "churches were not only being closed, they were being *blown up*." Russian nationalists felt that "Russian culture was being wiped from the face of the Russian earth." They noted that "societies for the preservation of monuments" had been created in Georgia, Armenia, and the Baltic "many years earlier than in the RSFSR." [21] In late 1964, immediately after Khrushchev's ouster, the new Soviet regime gave permission for establishment of a *Rodina* [Homeland] Club to promote study of Russia's monuments. In 1966 The RSFSR Council of Ministers decreed the establishment of the All-Russian Society for the Preservation of Historical and Cultural Monuments. This society, known by its Russian acronym, VOOPIK, grew by 1977 to 12 million members — 9.3 percent of the population of the

Russian Republic! High Soviet officials were among its directors, but some-times VOOPIK became too activist for the tastes of the Brezhnev regime. It and other groups sought to redirect not only Soviet cultural but environmental policies, both of which jeopardized the Russian patrimony.[22]

The Estonian Heritage Society (more precisely, Estonian Society for Preservation of Historical Monuments) was officially founded in December 1987 following a year of conflict with local authorities.[23] In 1988 the EHS began to issue its publication, *Sõnumid*. Like its Russian counterparts, the Estonian society aimed ostensibly at preserving the national heritage but soon concerned itself with shaping the present and future as well.

The Heritage Society in 1988-1989 devoted much attention to honoring those who fell in the battles for Estonian independence, 1918-1920. It elicited heavy support from young people and religious groups such as the Christian Union. The EHS displayed the prohibited national colors in Tartu on April 14-17, 1988. Many Estonians remember this time as the "Spring of the Blue-Black-White." Throughout the republic tens of thousands spent entire nights singing and waving tricolor flags. The Presidium of the Estonian SSSR Supreme Soviet legalized the flag on June 23, 1988, and some elderly Es-tonians declared that they could now die in peace.[24]

In early 1989 the EHS had about 10,000 members (annual dues, a trivial 1 ruble 50 kopeks). The society included not only Estonian but also Russian, Jewish, and Armenian chapters. It claimed the moral support of another 40,000 citizens.[25]

The Heritage Society Council on February 23, 1989 issued a declaration: First, it called on the Soviet and the West and East German governments to renounce the Molotov-Ribbentrop pact; second, it asked the Soviet Govern-ment to observe the 1920 Soviet-Estonian Peace Treaty as an expression of "new political thinking" in international affairs; third, it summoned all peoples to support Estonia's "parliamentary activity" to reestablish "Estonia's place in the family of European states"; and fourth, it asked all persons who were citizens of Estonia on June 17, 1940, "the day of the conquest of the Estonian Republic by the Soviet Union," and their descendants, to form an "all-Estonian Congress to discuss self-determination of Estonia." [26]

Throughout 1989 the EHS became more radical and often stood shoulder to shoulder with the independence movement.

Estonian National Independence Party (ENIP)

While the Heritage Society and the Estonian Greens discussed below could assert that their primary interests were cultural-historical and environmental, the promoters of Estonian independence openly challenged the Russian empire. Many of them were veterans of the gulag archipelago — political prisoners released only in February 1987. They had already defied Moscow when the Kremlin and KGB were more brutal than under Gorbachev. Neither their temperaments nor the new mood instilled caution.

The Estonian National Independence Party evolved from a "voluntary" organization known as the Estonian Group for the Disclosure of the Molotov-Ribbentrop Pact (MRP-AEG) that formed on August 15, 1987, and then convened the Tallinn rally on August 23. The demonstration's organizers — Tiit Madisson, Ms. Lagle Parek, and others — invited interested persons to join their "initiative group" after the rally. Madisson, Parek, and other MRP-AEG founders were harassed by Estonian police and the Estonian Interior Ministry both before and after the rally. Nonetheless, the MRP-AEG began to publish its *Info-Bulletin.*

On August 31 founding member Jüri Mikk sent a letter to Gorbachev and the two major Estonian Communist newspapers rebutting the charge that the August 23 demonstration had been organized by U.S.-sponsored radio stations in Europe. Because the regime still refused to publish the Molotov-Ribbentrop pact, Mikk began a hunger strike, which he ended October 31.[27]

Police harassment and extremely hostile press coverage of the MRP-AEG continued in late 1987, even though *Rahva Hääl* and *Sovetskaia Estoniia* shifted toward a more flexible treatment of ethnic problems, and Gorbachev traveled to Washington.

In this complex situation sixteen Estonians (not including Madisson, Parek, or Mikk) in January 1988 proposed the founding of the ENIP with a broad program: to restore historic truth; struggle for the "predominance and increased influence of the nationality indigenous" to Estonia; protect Estonia's environment; reorganize the economy into a free market; guarantee human rights; ensure Estonians military duty on Estonian soil or nonmilitary, alternative service; hold multicandidate elections; pursue Estonian representation in the United Nations and restoration of Estonian representation on the International Olympic Committee and diplomatic legations in larger foreign states;

and declare February 24, when independent Estonia was proclaimed in 1918, a national holiday.[28]

This proposal was sent to the Estonian mass media but none published it. It was then taken to Moscow and announced at a press conference on January 30. One signer of the proposal, Heiki Ahonen and his aunt, Lagle Parek, were attacked and beaten by unknown assailants on January 29. Ahonen and his mother, Eva, and other activists were expelled to Sweden or Israel in March.

When *Rahva Hääl* on August 11 and 12, 1988 finally published the secret protocol to the Molotov-Ribbentrop pact, the MRP-AEG folded and reemerged as the ENIP, founded in Pilistvere on August 20.[29] The ENIP and eight other independent organizations rallied in Hirvepark on August 23 to join the Popular Front's discussion of the Molotov-Ribbentrop pact. On September 14 the ENIP sent a memorandum to the United Nations detailing Estonia's problems under Soviet rule. On November 6 the ENIP appealed to the United Nations, asking for peacekeeping forces. On November 7, the anniversary of the Bolshevik Revolution, placards were seen across Estonia with such messages as "Communism is the Last State of Delirium." In November three ENIP members visited Georgia, where they attended the formal establishment of the Georgian National Democratic Party. ENIP information stands in Tartu and in Tallinn were dismantled at night by unknown persons in December.

Throughout 1989 the Independence Party became bolder. In January it sent a telegram to the European Parliament asking support for self-determination. With the Independent Information Center the ENIP cosponsored a forum, "What we should do to achieve independence" at the Tartu University. With the EHS the Independence Party urged a boycott of the elections for the USSR Congress of People's Deputies, charging that they concerned a foreign country. Both groups also objected to flying Estonia's tricolor flag on government buildings until Estonia was again truly independent. Both joined in picketing the Soviet airbase in Tartu on the site of a former national ethnographic museum. While the ENIP and Heritage Society worked together on many projects, ENIP leaders complained that the Greens tried to distance themselves from the independence movement; that the movement's existence was hushed up in the official media and ignored by the Popular Front and Intermovement.

The independence movement was termed "extremist" by leaders of the Communist Party and the Popular Front in 1989. But the ENIP leadership saw themselves as "centrist," backed by a broad native consensus, while Communists (including those in the Front) were "extremists" in their devotion to an alien cause.

An Estonian recalled a verse by Paul-Eerik Rummo:

> *Do we all know how to keep together*
> *do we know how to keep together*
> *like a frightened swarm of bees,*
> *do we know how to keep together*
> *and so doing, cross the ocean?*[30]

The answer was not clear at the end of the eighties.

Popular Front of Estonia

Creation of a Popular Front of Estonia (PFE) was proposed by a sociologist and former planning official, Edgar Savisaar, on a Tallinn television program on April 13, 1988. The motives of its members and supporters were complex. Some wished to uphold a modestly restructured status quo while others hoped for significant change that would occur slowly and cautiously. Here were a few of the permutations:

Some Estonian and Moscow-based Communists no doubt wanted to take the wind from the sails of the various groups demanding independence; they wanted also to generate support for Gorbachev and his perestroika programs.

Other Estonians, including some nominal Communists, saw the front as a safe way to edge toward national self-determination in many spheres: today, sovereignty; later, perhaps, independence. Risk-takers might demand independence now; cautious pragmatists might prefer less direct challenges to Russian empire.

Some bolder souls regarded the pragmatists as "collaborators" with an alien regime; some pragmatists, in turn, saw proponents of "independence now" as crazies. But many who at first wanted only to coopt or slow down national sentiments were later carried away by those very sentiments, often latent in their own hearts.

Some Communists who wanted only to do well in elections were pushed to talk as though they accepted the independence platform, but many revealed their preference for independence only when Soviet pressures eased. Discord among the Estonian natives, however, undercut their strength against the hegemonical power.

Some anti-Communists suspicious of the PFE remembered that to Venpopular fronts were endorsed by the Comintern in the years 1934-1938 as a device to unite all progressive forces against the threat of the day, fascism. The popular fronts' rationale differed from that of the "united" fronts from below backed by the Comintern line from 1921 until 1928 — educating workers while keeping Social Democrats at arm's length. The *Estonian Soviet Encyclopedia* (1974) stated that "the task of popular fronts in a socialist society is to mobilize the people to the building of socialism under the leadership of Communist parties." [31] Indeed, popular fronts were used to this end in the Baltic in 1940.

Suspicious anti-Communists noted the relative speed at which the PFE won the Establishment's approval — much more quickly than had the ENIP but more slowly than the Greens. Savisaar proposed creation of the PFE less than two weeks after a joint plenary session of Estonia's creative unions in which many writers and artists sharply articulated the rising national consciousness.[32] The next day, April 14, the proposal was given to the CPE Central Committee and Estonian Supreme Soviet Presidium, both of which approved the idea of public discourse on a popular front before the month's end. CPSU member Marju Lauristin announced a second initiative group in the university city of Tartu on April 15. By June 10 there were a reported 883 support groups. The Front obtained access to the media, to newsprint, to facilities that were denied the EHS and ENIP.

The CPE had been headed since 1978 by Siberian-born Karl Vaino, distinguished by his inability to master his ancestral language despite a forty-year residence in Estonia. Increasingly out of touch with the movement for reform in 1988, Vaino decided to *appoint* the Estonian delegation to the upcoming Nineteenth Party Conference in Moscow without holding multicandidate elections as called for by the CPSU central leadership. When the Popular Front called for a mass meeting on June 17 to meet with these delegates, Vaino asked Moscow for military support. But CPE Ideology Secretary Toome intervened and, on June 16, the Kremlin dismissed Vaino. Thousands celebrated the next day. The native Estonian over whom Vaino had been chosen in 1978, Vaino Väljas, now replaced him.[33]

At the Party Conference Väljas defended the PFE platform, including its call for economic autonomy. Väljas had served in the 1970s as CPE Ideology Secretary. Not given the job of First Secretary, he was drawn off to Moscow and proceeded to serve as Soviet ambassador to Venezuela and then to Sandinista Nicaragua until 1988.

The PFE, headed by its committee of seven, grew quickly and held its first national congress in October 1988, adopting a charter and an action program.[34] These documents outlined the basic strategy and tactics to be pursued by the Front.

Some 22 percent of the delegates to the PFE Congress in October 1988 were CPSU members. Addressing the Congress, Väljas said that he and Gorbachev had recently had a "prolonged comradely discussion in a spirit of complete mutual understanding [stormy applause]" and that he brought Gorbachev's greetings and wishes for success of the Congress. The PFE leadership, in turn, sent Gorbachev greetings "as the real [*deistvennogo*] leader of perestroika and wish you in your position as Chairman of the Presidium, USSR Supreme Soviet, success in implementing the Leninist slogan 'All power to the Soviets!'"[35]

Despite these positive auguries, the PFE was not officially registered until January 17, 1989 — a suggestion that some members of the Communist establishment doubted the front's utility.

The Popular Front of Estonia was open to all citizens of Estonia, but most of its members were Estonians. Its name was expressly chosen so as to reflect territory (Estonia) rather than ethnicity (Estonian). In October 1988 it claimed to have 60,000 members organized in local groups and backed by at least 250,000 supporters. By April 1989 it had 100,000 members, compared to 110,000 in the CPE, with overlapping membership of about 25,000.[36] Despite efforts to appeal to local Russians in the name of ecological and other territorial interests, the PFE membership remained overwhelmingly Estonian in 1988-1989.

The PFE issued no membership cards; assessed no dues; and made no attempt to maintain discipline. Membership was not based on party, religion or nationality. It sought cooperation with like-minded organizations within the

USSR and abroad, especially those representing "small nations" [*narody*]. Local chapters had their own bulletins and sometimes expressed disagreement with the national leadership, but tended to close ranks in emergencies.

Of the seven-member PFE executive board, five were CPE members in mid-1989. Several were delegates to the USSR Congress of People's Deputies while Savisaar served as Deputy Chairman, ESSR Council of Ministers, and head of the SSR State Planning Committee.

The conflicting interests of Savisaar and other board members, one scholar suggests, gave them the roles of both Luther and the Pope.[37] They purported to lead a populist movement while they shared the bed of the Establishment. In 1989 there were several cases of sharp discord between the Front leadership and its representative assembly, the *Rahvavolikogu*.

Most of the PFE leadership — 71 percent — and some 28 percent of the supporters claimed by the Front in 1989 were then Communist Party members. Since Communists in the republic's population numbered at most 10 or 11 percent (a fraction rapidly dwindling), the PFE had many more Communists than the general population. This reality, however, could be interpreted in opposite ways: as proof that the PFE was a tool of the old regime, or as evidence that many of the republic's most politically conscious stratum were leaving a sinking ship. A survey conducted in early 1989 (by a firm headed by Savisaar) showed that only 7.2 percent of Estonians would vote for the Communist Party in open elections.[38]

Greens

Spring 1988 was multicolored. On April 13 Savisaar proposed a popular front. A few days later, the EHS brought out the tricolor. On April 28 a decision was taken to create an Estonian Green Movement (EGM), which was founded on May 23. Environmental issues, along with the tide of Russification, had spurred a resurgence of national commitment in 1986. There was wide support for the Greens' objectives among persons who might otherwise stay away from politics.

The Estonian Green Movement focused on environmental issues, but quickly became involved also in political action. Thus, in 1988 the EGM Board demanded the resignation or removal of Estonian Council of Ministers Chairman B. Saul within a short period. It urged Greens and their fellow thinkers to charge local deputies to the Estonian Supreme Soviet with removing Saul. If that did not work, the board threatened that it would organize a mass meeting or pickets in front of the Council of Ministers Headquarters at Toompea Castle.[39]

By spring 1989, a year after its founding, the Greens claimed to have about 6,000 members. Their slogans were written in Estonian, Russian, and English on walls near Tallinn's historic center. Later in 1989 a Green Party split from the Green Movement, claiming that more direct political action was needed.

Other Reformist Movements

Illustrating the rapid growth of informal organizations were the signatures on an April 1989 letter from the "Tallinn Cooperation Team" to the Estonian Supreme Soviet regarding the law on making amendments to the Estonian SSR Constitution. Listed as signing the letter were the Tallinn branches of seven organizations: the Estonian Christian Alliance, the EHS, the Estonian Women's Union, the ENIP, the Green Movement, the Doctors' Union, and the Tallinn Independent Squad; also the PFE chapters of northwest Tallinn and three districts (*raions*); plus the Themis Democratic Association and the Independent Information Center.[40] The Estonian Christian Alliance had members both in the Heritage Society and the ENIP. There was also a Union of Labor Collectives at odds with the United Council of Work Collectives (OSTK) dominated by non-Estonians.

In spring 1989 an Estonian Council of Churches was established joining the leaders of all religious persuasions in the republic. The *Izvestiia* report of this event, published on April 22, 1989, stated that "the council's activity should promote the humanization of society, especially the church's participation in implementing charity ideas and in caring for the sick, elderly, and lonely." Council members were received by Indrek Toome, Estonia's Prime Minister.

Vaino Väljas in his May 4, 1989, report evaluated the various organizations on Estonia's political scene.[41] He praised the PFE as a "force that supports the renewal process" of perestroika, but lamented that the Front included few non-Estonians, a situation that generated its own antithesis. He also saw value in the Green Movement, because it "gave a powerful boost to the people's ecological consciousness," and acknowledged that the Heritage Society had worked to "restore our people's historical memories and reveal historical truth." But the Independence Party he condemned for its nationalist extremism, which pitted Estonians against outsiders. Some Heritage members, he noted, had been caught up in the ENIP frenzy, but—thanks to the Popular Front—their threat to political stability had so far been checked. The extremists favored separation and attempted "to create an alternative power structure that goes beyond the bounds permitted by contemporary laws." Väljas regretted that organizations whose purpose should be to unite people were in fact dividing them.

The Party secretary also took note of the newly formed Rural Union, created by state and collective farm managers. To this movement Väljas gave the otherworldly advice that "personal ambition and group interests should be decisively rejected by the wise peasant."

So long as Moscow did not intervene militarily, more pluralism was to be expected. In 1989-1990 a Social Democratic Party and a Christian Democratic group took root in Estonia as they did in much of Eastern Europe. The former attracted members of the PFE and ex-Communists, while the latter appealed more to long-term anti-Communists and proponents of free enterprise. Many in the ENIP were inclined toward conservative Christian principles, but the independence movement included persons of many viewpoints joined in their demand for independence. If and when independence was achieved, the ENIP might well split up.

A Citizens' Committee was formed in 1989 to register Estonian citizens to elect an Estonian Congress. The Congress, elected and convened in 1990, would then send delegates to Moscow to negotiate Soviet troop withdrawals and the reestablishment of an independent Estonian state. This approach— bypassing all existing Party and government authorities—was most menacing to Estonian Communist leaders. Its legitimacy would be broadly based and its independence from Moscow unquestioned. The Citizens' Committee approach was supported by the EHS, ENIP, the Greens, and the Estonian Christian Union. At first the PFE opposed the registration campaign, but most top leaders came to endorse it and run for Congress.

What Role for Estonian Communists?

What role could the CPE carve out for itself in the struggle between Estonian nationalism and Muscovite hegemonism? For nearly fifty years the CPE had slavishly carried out the will of the center. In the late 1980s it confronted possible extinction unless it could adapt very quickly and skillfully to the evolving challenges and opportunities of a rapidly changing environment.

Many Estonian Communists proved to be more nationalist than Communist and saw the PFE as a better vehicle than the Party for advancing Estonian interests. Some feared for their careers and joined the crowd rather than stay with a sinking ship. Some Communists, dedicated to Moscow or to Leninism, hoped to moderate a movement that could become quite radical.

Väljas in 1988-1989 attempted to identify the CPE with the moderate wing of the PFE, hoping that together they could restructure Estonia in ways acceptable to Moscow. As the CPE became caught up in the euphoria of Estonian nationalism, however, it permitted its ties with the Moscow Politburo to become frayed; and its relationship with the "international" immigrants deteriorated a great deal.

Under Väljas the size of the CPE Central Committee was reduced, leaving more than half its members native Estonians. Membership in the Estonian Supreme Soviet in 1988-1989 also shifted so that two-thirds of its members were Estonians, 186 out of 285.[42]

The Estonian Communist leadership clearly hoped that Estonians would come to see them as a vehicle for positive change — as Czechs and Slovaks did under Alexander Dubcek — rather than a brake on progress. Unlike Czechoslovakia twenty years before, however, the Estonian structure included a large non-Party "front" exerting a strong pressure for the Party to keep up with the mass movement.

PFE leader Marju Lauristin happily exclaimed in 1988: "Hitherto we Communists have always been forced to choose between our membership card on the one hand and honor, humanity, and Estonia on the other. But we Communists in the Popular Front are ready today, if the question is put in such terms, to choose honor, humanity, and Estonia."[43]

In the Baltic republics the local Communist parties could be displaced by nationalist or other reformist movements, as happened in much of Eastern Europe in 1989. Even in Moscow and Leningrad lapel buttons were sold proclaiming "I am joining the party (but not the CPSU)."[44]

To be sure, the Polish situation was both similar to and different from that in Estonia and the USSR as a whole. In Warsaw as in Estonia and some other

Soviet republics, the Communist regime was perceived as an alien import; in Russia, however, many (but not all) natives still saw the Politburo as "ours." (Non-Russian representation on the Politburo fell in 1988-1989 to one Georgian and one Ukrainian. Russians could say, "*la partie, c'est nous*." Unlike other Union Republics, there still was no "Russian" branch within the CPSU. (Efforts began in 1989, however, to correct this omission.) Poles, since 1956, had much more experience organizing against Communist rule than the Balts. Their numbers and the strength of their local armed forces were much more intimidating to the Kremlin than comparable elements in the Baltic. They had a history of rebellions against difficult odds.

Torn between Moscow's needs and the conflicting demands of its own population, the Estonian Party's future did not look bright. Either it would be eclipsed by local reformists or, as in Stalin's times, would become again a satrapy carrying out Moscow's commands.

Communists in Estonia, as in Russia and other republics, did not want to land in the dustbin of history. They feared that a domino effect might swing from Poland through the Baltic to Russia itself.

While it was soon to be transformed or supplanted, the Communist Party still dominated Estonian politics in 1988-1989. The next chapter examines in more detail the claims, demands, and actions of the PFE. Later chapters look at the ways by which Estonian Communists and the Kremlin tried to reestablish their own legitimacy and leadership.

NOTES

1. Note the letters quoted from Lithuania and other non-Russian republics in M. S. Gorbachev, *Perestroika: New Thinking for Our Country and the World* (New York: Harper and Row, 1987), pp. 69-72. For background, see Walter C. Clemens, Jr., *Can Russia Change? The USSR Confronts Global Interdependence* (Boston: Unwin Hyman, 1990), chaps. 7, 8.

2. Why in the 1980s was the Baltic more nationalistic than Belorussia and the Ukraine? These two Slavic republics have been subject to Russia for a much longer period and are close culturally and linguistically. In Kiev less than 10 percent of the population uses Ukrainian in stores and at work. For other factors, see Alexander J. Motyl, *Will the Non-Russians Rebel? State, Ethnicity, and Stability in the USSR* (Ithaca, N.Y.: Cornell University Press, 1987). Ukrainian nationalism is much stronger in the west than in the eastern and southern parts of the republic. As in the Baltic, intellectuals and Greens have been active in the Ukraine, but have confronted a more rigid Party bureaucracy than in Estonia. The Ukrainian popular front, *Rukh*, held its founding congress in September 1989, about a year after the first congress of the Popular Front of Estonia. See Roman Szporluk, "National Reawakening — The Ukraine and Belorussia," in Uri Ra'anan, ed., *The Soviet Empire: The Challenge of National and Democratic Movements* (Lexington, Mass.: Lexington Books, 1990), pp. 75-93, and Jan Zaprudnik, "Belorussian Reawakening," *Problems of Communism*, 38, 4 (July-August 1989), pp. 36-52. In 1990 nationalist movements in Russia, the Ukraine, and Belorussia began to pull their republics away from all-Union, centralized controls.

3. This calculation is in Rein Taagepera, "Estonia's Road to Independence," *Problems of Communism*, 38, 6 (November-December 1989), pp. 11-26, at p. 24. Taagepera's comparisons proceed also from the case studies by Juris Dreifelds, "Latvian National Rebirth," *Problems of Communism*, 38, 4 (July-August 1989), pp. 77-95, at p. 82 and V. Stanley Vardys, "Lithuanian National Politics," ibid., pp. 53-76.

4. See documents in Michael Tarm and Mari-Ann Rikken, eds., *Documents from Estonia: Articles, Speeches, Resolutions, Letters, Editorials, Interviews Concerning Recent Developments, from April 1986 to March 1989* (New York: Estonian American National Council, 1989), pp. 7-18. The accounts there correspond with participants' descriptions to the author several months after the event.

5. Tarm and Rikken, *Documents*, pp. 17-18.

6. Toomas Ilves, "Baltic Area Situation Report," *Radio Free Europe Research*, 12, 50 (18 December 1987), pp. 5, 7.

7. Ibid., p. 9.

8. Ibid., pp. 9-10.

9. Ibid.

10. Taagepera, "Estonia's Road," p. 16.

11. A popular guidebook reported that *Rahva Hääl* had a circulation in 1985 of 149,000 and *Noorte Hääl* [*Voice of Youth*], 163,899. It did not even mention Russian-language periodicals. See *A Thousand and One Facts about Soviet Estonia*, 4th ed. (Tallinn: Perioodika, 1986), pp. 162-63.

12. Several cultural luminaries joined the editors for a roundtable discussion to which a whole page was devoted. Most of the guests had Estonian names, but at least two had Russian names. The participants included the chief editor for Russian-language literature from an Estonian publishing house, and a senior academic specialist at the State Museum of Theater and Music. See *Sovetskaia Estoniia*, 9 December 1987, p. 2.

13. See Walter C. Clemens, Jr. "Soviet Nationalism: Controlled or Spurred by Glasnost?" in Ladislav Bittman, ed., *Gorbachev's Glasnost: Challenges and Realities* (Boston: Boston University College of Communication, 1989), pp. 37-52.

14. L. Sher, "Intelligentnost' i internatsionalizm," *Sovetskaia Estoniia*, 6 January 1988, p. 2.

15. Interview conducted by Ia. Tolstikov, *Sovetskaia Estoniia*, 9 December 1987, p. 3.

16. Szporluk, "National Reawakening."

17. T. Kallas, "Eto sviatoe slovo — rodina [It Is a Sacred Word — Native Land]," *Pravda*, 4 January 1988, and *Sovetskaia Estoniia*, 6 January 1988, p. 2. One of the Russians who has written forcefully on ecological themes, Valentin Rasputin, talked about living according to one's conscience in an interview in *Literaturnaia gazeta*, 1 January 1988, p. 10. His conscience, however, became not just anti-Communist but Russian chauvinist.

18. Among the founders was Valentin Rasputin. See *Literaturnaia gazeta*, 23 August, 1989, p. 2.

19. See Bill Keller, "Yearning for an Iron Hand," *The New York Times Magazine*, 28 January 1990, pp. 18ff., cited information at p. 48.

20. See chronology in Tarm and Rikken, *Documents*, pp. 111-18.

21. O. M., "'Survey' o russkom natsionalizme," *Veche*, 9 [n.d.], quoted in John B. Dunlop, *The Faces of Contemporary Russian Nationalism* (Princeton, N.J.: Princeton University Press, 1983), p. 67.

22. Dunlop, *Faces*, pp. 69-92.

23. The antecedents to the EHS were local groups that in 1986 worked to clear overgrown churchyards. Broadening their objectives, they held a general meeting in Tallinn in February 1987 to work out the general ideology of the movement. In April a meeting chose the name Estonian Heritage Society [*Eesti Muinsuskaitse Selts*] by a vote of 289-0 over a proposal containing the word "socialist." Planned EHS meetings in Tarvastu in September 1987 and later in Tartu had been blocked by authorities prior to the December meeting.

24. Taagepera, "Estonia's Road to Independence," p. 17.

25. Information supplied in February 1989 by engineer Martin M. Kuusk, active both in the Society and the Popular Front of Estonia.

26. See "Deklaratsiia Estonskogo obshchestva okhrany pamiatnikov stariny k 71-oi godovshchine Estonskoi Respubliki," issued in Tallinn as a mimeographed sheet.

27. Text in Tarm and Rikken, *Documents*, pp. 22-24.

28. This "proposal" was sent to the Estonian mass media and the Council of Ministers. Text in Tarm and Rikken, *Documents*, pp. 43-47.

29. In Estonian, ENIP is *ERSP*, for *Eesti Rahvuslik Sõltumatuse Partei*.

30. Letter dated 2 December 1988, quoted in Tarm and Rikken, *Documents*, p. 104.

31. *Eesti Nôukogude Entsüklopeedia* (Tallinn, 1974), 6, p. 381, quoted in Tõnu Parming, "The Estonian Popular Front: Between Reformist Collaboration and Estonian National Aspirations," unpublished paper, Radio Free Europe/Radio Liberty Conference on the Contemporary Baltic, Munich, September 1989, p. 5, n. 10.

32. On the April 1988 meeting, see R. Guseenov, "Estonia: Lessons of Democracy," *Komsomol'skaia pravda*, 13 October 1988, p. 4. The PFE platform was printed in *Sovetskaia Estoniia*, 7 June 1988, p. 2. Similar ideas advanced by the Latvian Republic Writers' Union were published in *Sovetskaia Litva*, 11 June 1988, pp. 2-3, with critical observations by the Central Committee, Latvian CP. A week later the LCP CC presidium attacked recent "relapses into nationalism, chauvinism and anti-Sovietism," *ibid.*, 19 June, p. 1. The Estonian CP, by contrast, took a much more positive approach toward the PFE. Some 22 percent of

the delegates to the October 1988 PFE Congress were CPSU members. ECP CC member Indrek Toome told a Swedish newspaper that despite the constitutional crisis developing between Moscow and Estonia, "a split between the Party and the Popular Front is out of the question." *Svenska Dagbladet,* 2 November 1988, p. 4.

33. Taagepera, "Estonia's Road," p. 18.
34. See *Narodnyi kongress: Sbornik materialov kongressa Narodnogo Fronta Estonii, 1-2 oktiabria 1988 g.* (Tallinn: Perioodika, 1989). For names of those on the Board of Directors [*pravlenie*], the Council of People's Representatives [*upolnomochennykh*], the Control Commission [*Revizionnaia komissia*] and Program Committee, see pp. 159-160. The Charter, Program, and Congress Resolutions are given at pp. 161-221.
35. *Narodnyi kongress,* pp. 9, 221.
36. Much of the membership data given here and some other information about the various organizations are from Rein Taagepera, "A Note on the March 1989 Elections in Estonia," *Soviet Studies,* 42, 2 (April 1990), pp. 329-39.
37. Parming, "Estonian Popular Front," pp. 1-2.
38. Ibid., p. 3.
39. "Announcement of the Board of the Estonian Green Movement," *Noorte Hääl* [Estonian language paper in Tallinn], 22 October 1988, p. 3, and Foreign Broadcast Information Service, *Daily Report: Soviet Union* (Washington, D.C.) [*FBIS-SOV*], 2 November 1988, p. 66. For a description of the Greens' program and their green and white flag, see report by Karin Luts, TASS in English, in *FBIS-SOV,* 22 November 1988, pp. 51-52.
40. "Public Address of the Tallinn Cooperation Team to the Estonian SSR Supreme Soviet Presidium," *Rahva Hääl,* 23 April 1989, p. 2, *FBIS-SOV,* 10 May 1989, pp. 57-58.
41. Speech to the 14th ECP Central Committee Plenum, *Sovetskaia Estoniia,* 5 May 1989, pp. 1-3.
42. Interview with Tiit Käbin, Estonian Academy of Sciences, 9 March 1989.
43. Quoted in Harald Hamrin, "Estonia: New Challenges from the People's Front," *Dagens Nyheter* [Stockholm], 3 October 1988, p. 10, *FBIS-SOV,* 5 October 1988, p. 43.
44. "*Vstupliu v partiiu (krome KPSS).*"

7
The Quest for National Self-Determination

The claims and demands of Baltic reformers resembled but also differed from those of other nationalist movements in the USSR in the late 1980s. All shared a primeval quest for national self-determination. But Balts had few quarrels with existing boundaries as did the Armenians and the Abkhazians of Soviet Georgia; Balts were not displaced peoples such as the Crimean Tatars seeking to return to a lost homeland; unlike the Moldavians and some other peoples, Balts had not been forced to use Cyrillic instead of their ancestral alphabet. Balts, at least in the late 1980s, differed even from Georgians and Armenians in their confidence that they could make it on their own.

National self-determination could be achieved in different ways. The Estonian Heritage Society and Estonian National Independence Party, among other groupings, demanded independence. They wanted not secession or separation from the USSR but the *reestablishment* of the Estonian state that existed before summer 1940.

The initial demand of the Popular Front of Estonia (PFE), on the other hand, was for *sovereignty* in all domains — economic, environmental, cultural, political, and even in military affairs. The PFE leadership implied at first that sovereignty could somehow be achieved while Estonia remained part of the USSR. Many of them argued, however, for a new treaty of union based on free choice, not on Red Army coercion. Much of the PFE program came to be endorsed by the Communist Party of Estonia (CPE); some of it was enacted by Estonia's Supreme Soviet.

This chapter focuses on demands for sovereignty within the system and how Estonia's Supreme Soviet sought to implement some of these demands.

Political Sovereignty

The first goal of the October 1988 PFE Program was to break the "centralized administrative-bureaucratic system" formed under Stalinism and the "stagnation" years and to transform the USSR "from a formally federal state into a union of actually sovereign states based on the confederal principle." Second, the PFE called for creation of a law-abiding [*pravovoe*] state with specified rights and obligations; third, the decentralization of power and its transfer to cities, districts, institutions and enterprises; fourth, the transformation of the Soviets (councils of government) into legally competent assemblies of people's representatives with full powers regarding their territories.[1]

The PFE program demanded the right for Estonians to decide their own affairs without external interference. "Sovereignty is possible only when the priority of the Union Republics is clearly established over the Union as a whole." Estonia, the program stated, should specify by treaty the functions, "such as defense and diplomacy," that belong to the Union, but this would not exclude recognition of the republic's "political independence" by other states or international organizations such as the United Nations and UNESCO.

The program opposed the monopoly of any political organization not democratically elected and demanded a pluralism in which "political entities [in addition to the Communist Party]" could take part. It stipulated a system of free nominations and elections and a division of legislative, executive, and judicial powers. It wanted an end to the system by which a First Secretary of the Communist Party also headed the republic's government.

"Estonian Rifles" Only in Estonia

For years Baltic dissidents had called for radical measures of nuclear and conventional disarmament or, failing that, demilitarization of the Baltic republics. These calls gathered momentum and some official sanction in the late 1980s from Gorbachev's calls for disarmament and his actions to reduce Soviet missiles and to cut unilaterally Soviet armed forces.

But many Balts vented their feelings not just against the arms race but against Soviet military occupation of their lands. An émigré organization in Sweden estimated that there were a total of 122,480 Soviet military personnel in Estonia with 25,000 dependents, adding about 10 percent to the republic's population. They were stationed at seven missile bases and a number of air and naval bases. They included nearly every kind of imaginable unit — naval, mine, tank, coast guard, KGB border guards, and Interior Ministry troops.[2]

Baltic pickets in the late 1980s carried signs and banners saying: "Down with Soviet occupation forces!" "Out with the occupation army and militia!" "The Red Bear is tearing Estonia of the black-blue-white tricolor apart!" "We won't let our sons serve in the Soviet army!"[3] While these positions were not endorsed by the PFE, the October 1988 Congress discovered that military issues ranked just behind historical and religious complaints.[4]

The military airport at Tartu, a delegate to the PFE Congress in October 1988 complained, endangered not just the city but the entire region because its military cargoes sometimes "contacted" the ground in "unassigned areas." The presence of the airport led authorities to make the historical university town a closed city, cutting it off from the outside world. The airport and the demands of the "occupiers" — the Soviet Ministry of Defense — also made it impossible to reopen the Estonian National Museum in Tartu.[5] The delegate therefore proposed that a West European city in an analogous situation be identified and that the two military airports be abolished reciprocally. Local Greens, he added, had mustered 13,000 signers of a petition to make Tartu an open city.[6]

Following this logic, a resolution of the PFE Congress demanded that the Estonian government take steps with the USSR Ministry of Defense to open Tartu for external contacts and for protection of the city's historical and cultural legacies.[7]

Balts, Ukrainians, and other national minorities protested in the 1980s the deaths of their young men from hazing in the Soviet Armed Forces and from fighting someone else's war in Afghanistan. Many Balts protested clean-up duties at Chernobyl. Such sentiments fueled demands by Balts from many walks of life that their young men perform military duty only on native soil. The Soviet military press rejected such demands as unreasonable and complained about the rudeness that nonnative Soviet troops encounter from Baltic citizens.

Some PFE leaders asserted that there were only 300 Estonian officers in the Soviet armed forces and said that they should be recalled to head a revived

Estonian Rifles Corps based on native turf; if Soviet forces continued to operate in Estonia, they should lease the land.[8] The PFE program, however, stopped short of these demands and called only for demilitarization of "society" and inclusion of all Baltic countries in a "nuclear-free North."[9]

Estonian displeasure with the presence of non-Estonian military forces mounted in 1989 as balloting took place for the Congress of People's Deputies. The issue was participation of Soviet military forces temporarily stationed in Estonia as voters and candidates in elections, a problem that had arisen even in 1918. Estonian nationalist Tiit Made, a candidate for the Congress, noted that soldiers stationed in the republic for a brief time of their two-year term usually knew nothing and cared little about Estonia, its people, and their problems. They did not even know the candidates for whom they were voting — usually officers who also served today in Estonia and tomorrow in Murmansk or the Far East.[10]

Made complained in April 1989 that in the district where he ran as a candidate for the 1989 Congress of People's Deputies there was a large regiment of air force and engineer companies, which nominated Colonel General Nikolai Yessipenko as its candidate. "A year ago he was serving in Afghanistan. He is in Estonia now, and he will next be stationed in Karelia, perhaps."

With great difficulty Made got to address the troops. When they learned that he favored military duty only in the conscript's own republic, "some 700 young soldiers literally exploded into applause and this also won me some votes from them." Their officers probably "regretted the whole thing afterward."

Electoral procedures at the base were most undemocratic, said Made. After the election Made learned that candidate Yessipenko was himself at the polling station; that other officers told the soldiers to vote for Yessipenko; that some soldiers received ballots with the names of certain candidates struck off; and that some officers demanded to have names struck off before the ballots were handed over.[11]

Made suggested that if the military participated in national elections it would be better for the professional soldiers to select a set number from their ranks from the entire USSR and thus avoid interfering in local life. "Young Estonian boys doing military service have no special desire to vote and take part in the political life in Turkmenia. And why then should an Uzbek or a Ukrainian interfere in our republic's political life?"

An editorial in *Noorte Hääl* elaborated the dilemma: "The people are picketing, holding mass meetings, and sending letters of protest both to Moscow and Tallinn." In April 1989 protestors gathered in Tallinn's Town Hall Square and called for burning all call-up notifications from military commissariats. Some said: Do not join the occupation army. Youths trust the three top Party and government leaders as people, "yet at the same time do not trust them." Youths are "certain these men want to improve the situation but that they do not have sufficient power" to do so. The top leaders should promise that "from autumn onward our lads will stay in Estonia (more moderately, in the Baltic states) to serve in the Army, if they wish."

The writer lamented that many youths believed things could be changed only by boycott, because the Defense Ministry was like a state within a state, unresponsive to legal action. He called for new approaches by the Estonian parliament directed at the central power. A leader of the local Komsomol (practically defunct) was quoted as warning against a boycott, because a "law-governed state presupposes both legal means and forms of action."

Mindful of recent killings of Georgian civilians by Soviet troops, the Estonian paper carried a photo of a man carrying a placard: "Tbilisi night" and "Murder." [12]

The breadth and depth of local feeling was expressed in an appeal of the Estonian Women's Congress to Defense Minister D. T. Yazov. Protesting hazing, it said:

> "A system based on despotism and degradation produces cruel people who in civilian life beat women and children, raise their hands against their parents, and taunt the weak. Cruelty in relations between draftees can even arouse base instincts in those young men whose evil inclinations could never have been manifested in other circumstances."

The appeal demanded that Estonian draftees be allowed to serve in Estonia or the Baltic; that military medical commissions operate under public control; that students be allowed to return to higher education after one year's military service; that every soldier be granted leave during his service; that all military units be open to mothers, family members, and representatives of women's organizations to ensure public control over army service; that military units be responsible for environmental conservation; and that they vacate histori-cal/cultural sites.[13]

Affirmative Action: Demographic and Cultural Sovereignty

As in Sri Lanka, the still-dominant ethnic group in Estonia felt that an alien minority had become overrepresented in the economy and in political life, and that government should intervene to protect majority rights. Whereas the influx of Tamils from India to Sri Lanka stopped long ago, streams of Russians and other Soviet citizens poured into Estonia from the 1940s through the 1980s. Whereas many Tamils attained high standards of education, most Russian immigrants — at least in Estonian judgment — had few qualifications except the blessing of Moscow.

The demographic-political situation in the Baltic also resembled condi-tions in Northern Ireland and the Basque country, except that the Balts generally avoided any resort to violent means to promote their inde-pendence.

"Migration" became a code word for Russification. It was the target of a whole range of Estonian complaints and demands. By the late 1980s immigra-tion from other parts of the USSR, coupled with the demographic losses of 1939-1949, had reduced the share of native Estonians in the republic to just over 60 percent. In Tallinn, Estonians made up just under half the total population. Indeed, many industrial complexes and most military bases con-tained very few Estonians.

CPE leader Vaino Väljas noted in 1989 that the Kremlin sponsored large migrations of Russian and other Soviet citizens into Estonia, Latvia, and to a lesser extent, Lithuania, after 1945. Moscow's drive for extensive develop-ment required industrial workers, managers, and other personnel. Not only had the local population been severely depleted, but a large fraction of the most educated Balts had disappeared.[14]

In the 1980s migrants accounted for more than 60 percent of total Baltic population increase. Some arrived from the Caucasus and Central Asia, where they had come to feel unwelcome.[15] This situation led several Estonians to comment in 1988-1989: "We get some of the worst kinds of Russians — people who will go anywhere for money." Immigration coupled with the chaos of perestroika led to an increase in crime as well, especially in Estonia's factory districts with heavy immigrant populations.

Immigration led also to what Estonians perceived as unfair distribution of benefits and privilege. As Estonian sociologist and PFE board member Edgar Savisaar put it: "Social injustice is transformed into national injustice through the distribution of material advantages." He reported in 1987 that Estonians made up less than half the workers in republic industry, with almost no representation at large factories such as Dvigatel, a pattern becoming more acute in recent years. He estimated also that Estonians were underrepresented in the CPE by at least 10 percent relative to their numbers. He quoted Gorbachev to condemn the practice in many republics of mechanically placing a nonlocal as the "deputy" Party chairman, factory manager or minister—a practice by which Moscow had long shaped policy in the non-Russian republics.[16]

Underrepresented also in government and feeling themselves weak in the USSR Supreme Soviet—especially compared to Russians—Estonians lost confidence in their ability to improve their lives through political action. A survey published in 1987 showed that of highly trained Estonians living in cities, only 12 percent thought that they could influence important questions in the "collective." [17]

"Apartment policy" [*kvartirnaia politika*] also seemed unjust to Estonians and a spur to unwanted immigration. Outsiders, Estonians complained, were offered new or at least better apartments than most locals could ever hope for. Locals languished on waiting lists while migrants often bypassed the queue altogether. Retired officers and their families, Estonians reported, also took good housing that then became unavailable to locals.

Estonians, Savisaar conceded, were criticized by others (mainly Russians) for not pursuing industrial jobs. But they were stymied by many factors, he said, such as the nature of technical training high schools, which catered to migrants. In the 1980s Tallinn youth took up only half the places in these schools because of the tradition of using migrants in construction and industry; the low quality of the teaching; and the schools' poor material conditions.

Against such explanations, some Russians asserted that Estonians were effete and preferred desk jobs or piano training. Few applied even to the local police academy,[18] a situation that began to change in 1989. The Estonians, furthermore, did not welcome industrialization.

Because Estonians did not feel at home in their own cities, many were returning to the countryside in the 1980s, even though prices were higher there and government services only one-third of city levels. A third of city youth and more than half of country youth said that they preferred life in the countryside — reversing the preferences of most young people exposed to urbanization. This country-city polarization reinforced differences between Estonians and migrants, Savisaar reported.[19] Taken as a whole, however, Estonia was one of the most urbanized republics — 72 percent — by 1989. City dwellers increased by about 10 percent in the 1980s while rural population increased by a fraction.[20]

Estonians resented the indifference of migrants to their culture and language.[21] Polls taken in 1970 showed that only 14.1 percent of non-Estonians in the republic believed that they could freely use Estonian, a figure that declined to 13 percent by 1979.[22] In my own visits to Tallinn I met cultured Russians who had lived there ten to twenty years without learning Estonian. Even their children had only an elementary knowledge of the language, a situation their parents blamed on poor teaching and a paucity of good texts. Indeed, Estonians conceded that few of their youth wished to take up teaching Estonian to outsiders.[23]

Estonians also chafed at the huge share of Russian books in their libraries. Thus, of books acquired in 1986 by libraries of the Estonian Ministry of Culture, only 22.4 percent were in Estonian; 70 percent in Russian; and 7.5 percent in other languages — even though twice as many books in Estonian were read as in Russian. Another disproportion: Of books on industry published in the USSR in 1980, 99.3 percent were in Russian with only 0.6 percent in languages of other peoples of the USSR.[24]

Reflecting such concerns, the PFE Congress warned in October 1988 that "interethnic" [*mezhnatsional'nye*] differences could become sharper unless Stalinist and other ideological preconceptions were cleared away and it was understood that each nation has the right to protect its way of life.[25] The Congress endorsed the "defense of national identification and a halt to the process of assimilation." [26] The PFE Congress also demanded a battery of measures for the "suppression" [*presechenie*] of the migration that threatens to make Estonians a minority in their own land.[27]

Economic and Environmental Sovereignty

Several years before the founding of the popular fronts, Balts had taken heart from the campaigns of Russian scientists and literary intelligentsia to stop Soviet campaigns to reverse rivers and otherwise remake the face of the country. Estonian resistance had thwarted Moscow's plans to strip-mine more phosphates near the Baltic coast, build an oil terminal near Tallinn, and construct more oil-burning electric plants.

Reflecting the environmental concerns of many Estonian reformers, the PFE Congress in 1988 affirmed the "priority of ecology over economics."

Environmental and economic self-determination overlap. So long as Moscow could decide what enterprises operated in Estonia and under what terms, Estonians lacked control over their environment as well as their economic life. Thus, an Estonian delegate to the USSR Supreme Soviet complained that the "strained ecological situation in the northeast of the [Estonian] republic" was caused by pollution from the enterprises operated by the all-union ministries of Petroleum Refining and Petrochemicals, Power and Electrification, and Coal Industry—whose slow response to complaints had led to mass protests to shut down their plants.[28] Many Estonians paid less attention to motes in their own eyes, such as the ancient paper mill spewing smoke in the very heart of Tallinn or the cigarette smoke that filled many offices and flats with a blue haze. One writer rationalized: "Our water is polluted; our food and air are polluted. What's the difference if we add a little cigarette smoke, which brings us joy?"

Baltic nationalists were quite explicit about their economic demands, which, they asserted, harmonized with Gorbachev's call for cost accounting [*khozraschët*] and restructuring. The 1988 PFE program called for all activities in the republic to proceed under cost-accounting, all subject to the legal jurisdiction of the Estonian SSR. "To feel oneself master [*khoziain*] is an indispensable component of general democratization."

"IME" is the acronym for Self-Managing Estonia; *ime* is the Estonian word for "miracle." Estonians put great faith in IME. The Popular Front supported economic pluralism—cooperatives and private property, guaranteed in perpetuity by the constitution. It called for the transfer of government enterprises to cooperatives, regional institutions, and to individuals.

Economic life, the PFE program held, should proceed without interference from government agencies toward decentralization and deconcentration.

The Front supported "development of national seafaring and use of marine resources." Estonians should be able to use their "primordial right" to the sea and to free interaction with other Baltic peoples.

The PFE Congress called for strengthening of economic science utilizing international exchanges; the revitalization of farm life and the community; the defense of the consumer; and publication by the Estonian Council of Ministers of all information about the formation and implementation of the government budget.

From Sovereignty to Independence

Even before the PFE was founded, other Estonian groups demanded not just sovereignty within the system but independence outside the USSR. Although the independence movements regarded the PFE leadership as tame — perhaps as house pets for the Kremlin — the PFE program gave a legitimacy to calls for sovereignty in all domains. From these calls the leap to independence became shorter. The same arguments that Savisaar and others used to justify sovereignty could be taken a step further to reach more radical policy conclusions. A year after its founding congress called for sovereignty, the PFE leadership adopted an election platform calling for independence. By 1990 even top Estonian Communists tried to hop on the independence train.

NOTES

1. *Rahvakongress. Eestimaa Rahvarinde kongress 1. ja 2. oktoobril 1988* (Tallinn: Perioodika, 1989). The following analysis is based on the Russian edition: *Narodnyi kongress: Sbornik materialov kongressa Narodnogo Fronta Estonii 1-2 okt. 1988 g.* (Tallinn: Perioodika, 1989). The General Program is at pp. 171-97.

2. Data from the Relief Centre for Estonian Prisoners of Conscience in the USSR in Stockholm, 1984, reprinted in *Eesti Ekspress*, 5 (6), 27 October 1989, p. 3.

3. Observations of Lt. Col. M. Zakharchuk in "Questions Addressed to the Military," *Pravda*, 19 April 1989, p. 6.

4. Ülo Kaevats, chairman of PFE program committee, quoted by Zakharchuk, ibid.

5. Delegate Rein Kilk averred that the Soviet Defense Ministry regarded the ruins of the museum as a war trophy and demanded that, in exchange for releasing the site to Tartu, the town build six hangars. *Narodnyi kongress*, pp. 105-6.

6. Some Estonians contended in 1989-1990 that Tartu was not really closed, but my hosts at the Academy of Sciences never managed to schedule a visit there because of special permissions required.

7. *Narodnyi kongress*, p. 200.

8. While few young Estonian men volunteered for officer duty in the Soviet forces, all were obliged to serve. The front page of *Sovetskaia Estoniia*, 7 January 1988, carried a decree from the Military Commissar of the Estonian SSR ordering all men born in 1971 to report to military commissariats in their neighborhoods. In Tallinn in 1989 one could see posters appealing for release of Protestant believers incarcerated for conscientious objection to military duty.

9. *Narodnyi kongress*, p. 173.

10. Tiit Made, "The Role of the Military in the Election Campaign," *Svenska Dagbladet*, 13 April 1989, p. 2, Foreign Broadcast Information Service, *Daily Report: Soviet Union* [*FBIS-SOV*] (Washington, D.C.), 24 April 1989, pp. 68-69.

11. Made also criticized Yessipenko's primitive ideas. When the two of them appeared before an audience of 300 in Tapa, the Colonel General was asked against which enemy the Soviet forces in Tapa were preparing. His reply: NATO plus Sweden plus Finland, with which, he said, the USSR has been at war since 1939.

12. Tooman Sildam editorial, "A Serviceman Is a Human Being. How Can This Be Proved?" *Noorte Hääl*, 13 April 1989, *FBIS-SOV*, 24 April 1989, pp. 69-70.

13. *Sovetskaia Estoniia*, 21 April 1989, p. 3.

14. 9 May 1989.

15. See Ann Sheehy, Radio Liberty Research Bulletin RL478/87 (30 November 1987), pp. 3-5. She also reported that the back page of *Kommunist Tadzhikistana* (17 November 1987) carried ads for workers wanted at a ball bearing factory in Minsk and a woolen textile plant in Riga.

16. Edgar Savisaar, "O natsional'nykh otnosheniiakh v Estonii: 1970-1980-e gody. II." *Raduga* [Russian edition of *Rainbow*, published also in Estonian], No. 11 (1987), pp. 52-57, at pp. 52-53. This article summarizes and cites many sociological studies by Estonian, Russian, and Georgian analysts.

17. The comparable percentage within the RSFSR was not much higher, 18 percent. But trained specialists in the countryside were more optimistic: 20 percent in Estonia; 32 percent in the RSFSR. *Raduga*, No. 11 (1987), p. 54.

18. See B. Matveev, "To Better Our Common Home," *Sovetskaia Estoniia*, 18 December 1987, p. 2.
19. Savisaar, "O natsional'nykh otnosheniiakh," p. 55.
20. The RSFSR was most urbanized: 74 percent, followed by Estonia, 72 and Latvia, 71. *Naselenie SSSR 1988: Statisticheskii ezhegodnik* (Moscow: Finansy i statistika, 1989), pp. 3, 22.
21. For a summary, see Walter C. Clemens, Jr., "Soviet Nationalism: Controlled or Spurred by Glasnost?" in Ladislav Bittman, ed., *Gorbachev's Glasnost: Challenges and Realities* (Boston: Boston University College of Communication, 1989), pp. 37-52, at pp. 41-42 and Clemens, "Estonia, a Place to Watch," *The National Interest*, No. 13 (Fall 1988), pp. 85-92, at pp. 87-88.
22. Savisaar, "O natsional'nykh otnosheniiakh," p. 56.
23. The closest that the Republic's schools came to integration was to put Estonian- and Russian-speakers in one building, which only aggravated their tensions.
24. Savisaar, "O natsional'nykh otnosheniiakh," p. 54.
25. *Narodnyi kongress*, p. 195.
26. Ibid., pp. 201-2.
27. Ibid., pp. 197-98.
28. E.A. Paap, chairman of the Estonian territorial committee of Coal Industry Workers Trade Union, quoted in *Izvestiia*, 30 October 1988, p. 3. Some of the worst pollution and resulting illnesses occurred in the Russian enclave in northeast Estonia. At one school in Sillamae at least twenty pupils lost hair and suffered scalp sores. See *Sovetskaia Estoniia*, 10 March 1989.

8
Nonviolent Liberation: "Singing Revolutions"

Using the System to Change It

Some Baltic reformers counted on constructive change within the system and wanted their republics to remain part of a revitalized Soviet federation. Independence seekers split into those who would bypass existing institutions and others who tried to exploit the system to withdraw from it. All reformers, even the most moderate, risked provoking Moscow into coercive repression.

To change the system meant defying its defenders. Reformers needed to expunge paralyzing dread from their souls. Uncertain how Moscow would respond to their challenges, the bravest followed the maxim: "We act as though we are free."

The tactics used by most Baltic reformers were nonviolent, persistent, and generally calculated not to trigger a coercive crackdown by Moscow or its local agents. Indeed, they went far toward becoming a model of resistance to alien rule and active pursuit of national self-determination. Much in their approach might have appealed to Thoreau or Gandhi. But their tactics and strategy were basically improvised and suffered several shortcomings that will be discussed at the end of this chapter.

Baltic reformers exploited to the hilt four aspects of the Gorbachev program: economic reconstruction, glasnost, democratization, and a commitment to a law-governed society. Moderate reformers paid homage to Gorbachev and his program. Indeed, the full title of Estonia's broadest reform organization in 1988 was Popular Front of Estonia in Support of Perestroika, although the last four words were usually omitted. The PFE leaders initially purported to work for change *within* the system. Even so, they helped set in train revolutionary developments going far beyond what the Gorbachev team originally envisioned under perestroika.

Baltic nationalists used the media, mass demonstrations, and symbols to broadcast their message at home, to other Soviet republics, and abroad. They used their own legislatures to pass laws in defiance of imperial rule. They looked for constitutional and other legal reforms that would defend their sovereignty and perhaps their independence.

Using every form of communication, they sought to educate other Balts — and the Kremlin — on the need for and feasibility of national self-determination for the Baltic republics. But they gave little attention to the fears and interests of outsiders who had settled in the Baltic and now wished to stay.

Symbols and Reality

Beginning in 1987 Baltic nationalists organized "calendar" demonstrations to recall events important to them — the founding of their independent states, their first peace treaties with Soviet Russia, the Molotov-Ribbentrop Pact, Soviet deportations in 1941 — occurrences that Moscow had long sought to muffle or relegate to historical memory holes.

The demonstrations remained orderly even though Baltic (and Soviet Russian) sentiments on these matters ran deep. Outsiders and local Soviets could only be impressed by the style and content of these assemblies. The size of the crowds and their sobriety helped demonstrate the depth and breadth of Baltic opposition to sovietization. Thus, a crowd of some 150,000 persons came out for the June 17, 1988, Tallinn demonstration to recall the 1941 deportations, and 300,000 on September 11, 1988.[1] I witnessed an orderly crowd of perhaps 2,000 in the Tallinn Town Square on March 9, 1989, the first time the Soviet bombing of the city in 1944 was publicly commemorated. All that day memorial posters and flowers were placed in public places, giving the impression of a massive funeral; that night the demonstrators carried candles with black ribbons; speakers lamented the damage to the old city without any military purpose. Their style was more that of an analytical lecture than an emotional appeal. No exaggeration was needed to stir deep feelings.[2]

The "Singing Revolution"

As in the late nineteenth century, so in the late twentieth: Estonians reinforced and demonstrated their national solidarity by a kind of singing revolution. When choirs from different parishes came together in the 1860s and 1870s, they contributed to the idea of a common people, a common culture, a common destiny, one not shared with German or Russian occupiers. The first all-Estonian song festival took place in Tartu in 1869. Held nearly every five years thereafter, it has become one of Estonia's most important cultural events. The festivals flourished in the 1920s and 1930s, were of course suspended during World War II, and resumed in 1947. Under Soviet rule, however, the festivals were reoriented to underline the glories of *Soviet* Estonia. Indeed, singers were often compelled to carry pro-Soviet placards and pictures of Lenin. The festival usually opened with a lengthy speech by a Communist official extolling Estonia's place in the "friendly family of the Soviet Union." Many Estonian songs were dropped from the repertoire and replaced by Soviet ones, often in Russian.

The energy that Estonians devoted to their songfests implied a political imperative as well as a deep drive to live zestfully their own culture.[3] In December 1988 they celebrated the eightieth birthday of Gustav Ernesaks, the grand old man of Estonian choral music. His composition, "My Native Land, My Dearest Love," had become the unofficial anthem of Estonia.[4]

A Moscow commentary, however, charged that the powerful music tradition was being "squeezed out" by the political demonstrators who gathered at Singers' Field (*Kadriorg*) beginning in the "hot summer" of 1988 when more than 300,000 Estonians spoke out for change, for sovereignty, for "yes to the Estonian language."[5]

Affirming his nationalist credentials, Prime Minister Indrek Toome announced in October 1989 that the 1990 festival would not be devoted to anything. "It will just be a festival of Estonian music." For the first time under Soviet rule the authorities permitted the festival to be known by its sequential number—the twenty-first since 1869. For the first time under Soviet rule, expatriates were invited—nine choirs and two folk dance groups from abroad, making up 2,000 of 30,500 performers. For the first time, some highly nationalistic songs would be permitted and only one Russian song, a setting of a poem by Sergei Yesenin. Even so, some Estonian nationalists urged a boycott because the restructured festival could still serve Moscow's propaganda purposes.[6]

Estonian sensitivity to such issues was demonstrated in 1989 when Estonian cultural and PFE figures protested a U.S.-Soviet song festival planned for Tallinn in 1991. The organizers proposed to bring together 20,000 participants from the United States and the USSR. Noted Estonian choir director Tõnu Kaljuste objected that the 1991 event would simply underscore that Estonia remained a constituent part of the USSR. PFE leader Ingar Fjuk said that the festival grounds were a "sacred venue...closely associated with the defiant assertion of Estonian national identity." The interested parties therefore looked for another framework in which U.S. and various Soviet choirs could take part.[7]

The Living Past

Each Baltic people boldly resurrected its own culture, religion, and history.

Estonians and Latvians were probably not as deeply religious as Lithuanians. But Christianity—even though imported long ago from Germany—symbolized a world view different from Soviet Communism. Since Moscow had repressed religion, its expression symbolized national liberation. Thus, many Estonians rejoiced in late 1987 when the Lutheran and Russian Orthodox prelates were allowed to deliver Christmas homilies on the radio. Christmas services were televised directly in 1988 and Russian Orthodox Easter services in 1989.[8] By 1990 religious ceremonies and statements by clergy could be seen frequently even on central television from Moscow.

Balts restored their treasured symbols. The blue, black, and white Estonian flag of the interwar period originated with a student fraternity in the nineteenth century. It was unfurled at a demonstration in June 1988 and later displayed on many occasions. Indeed, by February 1989 it flew from the highest point in Tallinn, the Long Hermann Tower, standing near but *above* the Council of Ministers building where the Soviet Estonian flag hung. While most Estonians favored flying the tricolor, some thought it wrong to fly the national flag when Estonia was not yet independent. Nonetheless the tricolor was officially recognized as the national flag in June 1989.

While Estonian students in the late 1980s showed little interest in politics, their fathers and mothers argued about sovereignty and independence. But university students were not really apathetic, said Marju Lauristin, head of the journalism department at Tartu University. "They are interested in forms — restoring fraternities and embracing religion." [9] Despite such assurances, there was evidence of a generation gap, perhaps because the young had no basis for nostalgia.

In 1989 the Historical Museum in Tallinn staged the first exhibit since 1944 of Estonian life under independence. The exhibit was quite plain — a hall displaying a few uniforms, religious booklets put out by various faiths, bottles of Curaçao liqueur, a shoe wax named *Dollar*, and bathroom fixtures that sold well abroad. There were some graphics claiming that agricultural production climbed 75 percent as a result of land reforms in the interwar period. [10] But for a people starved for their own self-image, even this was impressive. The museum's "comment" book illustrated some reactions. One visitor wrote (in Estonian): "The little Estonian Republic reached a high level in twenty-two years. Where would it be if we had developed further? Regrettably Soviet Russia's occupation destroyed everything. I hate those 150 [*sic*] Estonian Communists — stupid hateful traitors of their people — who befriended Stalin's Russia and wasted their much-suffering people." Another used Latin and Estonian: "*Historia est magistrer vitae*! Thank you for an excellent exhibit which helped me to understand the significance of free Estonia." A Soviet military officer with his young son also toured the exhibit thoughtfully, ending his tour, as I did, pondering a huge diploma in the post-1944 display room: a Hero of Socialist Labor award to an Estonian farmer who achieved a high tobacco yield from three hectares, signed by Nikolai Shvernik, Chairman of the Presidium of the Supreme Soviet. Some Russian visitors, however, challenged the exhibit's objectivity and political thrust.

In 1988-1989 Estonia's first and last president in the interwar years, Konstantin Päts, was publicly honored for the first time under Soviet rule. His story could hardly leave an Estonian's consciousness untouched. Taken to Russia in 1940, he ended his days in a psychiatric institution in 1956. [11] Exhibits were set up in his native village and the Estonian Academy of Sciences, among other places. A 1939 monument to him was restored in June 1989.

Exploiting Glasnost

After 1985 some Baltic reformers gained increasing access to the mass media — not only copy machines but printing presses — little inhibited or limited by local or Moscow censors. Their greatest problem was physical: to obtain paper and persuade local publishing houses to disrupt their planned production schedules. Thus, Moscow officials interrupted Latvia's supply of newsprint in 1990 to warn what might follow if the republic broke its ties with the USSR. Estonia's dependency on Moscow was underscored in 1990 when the editor of a Jewish literary magazine in Tallinn had to plead with customs officials in Moscow for weeks for permission to accept a *gift* of high quality paper from Sweden!

Baltic popular fronts, seen as supporting perestroika, had far more access to the media than the independence parties and the Greens. Working for a time in peaceful symbiosis with the Baltic Communist parties, the fronts managed to dominate the media and leave the independence groups as lonely voices in the distant wilderness.

Communist Party control over television reduced nationalist access to that medium more than to the printed page. Lithuania's Sajudis was the only Baltic popular front to have its own television program in the late 1980s. Nonetheless, Estonian TV reported PFE activities in its normal programs and PFE leaders appeared often on television and radio, whereas independence spokesmen got very little publicity.

Soon after their founding the Baltic popular fronts began to issue newsletters typewritten and copied on rotary printers. Later they gained access to official printers, although local chapters still issue typewritten newsletters as well.

In July 1988 the PFE started publishing a newspaper, *Rahvarinde Teataja* [*Popular Front Gazette*], with a press run of 7,000, and a Russian-language version, *Vestnik Narodnogo Fronta*, in 5,000 copies. The newspaper was closed down in November 1988 but reappeared in only one issue in February 1989. Shortly thereafter authorities permitted publication of two PFE newspapers, *Vaba Maa* [*Free Country*] in Tallinn (print run of 15,000) and *Postipoiss* [*Postman*] in Tartu (also 15,000). The Heritage Society began a monthly newsletter in September 1988 with a 5,000-copy press run. Non-Estonian groups also produced newsletters such as the Russian language *Tvoi dom* [*Your Home*].[12]

Proceedings of the PFE congress were printed (in Estonian and Russian) by the publishing house Perioodika. The journal *Rainbow* (issued in distinct

Estonian and Russian editions, with only partial overlap) called itself the "literary-artistic and social-political monthly of the Estonian Komsomol Central Committee and the Writers' Union of the Estonian SSR, published since July 1986 by the publishing house of the CPE Central Committee.

Professors and others working in institutions with photocopying machines used them to reproduce all kinds of materials, from political testaments to the *Mahabharata*, although sometimes they had to pay 10 kopeks per sheet — not a trivial sum if multiplied a few hundred times.

Censorship was not entirely eliminated in the late 1980s. Thus, *Rainbow* was occasionally challenged for its content and graphics (such as grotesque nudes on the October 1987 cover). While the central press also became more freewheeling, *Kommunist* (Moscow) omitted major sections of Valerii Tishkov's essay on the national question in issue No. 1 (1989), despite his recent appointment as director of the Institute of Ethnography, USSR Academy of Sciences. There was also a widespread suspicion in the Baltic that mail continued to be read. "How else," people wondered in 1989-1990, "explain the delays of up to a month in air mail to and from the United States?" Inefficiency, or inefficiency cum censorship, were also possibilities.

Telephone connections help maintain outside contacts. When I visited Rein Veidemann, then a PFE board member and chief editor of *Rainbow*, in March 1989, our conversation was interrupted by a prearranged call from Radio Free Europe in Munich. Veidemann wanted to alter the tone of Radio Free Europe broadcasts, which he believed showed too much nostalgia for interwar Estonia instead of looking forward to a new era. A candidate for the Congress of People's Deputies, he rushed from our meeting to talk with his constituents. Although he had little hope of winning in his heavily Russian district, he wanted "in conscience" to argue his case thoroughly. For both Radio Liberty and his Russian voters he would quote Goya: "The sleep of reason produces monsters."

Veidemann expressed the belief that Russians want an enlightened despot to rule them, while Estonians seek pluralistic self-rule. But he also criticized the USSR Writers' Union newspaper *Literaturnaia gazeta* because it did not take clear stands, instead publishing a wide range of viewpoints. Reminded that many American newspapers make a point of publishing competing views on their opinion pages, Veidemann replied: "The United States can afford an ideological melting pot. This practice is too dangerous for us. No other nation stands behind Estonia." He and other PFE members also found no reason to praise *Sovetskaia Estoniia* for its attempt to promote an exchange on interethnic issues.

Veidemann's comments revealed the tip of an iceberg: Many self-proclaimed Estonian democrats were not tolerant of others' views — especially of those who had nearly destroyed democracy. Had they the opportunity, many would ban the Communist Party, as in the interwar years.

Freer Science and Communications

The Estonian Academy of Sciences revised its statutes in April 1989 to give "priority to the scholarly and scientific pursuits over management departments...and to development of democracy in scientific life." It abolished the distinction between members and corresponding members and established just one rank: member. It opened academy membership to creative individuals in literature and the arts.[13]

In this ambience the Tallinn Polytechnical Institute (Estonia's M.I.T.) changed its name to Tallinn Technical University. It abolished its Department of Scientific Communism in early 1989 and established what was probably the first Department of Politology (Political Science) at a Soviet institute of higher education.[14] At a time when most Soviet graduate students were still inclined to wait for some official exchange to study in the West, many Balts applied directly to American universities. One of them, Latvian-born Natalya Tsarkova, entered Harvard as a sophomore in 1989-1990 and quickly became a participant in conferences and classes on Soviet nationality problems in the Boston area and an intern at World Monitor Television.

Researchers in Tallinn discovered in 1990 that their colleagues in Moscow were breaking off or not continuing research contracts, because of political uncertainties. Some exchange programs with the West, however, depended upon Moscow's permission. Here was Catch-22 writ large!

In 1989 a congress of Estonian journalists voted to create a republican union of journalists. The charter envisioned a transition to contract-based relations with the journalist unions of other republics and that of the USSR. Estonians could belong to their republic union and the all-Union one.[15]

Estonia's activists and intellectuals drew upon information sources richer than any other Soviet republic: Four Finnish television channels as well as four Soviet (including Leningrad) could be seen in Tallinn and some parts of northern Estonia.[16] Since Estonian resembles Finnish, many Estonians can absorb the world news from Helsinki as well as practice their English on Hollywood films with subtitles. For Russians, however, Finnish could as well be Greek or Arabic. Perhaps in part for this reason, some Russians denounced the Western programs available from Helsinki as "pornography."

How to Resist? Nonviolence and Political Pressure

Baltic reformers generally pursued their objectives in a spirit of nonviolence. They exploited symbols and glasnost to win support for their cause. As noted in later chapters, each Baltic republic also utilized Gorbachev's emphasis on law and democracy to strengthen the role of republican legislatures and the weight of their views in the USSR legislative organs. Reformers linked hands across the Baltic, generating much more mutual support than Lithuania, Estonia, and Latvia had experienced in the 1920s and 1930s. They developed contacts within other parts of the Soviet empire and in the West that inhibited the chances for a violent crackdown on their liberation.

Most Balts observed a decorum that set them off in Moscow's eyes from the more emotional and unruly nationalists of the Caucasus and Central Asia. Balts generally avoided clashes with immigrant residents that could ignite military-police interventions. Like their forebears, many Estonians and Latvians seemed to feel more at home with the mild pragmatism of the German Enlightenment than with the zealotry of the French Revolution.[17] Lithuanians also kept their balance in the late 1980s, inspired by the step-by-step progress of Solidarity in neighboring Poland. Lithuania's March 1990 declaration of independence, however, signaled a much quicker pace than their Estonian and Latvian neighbors had followed.

Estonia's Popular Front in 1988 averred that it wished to resolve all disputes by peaceful means but it admitted that circumstances might make this impossible: "We reject coercion as a means of political struggle and hope that we will not be placed in such a position that the people is compelled to adopt desperate decisions." [18] Some PFE leaders expressed confidence that, in a showdown, all 900,000 Estonian natives would stand with them.

Coercive power remained in the hands of Soviet authorities — the Ministry of Internal Affairs as well as the Ministry of Defense. Balts feared massive Soviet intervention as had occurred in the Caucasus. They noted the demonstrations of Soviet military power on the streets of Baltic capitals in 1989-1990, especially after Lithuania's declaration of independence. They worried about Soviet charges that Balts were hiding weapons and forming "independent volunteer militias" to fight against established authority.[19] Analogous charges had preceded the August 1968 invasion of Czechoslovakia.

Altercations with "migrants" could also bring in the Red Army. The power of their organized militancy was seen when non-Estonians stayed off the job in August 1989 to protest Estonia's new voting laws. Estonian reformers sought to avoid fights with "migrant" groups lest this become a pretext for Soviet military repression. Street warfare between Estonian and Russian youth, common earlier in the mid-1980s, became rare as all parties seemed to appreciate the gravity of their confrontation.

Having suffered foreign occupation for half a century, many Estonians were impatient with others' perspectives. The 1988 PFE manifesto declared: "We are ready to hear out different points of view and to cooperate with different organizations and movements if they facilitate the humanization of society and the establishment of genuine popular power." Whatever the "migrants" said about their needs and views, however, tended to get short shrift from many PFE members and was dismissed as "illogical" or "inconsistent."

The Estonian Citizens' Committee in 1989-1990 registered only Estonian natives as citizens, but it invited non-Estonians to apply for Estonian citizenship. Thousands of non-Estonians registered and elected observers to the Congress of Estonia held in March 1990. Seven of these observers then became nonvoting members of the Congress Council. The Congress, as noted in a later chapter, rejected a resolution aimed at mollifying the anxieties of non-Estonian settlers.

The Balts' nonviolent revolution suffered from several shortcomings. First, no one had worked out a grand plan for liberation in the way that professional military planners and Communist revolutionaries had studied possible paths to success.[20] Rather, Balts improvised, adapting Solidarity's tactics that had proved useful in Poland and avoiding those that had triggered military interventions elsewhere in the Russian empire.

Second, reformers not only did not agree with one another on the best tactics and strategy, but they were also deeply intolerant of rival approaches. Radicals thought of moderates as collaborators; moderates thought of radicals as naive or crazy. These distinctions ricocheted in émigré circles abroad.

Third, leaders of popular movements attempted to win the masses to support the liberationist cause, but they did almost nothing to train the masses for the kinds of problems they could meet on the road to liberation.

Fourth, Baltic reformers had comparatively few material resources at their disposal. Defenders of the status quo had huge advantages in access to the media, instruments of coercion, money, and buildings in which to function. The buildings of the CPE Central Committee and Tallinn Party organization, for example, were huge, spacious, clean, and well equipped; those of Rein Veidemann and other editors of *Rainbow* were small, crumbling, dingy. When Russian factory managers urged their workers to protest Baltic nationalism, they could reward them with bonuses and move them around on buses. Foreign donations to the reformers — money, computers, even volunteers — helped, but still left a huge deficit in available resources.

Fifth, many — probably most — Baltic nationalists paid little heed to the perspectives of the Russian settlers, soldiers, and distant bureaucrats. Such attitudes came easily. As one nationalist put it: "Do you expect the colonized to sympathize with the colonizers?" But this disdain may have been unwise, if only because colonized and colonizers had become interdependent. Mutual gain might prove to be more feasible than zero-sum value-claiming. Also, Russian settlers were also human, in some respects also victims of the Soviet system.

NOTES

1. The latter demonstration was attended by "at least 200,000 of Estonia's 1.5 million inhabitants gathered just outside the capital, Tallinn, for a celebration in songs and speeches of their new right to run their own republic in their own way." *The Economist,* 17 September 1988, p. 50.

2. But I also witnessed an even larger meeting of Russian settlers and soldiers in Tallinn the following March. They also appeared determined and even better equipped with loudspeakers and buses. Their speakers were more demagogic and outwardly emotional. They addressed *fear;* the Estonian nationalists, *hope.* The Russians were paid to show up, on company time. The Estonians appeared on their own.

3. See A. Sukhonos, "To Respect One Another," *Trud,* 27 April 1989, p. 4, Foreign Broadcast Information Service, *Daily Report: Soviet Union [FBIS-SOV]* (Washington, D.C.), 5 May 1989, pp. 52-54, at p. 52.

4. It was Ernesaks who proposed the idea to build the Song Festival Grounds that has now become the most sacred place of the Estonian People. See "He Is a Symbol of Estonia," *Homeland,* No. 50 (207), 14 December 1988, p. 2.

5. Sukhonos, "To Respect One Another."

6. Tarmu Tammerk, "Song Festival Not Devoted to 'Anniversary of Soviet Estonia'," *Homeland,* 1 November 1989, pp. 1-2.

7. Tarmu Tammerk, "U.S.-Soviet Festival 'Can't Take Place in an Occupied Country'," *Homeland,* 8 November 1989, pp. 1, 2.

8. See also interview with Aleksius, Metropolitan of Leningrad and Novgorod, and head of the Tallinn and Estonian bishoprics, and president of the European Conference of Churches, *Homeland,* No. 30 (187), 27 July 1988, p. 2.

9. Interviewed in Tallinn, 9 March 1990. The editor of the youth magazine *Noorus,* Priit Hõbemägi, had a different idea. His readers, he said on 6 March, were apolitical and yearned for sex and consumer goods. Still, a recent issue featured stories on Konstantin Päts and Oswald Spengler! "Pop culture," said some sociologists at the Academy.

10. There was also a newspaper clipping from *Revalsche Zeitung,* 16 October 1939, about the German-Estonian Protocol, signed after two days of negotiations in Tallinn, on the "resettling of Estonia's German population [*die Umsiedllung der deutschen Volksgruppe Estlands*]" in the German Reich.

11. See "The Reminiscences of Helgi-Alice Päts," in Mari-Ann Rikken and Michael Tarm, eds., *Documents from Estonia: Articles, Speeches, Resolutions, Letters, Editorials, Interviews Concerning Recent Developments* (New York: Estonian American National Council, February 1990), II, pp. 58-68.

12. See Saulius Girnius, "Unofficial Groups in the Baltic Republics and Access to the Mass Media," *Report on the USSR* (Munich: Radio Liberty), 5 May 1989, pp. 16-19.

13. R. Kaera in *Literaturnaia gazeta,* 17 (26 April 1989), p. 2.

14. See Iu. Livshits, "Innovation: Politology," *Tallinna Polütehnik,* 27 February 1989. p. 3. Professor Livshits had in effect taught politology for some years before this formal change. His 1989-1990 syllabus, however, did not neglect Marxism.

15. TASS in English, 6 May 1989, *FBIS-SOV,* 10 May 1989, p. 59.

16. In the 1960s a special antenna was needed to receive Finnish broadcasts in Tallinn and northern Estonia. By the 1970s, this apparatus was no longer needed in some areas; in others,

a less technically complicated device could be used. But in the late 1980s Finnish TV was still not accessible in southern and central Estonia due to technical difficulties.

17. Robert von Dassanowsky-Harris, "The Philosophy and Fate of Baltic Self-Determination," *East European Quarterly*, 20, No. 4 (January 1987), pp. 493-504, at pp. 495-96.

18. "Manifesto of the EPF," *Narodnyi kongress*, pp. 220-21.

19. Such cases are alleged in a long article by V. Urban in *Krasnaia zvezda*, 18 December 1988, p. 2, *FBIS-SOV* 88-245, 21 December 1988, p. 68. "To prevent dangerous consequences," Urban reported, the Estonian KGB had "officially warned" the self-declared militia leader.

20. Gene Sharp, among others, has argued that nonmilitary resistance, planned with no less care than a military offensive, could make Europe unconquerable. See his *Making Europe Unconquerable: The Potential of Civilian-Based Deterrence and Defense* (Cambridge, Mass.: Ballinger, 1985). For discussion, see Stephen J. Flanagan, "Nonprovocative and Civilian-Based Defenses," in Joseph S. Nye, Jr., Graham T. Allison, and Albert Carnesale, eds., *Fateful Visions: Avoiding Nuclear Catastrophe* (Cambridge, Mass.: Ballinger, 1988), pp. 93-109.

9
Hands Across the Baltic, the USSR, the World

The Broad Context

The struggle between defenders of the status quo and proponents of change became more intense in the late 1980s. Baltic reformers became bolder, influenced by many developments. These included:

- The disintegration of local Communist rule and Soviet hegemony in Eastern Europe
- The worsening economic situation throughout the USSR
- The increasing intensity of ethnic conflict in the Soviet Caucasus and Central Asia
- Demands even within the USSR to eliminate the CPSU's constitutional monopoly on political power
- The steady improvement in Moscow's relations with the West — in commercial as well as security affairs — adding to Gorbachev's reasons not to risk detente by violent suppression of Baltic freedom movements.

Seldom had change occurred at a faster clip in the Baltic and other parts of the Soviet empire. Dominoes fell. Events since 1988 looked like a rapid replay, in reverse sequence, of the late 1940s. Opposition movements long underground emerged when Moscow eased up on repression. Dissident voices made their way into the official press. Independence movements called for steps to throw off Moscow's hegemony. Popular fronts were formed claiming to represent all forces favoring perestroika within the system. Electoral slates were broadened from one to many candidates. Although only the Communist parties could field candidates in 1988-1989, other political groups could bless their favorites. Non-Communists could be and were elected to parliament.

Where and when would the wheel stop? Anti-Communist revolutions and electoral trends in East Central Europe — Poland, Hungary, East Germany, and Czechoslovakia — strengthened prospects for similar developments in the Baltic. In the Baltic as in East Central Europe, pressures mounted for the withdrawal of Soviet troops. In both regions economic ties with Moscow weakened and those with the West increased, and even foreign investors worried about instability in the Baltic.

Baltic reformers in the Gorbachev years sought to avoid the narrow isolation and feuding that weakened the independent states of East Central Europe in the 1930s. They pursued cooperation with like-minded people in the USSR and beyond.

Despite competition among Communists, popular fronters, and independence groups in each Baltic republic, the secular trend in 1987-1990 was for them to coalesce on common ground against Moscow and against local settlers. Communist Party members not native to the Baltic tended to remain faithful to the Kremlin; native Balts became more nationalist.

Common Ground: August 23 and 26, 1989

A major force bringing all Balts together was their dislike for the Molotov-Ribbentrop pact, the Kremlin's reluctance to admit the existence and significance of its secret protocols, and Moscow's testy response to Baltic demonstrations regarding the pact. Hardly any Baltic residents (except a few stubborn "internationalists") could be found to justify the pact in the late 1980s.[1] The more that the Kremlin waffled on the pact, the greater the solidarity of all Balts, including Communists, against Moscow.

Massive demonstrations were held in each Baltic republic on August 23 in 1987 and 1988 to condemn the Molotov-Ribbentrop pact. In 1989 — the fiftieth anniversary of the pact — the popular front movements of Estonia, Latvia, and Lithuania jointly drafted a statement denouncing Soviet policy in 1939-1940 and calling for the right of the Baltics to determine their own political futures. Some two million Baltic citizens formed an actual hands-across-the-Baltic chain that ran the nearly 600 kilometers from Tallinn to Riga to Vilnius. Their massive demonstration was shown on Soviet television, with the strange observation that it should not be seen as "a manifestation of a separatist mood." In Moscow, however, at least seventy-five Baltic demonstrators were clubbed by riot police and detained.[2]

Representatives of each Baltic republic took part in the study of the pact commissioned in 1989 by the USSR Congress of People's Deputies. The group worked quickly and fourteen of its members signed its first report on July 20, 1989. The report was endorsed by the commission's two deputy chairmen, the Moscow historian Yuri Afanaseev and PFE leader Edgar Savisaar, but not by its chairman, Politburo member Aleksandr N. Yakovlev, who pleaded that he needed to obtain clearance from above.[3] The initial report asserted that the 1939 pact did indeed contain secret agreements to divide Eastern Europe and called on the Congress of People's Deputies to declare the Soviet-German accords of 1939-1941 null and void from inception.[4]

The facts of the German-Soviet accords and their legal implications were laid out critically in long articles in the Russian-language press of Estonia, one taking up a full page on the historic date, August 23, 1989.[5] The Kremlin, however, kept its silence.

Savisaar on August 23, 1989, condemned suppression of the commission's full report by the highest authorities in Moscow. Gorbachev, Savisaar said, thought the report "one-sided." The Kremlin leader did not reply to an August 9 telegram from Estonian deputies objecting to further delay in endorsing the report. The commission would continue, however, and proceeded to analyze the 1940 incorporation of the Baltic republics into the USSR.[6]

Without waiting for further studies, a commission of the Lithuanian parliament asserted on August 22, 1989, that Moscow's 1940 annexation of Lithuania was invalid. "Stalinism and Hitlerism destroyed independent states by secret deals. The independence of many of these states has been restored, but Lithuania, Latvia, and Estonia have not reacquired their independence." The commission spelled out: "The declaration of the People's Assembly of 21 July 1940 on the entry of Lithuania into the USSR, and the law of the Supreme Soviet of the USSR on 3 August 1940 on the incorporation of the Lithuanian Soviet Socialist Republic into the USSR are illegal."

On August 23, 1989 the 220 members of the Sajudis governing council called on Lithuania to "take the peaceful course to becoming an independent democratic republic once again." The resolution asserted: "Lithuania is no longer under the administrative or judicial jurisdiction of the USSR with immediate effect. Relations between Lithuania and the USSR must be built on the basis of the treaty of July 12, 1920." Although many delegates had wanted a call for immediate independence, the resolution stopped short of this step. As one delegate put it, the governing council, the Sejm, wanted to avoid provoking "a physical reaction from Moscow." [7]

In neighboring Poland the Polish Workers' Party Politburo distanced itself ever more from Moscow. On August 22 it said that the Molotov-Ribbentrop pact and its protocols "violated universally approved principles of international law." The door was opening to a wholesale reevaluation of the USSR's frontier from the Black Sea to the Baltic.

When the CPSU Central Committee shot back with a sharp warning on August 26 that separatist movements in the Baltic were driving the USSR to the brink of "civil conflict," [8] the popular fronts accused Moscow of employing methods of "political terror." Vytautas Landsbergis, leader of Sajudis and a member of the Congress of People's Deputies in Moscow declared that "we long ago decided that this is something we must do, to fight for our independence. We're not extremist and we are not violent, but we are determined." [9] Even before the Central Committee broadside, however, Landsbergis worried that "the Soviet mass media is paving the way for a coercive step against our plans." [10]

A Lithuanian polemicist speculated that the Kremlin advertised problems in the Baltic to distract Siberians and others from immediate food deficits and to make them forget about corpses piling up in the Caucasus.[11]

The August 23, 1989, hands across the Baltic demonstration was primarily the work of Baltic popular fronts, but Baltic political leaders of many persuasions denounced the CPSU admonition of August 26. Some debated whether Gorbachev had wholeheartedly signed it. His defenders surmised that the CPSU statement was the work of Kremlin conservatives looking to reverse perestroika. Whoever signed it or why, it grated on Baltic sensitivities.

Estonian First Secretary Väljas asserted that the Central Committee reproach took a shortsighted approach to the Baltic, neglecting the results of Stalinist and Brezhnevite deformations extending back many decades. Väljas admitted the existence in Estonia of "separatist tendencies" but claimed the predominance of "sound" views. He affirmed Estonia's right and intention to acquire "all the rights stemming from its status as a sovereign socialist country."

Because the CPSU had avoided making a "historical and legal assessment of these deformations," said another CPE leader, some Stalinists blamed the Estonian Communists for losing control while others — backers of bourgeois restoration — also condemned the CPE for policies made in Moscow.[12]

Estonian Prime Minister Indrek Toome complained that the Central Committee tended to treat the Baltic republics as one region. The reason? "The union mass media have done their bit."[13]

The ENIP compared Estonia's contemporary situation with the 1918-1920 period that began with a declaration of independence and ended with Soviet recognition of the new status in a peace treaty.[14]

But Estonia's Popular Front urged caution. Mart Tarmak, editor of a PFE newspaper said, "We are not going to react with any kind of demonstrations or mass meetings. That would only give Moscow an opportunity to move in."[15] The PFE canceled a huge rally planned for September 10 and called on all political movements to abstain that month from arranging any mass demonstrations. Instead the PFE and Greens urged participation in a "political bee," held under the tricolor flag, in which some people helped harvest potatoes, some repaired Tallinn's Song Festival Grounds, and some gathered apples for deliveries to hospitals, orphanages, and soldiers of the Soviet Army.

Referring to the August 26 warning, leaders of the three Baltic fronts meeting in Riga stated on August 31 that "there has been no such sinister and dangerous document for the cause of democracy since the death of Stalin and the 1968 events in Czechoslovakia." Its signatories "looked like the younger brothers" of the authors of the 1939 German-Soviet pact.[16]

Latvian legislators, like Lithuanian, sent telegrams to Moscow denouncing the August 26 statement as interference in local affairs. Crowds cheered as twenty lawmakers arrived at the Popular Front office in Riga where the Latvian telegram was drafted.[17]

In September the three Baltic fronts appealed to the United Nations for protection against "the threat of genocide, emanating from the Kremlin." A joint statement asked UN General Secretary Pérez de Cuéllar to send to the region an international commission to study how human rights were being guaranteed.[18]

A commission of the Estonian Academy of Sciences reported in September that the republic's 1940 annexation violated both national and international law.[19]

The upshot of all these developments was to strip away any legal justification for the Kremlin's 1939-1940 occupation of the Baltic. On December 24, 1989, the USSR Congress of People's Deputies, at last prodded by Gorbachev, declared the secret protocols invalid from the moment of their signing. They had been kept secret from the USSR Supreme Soviet and were not ratified by it. The protocols did not provide a new legal basis for relations between the USSR and third countries. Stalin nonetheless used them to deliver ultimata and put pressure on other states and to violate Soviet treaty commitments.[20]

Official recognition of the protocols did not prevent Soviet censors in December 1989 from banning further showing of a documentary film, *Hitler and Stalin 1939*, after trial shows in Moscow and Leningrad, where high-school teacher Nina Andreeva called the work "a lie." [21]

In March 1990, however, a program entitled "Where Is Estonia Headed?" on Soviet central television showed a convivial trio—Ribbentrop, Molotov, and Stalin—followed by a shot of Hitler beaming.[22]

Legislative Activity: Issues of Independence

Communists and popular fronters overlapped in the parliaments of each Baltic republic, producing varying mixtures of "internationalist" and nationalist behavior.

Some spokesmen for Baltic independence regarded the Supreme Soviets of the republics and the USSR as illegitimate abominations. But many Baltic reformers worked in the late 1980s to make the local and USSR legislatures into active players in the campaign for sovereignty; despite the odds, they also struggled to influence national politics through the Congress of People's Deputies and the USSR Supreme Soviet, where they combined forces not only with nationalists from other republics but with other foes of centralized power.

The PFE leadership in late October 1988 cabled Gorbachev protesting the high-handed way that constitutional changes were being rammed through the USSR Supreme Soviet. The Estonians protested not only the lack of consultation with Union Republics but the restrictions being placed on them. Proposed amendments to the Soviet Constitution's Article 108 would grant central authorities the exclusive right to alter the USSR's composition and make it easier for Moscow to replace elected governments in Union Republics and change their boundaries. The PFE requested that the draft laws be removed from the Supreme Soviet's immediate agenda and that these matters be considered by a state constitutional commission with representation from republics.[23]

These ideas were elaborated in a resolution of the Estonian Supreme Soviet on November 16, 1988. Noting that 861,000 signatures had been received from the republic's residents objecting to the draft changes in the USSR Constitution,[24] the Estonian parliament sent the USSR Supreme Soviet alternative language that included a Union Republic veto over changes in the USSR Constitution.[25]

The Estonian Supreme Soviet on November 16 also declared Estonia's sovereignty. It proclaimed the supremacy of the laws of the Estonian SSR on republic territory and claimed the right to review and veto any changes in the USSR Constitution or laws before their implementation in Estonia. It asserted Estonia's exclusive ownership of natural resources, the main means of production, transport, banks, state enterprises, and the urban housing stock. It also provided that private ownership form part of the economic system of the republic.[26] Various Estonian leaders — party, governmental, and PFE — added that "this does not mean that we intend to separate from the USSR."[27]

But the head may not always control the body. Furthermore, the PFE had seven heads, one of whom — Marju Lauristin — declared that "we intend to draft an alternative proposal. We demand that the Soviet Union develop into a union [*sic*] of sovereign republics held together by bilateral agreements between the central government and the constituent republics." If Moscow refused, "the current constitution gives us the right of self-determination." It had to be "made clear what limitations our republic intends to accept to remain part of this system."[28]

Protests against the centralizing amendments to the USSR Constitution also arose in October and November 1988 from Latvian and Lithuanian groups. Politburo member Vadim Medvedev traveled to Riga, in part to encourage support for the constitutional changes, but encountered demonstrations and demands for republic sovereignty.[29]

In Lithuania the Sajudis claimed 1,350,000 signatures for a petition to put off action on the proposed amendments.[30] When the Party leadership succeeded in preventing legislation comparable to Estonia's, Lithuanians staged protests and a transport strike. The presidiums of the Latvian and Lithuanian parliaments said that certain amendments to the USSR Constitution were unacceptable, but did not then go nearly so far as the Estonians.[31]

The USSR Supreme Soviet, as detailed below, eventually modified some of the amendments incorporated in the USSR Constitution. But the Kremlin rejected the Estonian Supreme Soviet claim to a veto power over USSR constitutional changes and laws adopted in Moscow. On November 26 the USSR Supreme Soviet Presidium declared invalid the newly adopted amendments to the Estonian Constitution.

Condemned by Moscow, the Estonian Supreme Soviet Presidium started to cave in, but the parliamentary majority did not. The presidium proposed a statement that Estonia would "take note of" and "be guided by" the legislation adopted by the USSR Supreme Soviet. Rather than yield to Moscow, however, the Estonian parliament by a two-to-one vote refused to "be guided by" the center and committed itself only to "take note of" the preferences of the USSR Supreme Soviet.[32] A minority in the Estonian parliament, however, denounced its veto claim as "juridical and political hooliganism." [33] The upshot was a constitutional impasse between Tallinn and Moscow.

At its December 5-7, 1988, session the Estonian parliament also declared that Stalinist reprisals in Estonia were acts against law and humanity; it called for criminal proceedings to commence against those involved in mass murders and deportations; and it set a March 1, 1989, deadline for drafting a plan to compensate victims of Stalinism. In March the Estonian government announced a plan to compensate victims of repression — expected to number at least 40,000 — or their heirs, who would be entitled to expropriated property as well as monetary compensation.[34] The Estonian parliament also submitted a draft *USSR* law on Stalinist repressions to the USSR Supreme Soviet for adoption. But Estonian observers did not expect quick acceptance in Moscow. Rarely had Union Republics used their right to initiate new laws.[35]

In December the Estonian parliament also adopted an environmental policy document. Deputy Juhan Aare, a leader of the Estonian Greens, said: "Never before has the Estonian Supreme Soviet adopted such a comprehensive document on environmental policy." Academician Endel Lippmaa commented: "We would not have been able to adopt this clause without the November 16 decisions of veto power over all-Union laws." [36]

In December 1988-January 1989 the Estonian Supreme Soviet adopted an amendment to the Estonian constitution making Estonian the state language of Estonia and requiring all residents in official positions to be able to use the language within four years. A January 8 article in *Izvestiia* was cited by Estonian sources as proof of Moscow's efforts to fuel opposition to the law among Estonia's Russian population.[37]

Latvia and Lithuania also made their languages official, but Lithuania allowed non-Lithuanians five years to acquire the language. A draft language law was also introduced in Moldavia requiring that government meetings be held in Moldavian but reserving Russian as the medium of "interethnic" communication.[38] Latvia's government tried to block further immigration. Backed by the Trade Union Council, Latvia's Council of Ministers ordered any firm importing labor from outside the republic after January 1, 1989, to pay a tax of 25,000 rubles for each worker and each member of his family.[39] Since this amount was about ten times the average yearly wage for Soviet citizens, the tax multiplied many times the wage-cost per worker.

In April the presidium of Estonia's Supreme Soviet proposed a law on citizens' associations. It provided state guarantees of the constitutional right "to associate voluntarily to develop unsponsored activity [*samodeiatel'nost'*]" and movements. Such associations, however, were banned from encroaching on the rights and legal interests of citizens and organizations and state organs. The law said nothing about organizing political parties.[40]

Estonia's Supreme Soviet proposed transforming the USSR Constitutional Oversight Committee into a USSR Constitutional Court, extending its competence to protection of citizens' constitutional rights.[41]

Estonian nationalists led by the Tallinn Cooperation Team pressured the Estonian Supreme Soviet to reject the USSR Supreme Soviet decree "On making amendments and addenda to the USSR law on criminal responsibility for state crimes and other USSR legislative acts" of April 8, 1989.[42]

The Estonian Supreme Soviet again challenged Moscow in August 1989 by adopting a law that limited the right of soldiers and other newcomers to vote or run in local elections. This law, as we shall see, led many non-Estonians to protest their disenfranchisement, and the Estonian government backtracked. More than six months after Estonia's Supreme Soviet demanded a veto over USSR legislation, Lithuania's Supreme Soviet on May 18, 1989, passed constitutional amendments similar to Estonia's. Indeed, the Lithuanian legislature went even further than the Estonian in emphasizing state sovereignty as a solution to the republic's aspirations.

Latvia acted more cautiously and did not pass a declaration on sovereignty until July 28, 1989. The once conservative First Secretary Janis Vagris presided over the Supreme Soviet session in the absence of Presidium chairman Anatolijs Gorbunovs. But the net result of the many amendments to the Latvian constitution was less radical than that of the new Estonian or Lithuanian laws.

By summer 1989 all three Baltic republics had changed their constitutions in support of sovereignty. These documents set out the supremacy of republic laws, asserted the need for treaty-based relations with the USSR, and defended republican property against all-Union.[43] In October 1989 the Lithuanian Supreme Soviet turned down a Kremlin suggestion to recognize publicly owned land as all-Union property subject to Moscow.[44]

The Congress of People's Deputies: Baltic Hope and Despair

The USSR's legislative system was revised in 1989 to provide for direct elections to a Congress of People's Deputies that would debate large issues and then elect a bicameral USSR Supreme Soviet. The Communist Party and some other all-Union organizations could elect representatives directly to the Congress. Republican bodies such as the popular fronts did not have this right. Indeed, in 1989 they could not even act like political parties and actively nominate their own candidates. Rather, they could only signify their approval of candidates — Communist and non-Party.

Despite these handicaps, the Baltic popular fronts proved very effective in mobilizing support for their preferred candidates for the USSR Congress. In Estonia and Latvia many of the persons backed by the fronts also belonged to the Party.[45] In Lithuania, however, most Communists were defeated. When the Party refused to assert republic sovereignty in November 1988, the Sajudis front and the public turned sharply against the Party.

About 87 percent of eligible voters turned out in Estonia and Latvia. Eighteen of the twenty-one candidates endorsed by the PFE were elected, including top PFE leaders Edgar Savisaar and Marju Lauristin (one of two women from Estonia to win a seat), Party First Secretary Väljas, head of state Arnold Rüütel, Prime Minister Indrek Toome, and Green leaders such as Juhan Aare. Seven candidates endorsed by Intermovement were also elected, including their top leader Evgenyi V. Kogan, who defeated PFE candidate Rein Veidemann in a runoff. (Here the ethnic confrontation was stark as only 1 percent of Estonians voted for Kogan and 5 percent of non-Estonians voted for Veidemann.)[46] The chairman of Estonia's KGB was defeated by the chairman of Tartu University's organic chemistry department, also backed by the PFE.[47] The poor showing of Intermovement removed some pressure on the CPE to appease conservative forces; the defeat or resignation of most remaining Stalinists among the CPE leaders consolidated the reformist core of the Party. Still, Estonians did not forget the Party's earlier role as a tool of Stalinism.[48]

A Baltic front meeting in Tallinn in May 1989 adopted five resolutions to guide the Baltic delegates to the Congress of People's Deputies in Moscow. They included support for perestroika and demands for a new Soviet constitution restoring sovereignty to each state of the union and the right of each to decide its own foreign policy. Marju Lauristin of Estonia warned that the Baltic deputies—which later reached a total of 137—could find themselves isolated among the 2,249 delegates to the Congress. She therefore urged the Baltic delegates to forge a coalition with progressives from other republics.

Communists and popular fronters overlapped in Moscow. Granted, some 87.6 percent of the USSR Congress of People's Deputies elected in 1989 belonged to the Communist Party.[49] But this did not ensure any monolithic support for a single "line," because many Party members were now ready to buck the center.

The 1989 electoral system for the People's Deputies contributed to an overrepresentation of Balts relative to Russians. By the analysis of Soviet ethnographer Valerii Tishkov, of total deputies elected, Russians numbered only 45.6 percent—about 5 percent less than their share of the Soviet population. Lithuanians made up 2.3 percent; Latvians, 1.9 percent; and Estonians 1.8 percent—all much more than their shares of the USSR population

(Lithuania, 1.1 percent; Latvia, 0.51 percent; Estonia, 0.38 percent). This pattern resulted from the method of delegate selection: one-third from territorial districts, one-third from national-territorial electoral districts, and one-third from public organizations. Russians were somewhat over-represented in the first and third categories, but smaller titular nationalities were significantly overrepresented in the second category, where Lithuanians got 3.6 percent of the delegates; Latvians, 3.5 percent; and Estonians, 3.3 percent. Concretely, 27 of 52 Lithuanian delegates came from these districts; 26 of 44 Latvian delegates; and 25 of 41 Estonian delegates.

Some small nationalities such as Karakalpaks and Kalmyks got their only representation through the national-territorial districts. Altogether, sixty-five nationalities were represented among the delegates, but several dozen received no formal representation.

The underlying reason for these disparities, Tishkov argued, was the formal status of the territory in question. The higher its status, the greater its quota in the national districts. This favored the small titular nationalities of the Baltic. Thus, 1 million Estonians had 41 deputies but 6.6 million Tatars had only 24 deputies and 2 million Germans, 10 deputies. Also, the population of districts varied immensely within each republic. A rural district in Latvia composed mainly of Latvians could contain 28,000 voters while a multinational district in Riga had 150,000 voters. In eight of fifteen republics the elections favored titular peoples. Latvians were overrepresented by one-fourth and Estonians by one-fifth relative to other voters in these republics.

Baltic republics also got more delegates than certain other republics with larger populations, because the Baltic peoples had more citizens of voting age per capita — a consequence of their comparatively low birth and death rates. They also sent more delegates from public organizations than Central Asian republics, because Balts were more active in such bodies.

Tishkov lamented that the Congress and its Supreme Soviet was more an "assembly of nations" than an "all-Union parliament," and that ethnic rather than other considerations played a large role in delegate selection and in the content of Congress debate. He pointed out inequities in the 1989 system and issues such as delegate rotation that could skew national representation in the future — perhaps overrepresenting Russians.[50]

Tishkov's perspective was that of Director, Institute of Ethnography, USSR Academy of Sciences, and he was concerned with preserving the Union. His ivory tower analysis neglected the reality that a Kremlin-orchestrated political machine dominated the life of the Congress and its Supreme Soviet. Balts and some other nations were overrepresented, but they had little clout compared to Russians, who had 45.6 percent of the delegates, and found a broad alliance with other delegates accustomed to favoring the Center.

The entire Baltic contingent amounted to less than one-twentieth of the 2,249 Congress delegates. National spirit brought many Baltic Communists to align with the popular front mentality. Balts endeavored to coordinate actions with other dissidents or free-thinkers, including Russians, but they made up a distinct minority. What shook the Kremlin in 1990 was not the inchoate opposition it faced within the Congress and Supreme Soviet, but active resistance *outside* the all-Union framework by popular fronts, parliaments, and other movements in individual republics — including the Russian — to Kremlin imperialism.

At the first session of the Congress some 260 deputies signed up as members of the Interregional Group (IRG) led by maverick Boris Yeltsin, historian Yuri Afanaseev, economist Gavril Popov, physicist Andrei D. Sakharov, and Estonian chemist Viktor Palm. Many other deputies backed the group, whose program could be called broadly "social democratic." Among the group members was East European specialist Oleg T. Bogomolov, who noted that the collapse of Polish Communists was brought on by their refusal to negotiate seriously with the opposition.

The IRG experience could in principle have strengthened faith in the possibility of progressive change within the Soviet system. But a number of problems emerged, underscoring the obstacles to increasing national self-determination within the new legislative arrangements.[51] The difficulties included:

1. Impotence. The IRG contained only about 400 of 2,250 deputies to the USSR Congress in late 1989. Some were discouraged by the difficulty of resisting the Gorbachev steamroller, especially after Sakharov's death in December left the movement without a distinguished leader.

The bicameral organization of the Supreme Soviet gave no real protection to smaller nations. The constitutional arrangements of 1989 maintained a

Soviet of the Nationalities, but left no way for small groups such as the Balts to filibuster or otherwise block the majority.[52]

2. Authoritarianism. Gorbachev's increasingly short temper and drive for supreme power raised fears about his ambitions and future behavior. Tradition reasserted itself as even Russian "liberals" argued for a "strong hand" to guide the country toward democracy.

The executive presidency that Gorbachev engineered and his election to this office by the USSR Congress in March 1990 did not ease the qualms of Baltic and other reformers. Such powers could easily be exploited to repress nationalist and other dissent. Indeed, Gorbachev immediately used his new authority against breakaway Lithuania.

3. Pluralism or chaos? If pluralism took hold within the USSR Congress and Supreme Soviet, minorities of all kinds could pool their strengths. A growing number of political forces within the USSR expressed their dissatisfaction with the CPSU and/or with Gorbachev. But they ranged from anarchists to monarchists. There was, at the onset of the 1990s, no clear-cut liberal faction in Russia with which Baltic nationalists could link arms. Could Baltic nationalists logroll with Russian monarchists? How could they win Azeri or Armenian support when they drew back from ethnic violence for any reason?

Baltic resistance to Russian dominion was different in style and substance from that of many other dissident groups opposed to Gorbachev or to central dominion. Most Balts concurred with those Russians wishing to chuck empire, but differed with Russian liberals seeking only to democratize the Union. By late 1989 most Balts wanted to depart the system, not just change it. They certainly differed with those Russian nationalists yearning to crack down and reimpose order throughout the empire. They differed from Caucasians and Central Asians ready to use force to get their ways. Unlike Azeris and Armenians, Balts pressed no major territorial claims.

But old claims may of course be resurrected. A 1989 paper by Olga Oliker at Emory University reported that from 1921 through 1980, there had been at least ninety transfers of territory among Union republics and an equally large number of territorial shifts to and from smaller autonomous units of the USSR. Some seventy of the changes among Union republics took place before 1940 — a suggestion that policies in the 1920s and 1930s were less rigid in some respects than later. Oliker's findings, based on studies of central Soviet government gazettes, also underscored the depth of feeling on border issues, often requiring lower level conferees to appeal to the highest authorities to settle disputes.

Suggesting that territorial issues may again become important, not just in the Caucasus and Central Asia, high officials in Riga in August 1990 indicated that they sought restoration of Latvia's pre-1940 borders with Belorussia and Russia. In September 1990 a unit of Estonia's revived home guard, Kaitseliit, erected border markers in two parts of the RSFSR—Leningrad Oblast and Pskov Oblast—"to demonstrate the will of the Estonian people to restore Estonia's old borders." The government in Tallinn condemned these actions and said they were not authorized. Lithuanians heard challenges to their borders in 1990 from some Poles and Belorussians—as Estonians did from Russians. Lithuania, of course, could mount extensive counterclaims, for example, to the right bank of the Niemen River. The spirit of Helsinki (1975) and of German reunification (1990) militated for making the best of existing borders. Still, since Gorbachev showed some flexibility to Oslo on the Barents Sea and to Tokyo on the Kurile chain, conditions might be ripening for territorial revisionism within the USSR. Indeed, Estonia's Supreme Soviet protested part of the German-Soviet treaty signed in September 1990: An article recognizing all present borders in Europe, said the Estonians, amounted to recognition by Germany of Soviet annexation of the Baltic (an interpretation denied by Germany).

For pluralism to take root and prosper in Soviet politics, three kinds of legal and constitutional guarantees were required. First, privileges needed to be stripped from the CPSU and CPSU-dominated organizations. This would dictate changes in voting laws to deprive the CPSU, the trade unions, the Writers' Union, the Academy of Sciences, and other such organizations of any assured seats in the Congress. These reserved seats gave some individuals five or six votes and others only one. They also discriminated against organizations such as popular fronts that were not "all-Union."

The CPSU Central Committee agreed in early 1990 to abrogate its constitutional monopoly on power, but this did not ensure that a viable multiparty system would emerge and function. First, Soviet citizens had no experience with real democracy since 1917. Many seemed to gravitate toward anarchism or a sentimental return to the strong arm of yesteryear. Second, how could other parties rival the Communists' wealth, organization, and control of communications?

Independent political movements needed guarantees that they would have the right to (a) collect funds; (b) publish and broadcast their own materials; (c) act as political parties, officially putting forward candidates, holding caucuses, etc. As Gorbachev increased his authority in 1990, his opponents could do none of these things.

Reflecting both their despair with the Soviet system and their confidence in Baltic liberation, many Baltic delegates to the USSR Congress in 1990 declared themselves to be mere observers. Since their homelands were reestablishing their independence, it would be inappropriate for them to vote on the laws of a foreign country.

Still, weakness at the center emboldened nationalists at the periphery. As the CPSU renounced its constitutional right to lead and as other parties vied for power in 1990, this created more leeway for Balts to seek their own objectives, whether in Moscow or on the periphery. The disintegration of CPSU hegemony meant that the border peoples had a better chance to influence politics at the center—or to quit the union and go their own way.

Baltic Economic Coordination

Balts collaborated powerfully with one another in the economic realm. Echoing the PFE progam, the state planning (Gosplan) directors of all three Baltic republics, backed by many economists, jointly demanded in 1988 that their republics have exclusive control over republic property—its land, minerals, waters, continental shelf, and all property created or purchased by the state. The directors called for all interrepublic enterprises, even those of the Ministry of Defense, to be put on a contract basis, with each local republic setting the tax rates. They insisted that the Baltic governments be empowered to decide all issues of economic development, price formation, taxation, wages, and economic incentives. The republics, they said, should establish their own currencies and set the rate of exchange with other currencies, including the USSR ruble.[53]

Economic reformers associated with the PFE rejected the idea that their republic—perhaps with Leningrad, Kaliningrad,[54] and Nakhodka—become a special economic zone of the USSR. Such arrangements, they said, would perpetuate Russia's domination of the Baltic. Economic sovereignty, they said, required that Estonia have the right to enter into trade and joint ventures with foreign firms without consulting Moscow.[55] An example of what could be done emerged in 1989 as a Finnish food-producing machinery company formed a joint venture with Estonian firms, the first case in which a Finnish company owned a majority (51 percent) stake in a Soviet enterprise. The company hoped to operate not only in the Baltic but in other Soviet republics and CMEA (Comecon) countries.[56]

Balts rejected any suggestion that their economic life be organized in the same way as that of Kazakhs, Siberians, Ukrainians, and other Soviet peoples. A Latvian analyst sarcastically noted in 1989 that the consequence of such "ironing out of differences has been rather 'successful' in the sense that the fertile soil of the Ukraine now approaches that of the North, while alcoholism, pillage, wastefulness [*bezkhoziastvennost'*] have become characteristic almost in equal measure for all regions of the country."[57]

Balts blamed some shortages of consumer goods on tourists and settlers who bought things locally and shipped them elsewhere. Borrowing a page from Czechoslovakia, Estonia on January 10, 1989, placed sharp limits on mailing or shipping packages of food, household appliances, furniture, and other "goods with a heightened demand" from Estonia to other parts of the USSR, leading to a sharp decline in parcel mailings.[58] Individual cities such as Tartu and Tallinn refused to allow nonresidents to buy key products such as batteries and light bulbs. And Prime Minister Toome criticized local cooperatives for fattening cattle with "concentrated feeds obtained from our republican quota" and then selling the meat elsewhere. There was talk of limiting purchases to persons with Estonian residence permits or Estonian credit cards.[59]

Similar restrictions were instituted in Lithuania on August 1, 1989. Goods quickly seemed to become more accessible for locals, at least temporarily, but serious questions were raised about this "pathetic situation" and the conditions that gave rise to it.[60]

More than 350 delegates from the three Baltic fronts convened in Tallinn in May 1989 to discuss a common approach to economic independence and what actions should be taken by members who were also delegates to the Congress of People's Deputies in Moscow. The Baltic Communist Party leaders were invited but were said to be at the Kremlin meeting with Gorbachev. No foreign Communists attended, but the Finnish People's Democratic League and the Greens were represented along with Sweden's Center Party. Some invited foreign guests did not get visas from Soviet authorities.

Seven draft documents had been prepared beforehand. They were more radical than the bevy of documents finally adopted after two days' debate. On the first day, however, the conferees appealed to the UN Secretary General to call an international conference to investigate the legality of the Soviet annexation of the Baltic countries. A Swedish commentator expressed the thought that the fronts aimed "to make the Baltic countries the next big foreign policy burden for Moscow now that the troops have been called home from Afghanistan." [61]

The conferees appealed to President Gorbachev, the UN Secretary General, and the CSCE states to meet their demands for independence from Moscow in a "neutral and demilitarized European zone." They specified "independence" rather than "sovereignty," as had been called for in the draft documents and by some speakers, who expressed confidence that Moscow would "not oppose restoration of state sovereignty" to the Baltic republics "through negotiations." They also avoided any reference to secession. They concentrated instead on the 1939 Soviet-German protocols, expressing confidence that Moscow would declare them null and void in 1989.[62]

The gathering agreed also on joint declarations stressing the "right to self-determination of political status" and laying out guidelines for economic independence.

An upbeat report on the Baltic Assembly that appeared in *Izvestiia* only hinted at the sharp discussions held in Tallinn. It stressed the positive side of the Baltic demands for economic independence and even said that "the democratization processes are paving the way for the establishment of truly sovereign union republics." [63]

When Balts asserted economic independence in 1990, however, the Kremlin objected and used economic as well as other levers to thwart the process.

Within the USSR: Demonstration and Multiplier Effects

Interrepublic cooperation, whether tightly coordinated or merely parallel action, could add to the bargaining leverage of each republic. If only the Baltic

Reviewer comment!

republics had resisted Moscow's rule, the Kremlin might have been tempted to repress their common actions before the challenge to authority became too severe. This option was eliminated in the late 1980s as nationalist resistance emerged in many republics.

Cooperation extended from the Baltic to the other western republics and beyond. Most border peoples of the Russian empire faced similar problems arising from their dependency upon the center, problems ranging from environmental despoliation to Russification. Exchanges among these peoples could raise consciousness and generate ideas and plans for national self-assertion. Thus, a delegation of Estonian educators traveled to Kazakhstan in 1987 to compare teaching practices of the native language there with Estonia.[64]

With or without direct cooperation, the Baltic syndrome proved contagious. Popular fronts were organized in 1988-1989 not only in the Ukraine and Belorussia but also in Moldavia and the Caucasus. Sympathetic organizations mushroomed in Leningrad and other Russian cities as well.

Baltic leaders took an active interest in moderating and resolving ethnic conflicts in other parts of the USSR. The PFE Congress in 1988 called for a referendum in Nagorno-Karabakh.[65] In 1989 the PFE leadership expressed strong sympathy with the democratic forces in Georgia after the massacre in Tbilisi.[66] In January 1990 all three Baltic popular fronts, in a meeting at Riga, mediated differences between Armenian and Azeri nationalists.

The Azeris seemed to have picked up lessons from the Baltic popular fronts and the strikes of Russian coal miners, and fused them with their own traditions as they demanded greater autonomy for their republic in 1989-1990. Thus, the Azerbaijan Popular Front called for a strike after 80,000 Azerbaijanis demonstrated in Baku's central square on August 13, 1989. The strike threatened an asset, oil, more critical to the entire USSR than any Baltic product. The front demanded legal recognition, the recall of Azerbaijani deputies from the Supreme Soviet (saying they failed to represent local interests), an end to military rule, and assured Azerbaijani dominion over Nagorno-Karabakh. On August 12 demonstrators hoisted the flag from Azerbaijan's brief spell in 1919-1920 as an independent republic, and waved banners backing the Popular Front.

Balts generally sympathized with Christian Armenians over Muslim Azeris and most Balts repudiated the violence that has characterized ethnic strife in the Caucasus. Balts worried, however, that the dispatch of Soviet military forces to Azerbaijan in January 1990 could set a dangerous precedent for dealing with Baltic problems.

Nationalist activity of non-Russians evoked a wide range of response among Russian citizens and leaders. Some Russians concluded, "Let them go," or, "Let them kill each other." Others demanded order. Some Russian liberals, however, found inspiration in Baltic movements for democracy and environmental protection. Support groups for Baltic popular front and Green activities blossomed in Leningrad.[67] Even in Moscow in the late 1980s I found many Russians from different walks of life who expressed deep interest in and respect for the efforts of Estonians at self-determination. One Muscovite engineer showed me a video cassette program of Estonian paintings and cartoons illustrating the Soviet pillage of Estonia. While some Russian nationalists resented the special claims being made by the border nations, other Russians welcomed freedom wherever it emerged and hoped that it might spread to the RSFSR.

An example of the divided Russian response to Baltic demands arose at the USSR Doctors' Congress in 1988. When Estonian physicians called for a decentralization of medical services, they were subjected to considerable "name-calling by other delegates." A Russian physician accused the Estonians of pursuing "a nationalist health care policy." The Lithuanian platform, similar to the Estonian, was also attacked. A Moscow cardiologist, however, said later that he was ashamed of Russian chauvinism at the Congress.[68]

Cooperation Abroad: International and Transnational

Balts sought to multiply their transnational and international contacts. Some members of the Estonian Academy of Sciences traveled abroad a great deal — even more extensively than their Muscovite peers, the latter believed. Sociologist Tiiu Pohl, for example, visited Sweden and the United States several times in 1988-1990. She collaborated in a joint study of demilitarization sponsored by the Council on Economic Priorities and Soviet scholars. Tiit Käbin, political scientist in the Academy, visited the American Political Science Association National Meeting in 1988 and had an array of U.S. posters on his office wall, including a picture of small-town America proclaiming that the "road to the White House begins here." Pohl and sociologist Priit Järve gave papers at the International Studies Association in Washington in April 1990. Estonian-born American professor Rein Taagepera lectured in Estonia in the late 1980s on his academic specialty, electoral systems, and on alternative futures for Estonia's development. He contributed many articles to Estonian as well as Western journals.[69]

Balts maintained ties with their cousins abroad, concentrated in Sweden, the United States, Canada, Australia, and Finland. Tiit Käbin quoted Hemingway (*To Have and Have Not*, 1937) to the effect: "In every port you find an Estonian." He estimated that there were between 70,000 and 150,000 Estonians abroad, depending on how children and grandchildren were counted. They could follow Baltic affairs through a variety of publications. The Estonian language weekly *Kodumaa*, summarizing developments for foreign readers, also had a supplement in English, *Homeland*, later called *The Estonian Independent*.

Latvians, Lithuanians, and Estonians had strong organizations in North America, Europe, and even Australia. Thus, in the late 1980s there were about 26,000 U.S. citizens of Estonian extraction, 8,000-9,000 of whom supported the Estonian American National Council. Americans of Baltic origin let the White House know that they were no less concerned about their ancestral lands than Greeks, Jews, Poles, and other U.S. citizens. While officials of the Reagan administration met with Baltic Americans fairly often, the Bush White House did not authorize such a meeting until February 12, 1990. The Estonian American Council, however, arranged a talk by Tunne Kelam, cofounder of the ENIP at the Council on Foreign Relations on December 12, 1989. He visited North America again in spring 1990.

A slate of Estonian émigrés was included in candidates for election to the Congress of Estonia in March 1990.

Baltic political movements aligned with like-minded people abroad. Estonian Greens in 1988 joined the international Green movement. In April 1989 Baltic Greens sent delegates to the international congress of Greens convened in Paris. Renewed Social Democratic parties in Latvia and Estonia won support for their activities in 1989-1990 from companion parties in Europe and the Socialist International. Estonia's Liberal Democratic Congress in March 1990 was endorsed by European conservatives.

In 1989 the Estonian Supreme Soviet hosted a delegation of European parliamentarians, much to the chagrin of *Pravda*'s Yuri Zhukov.[70]

Baltic nationalists became skilled at giving interviews and writing for Swedish, Finnish, Italian, and other foreign newspapers. Marju Lauristin, interviewed by *Svenska Dagbladet*, appealed to the Swedish public: "We expect our Nordic neighbors to understand the situation that has arisen." If Sweden supports "our call for constitutional guarantees, and Moscow realizes that Sweden does so, it would be very important." [71]

In short, Balts linked hands not only with other Balts but with kinsmen and neighbors across the Baltic Sea and even the world's oceans. They also supported and drew support from and supported some nationalists and reformers in other parts of the Russian empire.

also explained so much

NOTES

1. Still, an educated Russian woman living in Tallinn asked in March 1990: "Why have we given Czechoslovakia and Poland back to the Czechs and Poles? They did not liberate their countries, we did." Such attitudes were common in Russia, even among otherwise liberal citizens in nearby Leningrad.

2. Esther B. Fein, "Baltic Citizens Link Hands to Demand Independence," *The New York Times*, 24 August 1989.

3. Heiki Lindpere, assistant to Savisaar on the commission and other matters, interviewed in Tallinn, 12 March 1990.

4. "Half of Pact Commission Sign First Findings," *Homeland*, 23 August 1989, p. 2.

5. See Igor Gräzin and Heiki Lindpere, "V razgare leta 1940-go," *Molodezh' Estonii*, 17 May 1989, and Lindpere, "Byla li al'ternativa dogovoru SSSR s Germaniei?" *Sovetskaia Estoniia*, 23 August 1989.

6. Joel Aav, "Kremlin Fails Courage Test on Pact, 'Not Ready for Truth'," *Homeland*, 30 August 1989, p. 1.

7. James Blitz, "Lithuania Heads for Break with Moscow," *Financial Times*, 24 August 1989, p. 2.

8. Excerpts in *The New York Times*, 27 August 1989, p. 18.

9. Esther B. Fein, "Unrepentant Movements in Baltics Decry 'Political Terror'," *International Herald Tribune*, 28 August 1989, p. 1.

10. James Blitz, "Lithuanians Ponder How Far They Can Push Moscow," *Financial Times*, 26 August 1989, p. 2.

11. Algimantas Cekuolis, *Gimtasis Krastas*, No. 38 (21-27 September 1989), p. 2, Foreign Broadcast Information Service, *Daily Report: Soviet Union [FBIS-SOV]*, 17 October 1989, pp. 83-84.

12. Indrek Toome, Chairman of the Estonian Council of Ministers, reporting on Väljas's remarks to the CPSU Central Committee. Interview in *Sovetskaia Estoniia*, 21 September 1989, p. 1, *FBIS-SOV*, 17 October 1989, pp. 87-88.

13. Ibid.

14. See summary by Tarmu Tammerk in *Homeland*, 6 September 1989, pp. 1-2.

15. Esther B. Fein, "Unrepentant Movements in Baltics Decry 'Political Terror'," *International Herald Tribune*, 28 August 1989, p. 1.

16. Ibid.

17. AP and Reuters reports, compiled in *International Herald- Tribune*, 29 August 1989, p. 1.

18. *Homeland*, 13 September 1989, p. 1.

19. *Homeland*, 20 September 1989, p. 1.

20. See A. N. Yakovlev, "Political and Legal Appraisal of the 1939 Soviet-German Nonaggression Treaty," and the Congress decree on this matter, *Vestnik Ministerstva inostrannykh del SSSR*, No. 2 (60) (31 January 1990), pp. 7-13.

21. The film was released on 23 August 1989 and shown in the Baltic and Georgia. Its makers estimated that the ban would cost them 1.5 million rubles. See *Homeland*, 27 December 1989, p. 1.

22. This marked the first time, according to sociologist Tiiu Pohl, that central TV had shown a sympathetic portrait of Estonia's quest for independence. The program also showed riveting shots of "hands across the Baltic" and the region's polluted waters.

23. Documentation and analysis in Toomas Ilves contribution to "'Baltic Area' Situation Report," *Radio Free Europe Research*, 13, 47 (25 November 1988), part II, pp. 3-5.

24. This number would represent practically the entire population of Estonian natives, including children, the lame, the elderly. It could of course draw also upon non-Estonian residents, but most of them would be inclined to approve the draft amendments or be apathetic. There is reason also to question other numbers alleged by Estonian nationalists, such as the circulation of their publications and the size of their rallies. One PFE member told me that the print run of the Russian edition of *Rainbow* was about five times higher than that published in a recent issue.

25. Text in *Sovetskaia Estoniia*, 19 November 1989, p. 2.

26. For a Moscow summary of the Estonian legislation, see *Pravda*, 28 November 1988, p. 2.

27. See explanation by Arnold Rüütel, Chairman of the Estonian Supreme Soviet Presidium at the 26 November 1988 session of the USSR Supreme Soviet Presidium on Moscow television, 27 November 1988, *FBIS-SOV*, 28 November 1988, pp. 48-49; also interview with PFE leader Hasso Nurm in *La Repubblica*, 18 November 1988, p. 3, *FBIS-SOV*, 22 November 1988, p. 49; and interview with Estonian Prime Minister Indrek Toome in *Avanti!*, 19 November 1989, *FBIS-SOV*, 22 November 1988, pp. 50-51.

28. Interview in *Svenska Dagladet*, 2 November 1988, p. 4 in *FBIS-SOV*, 9 November 1989, pp. 67-68.

29. Dzintra Bungs in *Radio Free Europe Research*, 13, No. 47 (25 November 1988), pp. 15-16.

30. See Saulius Girnius, ibid., p. 35.

31. See reports from Vilnius by *Pravda*, *Sovetskaia Rossiia*, Lithuanian, French, German, and other sources, *FBIS-SOV*, 21 November 1988, pp. 48-54, and reports from Latvia, pp. 54-57.

32. See Joel Aav, "Estonian Parliament Does Not Shrink Back," *Homeland*, No. 50 (207), 14 December 1988, p. 1; interview with Tiit Käbin, ibid., pp. 1-2; commentary by V. Urban in *Krasnaia Zvezda*, 18 December 1988, p. 2.

33. See *Homeland*, No. 3 (212), 18 January 1989, p. 1.

34. Exonerated persons would have priority in getting free housing and various pension benefits. See A. Rüütel announcement in *Sovetskaia Estoniia*, 24 March 1989, p. 1. Destalinization and democratization became fodder for Soviet propaganda. News of the compensation plan was broadcast by Moscow in English to Great Britain and Ireland, 20 April 1989, *FBIS-SOV*, 21 April 1989, p. 80.

35. On "Memorial" activities in Moscow, see Walter C. Clemens, Jr., "Remembering Stalin's Victims," *World Monitor*, 3, 3 (March 1990), pp. 54-55.

36. *Homeland*, 14 December 1988, pp. 1-2.

37. For background see Tarmu Tammerk in *Homeland*, No. 3 (212), 18 January 1989, pp. 1-2.

38. See sympathetic articles in *Komsomol'skaia pravda*, 4 April 1989, and *Izvestiia*, 6 April 1989, p. 4.

39. Roundtable, "To Listen to One Another," *Kommunist*, 6 (April 1989), pp. 62-80, at p. 68.

40. It was signed by A. Rüütel, chairman of the ESSR Supreme Soviet Presidium and V. Vahkt, its secretary. See *Sovetskaia Estoniia*, 9 April 1989, p. 2.

41. R. Vare, "The Road to Sovereignty," *Sovetskaia Estoniia*, 2 April 1989, p. 3, *FBIS-SOV*, 24 April 1989, pp. 70-72.

42. See *Rahva Hääl*, 23 April 1989, p. 2, *FBIS-SOV*, 10 May 1989, pp. 57-58.

43. Dzintra Bungs, "A Comparison of the Baltic Declarations of Sovereignty," *Radio Free Europe Research*, 14, 37 (15 September 1989), part 5, pp. 17-24.

44. Deputies complained about tendencies toward unitary government favored by Gorbachev and others at the center. Report on Vilnius in English to North America on 19 October 1989, *FBIS-SOV*, 23 October 1989, pp. 90-91. For the text of various changes in the Lithuanian Constitution, see *Sovetskaia Litva*, 10 October 1989, pp. 1, 2, *FBIS-SOV*, 23 October 1989, pp. 91-97.

45. In Estonia voters had to elect four deputies from large territorial districts for the Soviet of the Union and thirty-two from smaller national-territorial districts for the Soviet of Nationalities. Some districts were uncontested, but most had two or three candidates running for one position. In Moscow, by contrast, there were several districts for the Soviet of the Union but a single district for the Soviet of Nationalities.

46. The ethnic origins were implied by whether the voter chose a ballot in the Latin script or Cyrillic. On this and other nuances, see Rein Taagepera, "A Note on the March 1989 Elections in Estonia," *Soviet Studies*, 42, 2 (April 1990), pp. 329-39; also his essay on Baltic elections scheduled for *Electoral Studies*, December 1990.

47. Dzintra Bungs, "A Victory for Reformers in Estonia and Latvia," *Report on the USSR* (Radio Liberty), 1, 17 (28 April 1989), pp. 15-17.

48. Taagepera, "A Note on the March 1989 Elections."

49. See "List of USSR People's Deputies Elected from Territorial and National-Territorial Okrugs and From Social Organizations," *Izvestiia*, 5 April 1989, pp. 2-12.

50. Valerii A. Tishkov, "An Assembly of Nations or an All-Union Parliament?" *Journal of Nationalities*, 1, 1 (Spring 1990), pp. 101-27. See especially Table 1. On Russian-Baltic cooperation, see interviews by Boris Yeltsin with *Excelsior* (Mexico City) and his adviser M. N. Poltaranin in *Profil* (Vienna), *FBIS-SOV* 063, 4 April 1989, pp. 43-44. Earlier, Yeltsin granted *Sovetskaia Estoniia* an interview, which was treated as a journalistic and political

coup in Tallinn. The President of the Estonian Academy of Sciences, K. Rebane, was one of only eight academicians receiving a majority vote in the first round of nominations for the Congress at the USSR Academy of Sciences. See T. Iakhlakova, "Twelve Seats Are Available," *Sovetskaia kul'tura*, 25 March 1989, p. 2.

51. For analysis of the USSR legislature in 1989, see Dawn Mann, Robert Monyak, Elizabeth Teague, *The Supreme Soviet: A Biographical Directory* (Washington, D.C.: Center for Strategic and International Studies, 1989).

52. Lithuanian delegates have complained about "a fictitious division of chambers in the Supreme Soviet." Vilnius in English to North America, 19 October 1989, *FBIS-SOV*, 23 October 1989, pp. 90-91.

53. See protocol signed in Riga by the chairmen of Gosplan in Estonia, Latvia, and Lithuania and other economic specialists from these republics, published in *Sovetskaia Estoniia*, 27 September 1988, p. 2. The Gosplan head of Belorussia also helped convene the Riga meeting but did not appear there, according to Rein A. Otsason, chairman of Estonian Gosplan (interview, ibid.). Otsason added that some 200 specialists took part in the meetings, which were the most active and least indifferent he had ever witnessed. Only the Estonian delegation "had a unified concept and defended it unanimously," but the other two delegations finally gravitated toward the Estonian view. All recognized that changes in the USSR Constitution would be needed if only because of ambiguity in the term "state property."

54. Squeezed between Lithuania and Poland, Kaliningrad (formerly Königsberg, East Prussia, taken by Russia in 1945) was discussed as a special German-Soviet trade zone and a homeland for Soviet Germans forcibly moved to Kazakhstan in the 1940s. The idea was floated during Gorbachev's visit to Bonn in June 1989 and endorsed by Chancellor Helmut Kohl in July. Germans whom I met in Kasakhstan in May 1990 expressed no interest in moving to Kaliningrad. If they moved, it would be to Germany.

55. For a draft decree of the USSR Supreme Soviet Presidium on a special economic zone for the Estonian SSR, see *Molodozh' Estonii*, 15 October 1988, p. 1. For the positive appraisal of the idea by Academician Arno Köörna and a rebuttal by the IME Research Council of the Estonian Academy of Sciences, see *Homeland*, No. 43 (200), 26 October 1988, pp. 1-2.

56. Enriqué Tessieri, "Finns to Help Develop Estonian Food Processing," *Financial Times*, 17 August 1989, p. 4.

57. K. Prunskiene, participant in a roundtable published as "To Listen to One Another," *Kommunist*, No. 6 (April 1989), pp. 62-80, at p. 65.

58. See "Shortage of Goods Prompts Ban on Postal Parcels," *Homeland*, No. 3 (212), 19 January 1989, pp. 1-2.

59. Quentin Peel, "Baltic Bar Comes Down on Consumer Imports," *Financial Times*, 14 February 1989, p. 2.

60. P. Keidoshius, "Tol'ko po pasportu," *Literaturnaia gazeta*, 23 August 1989, p. 2. The article asked: "What has happened to Lithuanian hospitality?" The paper also pictured a block-long line of persons waiting to buy soap in Moscow.

61. Stockholm Domestic Service, 14 May 1989, *FBIS-SOV*, 15 May 1989, p. 74.

62. This analysis compares the original drafts with accounts on the assembly by Helsinki International Service in Finnish, 13 May 1989; Vilnius in English to North America, 13 May 1989; and Paris Agence France-presse in English, May 15, 1989; all in *FBIS-SOV*, 15 May 1989, pp. 73-74.

63. I. Livinova and L. Levitskii, "Baltic Assembly," *Izvestiia*, 16 May 1989, p. 6, *FBIS-SOV*, 19 May 1989, p. 79.

64. The Estonians were shocked to find how few Kazakhs knew their native tongue well. For corroboration, see John Soper, "Problems in the Kazakh Educational System," *Radio Liberty Research Bulletin* RL 488/87 (2 December 1987), pp. 2-3.

65. The EPF Congress called for a referendum in Nagorno Karabakh. See *Narodnyi kongress*, pp. 219-20.

66. Text in *Noorte Hääl*, 22 April 1989, p. 1, *FBIS-SOV*, 10 May 1989, pp. 58-59.

67. Illustrating sentimental ties between Russia and Estonia, a Leningrad poet began his reminiscences about Tallinn: "In Leningrad I Dream of Estonia." See Vsevolod Azarov, *Vesna v starom gorode* (Tallinn: Eesti Raamat, 1987).

68. See Joel Aav, "When Doctors Disagree," *Homeland*, No. 46 (203), 16 November 1988, p. 2. A Russian doctor in Tallinn told me in 1989 that medical care and environmental conditions in the entire country were a disaster — even within the armed forces — and had been so for decades.

69. Some critics of the PFE — including Intermovement as well as some ENIP backers — called Taagepera the front's "spiritual father." For a reference to this viewpoint, see the editor's introduction to Taagepera's "Kto agitiruet za nesavismisost'?" ["Who is agitating for independence?"] *Vestnik Narodnogo Fronta*, No. 4 (May 1989). Taagepera's essays appeared also in *Postipoiss*, 22 March 1989; in *Edasi*, 28 and 29 March 1989; in *Rainbow* [*Raduga*], February and March 1989 issues; and in a Leningrad publication. Some of his views appeared in English in *Homeland*, 31 May and 21 June 1989. See also "View of the Foreign Expert," interview with Taagepera in *Tallinna Polütehnik*, February 1989, p. 4.

70. See letter from A. Rüütel, M. Titma, and A. Green in *Sovetskaia Estoniia*, 18 March 1989, p. 3, regarding Zhukov's "Guests Came to the Baltic," *Pravda*, 11 March 1989.

71. Ingmar Lindmarker, "Estonia's Popular Front: We Are Moving Toward a Crisis," *Svenska-Dagbladet*, 2 November 1988, p. 4, *FBIS-SOV*, 2 November 1988, p. 4.

10
"Internationals": Resist or Join Baltic Independence?

Baltic independence could help or harm the vital interests of non-Balts — Russians, Poles, and others — living in Estonia, Latvia, and Lithuania. Some had lived in the region for centuries; most, for decades or just several years. The initial response of many nonnatives to demands for Baltic independence was to prefer the familiar status quo; with time, however, a growing number thought that Baltic liberation could also entail their own liberation.

The outsiders' security and complacency was challenged by new forces unleashed in the late 1980s. Many began then to call themselves "internationals," although most spoke but one language, Russian. Some locals, however, termed them "migrants," "illegal migrants," or "occupiers."

Many non-Balts lacked roots. Most were Russians who felt themselves at home in nearly every Soviet republic. These Russians expected, much like Americans, that they could settle in any part of their country, speak the dominant language, use their own money, and enjoy the same privileges as in their birthplace. Unlike Americans, many Russians also expected to enjoy special privileges when they settled in remote areas away from their native region. They felt at home; they were members of the master race, fluent in the language of "inter-national" communication. Toward Muslims, Russians generally considered themselves culturally and materially superior; toward Armenians and Georgians, they extended at best a grudging respect for cunning. The entire malaise, captured from an Azeri perspective, was set out in *Ali and Nino*, a novel written under the pen name "Kurban Said."

Russians' attitudes toward Balts were complex. Most Russians — those in Russia as well as those in the Baltic — regarded the Balts as more Western and more materially advanced than Russians. This recognition evoked mixed emotions. Some Russians thought that they should learn from and emulate the hardworking Balts. Others nursed a kind of inferiority complex toward Balts that contained both envy and respect. Some Communist or chauvinist Russians regarded themselves as ideologically and perhaps morally superior to Balts: Uzbeks and Azeris might need Russian technology; the Balts needed Russian defense capabilities, raw materials, and manpower. Above all, however, the Balts needed Soviet ideology so that they did not succumb to bourgeois, Fascist, or anti-Communist tendencies. In short, many Russians thought that they were doing the Balts a favor by cohabiting with them.

Some Balts saw the Russians not as settlers or even as migrants seeking personal gain; rather, the Russians were colonizers working for the interests of a distant metropole. From this standpoint, the Russians were more like the first Europeans who came to the Caribbean than those who settled New England. "Settlers develop the land for the future of their children; colonizers exploit it for the aggrandizement of the metropolitan power. Settlers build institutions to facilitate long-term development of their settlement; colonizers build institutions to facilitate exploitation." [1]

In reality, many Poles in Lithuania were the offspring of Polonized Lithuanians or Belorussians. Non-Balts in the Baltic included many diverse types: true settlers — Russians as well as Germans — who had been there for generations, even centuries; recent settlers who hoped to put down roots; venal migrants with no aim except a quick ruble or illicit dollar; and agents of Russian imperialism. But most quickly acquired the same outlook as that of Europeans who settled in Johannesburg, Madras, or Hong Kong. Many "Europeans" born in Africa or Asia thought of themselves as belonging there, with certain inalienable rights. Even those who came as adults on a *mission civilisatrice* or for self-seeking ends could not fathom how or why locals might want them to leave.[2]

The demographic picture was not black and white, of course, but included also grays and browns. As in the Third World, so in the Baltic: Many outsiders had settled and assimilated quite well with the native population. This assimilation occurred sometimes through intermarriage. In the 1960s Estonians and

Latvians married people of other nationalities more often than did the people of many other Union Republics.[3] Between 1979 and 1989, however, the tendency for natives to marry natives rose in each Baltic republic.[4]

Some migrants to the Baltic learned the language and came to esteem local ways, sometimes preferring them to those of Russia. Many Jews assimilated well, perhaps seeking a haven from anti-Semitism in the Slavic lands. But so did many non-Jews — for example, intellectuals who took up teaching positions at Baltic universities in the 1950s and 1960s.

Such assimilation was the exception rather than the main trend. Most settlers were laborers, party hacks, or lieutenants rather than university professors; some military men served only a year in the Baltic. Most settlers did not learn the local language; many regarded the Baltic cultures not just as alien and difficult but as degenerate; most remained in their own enclaves, something like U.S. or (still more) Soviet troops in occupied Germany.[5]

Nonnatives in Estonia

In addition to 963,000 indigenous Estonians in the late 1980s (about 30,000 less than in the 1930s) there were about 602,000 persons of other ethnic backgrounds living in Estonia — Russians, Ukrainians, Belorussians, and others.[6] Some occupied elite positions but most were factory workers, many unskilled. Some were born in Estonia; many had lived in Estonia for decades; but very few had acquired a working knowledge of the language.

Pavel Panfilov, then Second Secretary of the Tallinn CPE organization, told me on March 7, 1990, that he came to Estonia twenty-one years before. Having finished his chemistry studies in Kalinin, he was offered a job in the oil shale industry near Narva.[7] Soon he was asked to head the Komsomol organization. Then he became part of the *nomenklatura* and became immersed in party work. But in 1990 at age forty-five Panfilov had never studied Estonian and showed no signs of wanting to begin. Two sons, aged eighteen and twenty-one, had not studied Estonian, but another, aged nine, was beginning to. Panfilov explained: "It was simply not necessary for us to learn Estonian when I came. Even now, about 68 percent of Communists in the Tallinn organization are Russian-speakers. Had I been told twenty-one years ago that I must learn Estonian to work here, perhaps I would have made a different decision. Perhaps I would have preferred to study English or another language with wide use." Recently he asked all three sons about the future: each wanted to remain in Estonia, as did their father.

In 1989 Panfilov had called for condemning — probably he meant banning — the Citizens' Committee registration campaign for the Congress of Estonia. But authorities took no action and the citizens' campaign continued, aggravating relations between Estonians and Russians. "Now they think that they are the only law."

As noted earlier (chapter 7), Panfilov seemed disinterested in the hazing of Estonian draftees in the military, even though this practice made his job harder.

When most of the CPE voted to split with Moscow in late March 1990, Panfilov became one of two chairman of the holdout CPSU faction. How could he support a group whose language he could not speak?

As in the Third World, relations between conquistadores and subject peoples were complex, sometimes involving hate-love polarities.[8] One activist in Estonia's Heritage Society was quite anti-Russian as well as anti-Soviet. Still, he married three times, always a Russian! The third wife, interviewed in 1989, seemed to have embraced her husband's nationalist cause.

Symptomatic of the growing hostility toward the outsiders, fewer Estonians polled in the late 1980s admitted to knowing Russian well than in the 1970s. Many Estonians in service jobs refused to answer queries in Russian.

Estonian nationalism asserted itself in many ways threatening to settlers from outside. Not only did Estonians seek to break from Moscow's economic and political controls, they sought to be masters in their own land: In the late 1980s they passed laws saying that anyone who served the public would have to speak Estonian within a few years; anyone who wished to vote or run for office would have to satisfy a residence requirement; anyone who wished to purchase goods in short supply would have to prove his or her local residence. The Estonian Supreme Soviet passed such laws in 1988-1989. Often it backed down and limited their scope, but the intent and thrust of Baltic nationalism was clear. Lithuania, Latvia, and other Soviet border republics began to endorse and enact similar laws.

Outsiders responded to local nationalism in many ways. Factory managers, themselves Russian, mobilized their workers to protest and resist. Some Russians sympathized with the Estonians but felt unwelcome and decided to move away. A few sought to bridge the gap between native nationalists and outsiders so as to reach a modus vivendi useful to all sides.

As Communist Party leader Vaino Väljas put it on May 4, 1989, many non-Estonians in the republic viewed Estonia's perestroika with deep misgivings: They saw it as a "deviation from socialism or even as discrimination on nationality grounds." In consequence, some non-Estonians struggled "against the slightest changes in Estonia's life from great power positions condemned by the policy of restructuring."

Non-Estonians formed a United Council of Labor Collectives (*OSTK — Ob"edinennyi sovet trudovykh kollektivov*); an Intermovement (International Movement of Workers in the ESSR — *Internatsional'noe dvizhenie trudiashchikhsia ESSR*); and an organization of veterans (*Estonskaia organizatsiia veteranov voiny*) from Afghanistan as well as earlier service.

OSTK initially arose as a protest against the Estonians' wish to place all economic activity, including industry, under the control of local authorities. The United Council was formed mainly by directors, followed by their workers (most of them non-Estonians), of large plants and other enterprises subordinate to all-Union ministries in Moscow.

Two Intermovement leaders, Vladimir Yarovoi and Igor Shepelevich, were factory directors working for all-Union ministries. Evgeny V. Kogan, the third member of the leadership troika, was an engineer, not a manager. Intermovement was concerned not just with economics but also with the broader challenges Estonian nationalism presented to non-Estonians. Thus, Kogan expressed dismay in 1988 that PFE leaders had not dissociated themselves from slogans carried by pickets at the Supreme Court office that proclaimed: "We Are Relinquishing Soviet Citizenship!" [9]

When Kogan was injured in an auto accident during the 1989 campaign and forced to use crutches, his physical plight aroused much sympathy among voters, which he did not disdain. He quickly "learned and appreciated the value of scathing words...that wrench tears of sympathy from kind hearts." [10]

Kogan and Yarovoi were elected deputies to the People's Congress in 1989. Kogan was called often to the speaker's podium by Gorbachev, where he often railed against discrimination against non-Balts in the Baltic. Asked for a specific example, he cited the case of a woman "thrown out of her flat with her small son after her divorce." Investigators discovered that the man in question was a Lithuanian invalid seeking to evict his former wife (who also had a Lithuanian name). "I do not know why the MP from Estonia should pin a political label on a family drama," said a spokesman for the USSR Procurator's Office.[11]

Intermovement members were among those who charged "creeping counterrevolution" when the tricolor national flag was hoisted over Tallinn. Their opposition to perestroika extended to forming strike committees within the republic, actions that Väljas in May 1989 termed "not acceptable."

Väljas was especially incensed by the OSTK Ideological Commission demand in February 1989 for a Communist Party meeting within ten days, prescribing also the agenda and the norm for representation. "This was an unprecedented step—a social movement issuing instructions not only to the Central Committee but to the republic's entire Communist Party. The Constituent Congress of Intermovement was held in a similar spirit on March 4-5, 1989, in Tallinn and often voiced crude insults and threats instead of constructive criticism." [12]

There was no automatic overlap, however, between OSTK and Intermovement. Sometimes OSTK leaders supported, sometimes condemned, sometimes ignored actions and statements by Intermovement. As Estonian nationalists became more influential, however, Russian chauvinists tended to coalesce.

While most non-Estonian organizations sought to defend the status quo, some wished to abet Estonian independence in a spirit of interethnic harmony. This was the idea motivating a very small committee of non-Estonian intellectuals calling itself Political Club Referendum. Founded in autumn 1988, Referendum had about fifty members in early 1989, some of them associated with the Estonian Academy of Sciences. While the group referred to its members as Russian intelligentsia, they included Belorussians, Ukrainians, and other persons neither Russian nor Estonian. They disdained Intermovement as chauvinist and uneducated, led by high-school teachers of history and by bureaucrats who cried crocodile tears for their "workers."

In March 1990 founding member Oleg Samorodnii told me that Referendum had gotten nowhere.[13] He and like-minded non-Estonians had then founded a newspaper, *Respublika*, in December 1989. Its editors wanted to transcend ethnic barriers in pursuit of a larger aim: the principle of "people's power." [14]

Many non-Estonian democrats worked in 1990 for the election to the Estonian Supreme Soviet of nonchauvinists in Russian-dominated electoral districts, for example, engineers who thought that their own professional and personal objectives could be enhanced by an independent Estonia.

Despite such efforts, Russian democrats sympathetic to an independent Estonia fared poorly in the March 1990 elections to the Estonian Supreme Soviet. They were defeated by hard-line representatives of Intermovement and OSTK. Many Russian democrats backed the PFE but asked the Front not to endorse them. They were unknown to voters or rejected in favor of candidates endorsed by factory bosses. But pro-Moscow loyalists controlled less than 30 percent of the votes in the new legislature.[15]

Many non-Estonians were not active in politics one way or the other. Some were passive and let matters drift. Some assumed that they would somehow be accepted by an independent Estonia, if such emerged. Others expected to leave and take up their lives in another part of Russia's domain.

Some non-Estonians felt disenfranchised — let down by the CPE, which increasingly sided with the PFE, they were too proud to join the Intermovement, which they found to be too chauvinist or too proletarian.

To find a home and job elsewhere, however, was not so simple. One Russian-born physician now retired from a career in the navy said in March 1989 that he planned to move to Rostov-on-Don. Why there? Is the air better than Moscow? "No, it is worse. But my father has a small house there." This was the answer of a retired naval officer with a wife and small son. He liked Estonia, but found it unpleasant to remain. He understood the Estonians' hostility to Russians and did not wish to suffer from it. As a medical man he had contempt for Soviet politics, because it had shortchanged even the navy, not to speak of civilian health allocations. Still, even though the air was bad and the politics uninspired, he would return to Rostov-on-Don.

Another Russian, a journalist, considered returning to Russia, but did not know where to go. In the big cities the competition for jobs was intense and elsewhere there was not much demand for journalists. Why not open up a new paper in his native Siberia? "It's all too uncertain — both perestroika and glasnost — and I have no experience as an entrepreneur."

As Party leader Väljas observed, non-Estonians felt a deep uncertainty about their future. "It is quite natural for this uncertainty to emerge as a reaction to Estonians' desire to be masters in their own land." He regretted that "criticism of Stalin and violence against Estonians has developed into criticism of the Russian people." This, Väljas said, was unfair, because the Russian people had also suffered from Stalin and "the local Russians, Ukrainians, and Belorussians are not to blame for the violence against the Estonian people." [16]

Non-Russians in the Baltic drew some support from many quarters in Russia. The military newspaper *Red Star* and the trade union organ *Trud* [*Labor*] often criticized the nationalist fervor of the Balts. In April 1989 an essay in *Trud* called for mutual respect between Balts and internationals. Around the major confrontation between the PFE and Intermovement, the article stated, "there is now an entire 'wreath' of informal tendencies." They included "the Estonian Christian Alliance, Independent Info, the Free and Independent Youth Column No. 1, and other 'fringe' groups." *Trud*'s correspondent discovered that there were young Estonians—"rascals," he called them, demanding "revolution." They insisted "that the memory of the 'freedom fighters'—White Estonians who fought Estonian Reds, 1918-1919, be immortalized. The young Estonians' slogans called "Down with the Soviets!" and "Get the Communists out of Power." [17]

By inclination and circumstance the republic newspaper *Sovetskaia Estoniia* also defended the rights of its readers, Russian-speakers in Estonia. Its editors had tried, beginning in 1987, to bridge the gap. Pressed to choose, they sided with the settlers. Although some of the editors disagreed with the extremist tone of many speeches at Intermovement congresses, they published them anyway.

As polarization of Baltic societies increased, the Party press began to diverge on national-linguistic lines. Leaving its Estonian-language sister *Rahva Hääl* to reflect local views, the Russian-language *Sovetskaia Estoniia* in 1988-1989 gave coverage to long speeches made by members of Intermovement while giving only spotty attention to views and happenings at odds with "internationalist" perspectives. Thus, it did not report the March 9, 1989, demonstration (commemorating the 1944 bombing of Tallinn) and failed to print a conciliatory letter from Referendum, the Political Club of the Russian Intelligentsia.[18] Estonian radio carried the October 1988 PFE Congress live but not the Intermovement proceedings of March 1989—one reason why

Sovetskaia Estoniia decided to publish them, even though some editors concurred with "only 10 percent" of the speakers' opinions.

Although some non-Estonian locals believed that the CPE had betrayed "international" interests, *Sovetskaia Estoniia* did not forget them. How could it when, of four editors and one journalist I met there in 1988, all carried Russian nationality in their passports even though one was half-Estonian and others partly Ukrainian or Belorussian? Even though they worked in mass communications, several did not know the local language despite a long residence in Estonia.

Some Soviet publications, probably with cause, blamed both Estonians and non-Estonians for failing to consider each other's needs.[19]

An essay by Dr. I. Rozenfeld in *Sovetskaia Estoniia* in March 1989 took umbrage at the "reopening of the Estonian Student Society, which was closed in the 'forties." Its members' thoughts were expressed in "all their primordial nature." "Every young member of the society," the writer Jaan Kross told them, "must set himself the task of joining at least the Estonian elite in his field. And also — why not — yes, tell me why the hell not — the world elite too?"[20]

Rozenfeld said the student society speakers expressed themselves in "a vigorous national style" that has become a "symbol of revolutionaries and radicalism." This was not a "tricolor" style, he charged, but two-color: "'white' heroes of a liberation war who dreamed of a right-wing ('black') dictatorship." These people, Rozenfeld asserted, lacked the "tolerance toward other viewpoints" associated with the tricolor and bourgeois pluralism.

Such accusations flowed from a polarization mirrored in the Estonian press. Increasingly the Russian-language media reflected the views of outsiders while the Estonian media represented native perspectives. As of October 1989 no Estonian nationalist leader had written an article for or been interviewed by *Sovetskaia Estoniia*; no Intermovement or OSTK leader had written for or been interviewed in the Estonian-language papers. A correspondent for *Vechernyi Tallinn* proposed an exchange: *Rahva Hääl* would print Kogan's interview in *Sovetskaia Estoniia* (September 30, 1989), and *Rahva Hääl* would carry Edgar Savisaar's interview (October 1). But such exchanges proved difficult to implement.[21] On the other hand, *Sovetskaia Estoniia* carried a full-page essay on the Molotov-Ribbentrop pact on August 23, 1989, by an

Estonian lawyer, and an American professor's advocacy of an Austrian solution for the Baltic on November 22.

Estonia's CP was caught not only between the demands of the native population and the distant imperial metropole; it had also to care for the nonnative settlers who looked to it for protection. How to satisfy the competing demands of these three quite different interest groups?

The Communist Party's sharpest problem in 1988-1989 was not with the PFE or the Kremlin but with the non-Estonians in Estonia — Party members and others. With the Party leadership dominated now by Estonian nationalists, Russians and others in the ranks became increasingly uneasy. In April 1989 the secretary of the Tallinn city party committee, J. Saarniit, warned that the CPE could not hold an extraordinary congress soon because it would mean an open split within the party. The situation in the capital, he said, was especially precarious. In Tallinn native Estonians made up 47 percent of the population but only 32 percent of CPE organizations. This gap he explained by different ways of viewing problems and their solutions. "We are now paying," he said, for the self-deception that national frictions had ended.[22]

Natives and other residents of Estonia viewed many things differently, said Saarniit, such as the tricolor on Long Hermann. Decisions on many topics were not properly explained to the Russian-speaking work collectives. It was especially important to explain to them that *IME* (self-management) and accountability "constitute a real basis for consolidating and pooling the efforts and interests of all national and social groups in the population." The Tallinn city committee (*gorkom*) debated these issues. "We wanted people to speak out and try to listen to each other. And do you know the conclusion?" Saarniit asked. "We do not know each other. I am speaking of Estonians and Russians even at the level of members of the same *gorkom*. We do not know what is of concern to whom and why. A party committee secretary at a Russian-speaking enterprise was very surprised that Estonians are concerned about 23 August....They have quite different assessments of events." Some believed that the chairman of OSTK had fueled the present troubles; others blamed PFE leader Savisaar.

"In general there is too much emotion," Saarniit complained, "too many spontaneous and unpredictable actions. Not even secretaries of large party committees are able to forecast and reckon up the situation. This is bad. What we need now is more considered, better thought-out action."

Saarniit had recently told a party group that its "critical attitude [of] impatience and dissatisfaction with the leadership can be...understood. But if we continue wallowing in recriminations, insults, and skirmishes, it could happen that in the fall I, as gorkom secretary, or another party leader will no longer be addressing you here."

It was especially important to avoid a split within the CPE, he said, because the Estonian National Independence Party (ENIP) and Heritage Society were striving to seize political power through alternative institutions. The Tallinn gorkom believed the Party had been "too liberal" toward such provocateurs and demagogues.

The interviewer from *Sovetskaia Estoniia* interjected: "People expect such principled party assessments to be made at the upcoming Central Committee plenum. Otherwise there will be bitter disappointment."

Saarniit then quoted a few lines from the draft theses prepared by the Tallinn gorkom for the upcoming CPE CC plenum: "The situation...requires the Party organizations to combat attempts to create an opposition to the Party, to impose extremist views, to disparage the Party's role and prestige in the republic's social life." He himself criticized the draft program put forward by four CP first secretaries and other draft documents circulating in collectives and in party organizations. He wanted clarity on the official line, followed by energetic efforts to propagandize it.

He also called for agreement on terminology: What is a federation, a confederation? "Chauvinism, nationalism — how are they understood? Sovereignty — what lies behind all that." Clarity on these matters, Saarniit concluded, was essential for trust and mutual understanding.

At the May 1989 plenum of the CPE Central Committee, however, First Secretary Väljas attempted to establish a middle course identifying the CPE with Gorbachev's version of perestroika and glasnost. Any other approach, including that of some Estonian gorkoms and local Party cells, amounted to a deviation. Väljas expressed alarm that CPE membership declined in 1988 by 1,126 members, with Estonians leaving in large numbers; new admissions to the ranks were insufficient. Party cells in shop organizations declined by one-fourth in recent months. Why? Many Communists, said Väljas, were "'ashamed' to champion the Party line in the collectives and have stopped doing real ideological work and publicizing and implementing Party decisions." Many tried instead to "blend in...with the nonparty mass." For others, Party membership had become secondary while they gave priority to membership in some new organization whose rules meant more to them than the CP statutes and program. Some ran for election to the Congress of People's Deputies on platforms not those of the CPE. "We are opposed to Communists heading so-called strike committees or joining 'Citizens of Estonia' committees and other antirestructuring associations." If Communists violate our rules, they should be replaced.[23]

Although worried about the Party's declining membership, Väljas announced a purge. He recommended that the Central Committee "approve the requests to be removed from the CPE elected organs" by a group of CC members and candidate members and also members of the CPE Auditing Commission who "have retired on pension or have left the republic." Those leaving the republic presumably included Russians and other immigrants who felt themselves out of place amid Estonian nationalism.

Väljas noted that some comrades feared the CPE was "losing the initiative" and "tailing" other movements; they wanted an extraordinary congress or conference. Haste and impulsiveness of this kind, however, could be costly. The CC Bureau opposed holding an extraordinary congress now, because conditions were not ripe. Instead, a Party action program should be drafted, discussed, adopted and implemented. Broader understanding of each ethnic group's problems was needed rather than unfettered polemics. Väljas chastised some local Party newspapers and even *Sovetskaia Estoniia* for giving voice to extremist positions and various materials casting doubt on CPE strength and unity.

The specific actions endorsed by Väljas and the Central Committee, however, differed little from those championed by the PFE except that the Party endeavored to establish limits to change. Thus, Väljas made clear that Estonia's place had to be *within* the Soviet Union. The Central Committee, he said, sought "the development of Estonia's autonomy within the USSR and regards the attainment of sovereignty for the Estonian SSR as one of the main tasks of restructuring." The CPE cooperated with all social movements supporting perestroika and opposed any attempts forcibly to impose its own vision on the organs of power and government. But it condemned the recent PFE declaration "On National Self-Determination" calling for movement toward pre-1940 independence as unrealistic. World history, Väljas declared, provided no cases in which a state that de facto ceased its existence fifty years before "has been revived." Somehow the would-be historian was oblivious to the resurgence of nearby Lithuania, Poland, and other parts of Eastern Europe, not to speak of Egypt and other parts of the former Ottoman Empire.

Seeking to straddle a golden mean, Väljas declared that the "legal basis for the USSR as a union of states could be provided by a Union Treaty" defining the respective jurisdiction of the center and the periphery. He also welcomed the "registration of people's movements, recognizing them as partners in cooperation to resolve republican affairs." He wanted them also to have access to channels of mass information. But this only applied, he warned, "to those movements that operate within the framework of the Fundamental Law and existing legislation."

At the one extreme, Väljas charged in May 1989, were those who wished to solve all problems by reestablishing order; at the other extreme were those who sought a panacea in immediate and complete secession from the USSR. Both extremes would be detrimental to Estonia's restructuring, he declared.

Commenting on the work of the CPE CC plenum, *Izvestiia* stated that, "under the conditions of the already existing competition with social movements," the Estonian Communists had mapped out a course to ensure that the Party "does not let slip the initiative on all the key social problems of the republic's life." They would try to stabilize social ties and political life at all levels — rural, district, city — "so as to hold local elections already in November [1989]. They are to be followed by republic elections in which the possibility of direct election to the [Estonian] Supreme Soviet cannot be ruled out."

Continuing to whistle in the dark, *Izvestiia* reported the confidence of CPE leaders based on the fact that over 90 percent of those elected in March 1989 to the Congress of People's Deputies were Communists. Ten of the Party members elected belonged to the PFE; one to Intermovement; and four to other social organizations. All this showed that "the attempts of extremists to play on national feelings during the election campaign failed." [24]

Litmus Tests: Estonians and Non-Estonians on Pluralism/Communism

The perspectives of the various groupings were summarized in a survey of Estonian public opinion conducted in April 1989. Not surprisingly, Estonian natives tended to favor political pluralism and to oppose Communism. Some 80 percent of Estonians favored abandoning the one-party system, a view supported by only 43 percent of non-Estonians. If there were a multiparty election, half of the Estonians would vote for the PFE and only 7.2 percent for the Communist Party. About a third of non-Estonians would vote for the CP; 17.8 percent for OSTK; and 10.9 percent for Intermovement. Still, a substantial number of non-Estonians would vote for the Greens (11.5 percent) and even for the PFE (8.9 percent).[25]

The polls demonstrated also that Intermovement and OSTK enjoyed almost no support among Estonians and little popularity even among non-Estonians. Only 11.7 percent of the overall population backed Intermovement and OSTK and by only 28.7 percent of the non-Estonians, a fair number of whom endorsed the Greens (11.5 percent) and even the PFE (8.9 percent). The Estonian KGB chief, Karl Kortelainen, however, declared in his election campaign in 1989 that he agreed with all Intermovement's demands except ceding northeast Estonia (heavily populated by Russians) to the RSFSR.[26]

Even the answers on whether to fly Estonia's tricolor from the government tower did not elicit a uniform *nyet* from non-Estonians, because 24 percent of them approved and 30.2 percent were indifferent. Only 31.1 percent were clearly against. That 88.15 percent of Estonians favored flying the tricolor, however, actually understated national feeling, because some opposed putting the national flag to wave until Estonia became independent.

Over half the native Estonians, 55.5 percent, wanted an independent Estonia; 38.7 percent wished Estonia to be a sovereign republic within a Soviet confederation. A clear majority of non-Estonians, 54.1 percent, favored the status quo: Estonia to remain a constituent republic of the USSR; but 25.1 percent endorsed Estonian sovereignty within a confederation.

The April 1989 poll suggested that the native Estonians strongly favored democratic reform and independence and opposed the Communist Party; about a third of non-Estonians supported an anti-reform, anti-Estonian orientation and a quarter to one-third endorsed Estonian aspirations in some ways. Overall, at least two-thirds of the total (mixed) population favored a multiparty system and a major decentralization of the current constitutional relationship between Estonia and Moscow.

Backing for the three overtly proindependence groups (ENIP, Heritage, Estonian Christian Union) totaled 18 percent. Their supporters implicitly rejected the tamer demands of the Popular Front leadership, which did not demand independence. The PFE rank and file, however, was more radical than its leadership.

Other polls conducted by CPE newspapers in fall 1989 showed some rise in the Party's popularity, among Estonians as well as Russians. Estonian nationalists as well as the Internationals were showing some fatigue from continuous emotional stress and deteriorating economic conditions.

In these conditions a potentially important revelation occurred when the editors of *Sovetskaia Estoniia* in autumn 1989 met with three members of OSTK—a worker, an engineer, and a deputy director from three different heavy industries in Tallinn. The worker, a highly skilled machine tool operator, remarked that if the PFE leaders gave less attention to publicizing their latest novelties and spent more time visiting non-Estonian audiences to explain the essence of their plans, *at least half of the Russian-speakers of the republic would vote for the exit of Estonia from the USSR.*

To this the deputy director of another plant phlegmatically commented, "They're already in favor of that [*Da oni uzhe seichas za eto*]!"

These opinions had to be given much weight, one editor suggested, because they were based on intimate knowledge of the Russian workers' mood.[27]

If so, added to the idealistic Russians who believed Balts had a right to self-determination and those who favored Green activity, some Russian workers—perhaps a majority—might favor Estonian independence if they were not excluded from its benefits.

The contradictory sentiments of Russian settlers were reflected in surveys conducted in 1988 and 1989 in which they were asked to list the public figures who had done the most to promote the well-being of Estonia and who had done the most harm. Topping the first list for both years was CPE leader Väljas, followed by Marju Lauristin and Edgar Savisaar in 1988. The next year, however, the two PFE leaders had fallen to fifth and sixth places after Prime Minister Toome and President Rüütel. Intermovement leader Kogan placed sixth or seventh each year while OSTK leader Yarovoi came in fourth in 1989.

Who had done the most harm? Kogan topped the list each year, followed closely by Savisaar, Lauristin, and—only in 1989—by Tiit Made and Yarovoi.[28]

In short, one man's sweetness was another's poison. Heroes and heroines for one set of non-Estonians were villains for another set.

Surveys taken in the late 1980s indicated that 80 to 85 percent of Soviet immigrants to Estonia intended to remain if the republic became independent. Another 10 to 15 percent would prefer to live in Moscow or Leningrad, and 7 percent would like to live abroad, but almost none wanted to return to homes in other parts of the USSR.[29]

Into the Streets?

Estonian nationalists feared that a massive Soviet repression could be sparked by various factors, including a provocation by Intermovement.[30] Some Heritage Society members made it a point to observe Intermovement demonstrations while discouraging other Estonians from attending, lest complications ensue. They worried also about the charge in *Red Star* that some Estonians were trying to form an "independent volunteer militia" with arms to establish the country's independence,[31] because similar charges had preceded the August 1968 invasion of Czechoslovakia.

Violence from the "migrants" would be more likely if their encirclement mentality grew. Despite being outnumbered, they might resort to desperate acts, especially if egged on by manipulative factory managers or KGB operatives. If push came to shove, the Soviet army would probably side with "internationals." In June 1989 leaders of Intermovement and OSTK called a large meeting in Tallinn. On the eve of the assembly the PFE warned that Soviet tanks might appear in the streets, summoned by the meeting's organizers. Television commentators warned Estonians to keep their children off the streets.

When the meeting proceeded smoothly and in a disciplined way, several television workers breathed a sigh of relief. One told a friend: "Thank God that at the head of the Intermovement is Evgeny Kogan and not someone worse." A *Sovetskaia Estoniia* editor agreed, noting that Kogan stood as a barrier to the formation in Estonia of extremist organizations such as Pamiat, active in Leningrad and elsewhere. The danger that such organizations could take shape in Estonia, he added, was real.[32]

Settler power was seen in August 1989 when many of the Russian-manned factories stopped work to protest new Estonian laws setting residence requirements for participation in elections. About 18,000 workers from twenty-six enterprises took part in the strike, or more properly, lockout, since the actions were manager-sponsored and the workers suffered no pay loss. Although only 5 percent of the republic's labor force was involved, the action shut down not only supplies for all-Union ministries but interfered with transport and other local activities.[33]

The extent of central manipulation was suggested when an Estonian Radio reporter asked a striker outside the Dvigatel plant when the action would end. "I don't know," he replied. "We'll be told from Moscow." Other reporters saw on the locked door of this plant a notice that officials in Moscow had allocated for striking workers a ton of tea, refrigerators, and washing machines. Kogan, however, told a Leningrad television audience that "our workers who resolved to go on strike...are now suffering excessive hardships." They needed "not only moral but material support." [34] Meanwhile, workers at the Tapa railroad junction threw out Kogan when he tried to instigate a strike there. Some observers asserted that Kogan's agitation was incompatible with his position as deputy to the USSR Congress.[35]

The USSR Supreme Soviet Presidium backed the strikers with a decree asserting that Estonia's voting law did "not correspond to the USSR Constitution and the international legal commitments of the USSR." The Presidium called on the Estonians to amend the law by October, but an official of the Estonian parliament averred that reconsideration of the law was out of the question. "It has already been passed and is in effect."

Still, the strike sobered Estonian reformers who had at first discounted its consequences. Party leader Väljas said that the voting law may have been drafted too hastily and without sufficient thought to the needs of non-Estonians.[36] The strikers returned to work but threatened to strike again unless their franchise was assured. Väljas conceded on September 1, 1989, that the CPE was partly to blame for the August strikes because it had not paid sufficient attention to the speeches and complaints of Intermovement and OSTK leaders.

Estonian nationalists, for their parts, saw the settlers' interests as no more righteous than those of the French *colons* who settled in Algeria for many generations or those of the Nazis who occupied France during the war.

I witnessed a demonstration organized by OSTK and Intermovement in March 1990 two days after the Congress of Estonia asserted its legitimacy. Although denied permission by city authorities to use a particular square, the group blocked it off as many buses carried in demonstrators from local factories. A crowd estimated at from several thousand to 50,000 (TASS) filled the square and the hills sloping up toward the castle. Many uniformed army and naval officers with their families were present, although usually at a small distance from the proletarian men and women who stood closest to the microphones. Taking a cue from Beijing, banners proclaimed: "The Army [no longer the Party] and People Are One." Another poster exhorted: "Support the Committee for Defense of Civil Rights." Speakers warned that actions should have been taken a year ago, before the anti-Soviet forces could mobilize. Now the hour was late, and action rather than words would be needed.

A Russian lady next to me, who has married into the Estonian elite, sobbed: "Look at my people — all in gray, smoking cigarettes constantly, their faces flushed from alcohol, their bodies distorted by nothing but potatoes and greasy meat. They are afraid and don't know where to turn."

As their work day ended, many Russians turned away from the scene while the demagogues continued. Many others lingered, including some young men in whom rudeness and chauvinist passion seemed to feed each other, and with whom dialogue would not proceed easily.

Lithuania

Even though, or because, Lithuanians made up roughly 80 percent of the republic's population, ethnic relations became quite strained in the late 1980s. Charges and countercharges filled the air in 1989: Anonymous posters were reported in Lithuania declaring "Under the flag of Great Russia we shall overpower Lithuania. The only good Lithuanian is a dead one." [37]

The other side of the ethnic divide was reflected in a note by Senior Ensign V. Grinkevich to *Red Star*. On three occasions, Grinkevich reported, he was challenged by local nationalists. Recently at a streetcar stop in Vilnius two middle-aged men called him an "occupier" who had no business in Lithuania. The ensign replied in Lithuanian that he was born in Lithuania although his nationality was Polish. They replied: "So you are an occupier three times over! First, you have betrayed Lithuanians. Second, you are a Pole. Third, you serve in the Red Army." To avoid a showdown and to escape from thugs breathing down his neck, he walked to a phone, dialed, and described the situation to the police. They replied, "Deal with it yourself. You are a soldier, so defend yourself." [38]

As can be seen from this encounter, Lithuanians' relations were tense with Poles as well as with Russians. Part of the problem, of course, was that Lithuania's present capital, Vilnius, had been controlled by Poland from 1922 until 1939.

"Can Lithuanians Trust Poles?" a Lithuanian literary publication boldly asked in 1989. The author reported that many Polish clubs were sprouting up in Vilnius. Some members alleged that nothing constructive had ever been accomplished by Lithuanians. Some quoted West Germans (without irony) lamenting how few Poles remained in Vilnius after World War II. "It is no secret that the Poles have long been known for their inflated feeling of national pride. Perhaps they are all convinced that if anyone had invented anything worthwhile, he surely must have had some Polish blood or had some other connections with Poland. When they talk about Vilnius, one gets the impression our old capital is beautiful and pleasant only because it had been ruled at one time by the Poles." [39]

A more constructive perspective, the Lithuanian author continued, was heard recently in Warsaw, at a club promoting Polish-Lithuanian understanding. A Polish historian there explained that "Lithuanians do not have much reason to respect and love Poles....Lithuanians are especially sensitive to Polonization....Until the Lublin Union [of 1569] Lithuania was a very powerful nation....much more powerful than Poland. Following the union, the Poles began Polonization....Vilnius was seized from Lithuania by force by Poland [in 1922]....[Today] the Poles are obligated to learn Lithuanian if they constitute a minority in Lithuania....Why does [the Polish newspaper] *Zycie Warszawy* dare to state that Lithuania's Poles don't want to and should not support Lithuanianism? Why then do they wish to support and do support Russification?"

One club in Poland, Friends of Lithuania, rejected chauvinistic Poles for membership. Its slogan: "Free with free, equals with equals." [40]

Some Lithuanian citizens wanted their districts to be transferred to Russia or to Poland. A Sajudis editor replied that if Lithuania had a "pure democracy," each district would certainly have the right to autonomy. But such democracy did not yet exist in the republic. And Polish-Lithuanian conflicts had a long history. Probably some other solution would be better, based on positive steps to rectify present difficulties.[41]

Smaller minorities—Jews, Belorussians, Tatars, Karaims, and others—generally backed nationalist reforms. Many Russians and Poles, however, joined in 1988 to form an alliance known as Unity [*Vienybe-Edinstvo-Jednosc*]. Unity supported the Party's leading role, backed Moscow's version of perestroika, and favored "mutual enrichment" of national cultures without discrimination. It vehemently opposed any requirement to make Lithuanian the official language. Members threatened workers' strikes and refusal to pay CP dues if the November 1988 decree on the Lithuanian language was not rescinded. The smaller minorities called such positions "Great Russia chauvinism" and backed Lithuanian as the official language.[42]

In the 1989 elections to the USSR Congress of People's Deputies Sajudis candidates won in thirty-six of forty-two electoral districts. One of the movement's candidates was a Russian professional, elected in a heavily Lithuanian district of Kaunas. Another was a Jewish writer elected in a run-off in Vilnius. But the ethnic factor seemed to benefit a Russian nominated by the Communist Party in Vilnius and a Polish professor from the Vilnius Pedagogical Institute supported by Unity.[43]

Prospects for easing Lithuanian-Polish conflicts were better than between Lithuanians and Russians. Polish party leader Wojciech Jaruzelski and Lithuanian party chief Algirdas Brazauskas signed an agreement in June 1989 committing their parties to extensive cooperation.[44]

Despite signs that Polish-Russian solidarity might weaken, Valerii Ivanov, leader of Unity, claimed in 1989 that his organization represented all ethnic groups in Lithuania. In October 1989 he was summoned to the Vilnius City Procurator's Office and officially warned that he had broken the law when, the previous month, he appeared at a Vilnius plant and urged the workers to go on strike immediately. Some workers did in fact strike, leading other workers to complain to the Procurator and demand compensation by Unity for losses incurred.[45]

Ethnic conflict combined with other factors to increase street crime and illegal collecting of firearms in the Baltic and elsewhere.[46] Lithuania's

Minister of Internal Affairs confirmed that in February 1989 the USSR MVD had ordered internal affairs organs in all republics to pay special attention to the intensification of interethnic relations "which have taken on extreme forms." Moscow directed local organs to take steps to strengthen security of weapons and combat supplies. The Lithuanian minister, speaking in October 1989, stated that in the last eight months his forces had found 400 pieces of illegally stored firearms. Secrecy was often necessary, he went on, as when the ministry attacked a "so-called peasant mafia terrorizing the heads of farm enterprises." By law, he added, the Lithuanian MVD worked closely with those of other republics. It informed Lithuania's Communist Party Central Committee of its work, but also the general public. It was not qualified, however, to "present information about the public-political situation in the republic either to Moscow" or to the local Central Committee.[47]

Latvia

Nonnatives in Latvia numbered almost half the republic's population by the late 1980s. Proportionately stronger than in Estonia or Lithuania, the Russian settlers in Latvia had a greater capacity to oppose independence activity than they did in the other Baltic republics.

Responding in part to the sheer numbers of the non-Latvians, two tendencies competed within the Popular Front of Latvia (PFL) from its founding in October 1988. One focused on defending Latvian rights, the other on individual civic rights. While the former tendency was stronger in the late 1980s, the Front sought to prevent the fracturing of Latvian society into diverse ethnic parties. Beginning in November 1988 it sponsored the formation of Latvia's National Culture Associations to promote the languages and cultures of Russians, Ukrainians, Jews, Lithuanians, and other minorities.[48] The Front's advocacy of cultural pluralism meshed with its opposition to the denationalizing tendencies of Sovietization and Russification. The Front and the Communist Party of Latvia in December 1988 organized the People's Forum, a conference to air ethnic grievances.[49]

The PFL tried also to exert a calming influence on non-Latvians by its weekly newspaper *Atmoda*, published in both Latvian and Russian. Approximately two-thirds of its articles were identical, but some articles in the Russian edition explained details of Latvian history or focused on specifically

Russian themes, such as the Orthodox Church or Leningrad intelligentsia. *Atmoda* tried to persuade its readers that independence would benefit their diverse interests.[50]

Despite Latvian efforts to reach out, many non-Latvians responded defensively to the Popular Front and other nationalist movements. Proceedings of the Front's founding congress, October 8-9, 1988, were televised and sparked indignant reactions from those comfortable with the status quo. On October 18 representatives of 153 firms and a total of 813 persons gathered at the Riga Civil Aviation Engineering Institute to create the Latvian International Working People's Front (Interfront) to counter deviations from party norms and "ideal" ethnic relations.[51]

Formation of Interfront seemed to stimulate support for the People's Front, particularly in rural areas. A poll taken in late 1988 indicated that 48 percent of Russians in Latvia believed there was a need for Interfront compared to 6 percent of Latvians. The People's Front was endorsed by 74 percent of all Latvians but only 10 percent of Russians in the republic.[52] Reflecting divisions in the whole society, the Latvian Communist Party split into Latvian-oriented reformers and Russian-oriented traditionalists.

Because the demographic balance was nearly even between Latvians and Russians, the tilt of other minorities could sway the distribution of power. The Popular Front supported and won the support of Jewish, Polish, Ukrainian, Belorussian, Gypsy, and other cultural societies and clubs in 1988-1989; Interfront, however, snubbed these minorities, generating fissures within the Russian-speaking community. Thus, Latvian Poles leaned toward the Latvian cause whereas Poles in Lithuania tended to align with Russians. A poll in late 1988, however, showed that over one-third of Latvia's non-Russian minorities showed little enthusiasm for independent initiatives by groups claiming to represent Latvia's national minorities.[53]

Surveys in late 1988 showed that readers of Russian-language newspapers tended to regard the activities of "informal groups" in the republic as damaging to interethnic relations; only one-third of readers of Latvian-language papers felt the same way.

Even before changes in Latvia's language and immigration laws were implemented, they aroused negative responses from many segments of the non-Latvian population. Interfront sparked mass rallies in February 1989 and calls for a general strike by industrial workers. Since 62 percent of industrial workers were non-Latvian, the potential for serious confrontations remained, limiting the options of Latvian nationalists.[54]

Interfront probably did not represent the majority of Latvia's Russians but only the most conservative of them. But this group became more anxious in 1989 as it witnessed the formation of Citizens' Committees in March and more active support by the PFL and Latvia's National Independence Movement for independence rather than mere sovereignty.

The PFL in July 1989 tried to assuage non-Latvian anxieties by a firm statement calling for all nationalities to take part in shaping, evaluating, and implementing the program for an independent Latvian state. It said that all residents who "have chosen freely to support the creation of an independent Latvia become citizens of Latvia." Indeed, all permanent residents who, at the time of registration, had lived in Latvia for ten years should be granted citizenship, according to the PFL platform.[55]

If Latvian nationalists managed to enlist Russian settlers in the cause of independence, this could hurt Soviet objectives. In March 1990 publication of the Latvian and Russian newspaper *Atmoda* was suspended by Latvian Communists who owned and controlled the building where it was published.

Value-Claiming and Value-Creating

The ideal approach to bargaining, one school of thought holds, requires that the parties endeavor to create values useful to both sides rather than to claim them as in a zero-sum encounter.[56] But such attitudes are difficult to develop where there has been a long history of exploitation. Furthermore, there may be a zero-sum conflict between the cultural and physical survival of the Baltic peoples and the existence of a large Russian settlement. If so, the only thing to negotiate peacefully could be the terms of its departure. Deportations—usually brutal but decisive—had often been used in living memory to cope with ethnic and political disputes in the Baltic and Eastern Europe.

An émigré "Russian Jewish poet," writing to Moscow's *Literaturnaia Gazeta* from Boston, warned Balts to go slow. "All of us are harnessed to the same chariot, and nobody can unhitch from this harness [while] in motion without pain for himself and others. Everything will get entangled, all will be crushed. We have to reckon with others." If extremists prevailed and "everything collapses," Balts as well as non-Balts would suffer.[57]

But such appeals made little impact on Balts who felt exploited not just by Moscow but by the Russians who had moved into the Baltic. The Kremlin and most Russian settlers had not asked, "What can we create together?" but, "What can we get for ourselves from the Baltic?" The attitude was similar to that which European imperialists had taken to Asia and Africa in previous centuries. Gorbachev's perestroika team wanted to put everything on a new and healthier footing, but the hour was late. Damage had been done — physical, psychological, moral — that Balts would not soon forget.

Like French *colons* in Algeria, many Russians in the Baltic panicked at the prospect of local independence. Especially in Latvia and Estonia, the settlers were far more numerous than Europeans had been in India, Angola, or Algeria relative to the native population. Their qualitative impact on local affairs was also heavier than that of Europeans in Asia or Africa. Whereas the French felt themselves culturally superior to the natives, Balts perceived themselves to be culturally and materially above Russians. If the Russians resisted, joined the independence movement, or moved away, the effects, negative and positive, would be great, adding to or ameliorating other dislocations.

The Baltic confrontation also resembled and differed from the ethnic conflict in Sri Lanka, where the Sinhalese majority sought to undo the privileges acquired by the Tamil minority in the decades before independence in 1948. Once the British departed, the Sinhalese used their power to reduce the presence of Tamils in the civil service, the professions, and the universities, and to make Sinhala the one official language. Unlike the Estonians and Latvians, the Sinhalese made up a decisive majority in their land — on a scale similar to the Lithuanians. Unlike the Russians, most of whom came to the Baltic in recent decades, the Ceylonese Tamils had arrived in Sri Lanka more than 2,000 years before. Even the "plantation" Tamils — tea pickers — had been there since the turn of the century. The Ceylonese Tamils reacted violently to perceived discrimination. The most recent bout of ethnic strife, launched in 1983, shattered what many observers had portrayed as a model developing country.

The Balts' sentiments toward Russian "occupation" were understandable. But was it in their own best interests to claim values and not to consider creating them *with* local Russians and with Moscow? The Estonians and Latvians made up a much smaller majority of the population in their lands than did the Sinhalese in theirs. And the Russians were backed by a super if sick power, not just a badly divided India. If Moscow let the settlers fend for themselves, of course, the "internationals" would be less formidable.

NOTES

1. Ransford Palmer, "The Commonwealth Caribbean: Crisis of Adjustment," in Roy Glasgow and Winston Langley, eds., *The Troubled and Troubling Caribbean* (Lewiston, N.Y.: Edwin Mellen, 1989), p. 15.

2. For portraits of such expatriates, see V. S. Naipaul's books *In a Free State, Guerrillas, A Bend in the River* (New York: Knopf, 1973, 1975, 1979). Many Baltic Germans tried to hold onto their own lifestyles in the nineteenth century, but many joined the tsarist government and married Russians. See John A. Armstrong, "Acculturation to the Russian Bureaucratic Elite: The Case of Baltic Germans," *Journal of Baltic Studies*, 15, 2/3 (Summer-Fall 1984) pp. 119-29.

3. In 1969, 76.7 percent of Estonians and 74.7 percent of Latvians lived in ethnically homogeneous families, compared with 81.6 percent of Russians and 94.1 percent of Armenians. A separate study of Latvians showed that, if exogamous, they were most likely to marry a kindred group — Lithuanians. See Rasma Karklins, *Ethnic Relations in the USSR: The Perspective from Below* (Boston: Unwin Hyman, 1986), pp. 157-60.

4. See above, chap. 5, summarizing *Naselenie SSSR, 1988: Statisticheskii ezhegodnik* (Moscow: Finansy i statistika, 1989), pp. 276, 286, 318. There were also strong trends for Russians in the Baltic to marry other Russians that did not weaken appreciably in the 1980s. See the tables for Russians immediately following those for Balts.

5. About 500 interviews of Soviet immigrants in Tallinn conducted by the Estonian Heritage Society in April 1988 indicated that 90 percent of non-Estonians who had lived there up to three years did not know any Estonian. Among those who had lived in Estonia for more than eleven years, the percentage was 54. Some 42 percent of non-Estonians born and raised in Tallinn did not know Estonian. After passage of the Estonian Language Law in January 1989, 75 percent of Tallinn respondents expressed a willingness to attend Estonian language classes. *Homeland*, No. 13 (274), 4 April 1990, p. 2.

6. Preliminary reports from the 1989 census in *Rahva Hääl*, 19 September 1989, p. 2.

7. Oil shales in the United States are more caloric than Estonian, but Americans do not try to exploit them. "You are wiser than we [*Vy umnee nas*]," said Panfilov, who noted that Estonia depends upon oil shales for much of its electrical power.

8. These polarities are well portrayed in Naipaul's novels, cited in note 2, above. On the complex relations between Mexicans and their Spanish heritage, see David C. McClelland,

Power: The Inner Experience (New York: Irvington, 1975), chap. 5; on the outlook of "Empire-Builders," see chap. 8.

9. On the origins of Intermovement, see interview with E. V. Kogan in *Molodezh' Estonii*, 11 August 1988, p. 2.

10. Rumors spread that he was injured by a PFE conspiracy. Kogan did nothing to "dispel the crown of thorns on his head, knowing all the time that the accident was caused by a bald tire that always made his car lurch left when he stepped on the brakes." Grant Gukasov, "Yevgeny Kogan's Style," *Moscow News*, No. 13 (8-15 April 1990), p. 11.

11. Quoted in Gusakov, "Kogan's Style," p. 11.

12. Väljas in *Sovetskaia Estoniia*, 5 May 1989.

13. An extremely cosmopolitan person, Samorodnii was born in the Ukraine. He worked in Kampuchea as an interpreter in a Soviet aid mission before moving to Estonia with his Estonian wife.

14. Editors' statement to readers in *Respublika*, No. 1 (December 1989), p. 1.

15. "Estonia Elects a Pro-independence Supreme Soviet," *Homeland*, No. 12 (273), 28 March 1990, pp. 1,4, at p. 4.

16. Väljas in *Sovetskaia Estoniia*, 5 May 1989.

17. A. Sukhonos, "To Respect One Another," *Trud*, 27 April 1989 p. 4, *FBIS-SOV*, 5 May 1989, pp. 52-54, at p. 53.

18. "Otkrytoe pis'mo Estontsam ot russkoi intelligentsii politkluba 'Referendum'" appeared in the Russian language *Vechernyi Tallinn*, 11 March 1989, p. 1. "Did you give the letter to *Sovetskaia Estoniia*?" I asked Samorodnii. "Three of us divided up the task of circulating the letter," he replied, but hinted that he and his colleagues had little hope it would appear in the Party newspaper and so may have not even delivered it there.

19. But a report in *Trud* gave examples that put only Estonian nationalists in a bad light. The article denounced what it termed the mob response to a hunger strike by Tamara Nikolaevna Buslovich in Tallinn to protest an administrative arbitrariness—a firing. "Popular Front activists took her hunger strike as support for Intermovement....Soon they began calling her a stool pigeon." The author also condemned Edgar Savisaar's allegedly "disrespectful statement about the Red flag" when the national tricolor was raised over Long Hermann tower on 24 February 1989. "Why wasn't this event preceded by a broad democratic discussion...to avoid the resentment...associated with the lowering of the Estonian SSR state flag?" See L. Vaino, "In the Heat of Mutual Resentment," *Trud* (Moscow), 30 March 1989, p. 2.

20. I. Rozenfeld, "National Idea and 'New Vapsid'," *Sovetskaia Estoniia*, 28 March 1989, p. 3, *FBIS-SOV*, 20 April 1989, p. 75.

21. Viacheslav V. Ivanov, "Natsional'noe samoopredelenie na Baltike: Poiski Estonii," unpublished ms., Tallinn, written 16 October 1989, pp. 4-5.

22. Interview with Saarniit by N. Kuznetsova, *Sovetskaia Estoniia*, 12 April 1989, p. 3.

23. Väljas in *Sovetskaia Estoniia*, 5 May 1989.

24. M. Kushtapin, "Estonia: Firsthand Information," *Izvestiia*, 14 May 1989, p. 2, *FBIS-SOV*, 17 May 1989.

25. Conducted for a Finnish newspaper by a social science institute in Tallinn, the survey posed roughly 100 questions to 930 people, and was published in *Iltasanomat*, 3 May 1989. For a summary, see Toomas Ilves, "Estonian Poll on Independence, Political Parties," *Report on the USSR* (Radio Liberty), 1, 22 (2 June 1989), pp. 14-16.

26. Quoted in Ilves, "Estonian Poll," p. 15.

27. Ivanov, "Natsional'noe samoopredelenie," p. 12.

28. Aleksandr Podves'ko, "Neestontsy v Estonii,"*Respublika*, No. 2 (3), January 1990, p. 7.

29. *Homeland*, No. 13 (274), 4 April 1990, p. 2.

30. For an account of Soviet military action against demonstrators in Tbilisi, see Walter C. Clemens, Jr., "Why Gorbachev Has Georgia on His Mind," *World Monitor*, 3, 9 (September 1990), pp. 52-58.

31. Such cases are alleged in a long article by V. Urban in *Krasnaia zvezda*, 18 December 1988, p. 2, *FBIS-SOV* 88-245, 21 December 1988, p. 68. "To prevent dangerous consequences," Urban reported, the Estonian KGB had "officially warned" the self-declared militia leader.

32. Ivanov, "Natsional'noe samoopredelenie," p. 11.

33. The managers seemed to support and even sponsor the strike and did not penalize strikers with pay cuts. See Grant Gukasov, "Mutual Wisdom and Flexibility Necessary," *Moscow News*, No. 35 (3-10 September 1989), p. 9; see also his earlier report, *Moscow News*, No. 34, p. 13.

34. Gukasov, "Evgeny Kogan's Style."

35. Tarmu Tammerk, "Thousands of Russians on Strike in Estonia," *Homeland*, 18 August 1989, pp. 1,2.

36. See James Blitz, "Kremlin in Feud over Estonian Law," *Financial Times*, 17 August 1989, p. 2 and Blitz, "Estonia Hands Kremlin Chance to Hit Back at Nationalist Groups," *Financial Times*, 18 August 1989, p. 2.

37. Vilnius to North America in English, *FBIS-SOV*, 7 April 1989, p. 66.

38. V. Grinkevich, "Deal with It Yourself," *Krasnaia Zvezda*, 17 October 1989, p. 1, *FBIS-SOV*, 18 October 1989, p. 72.

39. Edita Degutiene, "Can Lithuanians Trust Poles?" *Literatura ir Menas*, No. 21 (20 May 1989), p. 7, *FBIS-SOV*, 18 October 1989, pp. 74-75.

40. Ibid.

41. Lyubov Chernays, editor of Sajudis Russian-language newspaper, interviewed on Moscow Domestic Service, 18 October 1989, *FBIS-SOV*, 20 October 1989, pp. 54-55.

42. V. Stanley Vardys, "Lithuanian National Politics," *Problems of Communism*, 38, 4 (July-August 1989), pp. 53-76, at 59-60.

43. Ibid., p. 71.

44. Ibid., p. 60.

45. Vilnius in English to North America, 6 October 1989, *FBIS-SOV*, 18 October 1989, p. 74.

46. The USSR Ministry of Internal Affairs reported in October 1989 that the rate of street crime was increasing, particularly in Estonia, Lithuania, the Mari and Tatar autonomous soviet republics, and in Leningrad and Moscow. This was part of a situation throughout the country in which serious crimes increased by 42.4 percent, crimes against property by 54.1, and street crime by 77.1 percent in the first nine months of 1989. "Economic" and drug-related crimes were also increasing. MVD briefing reported on TASS International Service in Russian 10 October 1989, *FBIS-SOV*, 17 October 1989, pp. 100-1. On cargo theft, see *Sovetskaia Kul'tura*, 28 September 1989, p. 2.

47. Marijonas Misiukonis interviewed and reported in *Sovetskaia Litva*, 10 October 1989, p. 2, *FBIS-SOV*, 20 October 1989, pp. 55-56. The head of the KGB in Lithuania was also interviewed, but answered in less detail.

48. There were at least seventeen such societies in early 1990.

49. See Nils R. Muiznieks, "The Latvian Popular Front and Ethnic Relations," *Report on the USSR* (Radio Liberty), 1, 42 (20 October 1989), pp. 20-21.

50. The editor of the Russian edition, Alekseys Grigorjevs, was of Latvian-Russian heritage. Interviewed at Harvard University, 18 April 1990. His operation also published democratic material from Russia and other republics, including Moldavian texts in the Latin alphabet.

51. Juris Dreifelds, "Latvian National Rebirth," *Problems of Communism*, 38, 4 (July-August 1989), pp. 77-94, at p. 86.

52. Ibid.

53. Ibid., p. 91.

54. Ibid., p. 93.

55. Quoted in Muiznieks, "The Latvian Popular Front," p. 21.

56. David A. Lax and James K. Sebenius, *The Manager as Negotiator: Bargaining for Cooperation and Competitive Gain* (New York: Free Press, 1986).

57. Naum Korzhavin, "To All Those Who Want to Listen to Me in the Baltic Area," *Literaturnaia gazeta*, No. 40 (4 October 1989), p. 12.

11
Baltic Nationalism and Communism: *Kto Kovo?*

who over whom?

Could Soviet-style Communism and Baltic nationalism be reconciled? If not, *Kto kovo*? "who would overcome whom?" By 1990 a compromise between the two looked unlikely.

It became increasingly difficult to run for office as a Communist in the Baltic and get elected. It was easiest in Estonia, where many top Communists early blessed the popular front, and hardest in Lithuania, where the Party held out longest against popular independence movements. Communist prospects in Latvia hovered between these extremes.

The upsurge of Baltic nationalism pressed local Communists to make a choice. Join or oppose the nationalists? Maintain fealty to Moscow or behave like a free person? Seven alternatives danced on the horizon as the Russian empire quaked:

1. Baltic Communist Parties (CPs) could coopt Popular Fronts (PFs) and use them to serve Moscow's interests *within* the system.

2. Baltic Communists could coopt PFs and seek to lead *national Communist* movements as Tito once did.

3. PFs could coopt CPs and use them in a campaign for national liberation fending off Kremlin repression.

4. CPs, backed by Moscow, could try to eliminate PFs and other nationalist groups, and monopolize power again.

5. CPs and PFs could each go their own ways, competing against one another and against independence parties for popular support.

6. CPs could split into nationalist and pro-Moscow factions, the latter attracting support from Russian and other "internationalist" settlers in the Baltic.

7. Independence-minded nationalists could discredit PFs and CPs and win broad support, compelling the fronts and Communists to join their cause or lose all credibility.

Each approach had its day at different times and places throughout the Baltic, reflecting a welter of personal, cultural, ethnic, idealistic, material, and political considerations.

The competition between Communist "internationalism" and local nationalism dated from the previous century. From Lenin's attacks on the Jewish Bund to Gorbachev's on Baltic separatism, orthodox Communists supported "internationalism" over nationalism, including both national communism and Communist nationalism.

The juggernaut of independence, the seventh option, rose from initial obscurity to overshadow all other approaches in 1989-1990. It led CPs as well as PFs to climb onto the independence bandwagon. Not just Baltic natives but many nonindigenous settlers came to endorse this approach, because Baltic freedom could mean their personal freedom. The trend by 1990 was toward the victory of nationalism over communism.

Independence drives were fueled by the "now or never" mentality of Balts anxious to preserve their cultures and gene pools, and hopeful that Gorbachev's Kremlin would not or could not act forcefully to thwart their ambitions.

Dynamics of Independence

The direction of change in the Baltic was determined by six factors:

1. Democratic procedures within each republic became a possibility in 1989 with the institution of multicandidate elections. By 1990 alternative parties were able to articulate their own platforms and support their own candidates.

2. Baltic politicians and voters splintered into the usual alignments of European politics — not just "social democrats" and liberals but freeholders, Christians, and even a few monarchists. The multiplicity of competing factions weakened their hand against Moscow. Alignments and coalitions were unstable as each tested the wind. Optimists expected that, after a time, the

contending groups would coalesce into two or three major groups of conservatives, moderates, and social democrats.

3. Despite their differences on other matters, the majority of voters in each republic favored independence from the Russian empire.

4. Repeated assertions by Gorbachev and other Politburo members in 1989 that Moscow would not use military force to resolve its disputes with Baltic nationalists emboldened Baltic reformers.

5. Established institutions had both liabilities and assets. Communist Parties, for example, were saddled by their reputation as collaborators, but they also controlled buildings, communication networks, and funds that rival groups lacked.

6. As the prospects of Baltic independence improved, some "internationalist" settlers stepped up resistance to what they saw as disaster; some planned to move elsewhere; some welcomed or at least accommodated themselves to new realities and sought to influence them.

The spring 1989 elections the USSR Congress of People's Deputies showed that Communists could be routed by non-Communists. So long as elections remained that open, Baltic politicians had to ponder: What platform will get me elected? What changes, what compromises must I make to stay in the running?

Baltic Communist Parties Independent of Moscow

Several developments in late 1989 opened the way to dismantle the dictatorship of the Russian-dominated Politburo in Moscow over the rest of the country. Pressure to dethrone the Communist Parties arose first of all from popular revolutions in Eastern Europe. On the run, most Communists there tried to drop their "internationalist" dependency on Moscow and even renounced their constitutionally guaranteed "leading role." Many also changed their party's name and program.

The Hungarian Communist Party called itself "Socialist" to break with its past and to assert an identity apart from the center. But only a tiny fraction of former Communists renewed membership in the Hungarian party and the new "Socialists" did poorly in March 1990 elections. An Estonian Communist reflected that more than a name change for the former ruling party would be needed to deal with real problems; policies needed "new contents." [2]

The impact of these events in the Baltic was profound. As a Lithuanian Communist told the Party's Central Committee in December 1989: "Lithuania is a volcano of passions, where political tension has reached the culmination point. The stormy waves of revolution, national rebirth, and the renewal of socialism coming from East Germany, Czechoslovakia, and Bulgaria are turning into passionate and sometimes irreconcilable arguments over what path the Party ought to take and where the republic should be heading. These waves are sweeping away party hierarchies and dogmas, one-party monopoly, and those leaders who were afraid of their own peoples." [3]

The Lithuanian parliament on December 7, 1989, changed the republic's constitution to legalize a multiparty system.[4] On the same day the Estonian CP Central Committee agreed that Article 6 of Estonia's Constitution should be annulled, thus removing the legal guarantee for CP preeminence in the republic. The Baltic example multiplied pressures for analogous actions in other Soviet republics and for the USSR as a whole. Sentiment mounted among Communists in each Baltic republic to split from the CPSU so that they could behave as free agents without obligations to a foreign power.

Politburo member V. M. Chebrikov (former chief of the KGB) on September 1, 1989, chastised the "many" Baltic Communists ready to give up party principles. For his part, General Secretary Gorbachev tried both in public warnings and private talks to halt the breakup of the CPSU.

What Gorbachev could not stop, he decided to join: Taking a page from Eastern Europe and the Baltic, Gorbachev in February 1990 urged that the CPSU give up its monopoly on power. While still leader of the party, he sought to rise above it, first creating and then filling the position of *prezident* to bypass vested interests and push ahead with perestroika.

The CPSU in February 1990 adopted a new platform conceding that "the development of society does not preclude the possibility of forming parties. The procedure for their formation will be established by law and reflected in the USSR Constitution." Moreover: "The Soviet Communist Party does not claim a monopoly and is prepared for a political dialogue and cooperation with everyone who favors the renewal of socialist society." The party wanted to "combine the advantages of the Soviet system with the advantages of parliamentarianism."

With the big picture in mind, let us analyze the zigs and zags toward independence in each republic.

Estonia

Gorbachev hoped in October 1988 that the PFE would draw support away from the radical independence groups.[5] The Communist Party of Estonia (CPE) tried to ride with the Front on its rising crest of popularity, guiding it away from shoals, undertows, and other dangers.

By comparison with other Estonian nationalist groups, the PFE leadership appeared moderate for many months. Some members of independence groups accused the PFE of selling out to Moscow and exercising a monopoly over the media. For a time Estonian Communists might have preferred the PFE as a lesser nationalist evil. But the PFE was pushed by the "independence now" groups to take more radical positions. Conditions in 1989 looked much different from one or two years earlier. The ENIP had called for independence and had not been repressed. Its demands had revealed wide support among Estonian citizens for independence. If the radical pronouncements of the ENIP did not elicit a Soviet crackdown, perhaps the PFE could get away with similar statements. (Had the ENIP been repressed, the PFE might have survived to continue its more gradual quest for national self-determination.) In short, without the pressure from the ENIP and the EHS, the PFE may well have traced the same course, but at a slower pace. As the Communist regimes in Moscow and Tallinn lost their bite, the PFE was able to build up its structure and accumulate a record of successes, step by step.[6] Similar dynamics drove Lithuania's Sajudis movement and the Popular Front of Latvia toward overt support for national independence. Moderates in Georgia and in other republics also moved toward independence platforms.

The situation for Estonian Communists was difficult, said the CPE ideological secretary in October 1989. Marxism-Leninism no longer seemed relevant to Estonians, because they searched for a "practical approach to social questions." The party secretary wanted the CPE to have a certain independence from Moscow, but believed that the CPSU should remain the central authority of the country. In any case, he went on, the CPSU had not lost control because "the army still works."

He predicted that the PFE would win half the seats in forthcoming local elections. He asserted, however, that the relationship between the PFE and CPE was "rather good", with PFE members in the highest bodies of CPE and leading Communists members of the PFE.[7]

Neither the PFE nor the CPE was monolithic. The leadership of the PFE was more moderate than many members and local chapters. On the other hand, the Tallinn CP organization was more critical of the PFE than the top Party leaders, who were quartered in an even more modern building a few blocks away. Both groups are affected by the heavy concentration of Russians and other non-Estonians in the republic's northeast, including Tallinn. Pavel Panfilov, Second Secretary of the Tallinn organization, said in March 1990 that 68 percent of its membership was non-Estonian. Many of them, he went on, blamed Gorbachev for instigating the troubles that beset them and the republic.[8]

For the PFE and other Estonian nationalists there was the persistent question: How should we treat the non-Estonian population? The chairman of the board of the Society of Russian Culture, said: Estonians "cannot be effectively included in the European home [to which they aspire] if they are not an internal model of the home of the multinational civic world [*mir*]." Estonia, he said, needed civic peace, not civil war. It needed *mir* — peace and community. The Russian-speaking section of the PFE adopted the slogan: "the 'Russian question' must be resolved by the Russians themselves." Intermovement, said the chairman, a sociologist, might collapse because it lacked any bearings except negativism.[9]

For local nationalists there were strong reasons to link arms across the Baltic. Local Communists, on the other hand, tended toward the psychology of Rousseau's stag hunt: Each man and each party for itself in an increasingly desperate situation.

As PFE leader Rein Veidemann noted in October 1989, in Estonia and Lithuania a wing was "becoming prominent, pressing fairly persistently for the Communist Party to become independent [as] in the countries of people's democracy."[10]

The PFE adopted an electoral platform in October 1989 that called not just for sovereignty but independence. Veidemann predicted that all three Baltic popular fronts would operate "as a compact political force, and the main ideology of this force is that the popular fronts are ready to have a share of power in the way of real political forces and to be held responsible for implementing this power." The Latvian and Lithuanian PF electoral platforms, he noted, were similar to that of the PFE.[11]

The tone of Estonian Communists was less ebullient — especially after the "viability" threat issued by the CPSU Central Committee on August 26, 1989.

Political movements splintered and new groupings mushroomed in 1989-1990. Public opinion polls (combining non-Estonians and Estonians) showed increasing disillusionment with virtually all political groups in the latter half of 1989. From April to December 1989 backing for the CPE declined from 16 to 9 percent; for the PFE, from 35 to 24 percent; for the Green Movement, 12 to 10 percent; Intermovement, 4 to 1 percent; the Heritage Society, 4 to 3 percent; the ENIP, 6 to 4 percent. The Estonian Citizens' Committees, recorded only after September, rose from 3 to 4 percent by December, and the OSTK rose from 2 to 4 percent, April through December.[12] The newly founded Social Democratic Independence Party immediately became number two for Estonians, getting 22 percent of support in a January 1990 poll, just behind the PFE, which had risen to 27 percent.[13] Since Marju Lauristin was a leader of both groups, confusion abounded.

Communist Party leaders, radicalized by the polls and Moscow's hard line, moved closer to the independence movement. In February 1990 some members of the existing establishment, headed by Prime Minister Toome, cut their ties with the PFE and created their own *Vaba Eesti* [Free Estonia] group. Competing in the March elections for the republic's Supreme Soviet, they stressed their experience and competence. CPE ideological secretary Mikk Titma joined *Vaba Eesti* and said he could no longer be part of the CP "totalitarian party-state machine."[14]

On February 2 Arnold Rüütel, president of Estonia's Supreme Soviet, presided over the Full Assembly of People's Deputies, made up of deputies to local councils, the Estonian Supreme Soviet, and the USSR Congress of People's Deputies. By an overwhelming majority — 2,973 for, 101 against, and 16 abstentions — the assembly declared that Estonia's independence should be restored on the basis of the 1920 Tartu Treaty.

Previously, calls for Estonia's lost statehood had arisen only from popular movements, but the February 2 declaration came from the republic's elected officials. Cautious, it set no timetable for opening negotiations with Moscow.

Estonian Communists had to choose between local values and those of the Kremlin. Natives of Estonia were tempted to go local, non-Estonians of Russian nationality — especially if they (and their families) did not know

Estonian — to seek safe harbor in empire. Those who were neither Estonian nor Russian, for example, Ukrainians, might decide based on whether or not they wanted their own native republic to be more or less independent. Intellectuals, especially if they spoke Estonian, tended to endorse Estonian independence.[15] "International" workers and soldiers, few of whom knew Estonian, were likely to oppose local nationalism. Estonian Jews interviewed in Estonia and the United States in 1989-1990 evinced no fear of anti-Semitism among Estonian nationalists.[16]

In January Marju Lauristin, firebrand of the PFE, led in the establishment of an Estonian Social Democratic Independence Party. It would be, she said, to the right of the British Labour and Swedish Social Democratic parties, less generous on welfare.[17] Willy Brandt and the Socialist International gave their blessings.

In early March a Liberal Democratic Party was established in Tallinn, a counterpoise to the Social Democrats that stressed free enterprise cum "humanism." Its meeting was attended by Swedish liberals, a Hungarian Free Democrat, and a Russian geneticist who said he belonged to a liberal "pre-party" in Moscow. Lauristin and members of other Estonian parties also attended and wished the Liberal Democrats well. What bound them together, they agreed, was greater than what divided them.

Overshadowing all other political movements, however, was the campaign to establish a Congress of Estonia elected by Estonian natives. The campaign, launched in March 1989, registered citizens who had lived in Estonia before June 1940 and their descendants. Non-Estonians could also apply for citizenship if they supported the principle of Estonian independence.

In November 1989 local committees formed a nationwide General Citizens' Committee chaired by Tunne Kelam, ideological leader of the Independence Party, with Heritage Society leader Trivimi Velliste as deputy chair.

Kelam was born in 1936, a preacher's son. He graduated from Tartu University in 1959 with a degree in history and languages. Fired from his job as an editor of the *Estonian Encyclopedia* in 1975 but not arrested, Kelam worked as a night watchman on a state chicken farm.[18] In 1989, however, he became coeditor of *Akadeemia*, a new monthly, and a contributor to the newspaper *Eesti Ekspress*, financed through a joint venture with Finland. In

December 1989 he met with officials in Washington and addressed the Council on Foreign Relations and various civic groups.

By early 1990 the campaign had registered more than 700,000 Estonian citizens (from an estimated total of 963,000, many of whom were too young or too feeble to take part) and nearly 30,000 applicants for citizenship. Estonians living abroad could also register, by mail or in person. Rein Taagepera from California, who left Estonia in 1944, registered in August 1989 at a booth set up in front of his old kindergarten. Behind him in line was a Russian immigrant who knew no Estonian, who received a card showing that he had cast his lot with his new country.

Setting up the machinery for an election is not easy in the best of circumstances. The General Citizens' Committee did so against the wishes of an administration in complete command of communication, transport, and finances.

In February over 90 percent of the registered citizens — 557,163 voters — elected a 499-member Congress from a slate of over 1,100 candidates, some of whom lived abroad. Applicants for citizenship, mostly Russian settlers, elected thirty-five representatives who also attended the Congress.

Persons affiliated with no party got the most seats, 109; PFE candidates won 107; the Heritage Society, 104; the ENIP, 70; the CPE, 39. This outcome was ironic, because the PFE had long opposed the very idea of a registration campaign. As noted below, however, PFE representatives did not score high when the Congress elected a council to direct its future activities.

Defenders of the status quo did what they could to thwart the Congress. Soviet consulates refused visas to two members of the European Parliament who planned to observe the elections; they denied visas to several overseas delegates, including California professor Taagepera. More ominous, intruders broke into the offices of the General Citizens' Committee on March 6, cut the telephone lines, and stole two personal computers containing the Citizens' register and election results. (Diskette copies remained.) The saboteurs used a fireman's ladder, not found in everyone's garage, to enter a second-floor window. When the local police [*milits*] refused to provide more protection, the Citizens' Committee organized a volunteer security force.

The power of the Balts' nonviolent revolution was almost tangible when the Congress convened on Sunday morning, March 11, 1990, in a gilded concert hall in Tallinn.

Balts are masters of political symbolism: Not politicians but musicians filled the stage — a symphony orchestra and a mixed choir. They did not dress in the shabby, dull dress of the Soviet empire but in tuxedos and gowns. Beneath brightly lit chandeliers they stood erect and proud. For this moment they were undiminished by the sovietization that has impoverished them while their neighbors — the Finns and Swedes — have attained among the world's highest living standards. Young men and women in traditional folk costumes marched up the main aisle carrying the blue, black, and white flag of the independent Estonian republic. They passed the first row where empty chairs were reserved for émigré delegates denied visas.

The Congress rose to sing Estonia's national anthem from the 1920s which, like the tricolor flag, had been banned until recently. The audience included both as guests and delegates many persons who had once been deported or who had fled. Many came from nearby Sweden, but some came from as far as Australia. Many eyes filled with hot tears as the music resounded, proclaiming that a small, brave people could survive and demand independence from Leviathan.

After the national anthem the orchestra and choir gave voice to the "Sanctus" of Estonian composer Rudolf Tobias, whose Mass was seldom performed until recently. A fusion of J. S. Bach and Arnold Schoenberg, its force filled the hall.[19]

The music and ceremonies ended, the Congress got down to business. The Congress claimed a legitimacy enjoyed by no other political body in the republic. It demanded that the USSR acknowledge Estonia's independence and withdraw its military forces. Congress chairman Endel Lippmaa left for Moscow to deliver this demand to the USSR Congress of People's Deputies.

On March 12, the second and final day of the meeting, the Congress elected a seventy-eight-member council (including seven nonvoting representatives of citizen applicants) to continue its work. The ENIP was most strongly represented in the council, while the PFE was poorly represented. This showing nearly reversed the popular sentiments as indicated in public opinion surveys conducted in 1989-early 1990 and differed sharply from delegate strength at the Congress. The discrepancy, Rein Taagepera has suggested, stemmed from elector rates: Each delegate could vote for eighteen council candidates. Had elections to the council followed what Taagepera calls the "square root" formula (as did elections to the Congress itself), each delegate could have voted for only eight council candidates — an approach that probably would have netted stronger representation for the PFE.[20] In any case the Council was dominated by persons whom some PFE leaders had earlier characterized as "radical." [21] No top Communists were in its ranks.

How the Congress would interact with the Estonian Supreme Soviet was unclear. Here was another case of *dvoevlastie,* "dual power", like that which preceded the October 1917 Revolution. The Congress was an alternative parliament, more legitimate in some ways than the Supreme Soviet — a creature of Stalinism, crippled even in 1990 by the fact that its members were selected by Russian settlers and soldiers as well as by Estonian natives. But some members of Congress planned to run also for posts in the Supreme Soviet. Sociologist Priit Järve observed that both bodies might serve the cause of independence: the Congress, because it seemed genuine to Westerners; the Supreme Soviet, because it could relate to Moscow. Both the Congress and the Supreme Soviet, elected later in March, asserted Estonia's right to independence and tried to persuade Moscow to renounce its claims.

The Congress had debated and rejected a declaration to allay the Russians' fears, proposed by Marju Lauristin.[22] "You cannot expect the colonized to sympathize too much with the colonists," some nationalists argued. Some Congress leaders attempted to approach the settlers, but they did so without a congressional mandate. Two journalists who traveled to the Russian-dominated town of Narva were told by local liberals that the silence of the Congress had made their life much more difficult.[23]

In April 1990 the Tallinn City Council voted to pay compensation for those who leave Estonia for permanent settlement in the Soviet Union and vacate their flats. The vote came after the RSFSR appealed to Russians to return to their native regions, many of which had become underpopulated.

The Congress of Estonia had a window of opportunity to assert if not seize administrative power from the lame-duck ESSR Supreme Soviet, which had been appointed several years earlier in choiceless elections. But a new Supreme Soviet was elected in late March 1990 and immediately over-shadowed the Congress. Acting like a real legislature, the new Supreme Soviet appointed a prime minister and set terms for negotiations with Moscow.

In April 1990 PFE leader Edgar Savisaar, age 39, was elected Estonia's Prime Minister by the republic's Supreme Soviet on a secret ballot by a slim majority—54 of 105. Having resigned from the CPE earlier in the year, Savisaar became the first non-Communist to head the country's government in fifty years. The PFE had already secured a majority in the Supreme Soviet Presidium and many legislative commissions. Another PFE leader, Marju Lauristin, assistant speaker in the legislature, had played a major role in guiding legislation through the body.

Savisaar probably won the votes of some Congress of Estonia members of the Supreme Soviet as well as those aligned more with the Popular Front. But relations between the Congress and the Supreme Soviet were strained, because some Congress members and leaders considered their mandate more pure, and wanted the Supreme Soviet to be a tool to pursue Congress programs. Savisaar also had to contend with old guard Communists in the Free Estonia movement, whose deputies predicted that his government would soon fall and injected their opinions into the main government newspapers. Commentator Kalle Muuli wrote in the Tartu daily *Edasi* that the chances for cooperation among these three groups were slim: "Some have been Communists for too long; others have been dissidents for too long." Some lacked a clean political record; others lacked political experience, he observed.

Savisaar in April appointed a new cabinet, including film-maker/writer Lennart Meri as Foreign Minister. Meri, like Savisaar and Lauristin, was also in the leadership of the Congress of Estonia.

"Are the Baltic republics in or outside the Soviet Union?" This was a key question in 1990. Further: "Which laws are valid if the USSR constitution no longer applies? If the Baltic states never joined the USSR voluntarily, how can their illegal government—the republican supreme soviets—negotiate on their behalf?" Meanwhile, pro-Soviet activists asked: "If the Baltic republics can revoke Moscow's rules, why can't we—at least in the areas where we dominate—revoke Baltic legislation?"

Infighting continued among Balts: The Council of the Congress of Estonia did not focus on proposing new legislation to the ESSR Supreme Soviet, which had about forty Congress activists in its ranks. Instead, the Council rapped the PFE because it dominated the Supreme Soviet but failed to implement resolutions of the Congress. The Congress of Estonia met a second time on May 25 and opted to oppose the Estonian Supreme Soviet and expand its own powers to include the right to pass legislation. Congress Chairman Tunne Kelam called for a "new definition of roles" based on equality for both bodies. Savisaar and other Popular Fronters, also members of the Congress, argued against expanding its authority, but were outvoted. Ex-political prisoner Enn Tarto commented: "This is a division between the haves and the have-nots. Some have just had the power while others have not. Why not change roles?" Defenders of the Supreme Soviet argued that pragmatists should rule, letting idealists uphold the legitimacy of the Congress.

"While we are arguing on how to turn the virginal de jure into the mature de facto, somebody else is oiling a gun around the corner," lawyer Arvo Junti told the Congress. Indeed, the very next day — May 26 — pro-Moscow deputies of the Estonian Supreme Soviet and local councils gathered in Kohtla-Järve to create still a third level of legislative bodies. Their aim: To keep Estonia within the USSR. They claimed not to be establishing an alternative power structure but only "an organ to guarantee the normal life for citizens of the USSR." They formed a bicameral Interregional Soviet of Deputies and Workers and a National Economic Council (*Sovnarkhoz*) chaired by Vladimir Yarovoi, who boasted of strong support from some Politburo members in Moscow. The meeting took place in Kohtla-Järve Communist Party headquarters, and was guarded by Soviet paratroopers. It was closed to outsiders who sought to observe — Marju Lauristin and reporters for Estonian radio and the liberal weeklies *Moscow News* and *Ogonёk*.

The Congress of Estonia and its Latvian counterpart wanted to be heard in negotiations with Moscow regarding Baltic independence. On May 25, 1990, Tunne Kelam, chairman of the Council of Estonia and A. Jirgens, chairman of the Council of Latvia, proposed to the presidents of the three Baltic republics consultations to agree on unified tactics in the negotiations. The consultations would include representatives of the two congresses and the three supreme soviets. On that date Kelam also sent a letter to Presidents Bush and Gorbachev, urging that they call an international forum of all parties concerned with the Baltic. The PFE also held a congress in May, which issued a new program and set up a "chamber of deputies" as a new subdivision within its leadership.

If the Congress of Estonia and the Estonian Supreme Soviet could not agree on what laws would govern, one lawyer cautioned, "the pro-Soviet Kohtla-Järve Council's version will be considered valid."

The Communist Party of Estonia at the end of March voted to separate itself from the CPSU, not immediately (as the Lithuanian Party had done the previous December), but after six months.

The Estonian Supreme Soviet on March 30 declared that it did "not recognize the legality of state authority of the USSR on the territory of Estonia." The parliament declared "a period of transition that will culminate in the formation of the constitutional organs of state power of the Republic of Estonia has begun."

Estonia's movement toward independence was more gradual and less precipitate than Lithuania's, but its momentum now increased, backed even by some top members of the Communist establishment.

Estonians such as Tunne Kelam, head of the ENIP, hoped that Russia would rather have "four Finlands" on its border than one Finland and three rebellious provinces.[24]

An economist at the Estonian Academy of Sciences argued that Estonia could break into world markets in biotechnology, lasers, cybernetics, and other fields if it only had the freedom to develop in these areas.[25]

If Russia punished Estonia, it would give itself a black eye economically as well as morally. In 1990 much of Leningrad's electrical power came from Estonia and a very large share of Soviet shipping, both imports and exports, went through Tallinn and other Baltic ports. This situation reflected not artifice but geographic reality. As early as 1920 the peace treaties that Russia signed with the three Baltic countries underscored their economic interdependence. As noted in chapter 3, Bolshevik diplomats wanted to ensure port and transit privileges for Soviet goods in the Baltic ports. They offered Estonia a concession to build a railroad to Moscow, but wanted electrical power for northeastern Russia from Estonian waters.

In April 1990 the Estonian government announced that the country's new currency, the kroon, would be printed and made available just before Christmas. Meanwhile, special purchasing cards issued in Estonia — following the lead of Latvia and Leningrad — did not help much in acquiring articles in short supply. Rein Otsason, president of the Bank of Estonia, said in June that introduction of the kroon would be the "only way to avoid financial crisis and quickly go over to a market economy." Some non-Estonians feared that the kroon would cut them off from the rest of the Soviet economy, but a convertible currency could link Estonia more firmly with the world economy and make Estonian ventures more attractive to foreign investors.

Savisaar's government decided to privatize service industries and state distribution networks within months. His aides said that ultimately only utilities, mining, railroads, and communications would remain state property. An Estonian-American Chamber of Commerce opened its doors to promote business in June 1990. It was housed in what had been the U.S. Consulate up to 1940.

In April 1990 all top Communist officials on the Estonian island of Saaremaa quit the Party. Soviet-style structures were replaced with councils more like those of the interwar years. Saaremaa's main city, Kuressare, became one of the three towns in Estonia to adopt a "self-sufficient" budget. Instead of passing revenues to Tallinn and then Moscow, most money now stayed in Kuressare, with an agreed percentage going to the regional and republican governments. Small businesses began to flourish among the island's 40,000 inhabitants, 94 percent of them Estonians.

The Estonian Supreme Soviet on April 11, 1990, passed a law making conscription into the Soviet armed forces illegal in Estonia and forbidding Estonian enterprises to help in the twice-yearly roundup of recruits. It annulled all Estonian criminal code articles concerning draft evasion and rehabilitated all persons convicted under these statutes. Another law, passed in March, encouraged a thirty-month period of alternative service for persons not wishing to serve in the Soviet armed forces. The Geneva-49 organization continued its campaign of draft resistance based on the 1949 Geneva Convention stating that citizens of an occupied country may not be forced to serve in the occupation army. In just ten weeks in early 1990, five Estonians were reported to have died in Soviet military service while twenty-three asked for psychiatric help.

Critics of independence fought back. In March the computer files of the Congress of Estonia were vandalized. In April 1990 an Estonian Lutheran pastor and his housekeeper were tortured and buried alive after their house was burned down — all money and church valuables untouched. The Rev. Harald

Meri had been drawing up a list of collaborators in the Soviet mass deportations of 1941 and 1949. In July burglars broke into the summer residence of Arnold Rüütel and — despite a fence and two guards — stole valuables including cameras and tape recorders.

On May 15 about two thousand pro-Soviet demonstrators met outside the Estonian Supreme Soviet building at Toompea Castle in Tallinn. Organized by Intermovement and other pro-Soviet groups, they demanded that the government rescind Estonia's independence declarations of March 30 and May 8. They tried to fly the Soviet Estonian flag side by side with the tricolor at Long Hermann tower and demanded the resignation of Arnold Rüütel as chair of the Supreme Soviet. When they tried to break down the door of the building, Prime Minister Savisaar broadcast a radio appeal for help. Several thousand Estonians appeared and trapped the pro-Soviet demonstrators in a courtyard. When the Estonians formed a corridor for the demonstrators to exit, they did so with no major altercations. Estonians then debated whether the Russians had attempted a coup d'état or only a show of force.

The next day, some two thousand men and a few women volunteered to join the unarmed Home Guard (Kodukaitse) to protect government buildings and communications. Kodukaitse received police powers and worked under supervision of the Estonian Interior Ministry. Aleksandr Klimov, a Russian born in Estonia, joined the guard, he said, to prevent Intermovement from provoking a split between Estonians and Russians.

Seeking to uphold Gorbachev's decrees on invalidating recent Estonian legislation, Soviet Interior Minister Vadim Bakatin ordered troops from his ministry to Estonia. On May 18, 1990, Prime Minister Savisaar phoned him and said that Estonia did not want or need Soviet forces to maintain order. Savisaar declared on television that Bakatin had withdrawn his order, but some observers believed that Interior Ministry troops came anyway. Soon, however, (August 2) Radio Free Europe's Estonian Service reported that Bakatin signed an agreement with Savisaar guaranteeing the Estonian government total control over law enforcement within Estonia. *Izvestiia* (July 31) reported that this approach was being discussed for all Union Republics.

A gathering of Estonian veterans of World War II and the 1918-1920 War of Independence was canceled in the central Estonian town of Tori on June 5 after what Estonian authorities protested as a show of disapproval by Soviet military authorities. Twenty-eight light tanks, nine supply trucks, and Soviet paratroop units traveled from Pskov through Tori to Pärnu. Savisaar called it a "provocation" to keep Estonia "on edge." Opponents of the veterans' meeting had called it a pro-fascist rally, but it was meant to include veterans who fought in the Red Army as well as with German forces. Organizers of a "Rock Summer '90 Freedom Fest" canceled the event because of the action by "occupation forces."

Thesis and antithesis: In June 1990 Estonian-speaking Aleksius II (born Aleksei Ridiger in Tallinn, 1929) became Patriarch of Moscow and of All Russia. He had been Metropolitan of Leningrad and Novgorod and head of the Tallinn and Estonian bishoprics. In 1961 he had been instrumental in saving the Orthodox nunnery in Kohtla-Järve from becoming a miners' resort. A member of the USSR Supreme Soviet, Aleksius helped draft the new law on freedom of religion. In 1991, however, he backed a repressive Gorbachev.

Estonia's Supreme Soviet supported both the symbols and substance of independence. It established a pair of national holidays: June 23, "Victory Day" in the 1919 War of Independence, and June 24, "Midsummer Day." On June 26 it passed a law severely limiting immigration of non-Estonians.

On June 30-July 1 the "Singing Revolution" attracted 500,000 persons to the Estonian Song and Dance Festival in Tallinn, a celebration in which 28,000 singers and 9,000 dancers took part, the twenty-first such gathering since 1869. In the week after the Tallinn festival other celebrations were held across Estonia, including on the island of Hiiumaa.

Surveys by the Mainor public opinion poll firm showed a significant growth in support for independence among Estonia's residents. In April 1989 only 56 percent of native Estonians and 5 percent of non-Estonians supported independence; in June 1990 these numbers had changed to 93 percent and 27 percent. Among Russians in Estonia, support for remaining a Soviet republic dropped from 54 to 16 percent; backing for a Soviet confederation rose from 25 to 48 percent.

Lithuania

Estonia moved toward independence in small steps; Lithuania, by 1989-1990, in giant strides. Estonia's registration campaign and Congress had endeavored to build legitimacy for those demanding independence. Lithuania's leaders, elected in free parliamentary elections in early 1990, claimed to be the people's voice. As such, they proclaimed Lithuania's independence on March 11. Estonia treated independence as a matter to be negotiated with Moscow; Lithuania in spring 1990 treated its independence as a fait accompli. Which approach would prove more effective would be decided by future events, including Moscow's response.

Red Star, like the trade union newspaper *Trud*, tended to portray Baltic nationalists as wild men. But most actors in the Lithuanian political spectrum shifted toward independence in 1989 — the Lithuanian Communist Party (LCP), the Supreme Soviet, the popular front Sajudis [Restructuring Movement], and a series of new organizations.

The tide for independence rose against demographic trends that favored outsiders over natives. In 1989 Lithuania's population totaled 3,690,000, an increase of 292,000 since 1979. The Lithuanian share of the total dropped by a fraction to 79.2 percent. The immigration of 193,000 people from other republics accounted for 34 percent of population growth. The share of Russians increased from 8.9 percent in 1979 to 9.3 percent in 1989, while the Polish share remained about 7 percent.[26]

Lithuanian Communists did not start their push toward independence from Moscow until they received a bad beating at the polls. Algirdas Brazauskas became LCP First Secretary in late 1988, some months after Vaino Väljas was recalled to head the Estonian Party. Local Communists and those in Moscow probably hoped that a more popular leader would help the LCP in the March 1989 elections for the USSR Congress of People's Deputies. The Party had lost support in November 1988 when the Lithuanian Supreme Soviet failed to follow Estonia's lead and demand sovereignty. Even under Brazauskas, however, the LCP continued its be-tough-on-nationalists stance. In February 1989 Brazauskas and the Party plenum tried to rein in nationalist manifestations during celebration of Lithuanian independence day.[27]

The Party suffered huge losses in the March 1989 elections as Sajudis candidates won thirty-six seats. The Party's ability to silence Sajudis declined as the front virtually obtained its own representatives in the all-Union Congress. Party membership declined throughout 1989 and the Party had trouble finding attractive candidates for local and all-Union elections.

Striving to compete, the LCP distanced itself from Moscow. At first its nationalist stance stressed only maximum autonomy *within* the USSR. The Party's flexibility was constrained from two sides. If it completely adopted the Sajudis program, the Party would be seen as opportunistic. For ideological reasons it could hardly preempt Sajudis by going even further toward nationalism. The orthodox wing of the Party got support from Russians, Poles, and other ethnic minorities in Lithuania, many of whom saw a Moscow connection as protection against local chauvinism. But these and other minorities were unlikely to shape Lithuanian politics in any major way, because only 20 percent of the republic's population was non-Lithuanian.

Lithuanian legislators became much more active in 1989. In May they approved changes in the Lithuanian Constitution making Soviet laws valid in Lithuania only after approval by the Lithuanian Supreme Soviet.[28]

Sajudis, like the other two Baltic popular fronts, was pushed toward more radical positions by other movements calling for independence. In 1989 these included the Lithuanian Freedom League, the Lithuanian Social Democratic Party, and the Lithuanian Christian Democratic Party. Another influence was the Tremtinys Association, active in memorializing victims of Stalinism.

The Lithuanian Komsomol, faced with challenges similar to those facing the LCP, split with the all-Union Komsomol in June. But this did not stop the growth of rival youth organizations such as the Scouts, "Young Lithuania," and the Catholic group "Ateitis." [29]

Many non-Lithuanians felt threatened by the resurgence of Lithuanian nationalism. Their major organization, *Vienybe-Edinstvo-Jednosc* [Unity], was popular among Poles as well as Russians in the republic, and got support from Moscow.

Periodic growls by the Russian Bear served to unite many Lithuanians in their quest for self-determination. When the CPSU Central Committee warned on August 26 that separatist movements in the Baltic were driving the USSR to the brink of "civil conflict," [30] Vytautas Landsbergis, Sajudis leader and member of the USSR Congress of People's Deputies, declared that "we long ago decided that this is something we must do, to fight for our independence. We're not extremist and we are not violent, but we are determined." Even before the Central Committee's broadside, Landsbergis had worried that "the Soviet mass media is paving the way for a coercive step against our plans." [31]

Lithuanian legislators immediately sent telegrams to Gorbachev and the Central Committee denouncing the August 26 statement as provocative interference in local affairs, insulting, and misleading.

The relationship between Sajudis and the LCP was complex. Throughout 1989 there continued to be a heavy overlap between membership in the two organizations. Their programs converged, although Sajudis tilted much further toward independence. The fact that they could compete at the polls gave individual candidates a vested interest in staking out a position most likely to attract voters.

One LCP official said in August that his party could not "stay in the stagnant condition it is in at present. It will not remain like the regional parties of Russia, Kazakhstan, and the Ukraine." He thought that the LCP might be "reestablished" separate from the CPSU.[32]

In early autumn 1989 there was a mutiny within the Party ranks in Lithuania's second city, Kaunas. An "open letter" appeared calling for a radical restructuring of the party and dropping sixty-four officials. The Kaunas membership had numbered over 23,000, but in the first nine months of 1989 some 465 persons resigned and only fifty-eight joined. A thousand members were late in paying their dues and there were calls to reduce dues. Some Kaunas Communists called for separation of the LCP from the CPSU, a view that some Muscovites disparaged as a call for the "good times" of the old bourgeois order.[33]

Three viewpoints on breaking with Moscow emerged at LCP Central Committee plenum in October 1989.[34] Conservatives wanted to follow the Kremlin; centrists headed by the current LCP leadership wished to improve the relationship between the LCP and the CPSU but avoid a break. Radicals wanted to split. They demanded a 4,000-strong meeting before the next LCP Congress to vote on the issue.

In September a draft program drawn up by a working group tried to straddle the centrist and radical positions. It called on the LCP to "work with all political forces which strive to realize the universal principles of humanism. Thus, the LCP, wishing to be a political force in the process of creating an independent, rule-of-law Lithuanian state, must also be an independent party." But its "independent political activity...must not be interpreted as splitting with the CPSU."[35]

Just before the LCP Central Committee met in October, Gorbachev and First Secretary Brazauskas talked by telephone. Gorbachev suggested delaying the LCP congress planned for December 1989 until spring 1990, after publication of the new CPSU draft program and rules. Brazauskas replied that the congress had already been democratically planned.

Amid this jockeying, Lithuanians seemed to become somewhat disillusioned with politics. This could be seen by comparing the results of polls conducted in May and in early October 1989 in which approval ratings could range from 100 to -100. Among all inhabitants of the republic, the Sajudis rating declined from 68 to 57; the LCP from 22 to 15; the Lithuanian Liberty League from 15 to -5. The ratings of Brazauskas and of Gorbachev also declined. The same trends appeared when pollsters separated the responses of the republic's Lithuanians, Russians, and Poles.[36]

A Sajudis editor blamed diminished interest in politics on worsening economic conditions. Also, euphoria evaporated because "everyone" had been dreaming of rapid independence but then saw that such things would not be so easy to attain.[37]

Some Lithuanians charged that Moscow was fabricating material with which to blacken the image of Lithuanian reformers and justify an intervention. This was the gist of the article "When You Wish to Hit Someone — Any Stick Will Do," by Algimantas Cekuolis, an editor and a deputy to the USSR Supreme Soviet. He said that *Pravda* sent staff members to Lithuania to collect trash to stop the "Lithuanian plague" from infecting the whole country. Thus, he charged, *Pravda* (September 13, 1989) accused Landsbergis of dictating to the LSSR Supreme Soviet how to hold elections; it exaggerated the extent to which non-Lithuanians would lose their civic rights; and it spread slander about desecrations of Red Army graves in Lithuania.[38]

Writer Leonidas Jacinevicius told the Lithuanian Writers' Association Party meeting in October 1989 that most LCP members believed Moscow would seek to maintain hegemony over the Baltic republics even if they became self-managing economically. If Lithuanian Communists continued to pussyfoot, they would have to tuck away the LCP slogan: "Lithuania without sovereignty is Lithuania without a future."

He agreed with LCP leader Brazauskas that two slogans should be renounced: "On leaving the USSR," and "Occupiers, get out of Lithuania!"

Instead of using the phrases that "arouse the center," the LCP should encourage the Lithuanian citizen to develop a sense of self-worth, expand tolerance, and throw off provincialism. "The intellectual forces within the Republic will thus assist in overcoming the slave syndrome, and no warning visits to Lithuania by high military officials will be capable of reviving it."

It was the CPSU that had discredited perestroika, the writer concluded. That was why "an independent LCP alone can be the authoritative force if it is to pursue goals in union with the nation." [39]

Responding to another plea from Gorbachev, Brazauskas on December 1, 1989, told the LCP Central Committee why the Lithuanian Party needed to become independent.[40] The Party's ranks were dwindling. The number of Communists resigning had increased tenfold. "Only by becoming an independent political party can the LCP gain real authority in society and direct its development toward the creation of a sovereign socialist democratic state." Without a change in the Party's status it would do poorly in the next elections.

Would such a change conflict with Leninism? Brazauskas replied that Lenin's attacks on "federalism" within the Party were written in 1913, 1914, and 1919 — in different circumstances from today — and that he was talking then about the Russian Social-Democratic Workers' Party, not the CPSU. Lenin opposed organizing parties on a nationality basis, but the LCP would be open to all nationalities living in Lithuania.

Brazauskas lamented the artificial wall built up between the CPSU and Social Democracy. The fact was that Lithuanian Communists and Russian Bolsheviks were "the offspring of social democracy."

An independent LCP, he said, would pursue cooperation with the CPSU as with all Communist Parties. The general orientation of the LCP and the CPSU, he said, was the same: democratic perestroika.

Independence or sovereignty? Brazauskas hedged. He foresaw many stages in reestablishing Lithuanian statehood. For the present, the goal was to reach, by contract, a "sovereign Lithuanian state in a new union of free republics."

The LCP Central Committee plenum was addressed also by CPSU ideological secretary Vadim Medvedev, who tried to derail the independence movement. His remarks were rebutted sarcastically by a member of the writers' union: If the LCP "which helped a neighboring state bury the independence of its own state, today takes a conciliatory, compromise position that indulges someone else, that will mean failure." [41]

Amid more warnings and pleas from Moscow, the LCP Congress voted on December 20 to become an independent political organization with its own program and statutes. The new program asserted that "restoration of Lithuania's statehood is a priority mission" of the Party. It called for an "independent," "democratic," and "socialist" Lithuania. It claimed to be guided by "the contemporary concept of the materialist dialectics of social development." It said that Communists had gone too far against "private property," but the document did not mention the crucial test: ownership of the means of production.[42]

Of 1,033 delegates to the Congress, 855 voted for independence. About 160 of the others decided to remain aligned with the CPSU. They included some forty delegates from military units stationed in Lithuania. The rump group claimed to represent at least a fourth of the republic's 200,000 Communists. They retained the CPSU program and formed their own Central Committee, rival to that of the independents headed by Brazauskas.[43]

The Moscow press noted that very few workers were among the Congress delegates and that Brazauskas and V. Beriozov had been elected as First and Second secretaries on a secret ballot but with no alternative candidates. It gave much space to the rump organization and said that the "battle of ideas did not end at the congress." [44]

An LCP majority tried to escape its own past by condemning past "crimes" of the Party and its leaders — their role in joining Lithuania to the USSR; in devastating the traditional culture; in mass deportations. These were Stalin's policies, but their "executioner" was also the LCP.[45]

Interviewed, Brazauskas admitted that for a time he had deliberately obstructed the separation of the two parties. At first he had delayed action because Moscow wanted to postpone the issue. But it could not be postponed further, because LCP members worried about the elections following the Party Congress.[46]

The CPSU Central Committee met December 25-26, 1989, to consider the Lithuanian split. Gorbachev said that "no part of the CPSU has the right to decide" on an independent existence without taking into account the position of the CPSU as a whole. Still, he said, the Lithuanian problem had to be settled "on the basis of civil peace, not civil war," using concessions and compromises. The Kremlin put off any decisive response to the Lithuanian split until a delegation led by Gorbachev could visit Lithuania in January.

In Lithuania the General Secretary made so many speeches and held so many conversations that they were published as a book in Moscow. He told a crowd: "Let's give you independence and establish world prices, and you'll bog down in a swamp immediately." But he also contemplated the possibility of Lithuanian independence when he, joined by other Moscow leaders, observed that the Supreme Soviet was drafting a law on the mechanics of secession, a process that had to consider defense, communications, and other issues.[47]

Despite his own oratory, Gorbachev got the message that the majority of LCP members approved of the new course. His visit to Lithuania probably contributed to Gorbachev's recommendation, expressed the next month, to further democratize Soviet life by removing Article 6 from the Soviet Constitution.

Brazauskas, meanwhile, sought quickly to enhance his party's and his own power in the republic. He asserted after the Party Congress that of all the political organizations in Lithuania, "only the Communists were capable of forming a government.... [This] work could be better done through the combined efforts of all rather than through having the various parties compete with each other or attempting to attain their own particular objectives." [48]

Immediately following the party's assertion of independence, its popularity surged. Surveyed immediately after the December congress, a cross section of Lithuanians gave a positive rating of 73 to the LCP and 65 to Sajudis — very different from their scores of 16 and 60 the previous November. In January 1990 it appeared that 38 percent in the republic would vote for the new LCP; 27 percent for Sajudis; and 8 percent for the Moscow-aligned Communists.[49]

Despite objections from Sajudis and other organizations, Brazauskas became Lithuania's president a very short time before elections to the republic's Supreme Soviet. Following a ritual from Stalinist times, the chairman of the LSSR Supreme Soviet Presidium, Vytautas Astrauskas, "asked to be relieved from his duties" on January 15, 1990, and proposed that Brazauskas be elected in his place. This then happened by a vote of 228 deputies in favor, four against, and nineteen abstaining.[50] This concentration of power resembled that which

Gorbachev had accumulated in recent years, ostensibly to promote a good cause. Brazauskas did not use these new powers to pursue a strong independence line. In late January 1990 he criticized demands voiced for withdrawal of the Soviet Army from Lithuania.[51] As to independence, he said that "there are very few proposals on how to achieve independence. We will never achieve independence in isolation." Such efforts should proceed slowly, he stressed.[52]

The first truly free elections ever held in the Soviet state showed that these tactics failed. In elections for Lithuania's new, 141-seat parliament, held February 24 with runoffs on March 10, 1990, candidates sponsored by Sajudis swept the field. The Sajudis slate included a mix of prosecession Communists, independents, and newly legalized Social Democratic, Christian Democratic, and Green parties. Brazauskas and a handful of his independent Communists were elected along with a smaller group of pro-Moscow Communists, representing enclaves of non-Lithuanians.

The parliament could have made Brazauskas its president but chose instead Vytautas Landsbergis. Born in 1932 into a family of the old intellectual aristocracy and a lifelong non-Communist, he represented a clean break with fifty years of Communist rule. A music professor and an accomplished pianist, he was known more for his firm convictions and moral principles than for his tact. Thus, when Gorbachev visited Lithuania in January 1990, Landsbergis greeted him as "the leader of a friendly neighboring country." Lithuanians selected a president who, as one school teacher put it, "is too much a Lithuanian ever to betray us or compromise." [53]

On March 11 the parliament proclaimed Lithuania independent. This action echoed in Moscow, where the Congress moved toward making Gorbachev executive president of the USSR. On March 15 the Congress declared Lithuania's proclamation illegal and invalid. The Kremlin then launched a multilayered series of psychological, economic, and military pressures aimed at bringing the Lithuanians to their knees. On March 16 Gorbachev sent Landsbergis a telegram giving Lithuania three days to rescind its decision. Soviet planes buzzed Vilnius. The Kremlin warned Lithuania against taking control of all-Union enterprises or setting up its own border posts. Moscow ordered two American diplomats to leave Lithuania. It instructed all foreign reporters to depart as soon as their visas expired.

The commander in chief of Soviet ground forces arrived in Vilnius. A column of armed vehicles drove by parliament as it deliberated in the early hours. Soviet paratroopers occupied Communist Party buildings and the Higher School of Marxism-Leninism. They arrested and beat up Soviet army deserters who had sought refuge in a hospital. Gorbachev directed Lithuania to halt formation of voluntary border forces and ordered army deserters to return to their units.

Gorbachev told Senator Edward Kennedy that force would not be used in Lithuania except to prevent bloodshed, but other Soviet spokesmen said it might be used to maintain public order. Lithuanians feared that disorder could be provoked either by the Soviet military or by non-Lithuanian settlers. Soviet helicopters dropped leaflets urging the settlers to attend a demonstration in Vilnius, but the rally was sparsely attended and no violence resulted.

An early April survey found that 6 percent of Vilnius residents supported *Edinstvo*, 8 percent the Moscow-aligned LCP, 10 percent the independent LCP, and 46 percent Sajudis. The first two organizations drew support almost exclusively from non-Lithuanians; the latter two were favored by 87 percent of the Lithuanians, 30 percent of the local Poles, and 20 percent of Russians.

Pollsters also asked Vilnius residents: "Would you like the Lithuanian Supreme Soviet to annul its decision on the restoration of statehood?" Among the Russians, 42 percent said yes, but the same number said no. Among the Poles, 30 percent said yes and 48 percent no. Among Lithuanians, 95 percent said no.[54]

Landsbergis made a virtue of Lithuania's military weakness, and appealed to the West for support. Lithuania, he said, wanted to negotiate with Moscow, but the Kremlin replied that "negotiations" may take place only between separate countries, whereas Lithuania remained part of the USSR. Lithuanian police collected some hunting rifles, as ordered by Moscow, but refused to turn them over to Soviet authorities.

Despite Lithuania's proclaimed independence, economic life remained basically under Soviet control, particularly transport and telecommunications links, big factories, currency, petrol, and raw materials. When Moscow began the blockade described in chapter 13, Landsbergis asserted that "Lithuania can hold out for 100 years without gas and oil." He told French television in April: "Until 1944 Lithuania lived on its own products and had a stable economy. It can survive." As Lithuanians began draconian rationing of fuel, their officials visited Norway, where petroleum companies offered to sell oil and gas for hard currency, but also queried how crude could be shipped from Klaipeda to Mazeikiai, Lithuania's sole refinery, 360 kilometers inland.[55] To supply Norwegian gas to Lithuania with no existing infrastructure could be even more problematic.

Still, economic warfare could hurt all parties. In 1990 Lithuania's single oil refinery supplied oil not just to Estonia and Latvia but also to Kaliningrad. Large all-Union factories in Lithuania, manned heavily by Russian workers, were among the first to suffer from the Kremlin's fuel embargo. Lithuania was a monopoly supplier to the USSR of some high-tech components and a large supplier of consumers goods, food, and cement. Probably the Kremlin could purchase these goods elsewhere, but only for hard currency. Lithuania depended upon oil and gas from Russia, but it exported more than twice as much electrical power to other Soviet republics as it received. Belorussia and the Leningrad region had become dependent upon Lithuanian meat, milk, and fish.[56]

Kazimiera Danuta Prunskiene, made prime minister in March 1990, cautioned the Kremlin that Lithuania took the "lead in supplying fuel equipment, picture tubes, integral schemes, household electric meters, high-quality drills, and cement." The republic's trade partners, including all-Union ministries, wanted to be sure trade ties were not severed. If Russia raised the price of oil, Lithuania would raise the prices of its exports.[57]

Other Balts wondered whether Lithuania had not gone too far, too fast, making it difficult for Gorbachev to acquiesce in its asserted independence. Some liberal politicians in Moscow thought that Lithuanians had alienated potential allies within the USSR by their aloofness and disregard for the fears of other ethnic groups, and their romantic, one-great-leap approach to independence.[58] A Soviet analyst contended that Gorbachev was responding to Soviet public opinion, which opposed Lithuanian separation. Also, Gorbachev had been insulted by Lithuania's move: "He is thinking, I gave them all these opportunities, and they spit in my face." [59]

Bowing to Moscow's pressures and West European suggestions, the Lithuanian Supreme Soviet on June 29 adopted a 100-day moratorium on its declaration of independence effective the moment that negotiations with

Moscow commenced. Prime Minister Prunskiene disagreed publicly with President Landsbergis on which of them would lead negotiations with the Kremlin.

In July President Landsbergis stated that talks with the RSFSR on Lithuanian independence might be as important as talks with the USSR. Prime Minister Prunskiene countered that it was the USSR, not the RSFSR, that controlled the army, borders, and other important spheres. Reports from Vilnius in August indicated that Landsbergis wanted to omit Prunskiene from the team negotiating Lithuania's independence with Moscow. He was also quoted as saying that if Moscow offered to negotiate with Lithuania alone, Lithuania could not refuse.

In July the border between Lazdijai, Lithuania, and Ogrodniki, Poland— closed since April—was reopened. People from both countries could cross without visas, but a passport and an invitation from the other side were needed.

In September Sajudis elected a new chairman, Juozas Tumelis, a librarian and historian, to replace Landsbergis, who had resigned in spring to become president. Prime Minister Prunskiene, meanwhile, continued her foreign diplomacy, meeting in Bratislava with Alexander Dubcek and with Slovak officials.

Latvia

In Latvia, where natives barely outnumbered "internationals," the struggle between defenders of the status quo and proponents of change was especially intense. As in Lithuania, however, the main thrust was toward independence.

The Popular Front of Latvia (PFL) was founded in October 1988 just after the Estonian. The first PFL congress elected a journalist, Dainis Ivans, as the Front's president. The Front's membership included not only individuals but associations such as Renaissance and Renewal, a religious rights organization. Within a year PFL membership grew to about 250,000 compared with 184,000 in the Communist Party of Latvia (CPL). The Front claimed in 1989 to have the support of 1.3 million people, at least half the republic's population. Popular Front membership was 85 percent Latvian, whereas Russians outweighed Latvians in the CPL, 43.1 percent to 39.7 percent.[60]

The immediate response of conservatives had been to seek illegalization of the Front.[61] Janis Dzenitis, prosecutor of the Latvian SSR, managed in January 1989 to have the Latvian Supreme Soviet Presidium revoke a decision of the

Latvian Council of Ministers to establish an Interdepartmental Commission which, among other things, was charged with registering otherwise unofficial organizations and had quickly registered the PFL. Dzenitis argued that all-Union rather than republican laws should govern such organizations. The PFL was deregistered along with six other groups including the Jurists' Association, founded in November 1988. Still, the Latvian Front continued to function.

Latvia's Interfront, founded in January 1989, claimed to be the true defender of perestroika in the republic. Its leaders denounced Latvian nationalism and played up fears of Russians and other outsiders in the republic.

The power of the PFL was shown in 1989 elections to the USSR Congress of People's Deputies. Three-quarters of elected deputies were supporters of the Front.

In May 1989 the Latvian National Independence Movement (LNIM), at its second congress, and the PFL board affirmed as their goal an independent Latvia. The Front leadership adopted a draft program in June 1989 calling for "Latvia's independent statehood" following "the traditions of the Republic of Latvia." It rejected one-party rule and called for a multiparty system.[62]

The draft program also called for guarantees of equal rights for all inhabitants of Latvia regardless of national or other affiliation. While many Russians and other non-Latvians were extremely anxious about Latvian nationalism, the PFL worked in 1989 to promote a variety of minority and religious rights. It claimed to have helped Jews to start their own schools, and Poles to institute instruction in their own language, and to have promoted experiments in teaching the history of religion in several schools.

Despite the desire of many Latvians to establish such guarantees, some Jews complained of a resurgent anti-Semitism.

Another approach to change was the signature campaign in support of independence organized in Riga by Visvaldis Brinkmanis. By August 1989 he had registered 480,000 signatures on a personal computer. As soon as 800,000 had signed (a majority of ethnic Latvians), Brinkmanis planned to summon a "citizens' congress" to declare Latvia independent. Only citizens of the prewar republic and their direct descendants were eligible to sign, although non-Latvians could register as "candidate citizens" if they accepted the goal of an independent Latvia.[63]

Ivans addressed the PFL Duma in August 1989. He asserted that the Citizens' Committees and registration campaign of the LNIM were unsound and unrealistic. He favored instead step-by-step parliamentary activity in Riga and Moscow. One could not expect the Kremlin or the United Nations to welcome plenipotentiaries from an independent Latvian republic. If Front members could win elections, the PFL would have influence in the future Supreme Soviets. It would be illegal and dishonest for the PFL to take part in citizen registrations or to become a party. Parties could be formed independently of the PFL. Also, the more radical course could hurt the Front in elections to Latvia's Supreme Soviet.[64]

Defying Moscow's admonitions, the PFL leaders at the end of August drafted a program calling for "full economic and political independence" for Latvia within the USSR, as a "state of transition to complete independent statehood." The program stipulated not just economic self-financing but total economic independence; that any economic and political deals with Moscow be negotiated by treaty; that Latvia be allowed its own internal legal code including laws on private ownership; and called for establishment of a special department to oversee the transition to independence. Front leaders claimed 240,000 members, some 60,000 more than the CPL.[65]

A Latvian Communist, Viktor Alksnis, deputy to the USSR People's Congress, accused the PFL of adopting the Stalinist principle "He who is not with us is against us." The Front would permit only those who shared its viewpoint to speak, Alksnis charged.[66]

The Front, he said, wanted secession. He commended instead the September 1989 CPSU draft program on ethnic issues as a sober guide for Latvian policy. The CPL, Alksnis declared, should work to prevent "weeds of nationalist and separatist sentiments making themselves felt in my homeland—Latvia." He told how Latvian nationalists blamed all problems on the center, on Russian bureaucrats whom they associated with the Russian people. The nationalists "have started to instill methodically into the consciousness of the people" the idea that the Russians are "an aggressive, grasping, and lazy people of poor intellect."

"A nationalist mine is being placed beneath perestroika," said Alksnis, "essentially negating the development of the republic within the USSR." The PFL program banned "national hatred" and demanded equal rights for "all democratic parties and sociopolitical formations," but it also wanted "to halt the activity of organizations and parties organizationally subordinate to the USSR."

Alksnis denounced the PFL because it looked to the West for training in "the world's leading economic schools" and for capital and entrepreneurial leadership, "particularly from Latvians living abroad." All this was unrealistic, he said. Who would assume repayment for what the USSR supplied to Latvia? The CPSU Central Committee plenum reported that the USSR was supplying the lion's share of Latvia's industrial needs: 96 percent of its fuel, 50 percent of its electrical power, 50 percent of its ferrous metals and 100 percent of nonferrous metals, 80 percent of its raw materials and chemicals, and 63 percent of its machine building. Latvia, said Alksnis, was "producing expensive industrial output from cheap raw materials essentially through the heavy labor of Uzbek children and women. But what if our egocentrism permeates to Tyumen, which supplies us with oil and gas for next to nothing, what if it also raises the question of bringing [oil] prices into line with world prices?"

Latvian nationalists, Alksnis declared, were launching a totalitarian regime with cruel national repression against non-Latvians, reducing their civil rights. The draft PFL program said not one word about socialism but promised that Latvians will become full citizens at home among the "civilized Europeans of the North." The Front is "a precisely organized ideological machine, *based outside the boundaries of the state*...delicately catching the balance of political forces and the mood of society and reacting instantaneously to changes" [emphasis added]. The 1989 PFL program, he added, was more radical than the previous year's. The recent draft guaranteed "equal rights and equal existence for all peoples that support the ideas of independence." Its meaning was "masked, but unambiguous: the right to citizenship is acquired in exchange for support for the idea of separation."

A similar critique was put forward by Janis Vagris, First Secretary of the LCP Central Committee, in September 1989.[67] But he emphasized the positive and told how in August 1989 the CPL had drawn up and adopted a new action program entitled "Along the Path to Latvia's Sovereignty." The basic idea was: "There can be no sovereign Latvia without perestroika, nor can there be perestroika without a sovereign Latvia." The CPL would definitely remain a part of the CPSU, said Vagris, but the Latvian Party would consider two alternative formats at its next congress, to meet in about a year. Vagris noted that the Latvian National Independent Movement proposed separation. This he denounced as pure adventurism. It was better to work within the framework of the known, he said, adding that in January 1990 Latvians would start working in conditions of republican economic autonomy.

The CPL leader rebutted charges that he had tried to drive a wedge to split Baltic unity. Both he and Estonian leader Väljas had responded similarly to the CPSU August 26 statement on the Baltic. But Vagris also implied that Latvia was better behaved than its neighbors. He complained that the August 26 warning aggregated the Baltic countries, as if Latvia were as unruly as Estonia and Lithuania. In fact, he said, even the August 23, 1989, human chain across the Baltic was quite orderly in Latvia, although that night the LNIM held a meeting where one speaker said that "Communist Party members deserve the hangman's noose."

Vagris also complained that the Kremlin's August 26 statement repeatedly mentioned "nationalism" and "nationalists." Indigenous Latvians, he noted, had developed an "allergy" to such terms because they associated them with the CPSU "Central Committee July 1959 plenum and its consequences. This fact is highly important in our republic and it aggravates the situation." The phrase "1959...consequences" referred to the purge of virtually every native Latvian from positions of higher responsibility because of an alleged "Latvian bourgeois-nationalist deviation." [68]

The second PFL Congress met in October 1989. Some 330 journalists including eighty from abroad covered the sessions. A correspondent for *Red Star* observed that the Front "largely determines the current political situation in the republic."

Of 1,046 delegates to the Congress, 24 percent were CP members and 94.5 percent were Latvians. [69] Whether the Congress would endorse the draft program was not at all clear, because some 45 members of the 100-man PFL council were Party members and many of them were having second thoughts about the draft program's endorsement of Latvian independence. Some complained that the program was too extremist, in effect backing the same principles as the LNIM. [70]

The program adopted did in fact endorse Latvian independence and a multiparty system, albeit without setting a timetable. It also demanded that the

Latvian Supreme Soviet recognize as illegal Latvia's 1940 incorporation into the USSR and that the Latvian parliament be authorized to suspend USSR laws in Latvia. It called for "suspension of organizations and parties organizationally subordinate to the USSR or other countries"; for "demilitarization of Latvia's territory"; and for legalization and encouragement of private economic activity.[71]

The *Red Star* and other Moscow reporters cited a Latvian academic's analysis of Latvia's economy "under emergency conditions." Such an emergency could last four to six months, it assumed. The Kremlin would probably order an economic boycott of Latvia the day after "Latvia has acquired full independence." Supplies of electricity and fuel could stop, rolling stock come to a halt, and food supplies become irregular. Latvia could not expect massive Western aid. The analysis nonetheless urged independence and Latvia's nationalizing all means of production, and the financial and other resources administered by the USSR, since "the cost of many of them was recouped long ago, and the USSR has, so to speak, lost its right to them."

Red Star's reporter took umbrage that some Latvians demanded a right to alternative military service on the basis of "religious, political, moral and ethical persuasions — No less!" He noted also demands that no draftees from Latvia be obliged to serve outside the Baltic unless they expressed in writing their wish to do so.

Red Star concluded that the Congress showed that the Front was deeply divided between moderates and radicals associated with the LNIM. Indeed, their position had been "consolidated." PFL leader Ivans himself complained that the Front's bulletin *Atmoda* "has practically become a publication of the independence movement." [72] Ivans, however, was reelected chairman, having defeated a challenger from the LNIM.[73]

Reflecting the nearly equal Latvian-non-Latvian demographic balance within Latvia, the republic's Supreme Soviet in October 1989 eliminated the residence requirements for voting privileges adopted earlier in the year and condemned by Interfront and the Kremlin. Military personnel stationed in Latvia would thus be able to participate in elections on an equal basis with long-term residents.[74] These decisions followed recommendations by Anatolijs Gorbunovs, chairman of the Latvian Supreme Soviet, and a leading Communist.[75]

On November 10, 1989, Latvia's Supreme Soviet designated three new public holidays: Christmas Day, Janis Day (or Summer Solstice, June 24), and the Proclamation of the Republic of Latvia Day (November 18).

To commemorate the founding of an independent Latvia, roughly half of all Latvians living in the republic converged on Riga on November 18, 1989, including Party leader Vagris who, only two years before, had denounced those who celebrated this day. The 1989 demonstrators appealed to the U.S. and Soviet presidents not to regard Baltic independence as an internal affair of the USSR and to promote its restoration in accordance with CSCE accords reached at Helsinki and Vienna.[76]

A major player returned to Latvian politics when the Latvian Social Democratic Workers' Party (LSDWP) held its twentieth congress in Jurmala on December 2-3, 1989. The last congress, the nineteenth, had been in 1934, when the Social Democrats were Latvia's largest party. Indeed, the 1989 meeting marked the first time since 1940 that any political party active during Latvia's independence era had formally convened. Long despised by Latvian Communists, the LSDWP had become a valued member of the Socialist International and continued its existence abroad for fifty years.[77]

Latvian Communist authorities sought to prevent a rebirth of a Social Democratic party but failed, thanks in part to visible support for the group from Willy Brandt, chairman of the Socialist International. Financial support for the December 1989 convention came from the Popular Front of Latvia, which the LSDWP saw as an umbrella organization for all reformist forces in the republic. The Twentieth Congress, with 180 delegates representing an active membership of about 600, agreed that the party would now be based in Latvia and that it should be regarded as the representative of all Latvian Social Democrats in the Socialist International. The party pledged itself to a "free and independent Latvia" and to various reforms, such as alternative service for Latvians not wishing to swear allegiance to the Soviet army or the CPSU. But the Social Democrats saw their immediate task as winning votes in elections to local councils and the republic's Supreme Soviet. This set them off from some independence groups that spurned participation in the electoral processes of an occupied land.

The overall situation had an impact on the Latvian Komsomol, in which membership declined from 300,000 in 1987 to 223,000 in 1989. First Secretary

Ivaars Priyeditis spoke bluntly: "Under conditions of a totalitarian state the Latvian Komsomol has turned from a democratic sociopolitical youth organization into a public monster with a vast bureaucratic structure." Its prestige, he said, was being maintained at a certain level thanks to economic and foreign-travel privileges granted to Komsomol members. If they dropped away, membership would plummet still further. Komsomol activists were debating some basic issues: Should the Latvian organization remain affiliated with the all-Union Komsomol? Should it remain a Communist youth league or become just a youth organization? Should it abandon Lenin's name, as had been done in Lithuania? Would it be supplanted by scouting or other movements recently reactivated? The scouts, he noted, had their offices in the same building as the Popular Front.[78]

On February 15, 1990, Latvia's Supreme Soviet adopted a declaration calling for the transformation of "the Latvian SSR into an independent Latvia." It established a commission to prepare for a referendum on restoration of independence and the drafting of treaties that would define Latvia's relations with other states. This resolution brought Latvia into line with similar declarations by the Supreme Soviets of Estonia and Lithuania on November 12 and 23, 1989.[79]

The February 15 statement was too weak for the pro-independence groups elected to Latvia's Supreme Soviet in March. The new body on May 4 issued a declaration proclaiming the reestablishment of Latvia's independence. The vote was 138 for, one abstention, and fifty-seven deputies refusing to vote, because the resolution was "unconstitutional." The declaration provided for a transition period before reestablishing the republic's de facto independence, to end with the convening of the parliament (Saeima) of Latvia. During the transition period Latvia's Supreme Soviet would exercise "supreme authority in Latvia." The declaration promised full political and other human rights, consistent with international standards, to Soviet citizens, non-Latvians, who wanted to continue living in Latvia.

Kto kovo?

Three Davids struggled against a Goliath determined to use the many levers of power it still controlled to thwart or at least delay their quest for independence. To repeat Stalin's question about the pope, "How many divisions" did Estonia, Latvia, and Lithuania have against the Kremlin? None.

The three Davids tried to develop a common stand. The Baltic Council of popular fronts, now meeting every month, convened in Vilnius in late March 1990. The popular fronts of Estonia and Latvia supported Lithuania and pledged to seek independence from the USSR side by side. The Council called on Moscow "to stop its military scare tactics and pressure toward Lithuania, and also inciting its citizens to break the laws of the Lithuanian government." The Balts urged Moscow instead to take up constructive negotiations.[80]

The three Baltic heads of government meeting in Vilnius in April signed an Agreement on the Baltic Market that, Estonian Prime Minister Savisaar said, had been discussed for a year and would be in force until A.D. 2000. "irrespective of whether or not all three republics are part of the USSR. A Council of Cooperation and a Commission would be headquartered in Riga. A common financial fund and an investment bank were also planned, but not a common currency.[81]

Estonian and Latvian delegations met with top Soviet leaders in mid-April, but went home disappointed. Arnold Rüütel reported that the Kremlin "did not want to listen" and no further talks were scheduled. Ivans said that Gorbachev did not "understand that the demand for independence is not confined to extremists, but is shared by the majority." Still, commissions of experts from the republics and from Moscow were tasked to work on the outstanding issues between them.[82]

On May 12, 1990, the presidents of all three Baltic Supreme Soviets signed an agreement renewing the pre-1940 Baltic Council. Meeting each month, the Council reaffirmed the Baltic states' interest in participating in the CSCE process and the Council of Europe. The Council called for international mediation to facilitate negotiations between the Baltic states and the USSR. The Council refused to "recognize any obligations...which may result from bilateral agreements" signed by Gorbachev and Bush at their June 1990 summit.

Savisaar broadened Estonia's contacts abroad in June 1990 by visiting Slovenia, the richest state in Yugoslavia, striving for more autonomy from Belgrade. In May 1990 the Slovenian parliament recognized the right of each Baltic parliament to declare its republic's independence. Savisaar signed an agreement with Slovenia's prime minister detailing future areas of cooperation between Estonia and Slovenia and calling for CSCE action to "influence positively" the restoration of Baltic independence.

On July 21, 1990, the three Baltic governments — freely elected and increasingly independent — denounced the fiftieth anniversary of the Soviet takeover. The Latvian Supreme Soviet's Council said that the date marked the beginning of "mass terror and genocide against the residents of Latvia."

On July 27 the three Baltic heads of state issued a declaration announcing that no representatives of their governments would take part in the drafting of a new USSR Union treaty. They also insisted that in drafting treaties with foreign countries or other republics, Baltic independence had to be recognized; that the three-plus-one principle was favored in Baltic-Soviet talks; that the Baltic republics had no territorial claims against one another; and that if any of the other twelve Union republics had territorial, property, or other claims against the Baltic republics, they should make them known within one month.

The Baltic Council meeting on July 28 was attended also by RSFSR President Boris Yeltsin, who had vacationed at the Latvian resort town Jurmala. The four parties agreed to sign bilateral treaties within two months on issues of mutual concern, including recognition of the independence of Baltic states. The Council reiterated Baltic refusal to take part in formulation of a new Union Treaty for the USSR.

Baltic officials also reached agreement to work toward a common economic market with Russia, Belorussia, Moldavia, and the cities of Leningrad and Moscow. They agreed to resist Soviet efforts to dictate economic policy from Moscow and condemned organizations such as Integral, created by the USSR Council of Ministers in July. Integral, a conglomerate of all-Union enterprises, joined Estonian organizations in an "independent industrial-economic complex" dealing directly with Moscow.

In August 1990 the autonomous republic of Karelia, linked to Estonia and Finland by a related tongue and history, declared its sovereignty. Home to 700,000 people, Karelia declared that its constitution and laws took precedence over those of the USSR and the RSFSR, in which it was located. Karelia's Supreme Soviet hesitated to confront and possibly derail Yeltsin's democratic course for the RSFSR. But Karelia's Popular Front asked: "After Yeltsin — What?" Some of its leaders believed that guarantees for Karelia's autonomy needed to be established in case Yeltsin's successors were less benevolent.[83]

In August the Latvian Supreme Soviet resolved to open a customs office on the border with Belorussia to stem the drain of items in short supply being taken by travelers to Belorussia.

That same month, Estonia's Supreme Soviet set out guidelines for independence talks with Moscow: The USSR Constitution with its secession clause did not apply to Estonia; Estonia would not take part in drafting a new Union treaty; the Soviet military presence in Estonia was illegal without a Soviet-Estonian agreement; the basis of talks had to be the 1920 Tartu Peace Treaty and other Soviet-Estonian accords prior to 1940, supplemented by recent Estonian laws. Two groups of deputies refused to take part in the vote, saying that the rights of all residents had not been considered.

With these guidelines to work on, Savisaar in August began talks with USSR Prime Minister Nikolai Ryzhkov and with RSFSR representatives. Ryzhkov was reported to approve Estonia's establishing its own customs controls on its border with the RSFSR, but the head of the Soviet customs administration said that legislation was being prepared to establish a unified customs system for the entire USSR. Officials of the RSFSR on August 16 agreed in principle to a political accord recognizing Estonia as an independent state under international law.

In 1990 the Scandinavian governments, Poland, and Germany moved toward setting up information or business centers in the Baltic. Parliamentarians from Czechoslovakia and Poland joined with Baltic counterparts to demand admission of the Baltic states to the CSCE process. But the formal agencies of power held back. The CSCE, Council of Europe, and European Parliament delayed giving a positive response to Baltic requests to rejoin formally the European community of nations. In September even the generally liberal government of Czechoslovakia refused to establish formal relations with Lithuania. Prime Minister Marian Calfa suggested, however, that Czechoslovakia's two constituent republics could promote their own ties with Lithuania. Prime Minister Prunskiene replied that she would favor direct relations with the federal government in Prague as well as with the Czech and Slovak republics. Baltic republics got more substantial results as they forged direct trade links with Leningrad, Kiev, and various regions of the erstwhile Soviet Union.

On September 5 the Baltic governments issued a statement welcoming the impending unification of Germany, but emphasized that the consequences of

World War II in Europe would not be overcome until independence was restored to the Baltic states. A Polish senator declared: "The only relic that remains from World War II, after German unification, is the denial of independence to the three Baltic republics."

How history would play out was unclear, but the moral and political contest between nationalism and communism was over. Communists fared even more poorly in republic elections in 1990 than they did in elections for the USSR Congress of People's Deputies a year before. Even when republic Communist parties averred their independence from the CPSU, they were tarred by their past. Individual leaders such as Lithuania's Brazauskas could still be elected, but their parties and programs were rejected.

As in East Central Europe, most Balts except for some Russian settlers rejected not only Moscow but Marx. They favored not just national self-determination and democratic politics but free enterprise. The collapse of Communist institutions to the west and south inspired and encouraged Balts, especially during the initial euphoria that preceded hardships and bickering as non-Communists tried to rebuild the life of Poland and other devastated countries. Even after the difficulties of starting afresh became manifest, Balts hoped that they might learn from the experiences of their neighbors.

NOTES

1. On the rationale, see J. V. Stalin's 1913 essay, "Marxism and the National Question," in Joseph Stalin, *Marxism and the National-Colonial Question* (San Francisco: Proletarian, 1975), pp. 15-99. For the later split between Stalin and Lenin, see documents in Richard Pipes, *The Formation of the Soviet Union*, rev. ed. (New York: Atheneum, 1968), pp. 282-93. For commentary, see Leonid Radzikhovsky, "Testament," *Moscow News*, No. 16 (29 April-6 May 1990), p. 6.

2. Mikk Titma, a sociologist, interviewed in *Der Standard* (Vienna), 12 October 1989, p. 3, Foreign Broadcast Information Service, *Daily Report: Soviet Union* [*FBIS-SOV*] (Washington, D.C.), 17 October 1989, pp. 86-87.

3. Romas Gudaitis in *Sovetskaia Litva*, 5 December 1989, pp. 2-3, *Current Digest of the Soviet Press*, 41, 49 (1989), p. 6.

4. The vote was 242 to 1, with 39 abstentions. Most members of the parliament were CP members and had been elected five years earlier. As amended the Lithuanian Constitution's

Article 6 stated: "Parties, social organizations and social movements are formed according to the procedure stipulated by law and function according to the constitution [and laws] of the Lithuanian Republic."

5. For statements by leaders of the Estonian National Independence Party and other groups more radical than the PFE, see Michael Tarm and Mari-Ann Rikken, eds., *Documents from Estonia...April 1986 to March 1989* (New York: Estonian American National Council, 1989). See also Tönu Parming, "The Estonian Popular Front: Between Reformist Collaboration and Estonian National Aspirations," paper, Conference on the Contemporary Baltic, Munich, September 1989. Estonians dispute how to translate *Eestimaa Rahvarinne* — PFE or Estonian People's Front or Estonian Popular Front.

6. See also Rein Taagepera, "A Note on the March 1989 Elections in Estonia," *Soviet Studies*, 42, 2 (April 1990), pp. 329-39. On the impact of glasnost, see Walter C. Clemens, Jr., "Estonia, A Place to Watch," *The National Interest*, No. 13 (Fall 1988), pp. 85-92.

7. Mikk Titma in *Der Standard*, 12 October 1989. For elaboration of his views — part sociology, part ideology — see his *Estoniia: Chto u nas proiskhodit?* (Tallinn: Perioodika, 1989).

8. That the "second secretary" of the Estonian Communist Party is Russian, Panfilov said, results from an "instruction [*ukazanie*]" from Moscow. Interviewed on 10 March 1990. The Tallinn CPE headquarters provided a gleaming and spacious contrast to the Estonian Academy of Sciences and various editorial offices I visited.

9. Dmitrii Mikhailov, interviewed in *Sovetskaia Estoniia*, 19 September 1989, p. 2, *FBIS-SOV*, 17 October 1989, pp. 88-89. C. Wright Mills might rejoice to find so many sociologists in Estonia's power elite: In 1989 they included Mikhailov, chairing the board of the Society of Russian Culture; Edgar Savisaar, early leader of the PFE (whose spiritual father, some believed, was political sociologist Rein Taagepera, University of California at Irvine); CPE ideological secretary Mikk Titma; also my hosts at the Estonian Academy of Sciences, Priit Järve and Tiiu Pohl. North American sociologist Tönu Parming was elected to the Council of the Congress of Estonia in March 1990. If these trends continued, Estonia might test Plato's wish that "philosophers become kings." In the Kremlin, meanwhile, the king, like his wife, claimed to be a philosopher. In May 1990 Savisaar became Estonia's prime minister.

10. Rein Veidemann interviewed on Tallinn Domestic Service, 15 October 1989, *FBIS-SOV*, 18 October 1989, pp. 85-86.

11. Ibid.

12. A few smaller parties also got some votes. See "On Political Scene, Interests Unravel," *Homeland*, No. 2 (263), 17 January 1990, pp. 1,2.

13. "Popular Front to Run Elections as 'Single Bloc'," *Homeland*, No. 6-7 (267-268), 21 February 1990, pp. 1,3.

14. "Estonian Communists Look for New Ways," *Homeland*, No. 6-7 (267-268), 21 February 1990, pp. 1,3.

15. See the Russian-language newspaper *Respublika* that commenced publication in December 1989, supporting a free and independent statehood for Estonia. The political and personal importance of knowing the local language came out in a survey of Baltic Germans: Rasma Karklins, "Ethnic Interaction in the Baltic Republics: Interviews with Recent Emigrants," *Journal of Baltic Studies*, 12, 1 (Spring 1981), pp. 16-34.

16. The Society of Jewish Culture in Tallinn published *Khashakhar "Rassvet"* in Russian. The 30 January 1990 number reported on the First Congress of Jewish Organizations and Communities of the USSR, held in Moscow in December 1989. The entire issue linked

Pamiat with Nazism and suggested some CPSU backing for anti-Semitism. One such article by Aleksandr Levin was reprinted in the PFE newspaper *Vestnik,* No. 4 (38), February 1990, p. 7.

17. Interviewed in Tallinn, 9 March 1990.

18. "This job greatly improved my education," he said. "I could read — under good light — for nine of my fifteen hours on the job." Pay: 150 rubles a month, close to the Soviet average. Conversation at Harvard University, 18 April 1990.

19. Tobias has been called an Estonian Sibelius or Smetana. To me his music is cleaner and less sentimental than theirs.

20. Personal communication. See also Rein Taagepera, "The Baltic States," *Electoral Studies,* 9, 4 (1990), pp. 303-11. For background, see Rein Taagepera and Matthew S. Shugart, *Seats and Votes: The Effects and Determinants of Electoral Systems* (New Haven: Yale University Press, 1989).

21. By the analysis of Tõnu Parming (a sociologist elected to the Council), ENIP members got the most votes to the Council (five of the top ten, nine of the top twenty), whereas no leading member of the PFE scored in the top five and only two among the top twenty. The Heritage Society, two Christian parties, and the Union of Workers' Councils got only one or two places each in the top rankings.

Without regard to top vote getters, the PFE won the most seats on the Council: 18, followed by the ENIP, 17; the EHS, 6; the Liberal Democrats, 3; Green Movement, 3; Union of Work Collectives, 2, Social Democratic Independence Party, 2; CPSU, 2; Conservative People's Party, 2; Christian Democratic League, 1; Christian Democratic Party, 1; others and independent, 14. See *Homeland,* No. 10-11 (271-272), 21 March 1990, p. 2.

The PFE's weak showing came in spite of the fact that it was the only faction to hold caucuses and to attempt disciplined voting during the Congress — another testimony to the importance of election rules.

For origins of the Union of Work Collectives, see *FBIS-SOV,* 8 January 1990, p. 51, and 5 February 1990, p. 89; for the CDU, *FBIS-SOV,* 17 November 1989, pp. 61-62; for the Conservative People's Party, *FBIS-SOV,* 5 February 1990, p. 88.

22. The resolution had been proposed by Marju Lauristin and was rejected in part because its style differed from other Congress documents. But the many speeches attacking the resolution seemed also to attack her, perhaps because her father had been a Soviet collaborator in 1940.

23. When the journalists went to a factory and asked to interview rank-and-file workers, they were presented — after a long wait — with men wearing newly pressed overalls and spouting the Intermovement line, a throwback to Stalinist times. Interview with Tarmu Tammerk, 14 March 1990.

24. Address at the Arco Forum, Harvard University, 18 April 1990.

25. Arvo Kuddo, "Can Estonia Make It Alone?" *Homeland,* No. 13 (274), 4 April 1990. p. 2.

26. Saulius Girnius, "Lithuania," *Report on the USSR* (Radio Liberty), 29 December 1989, pp. 25-26. For detailed analysis of events in 1988, see Alfred Erich Senn, *Lithuania Awakening — 1988* (Berkeley: University of California Press, 1990); on more recent developments, see Senn, "Toward Lithuanian Independence: Algirdas Brazauskas and the CPL," *Problems of Communism,* 34, 2 (March-April 1990) pp. 21-28.

27. See also V. Stanley Vardys, "Lithuanian National Politics," *Problems of Communism,* 38, 4 (July-August 1989), pp. 53-76.

28. James Blitz, "Lithuania Heads for Break with Moscow," *Financial Times*, 24 August 1989, p. 2. For details on Sajudis action, see above, chap. 9.

29. Saulius Girnius, "Lithuania," p. 25.

30. Excerpts in *The New York Times*, 27 August 1989, p. 18.

31. James Blitz, "Lithuanians Ponder How Far They Can Push Moscow," *Financial Times*, 26 August 1989, p. 2.

32. Valerijonas Balrunas, quoted by James Blitz, "Lithuania Heads for Break," p. 2.

33. *Sovetskaia kul'tura*, 7 October 1989, p. 2, *FBIS-SOV*, 17 October 1989, pp. 82-83.

34. Edvinas Butkus commentary on Lithuanian CP CC plenum in October 1989, Vilnius in English to North America, 12 October 1989, *FBIS-SOV*, 17 October 1989, pp. 80-81.

35. *Sovetskaia Litva*, 20 September 1989, p. 1, *FBIS-SOV*, 17 October 1989, pp. 81-82.

36. Vilnius in English to North America, 23 [*sic*] October 1989, *FBIS-SOV*, 20 October 1989, p. 54. For analysis and warnings about possible methodological failings, see Saulius Girnius, "Sociological Surveys in Lithuania," *Report on the USSR* (Radio Liberty), 10 November 1989, pp. 24-26.

37. Liubov [as given] Chernays interviewed on Moscow Domestic Service, 18 October 1989, *FBIS-SOV*, 20 October 1989, pp. 54-55.

38. Algimantas Cekuolis in *Gimtasis Krastis*, No. 38, 21-27 September 1989, p. 2, *FBIS-SOV*, 17 October 1989, pp. 83-84.

39. Leonidas Jacinevicius, "To Cross the Rubicon," *Literatura ir Menas*, No. 41, 7 October 1989, p. 2, *FBIS-SOV*, 24 October 1989, pp. 62-63.

40. Report in *Sovetskaia Litva*, 2 December 1989, pp. 1-2.

41. Romas Gudaitis, secretary of the Party organization in the Lithuanian Writers' Union, in *Sovetskaia Litva*, 5 December 1989, pp. 2-3.

42. Adopted December 21. Two weeks passed before the Russian text was printed in *Sovetskaia Litva*, 5 January 1990, pp. 1,2.

43. See Saulius Girnius, "The Lithuanian Communist Party versus Moscow," *Report on the USSR*, (Radio Liberty) 5 January 1990, pp. 6-8.

44. See *Pravda* (Moscow), 20 December 1989, p. 3; 21 December p. 3; 22 December, p. 3; *Izvestiia*, 23 December 1989, p. 12.

45. Resolution proposed on 23 December 1989 broadcast on Vilnius Domestic Service in Lithuanian, 23 December 1989, *FBIS-SOV* 26 December 1989, p. 55. See also the detailed exposition of these crimes and mistakes by historian Liudas Truskain, *FBIS-SOV*, 26 December 1989, pp. 54-55.

46. Vilnius Domestic Service in Lithuanian, 26 January 1990, *FBIS-SOV*, 29 January 1990 p. 73.

47. *The New York Times*, 12 January 1990, pp. 1ff.

48. Interview broadcast on Moscow World Service in English, 23 December 1989, *FBIS-SOV*, 26 December 1989, p. 54.

49. Nikolai Lashkevich telephone report: "Lithuania: Future Cannot Be Built on Foundations of Conflicts," *Soiuz*, No. 2 (8-14 January 1990), p. 2, *FBIS-SOV*, 29 January 1990, pp. 76-78.

50. Vilnius Domestic Service in Lithuanian on 15 January 1990, *FBIS-SOV*, 17 January 1990, pp. 116-17.

51. Moscow World Service in English, 28 January 1990, *FBIS-SOV*, 29 January 1990, p. 73.

52. Vilnius Domestic Service in Lithuanian, 26 January 1990, *FBIS-SOV*, 29 January 1990, pp. 73-74.

53. Three generations of the Landsbergis family have been involved in the arts and politics, struggling for Lithuania's independence. See *Baltiia: Daidzhest pressy respublik Pribaltiki* (Riga), May 1990, p. 4.

54. Alexei Levinson, "Vilnius Residents Polled," *Moscow News,* No. 16 (29 April-6 May 1990), p. 11.

55. The pipeline from Klaipeda to the refinery was designed for petrochemical products, not crude. Also, port facilities in Klaipeda were probably too small to handle large Norwegian tankers.

56. See Michael Kaser, John Lloyd, Robert Taylor and Karen Fossell in *Financial Times,* 20 April 1990, pp. 1,3.

57. Interviewed by Vladimir Gurevich, "Lithuanian Balance," *Moscow News,* No. 16 (29 April-6 May 1990), p. 11.

58. Bill Keller, "For Lithuania, Few Allies in Moscow," *The New York Times,* 27 March 1990, p. A12.

59. Leonid Mlechin interviewed by Linda Feldman, *The Christian Science Monitor,* 26 March 1990, p. 2.

60. Dzintra Bungs, "People's Front of Latvia: The First Year," *Report on the USSR* (Radio Liberty), 1, 41 (13 October 1989), pp. 25-27.

61. See Juris Dreifelds, "Latvian National Rebirth," *Problems of Communism,* 38, 4 (July-August 1989), pp. 77-95.

62. Other groups pressing for independence included the human rights group Helsinki 86 and the Republican Party.

63. Michael Dobbs, "Baltic Independence Groups, Gaining Strength, Predict Showdown with Moscow," *International Herald Tribune,* 28 August 1989, p. 6.

64. D. Ivans, "Our Path Is Parliamentary Struggle," *Sovetskaia Latviia,* 24 August 1989, p. 3, *FBIS-SOV,* 18 October 1989, pp. 77-78. Dates as given.

65. Esther B. Fein, "Latvians to Seek 'Special Status' within the U.S.S.R.," *The New York Times,* 1 September 1989, pp. A1, A8.

66. Like Gustav Husak and many other dogmatic Communists, Alksnis and his family themselves suffered from Stalinism: His grandfather was a deputy commissar of defense and chief of the Soviet Air Force. The air chief and wife were arrested in 1937. Alksnis's father was left alone but the boy was sent to a children's home. From 1941 to 1957 he worked in a Siberian mine. In 1957 he was rehabilitated. He found his grandmother and moved to Riga, but for years they could not talk of the dark past. Viktor Alksnis interviewed in *Sovetskaia Rossiia,* 1 October 1989, p. 3, *FBIS-SOV,* 24 October 1989, pp. 64-66.

67. Interviewed on the television program "Leadership's Opinion," 31 August 1989. Printed as "There Can be No Sovereign Latvia without Perestroika, There Can be No Perestroika Without Sovereign Latvia," *Sovetskaia Latviia,* 6 September 1989, pp. 1, 2, *FBIS-SOV,* 24 October 1989, pp. 66-68.

68. Similar purges occurred in Estonia and Lithuania at different times. Purges in Lithuania, however, were generally mild compared to those in Estonia and Latvia. See Alexander Shtromas, "The Baltic States," in Robert Conquest, ed., *The Last Empire: Nationality and the Soviet Future* (Stanford, Calif.: Hoover Institution Press, 1986), pp. 183-217, at pp. 199-200.

69. See reports in *Izvestiia,* 10 October 1989, p. 2; *Pravda,* 11 October 1989, p. 3; Moscow Domestic Service, 9 October 1989 — all in *FBIS-SOV,* 11 October 1989, pp. 67-68.

70. Bungs, "People's Front of Latvia," p. 27.

71. See especially the congress resolutions "On the Elimination of the CPSU's Monopoly of Power," and "On the Assessment of the Political Events of 1940."

72. Lt. Col. M. Ziyeminsh, "In the Grip of 'Emergency Conditions'," *Krasnaia Zvezda*, 14 October 1989, p. 2, *FBIS-SOV*, 18 October 1989, pp. 75-77.

73. Some readers of *Red Star* would probably prefer to read that a meeting was held in Riga to recall the "unforgettable events of fall 1944 when Soviet troops passed through the liberated capital" of Latvia. "The Memory of the Heroes Is Still Alive," *Krasnaia Zvezda*, 12 October 1989, p. 4, *FBIS-SOV*, 18 October 1989, p. 78.

74. "Amber Coast" radio program from Riga in Latvian to Europe, 8 October 1989, *FBIS-SOV*, 12 October 1989, pp. 49-50.

75. He opposed suggestions to add a Congress of People's Deputies to the existing republic government structure. He argued that it is good for Latvia that the commander of the Baltic Military District is a USSR People's Deputy. Citizens Committees, he agreed with Ivans, are a bad idea, saying that it is more useful to get on with our first free elections. He added, however, that a multiparty system is an idea whose time has come. The leading role of the Communist Party can be assured only by its political activity and the results of its work. Interview with A. Gorbunovs on Riga television, 7 September 1989, printed in *Sovetskaia Latviia*, 12 September 1989, pp. 2,3, *FBIS-SOV*, 18 October 1989, pp. 78-85.

76. Dzintra Bungs, "Latvian Independence Day: 600,000 Demonstrators Appeal to Bush and Gorbachev," *Report on the USSR*, (Radio Liberty) 1 December 1989, pp. 23-24.

77. Dzintra Bungs, "Twentieth Congress of Latvian Social Democrats," *Report on the USSR*, (Radio Liberty) 12 January 1990, pp. 24-27.

78. Karen Markaryan, "Every Day in This Spot," *Komsomol'skaia pravda*, 5 October 1989, p. 1, *FBIS-SOV*, 17 October 1989, pp. 85-86.

79. Text and analysis in Dzintra Bungs, "A Further Step Towards Latvian Independence," *Report on the USSR*, (Radio Liberty) 2 March 1990, p. 25.

80. Quentin Peel, "Baltic Nationalists to Seek Freedom in Three Republics," *Financial Times*, 26 March 1990, p. 1.

81. Gurevich, "Lithuanian Balance," *Moscow News*, No. 16 (29 April-6 May 1990), p. 11.

82. John Lloyd, "Gorbachev Sets Out on Collision Course with Estonia and Latvia," *Financial Times*, 20 April 1990, p. 1.

83. A commemorative edition of Finland's epic *Kalevala* (Helsinki: Otava, 1988) pointed out that most of the runos comprising the epic were collected in Russian Karelia where the Orthodox faith prevailed. An epic full of pre-Christian gods also honored cross pendants. A gourmet treat described in the poem was "sliver-sliced" bread which, in olden times, was made of wheat imported from Russia rather than the thick crusts of local rye.

12

The Center Does Not Hold: No Soviet Melting Pot

The USSR could in principle draw upon the strengths of Europe, Asia, and the Transcaucasus; on several forms of Christianity, Islam, Buddhism, Judaism, and other religions; and on cultures as diverse as Georgian and Mongolian. In practice, these diverse elements became a burden — part of Gorbachev's composite problem — rather than parts of the solution. They produced not synergy but entropy. The peoples of the USSR were not speaking the same language. The center did not hold. An empire based on coercion could not benefit from its cultural diversity. Joint value-creation for the empire's many peoples was difficult if not impossible.

Gone was Nikita Khrushchev's boast that the Soviet peoples were "merging" and Leonid Brezhnev's claim that they were at least "converging." The 1989 census confirmed that the Soviet "Union" was exploding, rent by centrifugal forces. Most of the major nationalities were turning inward, integrating less rather than more with those of other faiths, races, and regions.[1]

Final returns from the 1989 census, *The Estonian Independent* reported on April 18, 1990, showed that Estonia had the greatest mechanical population growth of any Soviet republic, with 36.6 new immigrants for every 10,000 inhabitants. Latvia had 36 and Lithuania 28.3. In the previous decade Estonian natives increased by 1.6 percent compared to 16.6 percent for non-Estonians in the republic. In January 1989 there were 1,572,900 people in Estonia of whom 963,000 were ethnic Estonians (61.5 percent), whose average age was

35.8 years. Russians made up 30.3 percent, Belorussians 1.8 percent, Finns 1.1 percent, and Jews 0.3 percent of the republic's population.

Estonia's urban population increased by 10.1 percent, from 69.7 percent in 1979 to 71.6 percent in 1989 — exceeded only by the RSFSR, where 74 percent lived in towns. Most of Estonia's Russians, Ukrainians, Belorussians, and Jews lived in towns or urban settlements, but only 59.4 percent of Estonians.

According to the census, 33.6 percent of Estonians spoke fluent Russian and 13.3 percent of non-Estonians could speak Estonian.

Estonia had the lowest illiteracy rate of any Soviet republic-0.3 percent. Of 1,000 inhabitants, 801 had higher or secondary education.

Over half of Estonia's residents — 54.3 percent — worked in the state sector; 25.8 percent were dependents; 17.1 percent, pensioners; 15.1 percent had two sources of income.

The census figures showed that the USSR's population grew by 9 percent in the 1980s, reaching 286.7 million in 1989. But this aggregate figure masked wide discrepancies, because the Muslim republics grew many times faster than the European. The Central Asian republics of Uzbekistan, Turkmenia, Kirghizia, and Tadzhikistan grew 22-34 percent; Azerbaijan, 17 percent; Kazakhstan, 13 percent. The European, traditionally Christian regions grew at less than the USSR average: the Russian Republic, Belorussia, and Estonia grew by 7 percent; Latvia, 6 percent; the Ukraine, 4 percent. Parts of central Russia grew only 1-6 percent, although scarcely populated parts of the Far East and Siberia grew 12-16 percent. Some regions of the Russian Republic, the Ukraine, and Belorussia lost population.

Most Muslim republics also experienced strong increases in rural population. In the 1980s it shot up by 23-39 percent in most of Central Asia, where unemployment was already high. In Azerbaijan it increased by 15 percent. Rural population increased slightly in Kazakhstan and in Christian Armenia and Estonia.

The USSR's rural population stood at 97.9 million, down 0.9 percent since 1979. Most rural regions of the Russian Republic and the Ukraine and all of Belorussia were depopulated, although the 1980s' hemorrhage was much less than in the years 1970-1978. Whereas 14.6 of 1,000 rural dwellers left the countryside in the 1970s, the flow slowed to 9.3 in the 1980s.

Central Asians were multiplying much faster than most other Soviets, but few moved to the Russian or other republics where most industrial jobs were concentrated. And almost none moved to the Russian countryside, where agriculture was losing needed workers. Rural areas in Central Asia with too many hands were getting more – a problem aggravated by military force reductions. In 1987 M. S. Gorbachev asked Dr. Alexander King, president of the Club of Rome, to investigate and recommend ways that the USSR could cope with its "pandemic unemployment problem in a humane way."

An urban-countryside divide was being added to the European-Muslim chasm. City populations increased relative to the countryside in most republics but not in Central Asia. In the entire USSR city dwellers increased to 188.8 million, up 15 percent since 1979. One-third of the increase came from country people moving to cities. The USSR in 1989 was 66 percent urban, compared with 62 percent in 1979. The most urbanized republics were the Russian (74 percent), Estonian (72 percent), and Latvian (71 percent), while Central Asia and Moldavia ranged from 33 to 47 percent in urbanization. Although the USSR had twenty-nine cities with million-plus populations in 1989, none was in the Baltic. Riga came closest, with 915,000 residents; Vilnius had 582,000; Tallinn, 482,000.

There was less grist for a Soviet *West Side Story*. Endogamy, marriage within the same ethnic group, increased in the 1980s. Nearly all Armenian men in Armenia married other Armenians – 98 percent. For Central Asians, the number was close to 95 percent. Kazakhs tended to marry Kazakhs even though they were outnumbered by Russians in Kazakhstan. In the Baltic the share of endogamous marriages went up after 1978: in Lithuania, from 92 to 94 percent; in Estonia, from 90 to 91 percent; in Latvia, the lowest ratio of all Union Republics, by less than 1 percent, to 80 percent. In Russia, however, endogamy declined from 91 to 90 percent. In most republics the ratio of women marrying their own nationality was slightly lower than these figures for men.

Some minorities did not hold their own. Tatars, living in their own Autonomous Republic enveloped by Russia, married their own kind only 61 percent of the time, down from 70 percent a decade before. In 1989 only 27 percent of Jewish men in the RSFSR married other Jews – down drastically from 41 percent in 1978.

Latvians and Estonians were being engulfed by Russians. Of all marriages in Latvia in 1989, 11,900 involved Latvian men; 9,143, Russian men. For Estonia, the numbers were 6,914 Estonian men; 4,526 Russian men, a 10 percent increase for Russians relative to Estonians since 1978. Even these numbers understated the Russian presence, since many Russians were already married when they moved to the Baltic republics.

Central Asian women had about five children on the average in 1989 compared with just over two in Belorussia, the Ukraine, the Baltic, and the RSFSR. Overall, the number of women having two or three children rather than one went up sharply, but the results were again skewed by Central Asia. For the entire country, rural women had 1.4 more children than urban. The more urbanized European sections, therefore, were likely to have low or no population growth while Central Asia soared.

More did not necessarily mean better, or richer. Average life spans in most European republics were longer than in most Muslim. As of 1989 the average Soviet citizen lived to be 69.5 years (64.8 for men, as against 73.6 years for the average woman, despite her many chores). As Soviet demographers point out, the average Soviet life span in 1989 was five to eight years shorter than in the U.S., Western Europe, and Japan. Comparisons in Turkmenia, Moldavia, and Kirghizia were still less favorable, because life spans there averaged only 66-68 years.

Soviet authorities acknowledged that mortality increased throughout the USSR in the second half of the 1960s and throughout the 1970s. This happened in part because the overall population aged, but people also started to die younger, especially working men. Alcoholism led to traumatic accidents and impaired blood circulation. The State Committee on Statistics claimed that the antialcohol campaigns started in mid-1985 quickly produced a 1.8 year gain in average life span, but said (equally implausibly) that these gains halted after early 1986.

Inequality reigned. Differences at every level — economic, ecological, educational — were reflected in rates of infant mortality. Little improvement in infant mortality was reported in the 1980s. By 1989 it averaged at least 24.7 deaths per 1,000 children in their first year — 2.5 to 5 times higher than in many "developed capitalist countries," the State Statistics Committee reported, probably undercounting Soviet death rates. Individual Soviet republics differed a great deal. The highest reported infant mortality was in Tadzhikistan — 49 per 1,000, compared with 11 in Latvia, 11.5 in Lithuania, 12.4 in Estonia and 18.9 in Russia. If Soviet physicians recorded infant deaths by international standards, Soviet infant mortality would probably have been reported as at least 25 percent higher.

The infant mortality figures suggested that Balts lived better in many respects than other Soviet citizens. The 1989 census also confirmed that Muslim peoples were increasing rapidly while most Europeans, including the Balts, barely reproduced themselves. The health standards of the Muslims were lower and the unemployment higher than among Europeans.[2] Ecological wild cards could become grim reapers: Belorussian scientists warned in 1990 that the toll from the nuclear plant meltdown at Chernobyl toll would be much larger than so far estimated. Central Asians worried about the effects of nuclear testing and about the drying up of the Aral Sea. Balts and others worried about air, groundwater, and their seas.

What Should Be Done? What Could Be Done?

The Kremlin faced the classic double bind of any exploitative regime: Continued repression was no longer cost-effective and could trigger a revolution, one that could be put down, but only at considerable damage to the regime's interests. Concessions, on the other hand, could feed appetites for greater change, producing a revolution of rising expectations.

In a two-party dispute, it is probably true that each can best enhance its own narrow objectives if both implement a strategy to create values for mutual gain. In the long run it is usually counterproductive to claim values for one side only, as in a zero-sum poker game.[3] This kind of bargaining depends, of course, on reciprocity. If only one side seeks mutual gain, it may be exploited by the other (the likely fate of one who always cooperates in game theory's Prisoner's Dilemma).

Value-creating is difficult, however, where one side is small and the other large, because asymmetries dominate every aspect of the relationship. The United States in the 1950s developed a relatively successful pattern of value-creating with Puerto Rico, but at the cost of the latter's pride, culture, and initiative. Operation Bootstrap achieved some of its aims, but left Puerto Rico psychologically and materially dependent upon U.S. handouts.

Each Baltic country, like Puerto Rico, is tiny compared to the regional hegemon. Each Baltic republic in 1990, however, was richer than Russia on a per capita basis but poor compared to Europe. Puerto Rico was materially poor compared to the United States although rich by comparison with its Caribbean neighbors. Each Baltic people, unlike Puerto Rico, still had a strong traditional culture to fall back on.[4] Far from being subsidized, the Baltic lands had contributed more to the USSR than they ever received. Most important, the Balts felt that they have been raped and pillaged by Moscow. They were in no mood to create values with the Russians. Most Puerto Ricans in 1990 wanted either a continuation of their present "commonwealth" status or U.S. statehood; very few preferred independence. Those that did want independence faced demands from Congress that U.S. Naval bases remain.

Gorbachev's Kremlin stressed its readiness to make amends and launch a fresh start. Some perestroika designers wanted to create values with the Balts, but decades of Soviet value-claiming had left deep wounds, both spiritual and material. Some Russians perceived this as a failed marriage from which the Balts wanted out; many Balts saw it as the aftermath of rape.

Regardless of past rights and wrongs, few if any Soviet leaders could view an end to empire with equanimity. How did they respond to the Balts' demands?

Revising Theory and History

The depth and breadth of the national question in the USSR was seen in one datum: The CPSU Central Committee received over 60,000 letters on this subject in the first eight months of 1989. Over 40 percent of these letters were signed by tens or even hundreds of people belonging to an organization. A sample was published in the Party's theoretical journal *Kommunist*. The only letter published concerning the Baltic came from Moscow, where A. Ivanov argued that the Balts have been cut off from their Western heritage. If Balts were allowed to make contact freely with the West once more, wrote Ivanov, they would see the advantages of remaining in "a strong united state" [*sil'nogo soiuznogo gosudarstva*].[5]

In the late 1980s Party leaders at all levels — Gorbachev as well as Baltic Communists such as Väljas — castigated past Soviet policies toward the national question. These policies, they said, had been too optimistic, ignoring real problems; often they added to nationalist discontent.

The Politburo consistently underestimated the power of nationalism in the Baltic as it had in other parts of the USSR. Moscow provoked riots in Kazakhstan in 1986 by replacing the local party leader with a Russian. The Kremlin ignored deep problems in Georgia, Armenia, and Azerbaijan for too long and then used excessive force to repress them. It acted as though the Balts could be talked out their insistent drive for independence.

A review in *Kommunist* of recent Soviet writing admitted that for decades "national self-determination" was treated as "odious" and "alien" to socialism. In the late 1980s, however, Communists saw that Lenin himself endorsed national self-determination and that this principle is an essential part of the law-abiding state. In the age of glasnost, the author declared, forms of direct democracy, including referenda, should be elaborated.[6]

Blending Glasnost and *Dezinformatsiia*

Wanting to avoid repression, the Gorbachev team sought to preempt or at least moderate Baltic criticism of past Soviet actions. The Kremlin *talked* as though many Baltic claims were legitimate reactions to past grievances and to the new demands of perestroika.[7] If Moscow confessed its past sins, perhaps the Balts would not go too far.

Moscow approved expression of Baltic claims and counterclaims while hoping to keep tempers and actions within acceptable limits. Within the Baltic countries, as in some other Soviet republics, this led to an unprecedented venting of emotion and assertion of perceived facts, but without the widespread bloodletting of the Caucasus or Central Asia.

The Kremlin was torn between accepting grass-roots political expression and condemning it. Thus, the Party press in Estonia and in Moscow treated one of the first large demonstration against Soviet power, that of August 23, 1987, in Tallinn, as the result of U.S. subversion. *Pravda*'s theme: "In a Foreign Voice — Afterword to the Nationalistic Actions of So-called Rights Activists in the Baltic Republics." [8]

But *Pravda* admitted that the same problems propagandized by foreign "voices" and by Baltic "chauvinists" were real. They included a decline in birth rates among indigenous Baltic peoples, a worsening of living conditions, and environmental degradation. The past disinclination of Soviet media to discuss these problems forthrightly created a vacuum that foreign propaganda exploited. Not until mid-1987 did the Baltic press respond seriously to the alien challenge; even then it did so only in a one-sided manner — completely "inadmissible" when inculcation of "internationalism" was at stake. Now, *Pravda* declared, it was time to emphasize that Soviet power and democracy are taking positive steps to deal with these issues. In Latvia, for example, birth rates were said to be rising in response to material assistance for larger families.

Baltic nationalists accused Moscow of mounting an "information block-ade" to distort or prevent news from the Baltic from reaching other parts of the USSR.[9] One aim, some feared, was to set the stage for a military or KGB crackdown. Another consequence was that "migrants" "got their information later than the Estonians, while some developments [were] hushed up altogether in the Russian newspapers." [10] Estonians brought criminal action against two TASS correspondents for "slander." Because the information was only wired to Moscow and never published, however, a court ruled this could only be a civil case. In another case the Estonian Telegraphic Agency, a unit of TASS, apologized for publishing incorrect information.[11]

Despite its pitch for clearing up blank spots, Moscow often minimized their dimensions, a form of damage control. Thus, the Kremlin was loath to admit the number of persons deported from the Baltic; the editors at *Sovetskaia Estoniia* denied during a January 1988 meeting that anti-Soviet partisan warfare had occurred in Estonia ("although there was anti-German activity during the war"); and, as noted above, the Soviet Foreign Ministry tried for a time to question the existence of the Molotov-Ribbentrop secret protocol because the original documents could not be found.

On the other hand, the theoretical monthly of the CPSU published in April 1989 an extremely frank roundtable discussion involving "scholars of the Soviet Baltic, representatives of the Communist Party Central Committees of Latvia and Lithuania, of mass social organizations, and creative unions." [12] The editors noted that despite two days of discussions in which sometimes polar opinions were expressed, the questions raised had not disappeared. "A monopoly on truth will no longer be tolerated — neither in the former 'apparatus' nor in the new 'radical-mass' form." The quiet voice of reason, they said, would be heard over loud voices and dogmatism.[13]

The Kremlin continued its own "propaganda about the friendship of the [Soviet] peoples, the patriotic and international education of the working class, and the improvement of interethnic relations outlined by the Nineteenth Party Conference." These were the goals, for example, of a new program — *Soiuz* [*Union*] — begun in April 1989 on All-Union Radio and Radio Orbita.[14]

Glasnost and accuracy seemed to shrink in Moscow's central press in late 1989-1990, probably a reflection of mounting economic and ethnic problems.[15] As some republics, Transcaucasian as well as Baltic, moved further toward independence, Soviet media prepared their audiences for military intervention. Lithuania — especially after March 11, 1990 — was displayed as a tinderbox ready to explode so that all humanitarians would welcome the restoration of order by Soviet forces. There was, however, no across-the-board consistency: Central TV offered a sympathetic, hour-long portrait of Estonia's quest late on March 6, 1990, followed on March 20 by a half-hour in prime time detailing an anti-independence rally in Vilnius.

Downgrading the Bourgeois Period, Upgrading Tsarism and Stalinism

Some Soviet apologists stressed that Balts tended to forget many dimensions of a shared historical experience. They should remember that medieval Russian princes often fought with Balts against Nordic and Germanic invaders; that Estonia's modernization commenced under Russian administration in the nineteenth century; and that Russians also suffered from Stalinism.

The trade union newspaper *Trud*, published in Moscow, often sided with "internationalists" against Baltic nationalists. Describing the 1989 exhibit of Estonian history in Tallinn a commentator in *Trud* made fun of an old woman who wiped away a tender tear saying, "What a uniform....How pretty the epaulets." The author sided instead with a man with an empty sleeve, apparently a veteran, who worried aloud: "I am afraid that Estonia might forget the Red barricades." *Trud*'s reporter noted a comment in the guest book that "this exhibition should be made permanent" to support the principle of "not living by lies." But the reporter endorsed other lines written in the "firm handwriting of a working man": "Nostalgia! If things were so great, why was there an uprising of working people in 1914? Why was there mass emigration from the

Estonian republic? The slowing down of industrial production? There is no need to blame your troubles on others."

The *Trud* commentator approved protection of "native roots" and the "roots of sovereignty." But he warned against "unhealthy isolation" and primitive "nihilism." [16]

Other Soviets argued that the now idealized "bourgeois" Estonian republic was politically unstable and depended heavily on trade with Soviet Russia. Many Russians lived in Estonia before 1918 and many more settled there in the 1920s. An Estonian economist reported that in the interwar years 8 percent of the Estonian population was Russian in a total of 13 percent non-Estonians. [17] Rein Taagepera's data suggest that the 8 percent figure could apply only to Estonia's pre-World War II borders; within present borders — after territorial shifts to the Russian Republic — no more than 5 percent were Russians. Seriously distorting the historical realities, Gorbachev commented on January 11, 1990, that 40 percent of Estonia's interwar population had been Russian! [18] Had the king been deceived by his courtiers?

In 1987 some authorities urged Estonian teachers to explain in kindergartens that "for various reasons not everybody can live permanently in his own homeland." [19]

Defenders of Soviet centralism also held that the Baltic economies were among the most flourishing, thanks in part to industries manned by "migrants" and to deliveries of Russian oil at bargain prices. [20] An essay in *Kommunist* noted the many problems that would arise from a republic's attempting to establish "economic sovereignty." [21] If decentralization went too far, the USSR could wind up like feuding Yugoslavia.

One Russian put down the whole idea of Estonian self-determination with the quip: "It's like Californians saying that their state is their country and only for them." A broad view was that Estonian culture had long been influenced by many cultures — Germanic, Polish, Scandinavian, Russian — and that Estonians and Russians alike should drop their chauvinism and see Estonia as part of world culture. [22]

The most sensitive historical issue was the 1939 Molotov-Ribbentrop pact with its secret protocols. Soviet apologists tried, at least until late 1989, to argue that the accord was forced on Moscow by circumstances. In August 1988 a Soviet spokesman cast doubt on the existence of the secret protocols by saying that the original documents did not exist in the USSR. In July 1989 the same official, Valentin Falin, head of the International Department, CPSU Central Committee, told a West German television audience that the treaty did have a secret annex. He could not confirm that the microfilm copy in Bonn's possession was genuine, but said history had proven that it was essentially correct. Foreigners got the new view first, but Falin's interview was then broadcast for Soviet audiences in August.

Soviet officials tried to separate the legal significance of the Molotov-Ribbentrop pact from the 1940 Baltic annexation accords. Thus, Aleksandr N. Yakovlev, chairman of a government commission examining the pact, stated in mid-August 1989 that it was "farfetched to seek some kind of interconnection between the present status of the three [Baltic] republics and the nonaggression treaty." [23] And Falin warned that attempts to redraw the boundaries of Eastern Europe could have a dangerous destabilizing effect. "If the striving to divide what cannot be divided continues, as was characteristic of the period before the previous two world wars, if lands and frontiers are being recarved while the lives and safety of people are neglected, the worst, and this time, the final disaster will be brought on." [24]

Commission head Yakovlev confirmed to the Congress of People's Deputies that the secret protocols did exist. On December 24, 1989, the Congress by a vote of 1,432 to 252 with 264 abstentions condemned the protocols as "legally untenable and invalid from the moment they were signed." [25] Some Moscow historians thought the pact was not needed even to protect Soviet security.[26]

Kremlin apologists continued to argue that the occupation and subsequent incorporation of the Baltic republics into the USSR did not hinge on the Molotov-Ribbentrop agreements and were legally correct. The Red Army had tried to save and later to liberate the Baltic from Nazis. The deportations and mass repressions of Baltic citizens were no worse than the genocidal tactics that Stalin used against other Soviet peoples including Russians. The Baltic in some respects suffered less from Stalinism and the stagnation period than other parts of the USSR.

Strong Center and/or Strong Republics?

Instabilities mounted as nationalists in other republics in the Soviet West, in the Caucasus, and in Central Asia asserted their claims for local tradition and interest against the center, against immigrants, or against their immediate neighbors. Thesis met antithesis with no peaceful synthesis in sight. Not only did popular fronts reproduce themselves, but so did Intermovements, as in Moldavia, where much of the population was Russian speaking and highly agitated by the prospect of discriminatory language laws and other assertions of Moldavian/Romanian nationalism.

Gorbachev in the late 1980s expressed a hope for a "strong center and strong republics," [27] but this was an unlikely outcome. At least in the near term, either the center or the periphery would become stronger at the expense of the other. Baltic analysts were uncomfortable with a formula implying a heavy burden for a weak economic mechanism badly in need of renewal.[28] In August 1989 the Supreme Soviet called on all republican parliaments, regional and town soviets to hold emergency meetings to discuss the mounting economic and political crisis of the country. The resolution reflected Gorbachev's high-risk strategy of using popular pressure to reform the ossified power structure of the USSR.

Later that month, however, the hand that gave showed that it could also take away. When Estonia set down residence requirements for suffrage, *Pravda* (August 15) denounced the move as infringement of human rights and said that "the popular fronts, which emerged due to the process of renewal in the country, have begun to drift away from the course of perestroika." On August 18 the USSR Supreme Soviet Presidium demanded that the Estonians amend their law by early October.[29]

On August 17 the CPSU issued its draft program on "The Party's Nationalities Policy in Present-Day Conditions." [30] The document called on the central government in Moscow to protect the rights of minorities in all republics. Backing "internationals," it called for a law "to guarantee the rights of citizens of the USSR living beyond the borders of their state territorial formations."

The draft called for a "radical transformation in the Soviet federation" but made no specific proposals for individual republics. "Without a strong union," the draft said, "there cannot be strong republics. And without strong republics, there cannot be a strong union."

"If a union law goes beyond the limits of the union's authority, then the republic has a right to raise questions about its abolition." But "republican law that also goes beyond the framework of competence of the republics can also be subjected to abolition by the union." This arrangement tilted sharply to the center: A republic could "raise questions," while the center could "abolish." Disputes would be resolved by a Constitutional Control Committee, probably structured to favor Moscow.

The draft admitted that republics should have ownership rights over their land and natural resources, but it also declared that the Union must "strengthen its right to use these resources, taking into account general interrepublican interests and the interests of the defense and security of the country." How resources could be owned locally and controlled centrally was left to some Hegelian synthesis.

Stung and alarmed by the increasingly sharp Baltic demands and moves for independence on the fiftieth anniversary of the 1939 pact, the CPSU Central Committee on August 26, 1989, issued its most pointed warning to date.[31] The statement began by noting the findings of the Lithuanian Supreme Soviet Commission studying the German-Soviet treaties and their consequences. Not only the Soviet-German treaties but the July 1940 declaration of the People's Sejm on joining the USSR and the August 1940 Soviet law admitting Lithuania into the USSR had been declared illegal and invalid — at the very time that the relevant Commission of the Congress of People's Deputies had not finished its work. The statement was "not accidental," but "directly linked with the separatist line that has been pursued in the past months...by certain forces in Lithuania, Latvia, and Estonia. Its high point came on August 23 [1989] when Popular Fronts and affiliated organizations held a mass action, whose political aim was to incite the peoples of the Baltic republics to secede from the Soviet Union."

The Central Committee charged that nationalist extremist groups had taken advantage of democracy and glasnost and steered their countries toward "disruption of longstanding, organically formed links with other Soviet nations." They become increasingly separatist, antisocialist, and anti-Soviet. Their organizations resembled political formations of the bourgeois and even the Nazi period. "Intimidation, deception, and disinformation became routine, and even moral terror and defamation of all who disagreed, all who remained true to internationalism and the idea of an integral Soviet Union." Foreign "organizations and centers" served as advisers. Vandalism and desecration of sacred things — graves of those who fell in the civil and Great Patriotic wars — had occurred.

The common people, the statement continued, had not called for disrupting links with the USSR, an "additional proof that the separatist movement reflects neither the interests of the Baltic peoples nor their true national patriotic awareness." Pulling out every code word in the book, the Central Committee declared: "Things have gone far. The fate of the Baltic peoples is in serious danger. People should know into what abyss they are being pushed by the national leaders. The consequences could be disastrous....The very viability of the Baltic nations could be called into question."

The Kremlin said that the perestroika process in the Baltic needed to be "cleaned...from extremism, destructive and harmful tendencies."

It called on the Baltic peoples to think clearly, consider the multitude of links with other parts of the country, take advantage of the Party's efforts to eliminate past distortions and create new opportunities, "defend the new revolution and uphold perestroika."

Since Gorbachev was on vacation when the text was issued, speculation arose as to his role in drafting it. Clearly he was not cut off from such matters. On August 22 he had telephoned the Polish Communist leader Mieczyslaw Rakowski urging the Polish Workers' Party to share responsibility in the new coalition government. Liberal on Poland, he was tough on the Baltic. On August 25 and 26 he telephoned Lithuanian CP leader Algirdas Brazauskas warning that "anticonstitutional" developments in Lithuania had "gone too far." On August 29 CPSU Politburo spokesman Gennadi I. Gerasimov said that the August 26 rebuke had been worked out with participation of all Politburo members, including Gorbachev.[32] Even so, the language seemed more characteristic of old than new thinking, and some wondered whether Gorbachev had little choice but to go along with its conservative sentiments. Still, the document formed part of an escalating pattern of Moscow's displeasure with Baltic self-determination.

On September 13, 1989, Gorbachev met with party and government leaders from the Baltic and urged "reasonable compromise." He warned against the "ruinous" step of separatist Communist movements but also emphasized the need to work out differences without confrontation. He said Soviet leaders had no right to abandon three principles: Soviet federation, party unity, and the equal rights of all nationalities.

Seeking to clarify the Party's August 17 draft resolution, Gorbachev on September 19, 1989, called for a "clear delimiting of the powers of central and republican bodies of power [to] enable the republics to decide all issues of their life on their own, except issues which they will voluntarily delegate for decision making by the Union and in the resolution of which they will, incidentally, take part." He urged abolition of "earlier procedures whereby the Union had the right to take up and decide virtually any issue, making the competence and sovereignty of republican authorities in many ways a mere formality."

He called also for ensuring "participation of all our peoples" in all levels of the government's apparatus.

But while Gorbachev offered concessions to his empire's various nations, he attempted also to establish limits. Noting that cases of ethnic discrimination were increasing, he denounced groups that played "the nationalist card" to channel dissatisfaction accumulated over decades into the sphere of interethnic relations. He threatened force against extremists who provoke interethnic clashes as had happened recently in Transcaucasia, the Fergana Region of Uzbekistan, and Novy Uzen in Kazakhstan.

Gorbachev spoke about the Baltic both directly and indirectly. He granted that the 1940 conditions in which Moldavia and the Baltic republics joined the USSR were complicated. But he said there were "no grounds to question the decision by the Baltic republics to join the USSR and the choice made by their peoples."

The indigenous peoples of every republic "undoubtedly have the full right to establish their tongue as the state language," but Gorbachev also recommended that Russian be given the status of "common state language across the USSR." All Soviet peoples need Russian, he said, the "means of interethnic communication." [33]

Despite Gorbachev's bow to "republics' rights," Balts continued to see the balance as rigged against them. In December 1989 the Lithuanian delegation led a walkout by a majority of all Baltic deputies from the Congress of People's Deputies in Moscow. It came after Lithuanian delegate Kasimiras Motieka demanded that negotiations on outright independence begin forthwith. The confrontation came at the end of a debate setting up a Constitutional Control Committee to ensure compliance with the USSR Constitution in the Union Republics. Many Baltic delegates as well as many other reformers argued that constitutional compliance could not be regulated until the Constitution itself was rewritten to be acceptable to all. Motieka declared that "the last traces of freedom and legislative power of the republics" would be removed by the new law.[34]

May a Communist Party Split from the CPSU?

The December 1989 decision of Lithuania's Communist Party to break from the CPSU provoked intense debate in Moscow. Even as Gorbachev praised recent changes in East Germany and Romania, he again denied the right of the Baltic or other nationalist movements within the USSR to self-determination. On December 25 he told the Congress of People's Deputies: "I am convinced that nowadays to exercise self-determination through secession is to blow apart the Union, to pit peoples against one another and to sow discord, bloodshed, and death," despite the existing constitutional right of secession guaranteed to the Union Republics.

The Congress of People's Deputies saw its president become more curt, rudely cutting off and deriding speakers from the Interregional Group (IRG) that made up about 400 of the 2,249 delegates. "The Interregional Group is constantly trying to spread the idea that our society is falling apart," Gorbachev said. "We can maintain our union." An IRG speaker whom he cut off shot back, "Doesn't Romania teach us anything?"

Using language that suggested a sort of Brezhnev Doctrine of limited sovereignty within the CPSU, TASS reported that the Politburo convened an emergency meeting of the CPSU Central Committee "on the basis that [the Lithuanian breakaway] concerns not only Lithuanian Communists but involves the whole party."

Addressing the plenum on December 25, Gorbachev blamed the Lithuanian CP because its inertia and stagnation had generated popular discontent. This sentiment was "skillfully used by antisocialist and left-wing forces whose efforts in the republic created numerous political associations....Comrade Brazauskas and the apparatus he leads [then] fell into another extreme" — "appeasement and endless concessions to ever harsher demands from Sajudis."

Ignoring repeated warnings from the CPSU CC, the Lithuanian Party leadership then supported various legislative acts designed to break the republic's federative links with the USSR.

Gorbachev complained that "emissaries of Sajudis and different political groups systematically go abroad" actively trying "to internationalize the so-called Baltic question." They address the United Nations and European Parliament requesting "influence on the Soviet leadership. They knock at the door of the American Embassy in Moscow. They knock at the White House."

"Not without the help of the Lithuanian Central Committee's leadership, public opinion was shaped in favor of secession."

The recent decisions of the Lithuanian CP congress, he said, "are illegal....The delegates to this congress were given a mandate for perestroika, not a split of the party....Therefore they are illegitimate." He was incensed that all Lithuanian CP members would automatically become members of the new party unless they turned in their party cards. "Only each member...has the right to decide for himself...which party to join."

Gorbachev recounted that at the Moscow plenum "a number of comrades" wanted to recognize the Lithuanian decision "as a fait accompli by allowing the events in the republic to take their own course...limiting our reaction to a political assessment." They accepted that the "logic of democratization" would sooner or later bring similar steps in other republics as well. Other comrades took up "harsh positions, believing that the integrity of the party and state is at stake....[and] that their preservation justifies any means. They propose...to disband the republic party organization and to carry out its re-registration."

Gorbachev seemed to align himself with the tough line, at least in theory: "We proceed from the fact that the independence of the Communist parties of the republics is as possible and desirable within the framework of the Communist Party of the Soviet Union as the sovereignty of the republics is within the framework of the Soviet federation." In short, republic parties could no more break away from the mother organization than could republics secede from the union.

If the single structure of the CPSU were ruptured, he said, "our party would turn into an amorphous federalist club consisting of separate independent party groups." If that line were crossed, "we will deliberately be heading toward the disintegration of the Soviet Union." Therefore "harsh necessity requires action to preserve the state and secure its unity." No one should have "any illusions" about the "intentions or the abilities of the central Government."

Despite these threats, Gorbachev welcomed a suggestion to send a delegation of national party leaders to visit Lithuania and assess the mood among CP members there. This decision, one CPSU CC member said, gave time for everyone "to cool down....Gorbachev seemed almost relieved to have this idea presented to him." Lithuanian sources reported that Gorbachev phoned Brazauskas after the plenum decision and said, "I shake your hand," saying he looked forward to a meeting in Lithuania.[35]

Lithuanian optimists hoped that Gorbachev's entourage would discover that most Lithuanian CP members favored the split and that it had not been engineered by just a few at the top. Some analysts believed the whole episode could help perestroika by demonstrating how profoundly Communist parties must change if they were to survive. Spokesmen for the minority wing of the Lithuanian CP (160 against 855) affirmed that they would remain loyal to Moscow and split from the majority wing.

The odds were that the Kremlin would have to accept a similar fait accompli in each Baltic republic and others as well. Vadim Medvedev, ideological supremo, told the press on December 26, 1989, that any use of force to maintain the union was still flatly rejected by the leadership. He pointed to recent Soviet condemnation of force against Czechoslovakia and in Afghanistan and added: "We did not do this in order to use military means to resolve problems in the Soviet Union." He pledged a quest for political solutions to interethnic problems in the USSR.

A Legal Way to Secede?

Faced with heightened momentum toward independence in the Baltic, Soviet lawyers hastened their efforts to write a constitutional amendment spelling out the procedure for secession. Second Secretary Panfilov had an early draft on his desk when we met in Tallinn in March 1990. He, like party chief Gorbachev, took a legalistic stance and said that Balts could become independent if they wished, but that this action had to be taken within the confines of the law — a law that did not yet exist.

Baltic nationalists scorned the assumption that they had to conform to a law not yet written, enacted by a state they had never chosen to join.

They spurned the constitutional amendment adopted in Moscow in April 1990, which they termed a "law against secession" rather than a law *on* secession. For a republic to secede, the amendment required that it cross a mine field: Two-thirds of the permanent residents in the republic would have to vote "aye" in a referendum (uncertain in Latvia and Estonia with their large nonnative populations); a debt settlement acceptable to Moscow would have to be reached (but what bill would the Kremlin present?); secession could take place only after a five-year waiting period (during which time the republic's economy and morale could collapse); and the Congress of People's Deputies would have to give its approval.

In April the Congress also passed a new law on responsibility for maintaining the USSR's territorial integrity. Independence leaders in the Baltic and elsewhere could be charged with criminal acts because they advocated reducing the territorial scope of the USSR. Still another law empowered the executive *prezident* to declare a national emergency and rule by decree. He could require forced labor; ban the use of copying machines; overturn the laws of local governments; and punish rumor mongers.

Goliath's sheer bulk against little David might not suffice. So Gorbachev was adding many arrows, spears, and battering rams to the giant's armory. Still, Baltic leaders hoped that their skills would enable them to outwit and outmaneuver the clumsy giant.

NOTES

1. The following analysis is based on the introduction and data throughout Gosudarvstevennyi Komitet SSSR po Statistike, *Naselenie SSSR 1988: Statisticheskii ezhegodnik* (Moscow: Finansy i statistika, 1989). The data omitted ethnic breakdowns for each republic and were characterized as "preliminary." But more than 200 pages were given to analyzing marriages and divorces by republic, broken down by nationality and age.

2. Such generalizations were less valid for urban Muslims, particularly those in Russian cities. See Walter C. Clemens, Jr., "Straddling Two Cultures: An Azeri in Moscow," *Christian Science Monitor*, 12 April 1990.

3. David A. Lax and James K. Sebenius, *The Manager as Negotiator: Bargaining for Cooperation and Competitive Gain* (New York: Free Press, 1986). In world politics the Marshall

Plan could be seen as an example of value-creating; the Molotov Plan as value-claiming. The United States invested about $13 billion in European reconstruction; the USSR extracted over $20 billion from East Central Europe. The investment helped generate a prosperous security community; the extractions, poverty and animosity.

4. Puerto Ricans maintained their language, despite U.S. attempts for several decades to replace it with English, but their Caribbean and Old World roots had become blurred in a blend of supermercados, fast food, and skyscraper hotels. Professor José Garriga-Picó, University of Puerto Rico, argued that if Russia's policies in the Baltic threatened ecocide, genocide, and the local culture, similar charges could be leveled at Washington's policies in its "Commonwealth." Interviewed in Boston, 5 April 1990.

5. "Iz pochty TsK KPSS: O natsional'nom voprose," *Kommunist*, No. 15 (October 1989), pp. 45-52, at p. 52.

6. See comments on five new books in B. Gabrichidze "Razvivaia teoriiu samoupravleniia naroda," *Kommunist*, No. 10 (July 1989), pp. 125-27.

7. For a basically positive appraisal of the Baltic fronts, see Leonid Mlechin, *Novoe vremia*, No. 43 (1988), pp. 25-28; also the views of CPE First Secretary of the Parnu district, Valter Udam: "Energichno dvigat' perestroiku," *Kommunist*, No. 4 (1988), pp. 77-84.

8. The 3,400-word essay was by special correspondents O. Meshkov, G. Ovarchenko, and D. Sniukas, "In a Foreign Voice: Afterword to the Nationalistic Actions of So-called Rights Activists in the Baltic Republics," *Pravda*, 1 September 1987. Similar arguments were put forward in *Sovetskaia Estoniia* on 25 and 27 August, 1987.

9. See "Estonia in the All-Union Mirror," *Homeland*, No. 30 (187), 27 July 1988, p. 1; "TASS Carries False Report," *Homeland*, No. 50 (207), 14 December 1988, p. 2. Because of dissatisfaction with TASS and the republic's official news agency, Lithuanians created the Sajudis Press Agency to give accurate information about local affairs. Vilnius in English to North America, 6 April 1989, Foreign Broadcast Information Service, *Daily Report: Soviet Union [FBIS-SOV]* (Washington, D.C.), 11 April 1989, p. 55.

10. Joel Aav, "Internationalist Front: Aiming at National Divide," *Homeland*, No. 30 (187), 27 July 1988, p. 2.

11. Interview with Tiit Käbin, 9 March 1989.

12. From Estonia came M. Bronshtein, head of political economy at Tartu University; V. Iarovoi, director of Dvigatel factory and chairman of the OSTK presidium; M. Lauristin, head of the journalism faculty at Tartu University; Klava Hallik, head of the Institute of Philosophy, Sociology and Law, Estonian Academy of Sciences; and G. Hazak, historian from Tallinn Polytechnical Institute.

13. "To Listen to One Another," *Kommunist*, No. 6 (April 1989), p. 80.

14. Announced on Moscow Domestic Service, 2 April 1989, *FBIS-SOV*, 4 April 1989, p. 51.

15. Instructions to Soviet censors, however, became more liberal. See Lya Pent in *Homeland*, No. 6-7 (267-268), 21 February 1990, p. 4.

16. A. Sukhonos, "To Respect One Another," *Trud*, 27 April 1989, p. 4, *FBIS-SOV*, 5 May 1989, pp. 52-54, at p. 54.

17. Arvo Kuddo, quoted in *Sovetskaia Estoniia*, 9 December 1987, p. 2.

18. "Estonian Communists Put Gorbachev Right on Nationalities Issue," *Homeland*, No. 3 (264), 24 January 1990, p. 1.

19. *Sovetskaia Estoniia*, 10 September 10 1987, cited in Ann Sheehy, "Migration to RSFSR and Baltic Republics Continues," *Radio Liberty Research Bulletin* RL 478/87 (30 November 1987), pp. 3-5, at p. 5.

20. Estonians calculated that the meat and other consumer goods they sold to Russia at low prices were worth far more than the subsidized oil they received.

21. S. Cheshko, "Economic Sovereignty and the National Question," *Kommunist*, No. 2 (January 1989), pp. 97-105.

22. L. Sher, "Intelligentnost' i internatsionalizm," *Sovetskaia Estoniia*, 6 January 1988, p. 2.

23. Interview with A. N. Yakovlev, *Pravda*, 18 August 1989, pp. 1-2.

24. Quoted in Bill Keller, "Annexation Void, Lithuanians Say," *The New York Times*, 23 August 1989, pp. A1, A5.

25. The Congress also condemned the use of force by security troops in Tbilisi in April 1989 and the Soviet armed intervention in Afghanistan in 1979. Key documents are in *Vestnik Ministerstva inostrannykh del SSSR*, No. 2 (60), 31 January 1990, pp. 7-16.

26. See M. M. Narinskii interviewed in *Profil* (Vienna), 14 August 1989, p. 53, *FBIS-SOV*, 21 August 1989, p. 101.

27. For optimistic reports on how this principle could be implemented in the economic sphere, see Iu. D. Masliukov: "Strong Center — Strong Republics," *Pravda*, 23 March 1989, p. 2; and interview with A.I. Smirnov, chief of the USSR Council of Ministers, Administration of Affairs National Economy and Capital Construction Territorial Development Department: "Toward Harmonization of Interests. Strong Center — Strong Regions," *Izvestiia*, 30 March 1989, p. 2.

28. See K. Prunskiene in "To Listen to One Another," p. 65; her anxieties were echoed by other participants in the discussion.

29. James Blitz, "Estonia Hands Kremlin Chance to Hit Back at Nationalist Groups," *Financial Times*, 18 August 1989, p. 2.

30. For analysis, see interview with A. V. Vlasov, chairman of the RSFSR Council of Ministers, in *Izvestiia*, 2 September 1989, p. 3; *Moscow News*, No. 35 (3-10 September 1989), pp. 8-9; and especially the roundtable "In Search of Balance," *Sovetskaia Kul'tura*, 16 September 1989, p. 4.

31. For text, see *The New York Times*, 27 August 1989, p. 18; for a precursor, see editorial in *Pravda*, 15 August 1989, p. 2.

32. See *The New York Times*, 23 August 1989, p. A1, A6 and 30 August 1989, p. A3. Also see *Financial Times*, 29 August 1989, p. 1.

33. Despite his intellectual brain trust, Gorbachev asserted that English (not Hindi) is the "state language of India."

34. Quentin Peel, "Lithuania's Conflict with the Kremlin Dampens Festivities," *Financial Times*, 23 December 1989, p. 3.

35. See Esther B. Fein, "Gorbachev Agrees to Go to Lithuania on Secession Move," *The New York Times*, 27 December 1989, pp. A1, 12.

13

Kremlin Dilemma: Concessions or Crackdown?

Which force would gain the upper hand? Acceptance of change in the Baltic or reassertion of central control? Surveys of Soviet citizens conducted in 1989 indicated a wide consensus that the gravest threat to Soviet life and society was the spread of ethnic conflicts. At public and private meetings many persons expressed alarm about the possibility of civil war and collapse of the state.[1] Could the Kremlin stave off the judgment that communism had died?[2] Would it try to do so with a bang, a whimper, or graceful concessions?

Moscow's options were shrinking. Rebukes and threats did not sway Baltic nationalists. The Balts seemed not to fear military reprisals or economic sabotage.

Cultivating "Internationalists" in the Armed Forces

Defenders of a strong center asked whether an "Estonian Rifles" corps would be very effective against a modern army. The Soviet Defense Ministry, for its part, stepped up efforts to "cultivate internationalists" in spite of great linguistic and cultural diversity among recruits.[3] Certainly it would be a mistake, the Ministry said, to station troops only in their home territory. How could Baltic soldiers ever learn to fight in the tropics?[4] Meanwhile, many articles in *Red Star* affirmed that it was not easy to be a "migrant" in the Baltic or carry out military duty there.[5]

A multifaceted analysis by Lt. Col. M. Zakharchuk appeared in *Pravda*, April 19, 1989. He reported that many extremists in Baltic countries demanded an end to the Soviet "occupation," but that they were not officially supported by the popular fronts. The fronts would continue conscription but wanted local boys deployed locally. This naive view, he said, ignores history: The present Soviet system defeated Hitler and liberated the Baltic. Other systems — the territorial militia, the extraterritorial, the international (mixed) approach, national military formations — had all been tried and found wanting. "Not a single one of our union republics is capable of creating and maintaining 'its own' army."

Zakharchuk bemoaned the burdens of military duty in the Baltic. "In Estonia, for example, officers and ensigns are hardly ever allocated housing, and they and their wives are refused registration at their places of residence."

But he blamed these conditions in part on the gross weaknesses of ideological work by army political workers, most of whom had "adopted a wait-and-see attitude." Higher-ups discouraged officers from having contact with the popular fronts. Such contacts should not be classified "like before,...as sedition." Instead of talking about "unbreakable ties between the Army and the people," Zakharchuk said, propagandists should assert that the Army *is* the people.

"The Army and People Are One." Posters and banners carried by non-Estonian demonstrators in Tallinn on March 14, 1990, displayed this slogan. Many Soviet officers, naval as well as army and border patrols, stood in that crowd, many with wives and children.

By 1990 Soviet authorities worried deeply about morale in the armed forces. Desertions were rising in many parts of the USSR. Against its better judgment, the Defense Ministry had increased the proportion of native conscripts stationed in the Baltic from several percent to about 35 percent.[6] Moscow probably worried that, as in Azerbaijan and Armenia, well-armed and trained guerrillas might someday operate in the Baltic.

When Lithuania declared its independence in March and summoned home its young men from Soviet forces, Moscow reacted vigorously. Soviet forces entered places of refuge and private homes in Vilnius to seize deserters, rough them up, and return them to their units. Moscow offered an amnesty to those who returned voluntarily, but got few takers. The Kremlin also warned Lithuania not to establish its own border patrols. It demanded that all firearms be turned over to Soviet officials, but got only a few hunting weapons.

Apart from issues of independence, hazing remained a sore point for Balts and many other peoples of the USSR. Letters to the editors of republic and central newspapers recorded many murders and suicides. While Russians also suffered, members of smaller nations felt they were punished for being different. Lithuanians complained of beatings provoked because their government wanted independence.

Asked why he did not importune military authorities to stop hazing, Tallinn Second Secretary Panfilov shrugged off the issue. "Boys will be boys" was his attitude. He seemed never to have considered complaining to the military authorities about hazing, even though it made his job much more difficult.[7]

Legal Carrots and Sticks

The Gorbachev regime played both tough and nice cop. Soviet and local security authorities were comparatively lenient toward nationalist demonstrations in the late 1980s, but they also created the legal basis for a crackdown. Decrees by the Presidium of the USSR Supreme Soviet on July 28, 1988 set out new restrictions on holding rallies and authorized the use of troops to maintain order, even giving them the right to enter homes. Following up on this trend, the Presidium on April 9, 1989 tightened the USSR law "on criminal responsibility for crimes against the state." While the decree aimed primarily at violence in the Caucasus, it could also restrict the political education and action campaigns in the Baltic. The decree set out escalating prison terms and fines for "public appeals for undermining and overthrowing the Soviet state and social system, as well as the publication or circulation of materials containing such ideas"; for such actions "committed repeatedly, or by an organized group of people, or with the use of copying facilities"; for "deliberate actions aimed at kindling interethnic or racial hostility and the restriction of citizens' rights depending on their race or nationality" — especially if these actions were "combined with violence and deception or committed by an official" or by "a group of people" with "appeals for high treason," or with acts of "terrorism or subversion."[8]

The central authorities endeavored to persuade Baltic nationalists to accept the changes proposed for the USSR Constitution in late 1988. The USSR Supreme Soviet Presidium declared the November 16, 1988 changes in

Estonia's Constitution to be invalid,[9] but took no immediate steps to compel the recalcitrant Estonians to remove their veto claim.

Perhaps perceiving the depth of nationalist opposition, the proposed amendments and additions to the USSR Constitution were withdrawn or moderated in the law adopted by the USSR Supreme Soviet on December 1, 1988.[10] The final version dropped the draft provision (Art. 108, Par. 2) that the Congress of People's Deputies could decide on "questions of the composition of the USSR" and the formation of new republics and oblasts, a provision that could have nullified the right of secession. Draft 108.12 was altered to take from the People's Congress the right to repeal legislative acts by the Union and Autonomous Republics if they conflicted with the USSR Constitution. A new paragraph worked into Article 119, however, stipulated that the Supreme Soviet's Presidium "exercises control over the observance of the USSR Constitution and ensures that the constitutions and laws of the Union republics conform to the USSR Constitution and USSR laws." This Damoclean Sword was shifted from the People's Congress to the Presidium, where it was even more likely to be wielded.

Still, Article 70 continued to specify that the USSR is based on "socialist federalism, the result of the free self-determination of nations and the voluntary uniting of Soviet Socialist Republics with equal rights." And Article 72 still affirmed the right of each union republic to secede from the USSR.

Furthermore, the final text improved representation of the non-Russian republics in the Soviet of Nationalities (Art. 111) and ensured their representation in a new USSR Committee for Constitutional Oversight (Art. 125). Union Republics were also assured the right (by Art. 125.2 and 125.4) to protest against laws and other acts of all-Union state and public organizations. Central powers were also constricted by Article 113.7 and 9 and Article 116 and the deletion of Article 113.10.

Taking account of Baltic objections, Article 114 was modified so that the presidium of a republic's supreme soviet had to be consulted before the USSR Supreme Soviet Presidium could declare a local state of emergency.

On balance, the alterations went some distance toward meeting the objections that Baltic nationalists put to the new amendments. But Kremlin spokesmen underscored that republics could not veto central legislation. Since the Estonian claim and Moscow's counterclaim were not resolved, a legal impasse resulted.[11] And Balts complained that "not a single republic jurist participated" in preparation of a Draft USSR and Republic Criminal Code Principles.[12]

The Kremlin exploited and stretched whatever legal instruments existed to rein in the breakaway republics. In March 1990, as noted earlier, Soviet prosecutors traveled to Vilnius to demand strict execution of Soviet laws. The prosecutor's office there became the first Lithuanian government building to be occupied by Soviet paratroopers.

TASS on March 30 announced another legal device to harass the Lithuanians: Belorussia's parliament announced that it would claim Vilnius and six other districts if Lithuania seceded from the USSR. What a tangled web: Poland occupied Vilnius during the interwar years, but *that* part of Poland was handed to Belorussia by the Red Army in 1939. Stalin then ordered Belorussia to give the disputed areas back to Lithuania in 1940. Fifty years later Belorussia's government wanted them back!

Regional Autonomy

The Kremlin endeavored to make some Union Republic ministries more meaningful, a wish no doubt shared in the republics. Thus, the Estonian Ministry of Foreign Affairs reported in early 1988 that it was busy helping to expand the republic's contacts in many spheres — commercial, cultural, tourist — with neighboring countries. Foreign Minister Arnold Green stated that, under perestroika, all the republics' foreign ministries were becoming more active. Of course, he added, Estonia did not go its own way but rather supported the single line laid down in Moscow. Still, Estonian officials studied foreign policy issues affecting republic interests and informed the USSR Foreign Ministry about them. The Estonian ministry was working closely with its Latvian and Lithuanian counterparts to organize conferences on regional problems. Green himself traveled widely in the late 1980s, three times joining USSR delegations to the United Nations, and leading Soviet delegations to the Yemen Arab Republic and to Madagascar.[13]

Moscow probably wondered and worried where and how to draw a line. If not in Estonia, surely in the Ukraine and Belorussia, the local diplomats must be thinking: "Today a consulate; tomorrow an embassy." [14] The 1936 Soviet Constitution was amended in 1944 to permit Union Republics to possess not only their own foreign affairs ministries but also their own defense ministries and defense establishments. This tack gave the appearance of more autonomy to the republics and also helped secure two extra seats for Moscow at the United Nations (if not for every Union Republic, as Andrei Gromyko proposed in 1944). Although the Kremlin welcomed acceptance of the Ukrainian and Belorussian republics as members of the United Nations, it spurned Britain's offer to establish diplomatic relations with them after the war. And the foreign consulates in these republics were accredited through Moscow, not through Kiev or Minsk.[15]

In 1988 the Baltic was in the sphere of foreign consulates based in Leningrad. But in 1989 negotiations were under way for reciprocal establishment of foreign consulates: Estonia and Latvia with Sweden; Lithuania with Poland. By March 1990, as I found in a visit to Estonia's Foreign Ministry, most officials below the aged foreign minister were actively planning an independent foreign policy and seeking useful contacts in Europe and North America.

In March 1990 the Lithuanian legation in Washington began to look again like the embassy of an independent republic, with the son of Lithuania's last ambassador at the helm. If the independent regime in Vilnius collapsed, he was authorized to succeed it.

Having established foreign ministries for each Union Republic, Moscow had to live with the reality that they might exercise the functions given them on paper.

Accepting Baltic Economic Self-Management as a Model

The ever weakening condition of the Soviet economy in the late 1980s gradually overrode Kremlin doubts and hesitations about Baltic aspirations for economic self-management. Baltic demands and proposals for economic sovereignty were much more specific than in most other spheres. And from Moscow's standpoint, they might serve as a stimulus or a useful model for other regions.

To be sure, even Gorbachev looked at Baltic economic aspirations with some alarm, especially when wrapped in the same package with a local right to veto all-Union legislation. Thus, after hearing Estonian president Rüütel address the Presidium of the USSR Supreme Soviet, Gorbachev on November 27, 1988, criticized "some people [who] regard the country and the world in general from their individualistic viewpoint."

The Estonian Supreme Soviet, said Gorbachev, had taken positions without subjecting them to all-round discussion. "Take, for instance, the problem of property. The amendments adopted by the Supreme Soviet of the republic say that Estonia's land, its mineral resources, the atmospheric air, inland and territorial waters, the shelf, forest and other natural resources are its exclusive property....Transport and communication facilities, state banks, trade, communal and other enterprises organized by the state, the available housing of the cities, as well as other facilities needed for the fulfillment of tasks by the republic of Estonia also belong to it.

"This is a principled deviation from the existing Constitution."

Denouncing idealized images of the Baltic's bourgeois past, Gorbachev called for broadening cooperation among the republics rather than weakening them. He acknowledged the legitimacy of many questions facing Estonia, and granted that "those areas where people work better should get more." But he emphasized that "we are one family...[with] a common home."

Less than a year later, however, on July 27, 1989, the USSR Supreme Soviet approved in principle the plans of Estonia and Lithuania to develop market-oriented economies independent of the central plan. Its resolution gave general approval to laws approved by Estonian and Lithuanian parliaments calling for the republics to take control over their budgets, tax policies, prices, financial markets, and foreign trade. Faced with opposition and sharp criticism from Yuri D. Masliukov, chairman of Gosplan, and other advocates of centralization, the Baltic deputies did not press for an immediate vote on the laws releasing them from central planning, settling instead for a general statement of support.

A key provision of the July 27 resolution provided that the two republics would be exempt, after 1989, from any central economic laws that interfered with their progress toward developing economic independence. The USSR Supreme Soviet delayed until October final action on new laws required to implement the resolution. The Baltic republics, moreover, still had to negotiate with Moscow such delicate issues as control of natural resources, railroads and power plants, and the fate of Baltic industries supplying all-Union ministries such as defense.

Some Baltic nationalists saw economic self-management as a step toward secession, but some Estonian and Lithuanian delegates to the USSR Supreme

Soviet said that their countries were too dependent on other Soviet republics for markets and as suppliers of raw materials to think now of severing their ties completely.

Baltic economists explained that Lithuania and Estonia had a long way to go before the quality of their exports would be widely acceptable in the West. "We plan to use the Soviet Union as our main market," said Mikhail L. Bronshtein, an Estonian economist who led the fight for the Supreme Soviet resolution. Some Balts hoped that their countries would develop economies based on agriculture and light industry, resembling Finland or Sweden more than the traditional Soviet model. Another Estonian economist, Tiit Made, explained that Kuznetsk miners, if they had control of their coal, could sell it at world market prices for Estonian meat and cheese.[16]

Estonian and Lithuanian deputies celebrated what they hoped would be the beginning of a broad loosening of centralized controls. They blithely downplayed imminent strikes by non-Estonians to protest discriminatory voting qualification laws adopted by the Estonian parliament. Tiit Made, an originator of the self-management plan, said Estonians were unconcerned about the strikes because the affected factories and shipyards provided goods primarily for ministries in Moscow rather than for local markets. Such bravado had a strangely familiar ring to anyone who experienced the euphoria of Czechoslovakia in spring and early summer of 1968. Hubris had undone more than one East European grasp for independence.

Estonian bravado became more sober as "internationalist" work stoppages (in effect, lockouts) spread to more than fifty enterprises around the republic and a Supreme Soviet commission flew from Moscow to Tallinn to investigate. In mid-August 1989 CPE leader Väljas acknowledged that Estonians had not paid sufficient attention to the legitimate needs and concerns of non-Estonians in the republic and had sometimes acted with undue haste. He promised that the election law would be reviewed. He assured the strikers that none would be punished if they broke no specific law. *Izvestiia* reported that the Popular Front of Estonia (reversing its earlier nonchalance) wanted a government back-to-work order enforced. *Pravda* denounced all the Baltic popular fronts for becoming too nationalistic and tolerant of anti-Soviet, bourgeois practices.

The magnitude of the work stoppage, however, may have been exaggerated. It affected only 5 percent of the labor force and probably caused less disruption than yearly contract negotiations in Finland.

The Estonian election laws, an official of the USSR Ministry of Justice explained to Westerners, were undemocratic, because they would replace the normal process of assessing candidates' qualifications with a formal residence requirement. The Estonians were ignoring the natural migrations of manpower and circumstances such as study and business trips. Article 32 of the Soviet Constitution and Article 32 of the Estonian proclaimed citizens' equality regardless of origin, nationality, language, and residence. Article 48 of the USSR Constitution guaranteed the right of every citizen to take part in the management and administration of state and public affairs. Article 95 proclaimed that public officials should be elected on the basis of equal suffrage. The Constitution also held that, should there be a conflict of interpretation between a law of a constituent republic and a national law, the latter would prevail (Article 74). "Even if we admit that there is a good deal of sense in the Baltic lawmakers' arguments insisting that local legislation should prevail over national as a key part of republican sovereignty...the current Soviet Constitution will remain in force until constitutionally amended."[17]

He added that the International Covenant on Civil and Political Rights, ratified by Moscow in 1973, guaranteed every citizen the right and opportunity, without any unjustified restrictions, to vote and stand for public office on the basis of universal suffrage. Further, the minimum residence requirements in France, Belgium, Japan, and New Zealand stipulated only three to six months residence to vote. By implication, the Estonian law was unreasonably tough on newcomers.[18]

The official's argument, if put into broader perspective, lacked force. Estonia could not be compared to France or Japan because its official language was unknown to most migrants, making it difficult for recent settlers to understand local issues. Gibraltar, a British colony rather than a "sovereign Union Republic," denies citizenship to Englishmen and all immigrants. Many American states have residence requirements for U.S. citizens who move from other states; and all deny voting rights to immigrants until they become citizens, a process requiring at least five years.

Economic Warfare

Moscow tightened the screws as the Baltic republics sailed, so they hoped, into the winds of economic self-management. Their planned venture in economic autonomy had been condemned in July 1989 by Yuri Masliukov, head of Gosplan (State Planning Agency), but supported by Leonid Abalkin, chairman of the committee on economic reform.[19] Closer to Gorbachev, Abalkin and his orientation seemed to be gaining the upper hand in late 1989-early 1990, the very time when most Baltic nationalists demanded not just economic self-management but political and economic independence.

Gorbachev on September 19, 1989, warned Balts not to forget that their postwar economic rehabilitation was assisted by the entire Soviet federation. All Soviet republics in 1989 depended on others, Gorbachev declared in a ninety-minute speech on the nationality question to the CPSU Central Committee. Latvia, he said, imported from other republics 96 percent of its fuel; 50 percent of its electricity; 90 percent of its ferrous metals; 100 percent of its nonferrous metals; 80 percent of its chemical raw materials; 63 percent of its machine-building production; and more than half of the concentrated grain fed to livestock.

Lithuania supplied other republics with computers and other light industrial products, but imported from them technological equipment, tractors, raw materials, and fruits.

If Lithuanians decide to upgrade the minibus produced there, parts suppliers from other republics have to be integrated in the process — another reason, he said, for economic decentralization.

Gorbachev endorsed economic self-management in the Baltic and elsewhere, but he also warned: "In modern conditions tendencies toward autarky and attempts by relatively prosperous republics and regions to isolate themselves and fence themselves off would be extremely dangerous. This can bring fairly negative consequences for those who embark on this road." He rebuked "demagogues" serving up slogans under the "pleasant sauce" of independence and secession, gambling with the destinies of the people. Only an adventurer would undertake to recarve a presently intertwined society.

Gorbachev started to make good on his threats. In 1990 the Kremlin staged a multiple squeeze play hinting at the consequences should the errant children stray too far. Most of these actions violated either the spirit or the law of the

USSR Supreme Soviet's November 1989 legislation providing for economic self-management in the Baltic.

The Kremlin centralized not just bank operations in Moscow but seized republic assets. On January 2 Moscow closed all foreign accounts of the Estonian and Lithuanian branches of the USSR Foreign Economic Bank. More than twenty Western banks that used to have direct operations with Baltic banks were compelled to go through Moscow, adding much time and cost to their operations. On January 4 the USSR Council of Ministers moved to transfer the Estonian division of the USSR State Savings Bank to Moscow. All of Estonia's savings, some 3 billion rubles, were thus taken out of Estonia.[20]

Grain allotted to Latvia was slashed by 40 percent in early 1990, which Communist leader Janis J. Vagris interpreted as a warning against Latvian moves toward independence.[21] Estonian officials complained that they had received only two-thirds the fodder needed for animal husbandry; therefore Estonia's deliveries of meat and eggs to Russia were below targets set in Moscow.[22]

Research teams in Moscow broke off contracts with Baltic institutes, saying that they had become undependable.

Oil deliveries to the Baltic became more irregular in 1990, causing break-downs in local transport.[23]

Delivery of metal for local industries also became erratic. Even the January 1990 decision of the Estonian Supreme Soviet decision to raise prices on alcohol and tobacco was declared null and void by Moscow. The price hikes were intended to increase the pay of workers in service industries as well as student stipends and pensions.[24]

Customs authorities in Moscow continued to insist on the right to approve and to tax goods imported by Baltic republics. The editor of a Jewish literary journal in Tallinn could not receive a gift of high quality paper from Sweden without Moscow's permission, withheld for at least three weeks despite repeated phone calls and fax messages.

Moscow ministries pushed aggressively to expand phosphate and oil-shale mining despite principled rejections by Estonian authorities who feared ecological disasters. How could Estonia manage its own economy if it had to obey a distant center?[25]

Soviet military authorities refused to pay for damages caused by enormous oil spills into Estonian lands and waters in late 1989-early 1990. Some 450

Soviet officers and their families were settled in the towns of Tapa and Rakvere and given ration cards without informing Estonian authorities.[26]

The Kremlin in March 1990 ordered all state enterprises in breakaway Lithuania to obey only orders from Moscow and to avoid negotiations with Lithuanian officials about transferring control. President Landsbergis, in reply, affirmed Lithuania's intention to honor all existing contracts, but said that Lithuanian claims to ownership of industries on its territory were "unquestionable according to international law." The whole issue, he added, should be solved at the negotiating table.

Moscow presented rebellious Lithuania with a bill for Soviet capital investments and subsidies over the years — 21 billion rubles, payable in hard currency, plus charges for contracted deliveries not made by Lithuania and costs of resettling any residents wishing to leave.

Responding to such value-claiming tactics, Baltic economists and demographers started to calculate their counterclaims. Not only would they charge Russia for goods and services extracted and for territorial changes made by Moscow, but for environmental damage and for the tens of thousands of lives destroyed by Soviet actions. Russians and Balts would have done better to turn their backs on the bitter past and make the most of a new future.

The Kremlin could try to follow President Charles de Gaulle's example of 1958 when departing French technicians ripped out the entire infrastructure of Guinea as the prize for its independence. Russia, however, needed the Baltic countries a great deal more than France needed Guinea. Even Leningrad depended on electric power generated in Estonia. And much of Russia's trade with Europe, both imports and exports, depended upon Baltic ports that were less clogged and more efficient than Leningrad. Russia, like other countries, needed cooperative neighbors for its ties with the outer world.

Balts tried to break their dependency on Moscow. In January 1990 Estonia obtained assurances from Finland that it could deliver 100,000 tons of petrol and diesel fuel that year. Finnish refiners also talked of building an oil refinery in Estonia, perhaps at Paldiski — since 1940 a Soviet naval base. Bypassing Moscow, Estonia in January also entered negotiations with Kazakhstan that could lead to direct imports of oil and cotton. Balts also took hope from the fact that, of 1,300 joint ventures in the USSR in 1989, sixty-eight were in

Estonia and twenty-three in Latvia.[27] Despite the many uncertainties, some foreign businesses were willing to make new deals with the Baltic.

The Use or Threat of Force

Terror went out of style in the USSR after Stalin's death, but its passing did not end official coercion and even violence, both of which have been employed against dissident elements from Brezhnev through Gorbachev.[28] The Kremlin retained the option to repress nationalist or other dissent with force. When Soviet troops (internal security or regular) were used against Kazakhs, Armenians, or Georgians, there was an implied message for the Baltic: "We may do the same to you, but you may be spared if you behave."

Given past repressions and deportations, Balts were quick to focus on even veiled threats. The four-day visit of Vladimir Chebrikov to Tallinn in November 1988 led an Estonian commentator to caution that Estonia should "prepare for the worst." He quoted the former KGB head as warning that "one may gain independence and lose everything else." When Chebrikov visited the Dvigatel military factory, the commentator noted, Estonian reporters were refused entry to hear non-Estonian workers "viciously attack" the new policies of the CPE.[29]

Anxieties rose when the Estonian Supreme Soviet proclaimed its right to veto Soviet legislation. As Tallinn Radio told its listeners, a "threatening note, couched in a serious tone, was circulated [in the media] to the effect that new Estonian laws" exceeded their competence. Estonian President Arnold Rüütel was summoned "very promptly to Moscow" to meet with the USSR Supreme Soviet's Presidium.[30]

Interviewed later that day, however, Rüütel told Estonians there were "no grounds for panic" because the USSR was moving toward a "law-ruled state." [31]

Still, the whole scene had an eerie resemblance to the moments in 1968 when the Soviet media reported anti-Soviet activities in Czechoslovakia and when, after Soviet tanks filled the streets, Alexander Dubcek was summoned to Moscow and other Czechs and Slovaks were discovered willing to denounce and replace the Dubcek team.

Thus, TASS broadcast an interview with Vasilii Koltakov, a turner at the Dvigatel plant, one of seven deputies to the Estonian Supreme Soviet who voted against the Article 74 amendment. He spoke of coaching and even threats by PFE activists to induce deputies to vote "aye" or abstain.[32] And a

Soviet newspaper interviewed three deputies to the USSR Supreme Soviet who termed the Estonian legislation illegal and against "democratic centralism, democracy." [33]

A few days after Soviet security troops killed some twenty Georgians in April 1989, Baltic residents were shocked to find armored vehicles rumbling through the streets of their major cities. Military authorities averred that these were merely routine training exercises, but they brought to mind the comradely Warsaw Pact maneuvers held in Czechoslovakia in the months before the August 1968 crackdown. The mayor of Tallinn, for his part, affirmed that city officials had not authorized treaded vehicles in the city streets. Estonia's traffic police tried in vain to prevent a column from entering Tallinn. When the police blocked a road with a car, the colonel commanding a tank column warned them to remove it or else "we'll run over your car." The traffic chief concluded that the military was arbitrary and held nothing sacred. The damage by the tanks and armored cars to the city streets was considerable. Many Estonians inferred the military had tried to intimidate popular movements. The PFE organization at Tartu University denounced this "use of the army for a public show of strength." [34] Soviet officials wished to avoid repression, if only because it would discredit Gorbachev's reforms at home and abroad and make more difficult the reconciliation of Balts and other Soviet citizens. As Andrei D. Sakharov cautioned a Pugwash meeting in Cambridge, Massachusetts, however, the 1989 massacres in Tbilisi and at Beijing's Tiananmen Square demonstrated that governments unfettered by law and truly democratic institutions are inherently dangerous and unpredictable.

When Soviet forces smashed into Baku in January 1990, their action was presented as a necessary step to stop ethnic violence. But Defense Minister D. T. Yazov later explained the intervention as a way to "destroy the organizational structure" of the Azerbaijan Popular Front and prevent it from overthrowing Soviet power in the republic.[35]

The withdrawal of Soviet forces from parts of Eastern Europe probably underscored for Moscow's strategists the importance of retaining forward bases in the Baltic. All supply routes for Kaliningrad (an extension of the RSFSR), the main base for the USSR Baltic Fleet, ran through Lithuania. All three Baltic states contained well equipped bases for mobile military units; they also housed surveillance centers to listen to and watch the West. Much territory of each Baltic republic was off limits even to locals because of its military significance.

In late March 1990 Soviet paratroopers and motorized convoys enveloped Vilnius in response to Lithuania's declaration of independence. Gorbachev said that force would not be used except to prevent bloodshed, but other Soviet spokesmen gave a wider warrant: force might be used to uphold public order. Soviet jets buzzed Vilnius; an armored column rumbled past the parliament in early morning darkness while it was still meeting;[36] paratroops occupied Communist Party buildings and the Higher School of Marxism-Leninism; and loyal troops snatched up and bloodied Lithuanian deserters.

If Soviet leaders wished to pound the mailed fist, it was poised. Rather than strike, Moscow might slowly strangle its victim. A team from the Soviet Prosecutor's Office in Moscow flew to Vilnius and demanded of their colleagues strict observance of Soviet law. The Kremlin's Deputy Prosecutor complained that Lithuania had just replaced its chief prosecutor without Moscow's approval. The Soviets then tried to install their own nominee. When the Lithuanian prosecutors rejected the implant, paratroopers took over their building. They also seized the printing plant, another Communist Party enterprise, for Lithuania's main newspapers.

An official of the CPSU Central Committee told a reporter that the Soviet military had plans much like those under which Soviet forces occupied Prague in 1968. They included seizure of the Lithuanian parliament, replacing its nationalist leadership, and imposing martial law.[37]

The Deputy Chief of the Soviet General Staff, Col. Gen. Vladimir Denisov, warned in *Trud* on April 13 that Lithuania's "secession policy is pregnant with danger not only for the Baltic republics and the USSR, but for all of Europe." Lithuania's secession would breach Soviet defenses and communications, he said, warning that if the Lithuanians did not listen to "reason, events could have painful consequences for everybody."

That same day (Good Friday) Gorbachev warned that the USSR would sharply reduce oil and gas deliveries to Lithuania if its declaration of independence was not retracted within forty-eight hours. The Monday after Easter the Lithuanians offered to compromise on some issues — residence for non-Lithuanians, optional military service in Soviet forces, perhaps even the effective date of their independence — but not on independence.

America's economic clout entered the ring, at least for a short time. Congressmen and even the White House hinted that if Moscow blockaded Lithuania, the United States might not grant most-favored-nation treatment to the USSR or go along with other steps to bring the Soviet Union into world commerce. For a day, the Kremlin seemed to back down. High officials said they had received no order to turn off the spigots.[38] But then oil deliveries to Lithuania's only refinery stopped and gas supplies were cut by more than 80 percent. Supplies of various raw materials were also curtailed. The White House suddenly retreated and announced that it would watch and wait longer before implementing any sanctions against the USSR. That same day — April 24 — the KGB sent reinforcements to guard Lithuania's borders. It stepped up patrols in the Baltic Sea to prevent weapons from being smuggled into the republic.

The United States was a paper eagle. But Gorbachev still seemed unhappy in new role as enforcer. When Paris and Bonn suggested in late April 1990 that Lithuania delay implementation of its independence declaration, Moscow approved the idea as the basis for conciliation and compromise.

On May 14, 1990, Gorbachev decreed invalid Latvia's May 4 declaration of independence. That same day Soviet army helicopters dropped leaflets on Riga urging that "Soviet persons" make their stand against the "counterrevolution." On May 15 several thousand opponents of Latvian independence tried to force their way into the Supreme Soviet building. The opponents included several hundred uniformed Soviet army troops and cadets, in civilian dress, from officers' training schools in Riga. They were met not only by Latvian civilians and local militia but by black beret riot control units of the USSR Ministry of Internal Affairs. Both sides turned to shouting slogans and singing nationalistic songs. Efforts by opponents of Latvian independence to organize a strike fizzled out. The confrontation in Riga was more tranquil than one in Tallinn the same day, where demonstrators broke into the parliament building and were driven back by independence supporters.

The CPSU Politburo adopted a secret resolution on May 28, 1990, condemning the Communist Party of Estonia for "losing control" of Estonia's drive to independence. Under the resolution, leaked to the daily *Rahva Hääl*, the CPE was to "rebuff" the independence movement and "consolidate all Communists on the platform of the Soviet Communist Party." The CPE was instructed to set up a Russian-language Communist Party channel on Estonian television.

Harry Roots, a secretary of the CPE Central Committee, said that the resolution aimed at "cutting all ties between Estonian and Russian Communists and thus inciting interethnic tension." The Estonian Party, following the lead of the Lithuanian and Latvian, had split into two factions some two months before — a reform- oriented, Estonian nationalist wing and a traditional, pro-Moscow wing. Reform Communists sought to use the resolution to recruit more members, but many Estonian Communists rejected the party in any form and simply returned their membership cards. Challenged on the May 28 resolution, ideologist Vadim Medvedev told an Estonian Communist that the Politburo would "reconsider" the matter.

In July Admiral Vitalii Ivanov implied that an obstacle to Baltic independence was Western opposition to naval arms reductions. The commander of the Soviet Baltic Fleet told TASS that while military tensions in Europe had decreased, the West refused to match Soviet cuts in naval forces.

Still, the Kremlin continued its efforts to open some Baltic and Pacific ports to the world. It announced that Novgorod would be added to the list of free economic zones being created in Leningrad, Vyborg, Kaliningrad, Sakhalin, Nakhodka, and Chita. In Kaliningrad the City Soviet in July 1990 agreed to allow tourists from West Germany to visit the city, thus breaching the atavistic Soviet rule keeping it a closed city. Meanwhile, discussions among Soviet Germans indicated that few would choose to resettle in Kaliningrad even if it did become a "German" republic.

In August 1990 as in 1989, Gorbachev's Crimean vacation was interrupted by events in the Baltic, leading him to sign or issue strong statements. On August 12, 1990, Gorbachev denounced the ESSR Supreme Soviet declaration that Estonia had ceased to be part of the USSR. He reiterated the presidential decree of May 14 stating that independence declarations by Estonia and Latvia were invalid. He also criticized as illegal Estonia's assertion that the presence of Soviet armed forces in Estonia violated its sovereignty.

Gorbachev's bent for centralization was partially checked in September 1990 when the Supreme Soviet's constitutional compliance committee ruled that the USSR president had exceeded his powers by trying to regulate political demonstrations in Moscow. Gorbachev had tried by decree to remove from the Moscow city council, dominated by liberals, the power to sanction rallies in the city center and give it instead to the USSR Council of Ministers. The compliance committee suspended the decree because it "narrowed territorially the powers of the Russian republic and the Moscow city council."

As the USSR's overall economic situation became more perilous in autumn 1990, Kremlin negotiators made some concessions to delegations from the Baltic republics. TASS reported progress in these meetings, but Moscow found it difficult to deal with its former vassals as independent countries.

The tangle of difficulties in creating a new Union Treaty were hinted at by Rafik Nishanov, chairman of the USSR Supreme Soviet Council of Nationalities. As reported by *Pravda*, September 6, 1990, Nishanov stated that twelve republics (none Baltic) had taken part in consultations to draw up a new treaty. Seven had presented drafts while the other five expressed their views in other forms. The majority of the republics, said Nishanov, favored federal ties, though some preferred confederal. Nishanov suggested that they should seek "an original solution." Major disagreements concerned the powers to be allocated the center and whether autonomous republics — many demanding "sovereignty" — should also sign the new treaty.

NOTES

1. See the report of sociologist Vladimir Shlapentokh, "Gone Are the Toasts to Mikhail," *International Herald Tribune*, 28 August 1989.
2. See Zbigniew Brzezinski, *The Grand Failure: The Birth and Death of Communism in the Twentieth Century* (New York: Charles Scribner's Sons, 1989).
3. See *Krasnaia Zvezda*, 30 September 1988, p. 1; on the polyglot nature of the Soviet Armed Forces, see Foreign Broadcast Information Service, *Daily Report: Soviet Union* [*FBIS-SOV*] (Washington, D.C.) 5 April 1989, pp. 67-68; for a discussion of languages of smaller peoples under socialism, see Evgenii Zeimal's, "Narodnosti i ikh iaziki pri sotsializme," *Kommunist*, No. 15 (1988), pp. 64-72; on Latgalia in Latvia, see p. 71.
4. To which Balts reply, "We have no business fighting in the tropics."
5. V.Verbitskii, "Is it easy to be a 'migrant'?" *Krasnaia Zvezda*, 15 February 1989, p. 4.
6. A Lithuanian newspaper reported in December 1989 that Defense Minister Yazov had pledged that 70 percent of Lithuania's youth would serve in the Baltic region, but only 20 or 25 percent did so — of whom only one-sixth served in Lithuania. Reprinted in *Respublika*,

No. 1 (2), January 1990 (Tallinn), p. 7. See also Stephen M. Meyer, "From Afghanistan to Azerbaijan, Discord Undermines the Red Army," *The New York Times*, 28 January 1990, p. E3.

7. Pavel Panfilov, interviewed 7 March 1990.

8. Quotes from text of Moscow TASS in English 9 April 1989, *FBIS-SOV*, 10 April 1989, p. 43.

9. "USSR Supreme Soviet Presidium Decree on the Nonconformity of the Estonian SSR Law 'On Amendments and Additions to the Constitution (Fundamental Law) of the Estonian SSR and the Estonian SSR Supreme Soviet Declaration on the Sovereignty of the Estonian SSR, Adopted 16 November 1988, with the USSR Constitution and USSR Laws," *Pravda*, 28 November 1988, p. 2. The decree was signed by M. Gorbachev, Chairman of the USSR Supreme Soviet Presidium, and by its Secretary.

10. *Konstitutsiia (osnovnoi zakon) Soiuza Sovetskikh Sotsialisticheskikh Respublik* (Moscow, 1988). For comments and debate by Gorbachev, Estonian representative A. Rüütel and delegates from other republics (some of them quite critical of Estonia's position), see Moscow television report in *FBIS-SOV*, 28 November 1988, pp. 42-51. See also analysis by Ann Sheehy in *Radio Liberty Research Bulletin*, RL 508/88 (21 November 1988), pp. 1-3, and RL 553/88 (12 December 1988), pp. 1-7.

11. The director of a large plant in Estonia reporting to an all-Union ministry suspended at his enterprise the language law adopted by the Estonian Supreme Soviet. Estonian activists then demanded that the republic prosecutor take action to uphold the law. The director replied: Did not the Estonian Supreme Soviet on November 16, 1988 take a similar decision on all-Union laws? To which the locals argued "administrative power is not the supreme power." And so on, as "mutual grudges piled up." See Vaino, "In the Heat of Mutual Resentment," *Trud* (Moscow), 30 March 1989, p. 2.

12. Vytautas Piesliakas, "Are We to Remain Simply Interpreters Again?" *Tiesa* [Vilnius], *FBIS-SOV*, 5 April 1989, pp. 82-83.

13. ETA report: "MID Estonii: vremia perestroiki," *Sovetskaia Estoniia*, 21 January 1988, p. 1.

14. First Secretary of the Lithuanian CP Algirdas Brazauskas commented that the USSR and Lithuanian constitutions permitted republics to maintain consular relations with other states, but that there was no precedent in Soviet diplomatic practice for a Union Republic to establish a diplomatic mission in another state. See *Tribuna Ludu*, 29 March 1989, p. 7, *FBIS-SOV*, 5 April 1989, p. 70.

15. For background and bibliography, see Alexander J. Motyl, "The Foreign Relations of the Ukrainian SSR," *Harvard Ukrainian Studies*, 6, No. 1 (March 1982), pp. 62-78. In 1990 there were still three kinds of ministries: All-Union, centered in Moscow; Union-Republic, with major offices in the republics as well as in Moscow; and Republic, based in the republics. The 1977 constitution, as noted earlier, generally reduced republics' powers. See also John S. Reshetar, Jr., *The Soviet Polity: Government and Politics in the USSR*, 3d ed. (New York: Harper and Row, 1989), pp. 210-14.

16. See report by Bill Keller in *The New York Times*, 28 July 1989, pp. A1, A4.

17. Vladlen Tishchenko, Institute of Research, Ministry of Justice, letter to *Financial Times*, 23 August 1989, p. 15.

18. Ibid.

19. Quentin Peel, "Soviet Chiefs Clash Over Plan for Baltic Economic Autonomy," *Financial Times*, 27 July 1989, p. 1.

20. "Moscow Dictating the Pace of Self-management," *Homeland*, No. 9 (270), 7 March 1990, p. 1.

21. This cut exceeded those reported in other republics due to grain shortfalls. See *The New York Times*, 10 February 1990, pp. 1,6.

22. "Less Meat to Russia," *Homeland*, No. 4 (265), 31 January 1990, p. 1.

23. Difficulties occurred also in 1989, some of them traced to the August 1989 strike of Russian workers in Estonia. Petrol shortages also struck even the oil-mining districts of Siberia!

24. Tarmu Tammerk, "Estonia's Price Rises Renew Conflict with Moscow," *Homeland*, No. 3 (264), 24 January 1990, p. 1.

25. Tiiu Taras, "Mining Projects Still in the Air," *Homeland*, No. 6-7 (267-268), 21 February 1990, pp. 2-3.

26. "Army Jet Fuel Contaminates Fields," *Homeland*, No. 9 (270), 7 March 1990, p. 1.

27. The number for Lithuania was not given. See *Homeland*, No. 6-7 (267-268), 21 February 1990.

28. See Alexander J. Motyl, "Policing Perestroika: The Indispensable KGB," *Harriman Institute Forum*, 2, No. 8 (August 1989), pp. 2-3. Motyl predicted a large and continuing role for the secret police and KGB efforts to penetrate popular fronts and other social organizations. Many persons I met in Kazakhstan in 1990 believed the KGB to be pervasive; in Estonia and Georgia the institution was virtually ignored.

29. Arved Jurgenson, "Politburo Member Visits Estonia," *Homeland*, No. 46 (203), 16 November 1988, p. 1.

30. Tallinn Domestic Service, 18 November 1988, *FBIS-SOV*, 21 November 1989, p. 39.

31. Ibid.

32. TASS in English, 20 November 1988, *FBIS-SOV*, 21 November 1988, pp. 42-43.

33. L. Perkina, "Proceeding on the Basis of Statewide Interests," *Sel'skaia zhizn'*, 20 November 1988, p. 5.

34. *Rahva Hääl*, 26 April 1989 and other sources reported in *Homeland* (Tallinn), 26 April 1989, p. 1, *FBIS-SOV*, 12 May 1989, p. 54.

35. Bill Keller, "Legislators Challenge Gorbachev On Use of Troops in Azerbaijan," *The New York Times*, 27 January 1990, p. A1; on historic animosities, see Walter C. Clemens, Jr., "Straddling Cultures: An Azeri in Moscow," *Christian Science Monitor*, 12 March 1990, p. 18.

36. A Soviet reporter felt terror but most Lithuanian legislators and Landsbergis responded fairly calmly to reports of the approaching tank column. See Oleg Moroz, "Vesenniaia noch' v Vil'niuse [A Spring Night in Vilnius]," *Literaturnaia gazeta*, 4 April 1989, p. 11.

37. See Craig R. Whitney, "Military's Voice Being Heard on Lithuania, a Soviet Aide Says," *The New York Times*, 15 April 1990, p. 10.

38. A day or two before U.S. threats mounted, a telegram from the regional gas headquarters in Belorussia warned Lithuania that supplies would be "sharply reduced from April 17." But on the appointed day a company spokesmen said that the telegram was meant only as a warning and that the 18 million cubic meters of gas used daily by the republic would continue to flow for the moment. See Lionel Barber, "US May Cancel Talks with Moscow," *Financial Times*, 18 April 1990, p. 22. But then Moscow's blockade began on 18-19 April.

14
Whither the Russian Empire? Models for Change

The challenges facing the Soviet system became clear to Soviet analysts. Readers of *Kommunist* learned in 1988 that the message of Paul Kennedy's *Rise and Fall of the Great Powers* applies to the USSR. Rejecting economic determinism, however, the *Kommunist* writers asserted that democratization of the Soviet political system was both possible and necessary and that it was essential for introduction of radical economic reform and to unleash the energies of "our multinational country." [1]

A year later the picture looked bleaker: Historian Mikhail Kozhokin granted that the onset of perestroika had temporarily halted the decline of Soviet prestige abroad. But, he asserted, the worsening crisis within the USSR left little time in which to halt the ebb tide of Soviet influence in Eastern Europe. His conclusion: An effective economy and democratic political structure in the USSR would "strengthen the authority and influence of our state in the world incomparably more than any kind of nuclear power." The difficulties, he conceded, were enormous and could be not be resolved by outside help. [2]

Despite Gorbachev's energies, radical reform of Soviet life and institutions proved difficult. Leading Soviet economists declared in 1990 that Soviet economic weakness exceeded CIA estimates: USSR defense expenditures consumed a fifth or even a fourth of a GNP no greater than 28 percent of American. Oleg Bogomolov averred that "the economic situation in our country does not allow any alternative" to reducing military expenditures.[3] He could have added: There is no choice but to reduce the burdens of empire.

Russia's empire spanned the USSR. It included not only an inner empire of contiguous countries, but also overseas clients from Cuba to Vietnam.[4] What alternatives might accommodate the interests of Russians, the border republics, and the East Europeans?[5]

In the late 1980s President Gorbachev condemned unrealistic fantasies and warned against secession efforts in the Baltic or other Soviet border lands. Instead he called for a "strong center and strong republics." [6] But Gorbachev did not spell out how this unity of opposites could be achieved. And many Baltic analysts were uncomfortable with the formula. Continued centralization implied heavy burdens for weak republican economies in need of renewal.[7]

As Eastern Europe in 1989-90 rejected Communism and Soviet tutelage, attitudes in Moscow began to parallel those that developed in Britain in the late 1940s and in France a decade later. The "self-evident" need to cling to empire gave way to an urge to let go its burdens.[8] Moscow had already withdrawn from active combat in Afghanistan; it was winding down aid to Cuba, Outer Mongolia, and Nicaragua. It began also to confront the likelihood of defections from within the USSR.

In 1989 Moscow no longer met Baltic calls for independence with a categorical *"nyet."* It replied in the negative, but added one-sided arguments.[9] In 1990 it said separation was possible but only if would-be secessionists followed Soviet constitutional procedures.

Historical Analogies

"History is future." So reads the sign in a Zurich book shop. To what extent did the problems and opportunities of the USSR resemble those of other large imperial systems — Athens, Rome, the Holy Roman Empire, the Ottoman Empire, the Austro-Hungarian Empire, or the Tsarist? To what extent did they resemble those of other large multinational states such as the United Kingdom, United States, Brazil, India, and others?

Athens

The Delian League was basically different from the Soviet empire in that one small polis, Athens, dominated other city-states by the force of its will, culture, and navy. But there were also similarities: Athens achieved its hegemony by leadership in what Stalin might have called a Great Patriotic War against Persia. When that war ended, Athens used its new prestige and power to exploit and dominate its allies, taxing them and subordinating them to satellite status. Athens became embroiled in a long and damaging conflict, some seventy years of cold and hot war with the other Greek superpower, Sparta. Weakened by this struggle, Athens was hard pressed to keep its allies and satellites in line. The Athenians, according to Thucydides, debated whether to maintain their empire by force and terror or by benevolent administration — alternatives that might be called value-claiming or value-creating.[10]

Soviet hardliners have argued, like Cleon, that sentiment should play no role in administering an empire. Cleon told the Athenians, "Your empire is a dictatorship exercised over subjects who do not like it and who are always plotting against you; you will not make them obey you by injuring your own interests in order to do them a favor; your leadership depends on superior strength and not on any goodwill of theirs."

Arguing for tough laws and against infatuation with "new thinking," Cleon warned: "And this is the very worst thing — to pass measures and then not to abide by them. We should realize that a city is better off with bad laws, so long as they remain fixed, than with good laws that are constantly being altered, that lack of learning combined with sound common sense is more helpful than the kind of cleverness that gets out of hand."

Speaking about the Balts, more prosperous than most Soviet citizens, Cleon might warn Moscow: "The fact is that when great prosperity comes suddenly and unexpectedly to a state, it usually breeds arrogance; in most cases it is safer for people to enjoy an average amount of success rather than something that is out of all proportion." Imperial powers should repress their subjects before they became arrogant, "for it is a general rule of human nature that people despise those who treat them well and look up to those who make no concessions." Moscow, like ancient Athens, needed to think also of its other subjects: A decisive intervention against one set of rebels might deter others from revolt. Do not let sentiment intrude: If subjects are justified in revolting, you must be wrong in holding power. But if you propose to hold power anyway, regardless of rights and wrongs, they must be punished. "The only alternative is to surrender your empire, so that you can afford to go in for philanthropy."

Cleon's opponent, Diodotus, prefigured the warnings of various Communist leaders about rushing to independence. Diodotus spoke out against "haste, that usually goes with folly, [and] anger...the mark of primitive and narrow minds."

Diodotus cautioned about the human condition in terms relevant to any imperial power faced with insurrection. "So long as poverty forces men to be bold, so long as the insolence and pride of wealth nourish their ambitions, and in the other accidents of life they are continually dominated by some incurable master passion or another, so long will their impulses continue to drive them into danger." In short, human nature "when once seriously set upon a certain course," cannot be "prevented from following that course by force of law or by any other means of intimidation whatever."

If the drive for freedom cannot be intimidated, how should empires deal with their subjects? Diodotus said that "the proper basis of our security is in good administration rather than in the fear of legal penalties....The right way to deal with free people is this — not to inflict tremendous punishments on them after they have revolted, but to take tremendous care of them before this point is reached, to prevent them even contemplating the idea of revolt, and, if we do have to use force with them, to hold as few as possible of them responsible for this." [11]

Soviet imperialism followed the maxims not of Diodotus but Cleon. And when V. M. Molotov advised the Balts in 1939-1940 to capitulate to Moscow, he bullied them as the Athenians did the Melians: In many cases men who devote themselves to "honor" fall into disaster, bringing dishonor through their folly. There is nothing disgraceful in giving way to a great power that offers you reasonable terms: "alliance on a tribute-paying basis and liberty to enjoy your own property....This is a safe rule — to stand up to one's equals, to behave with deference toward one's superiors, and to treat one's inferiors with moderation."

The Melians replied that they were unwilling to "give up in a short moment the liberty which [their] city had enjoyed from its foundation for 700 years." Whereupon the Athenians besieged their city; took it by treachery from within; and killed or enslaved the population. [12] The Balts, however, did not fight in 1939-1940, and still suffered a terrible fate. They lost their property and their liberty. Many were enslaved or killed.

By the time the Athenians considered Diodotus's proposition about the need for good administration and value-creating, the damage had already been done. Athens had already degraded itself in the eyes of its allies. Challenged on all sides, Athens leaned toward coercion rather than conciliation. One by one many of its satellites threw off the Athenian yoke. Increasingly isolated, Athens was defeated by the Spartan coalition including former members of the Delian League. Like Moscow, Athens had abused its power, trusting that to the victor go the spoils.

Many Soviet successes abroad derived from building up military power over decades and using it skillfully to intimidate, deter, or overwhelm foreign adversaries. But the threat of force and its actual use have also been the single largest sources of failure in Soviet foreign policy, from the 1920 Polish defeat to Afghanistan. Subjugation of the border republics and Eastern Europe netted few long-term gains for the USSR, but created profound vulnerabilities for the entire Soviet system.[13]

Rome

Like the Third Rome, the first Roman empire was built initially upon military conquests. It grew fitfully and with many reversals. It expanded out of insecurity — fear of hostile incursions — as well as expansionist designs. At its largest extent (when Emperor Trajan died in A.D. 117), the empire covered an area only half that of the modern United States — a quite manageable plot by comparison with the sprawling tsarist and Soviet empires. But in terms of days needed to reach a certain destination, medieval France was larger than the later Russian/Soviet empire and the Roman empire was truly gigantic.

The cosmopolitan character of the Roman Empire was its strength and its downfall, a feature basically lacking in the Russians' empire. Roman citizenship and participation in its civilization were offered to those who qualified. Honorary Romans were given major responsibilities throughout the empire, incomparably greater than the Uzbek or Moldavian first secretaries usually backed up by a Russian second secretary of the republic's Communist Party.

Rome's expansion subdued or drove back many peoples from the Black Sea to the Rhine. Border lines called *limes* were established to divide the law and order of the Roman empire from the other way of life beyond, analogous in some ways to the 1961-1989 wall between East and West Germany. The emperors depended increasingly on local mercenaries to maintain Rome's side of the *limes*. Like the East European members of the Warsaw Pact, however, the barbarians' dependability could not be presumed.

Ultimately the empire became overextended. There was a vacuum at its administrative heart. Still, Roman civilization left roads, aqueducts, and coliseums that, nearly two millennia later, were far more impressive than the Palaces of Culture or sports stadiums of the Stalin empire.

There have been brief moments of "internationalist" élan in the spread of Soviet communism — a messianic, crypto-religious spirit usually manipulated from on high — but these moments have been short-lived. Even the Georgian Stalin turned out to be a sort of Russian chauvinist. He and his cronies denounced "rootless cosmopolitanism," an epithet among Party ideologists even in the early 1980s. Putting most power in the hands of one nationality is one way to manage a multiethnic community. Rome's way was not Moscow's. Both approaches had strengths and weaknesses. In an age of nationalism, however, genuine cosmopolitanism would be less likely to generate resentment against the center than Great Russia chauvinism. The Roman Empire flourished for several centuries; the Soviet endured for less than half a century.

Ottoman Empire

The First Rome collapsed in the A.D. fifth century but the Second Rome — at Constantinople — lasted until the mid-fifteenth century, when it fell to the Turks, tempting Moscow to claim the mantle of Third Rome. The multinational Byzantine Greek empire, which had given Orthodoxy to Kievan Rus', had crumbled away for five hundred years. Its capital became the heart of the Ottoman Empire.

Like Romans, Ottoman Turks were a relatively small group at the core of a multinational empire. They were more tolerant than the Romans of local diversity and did not press most of their subjects to accept Islam or Turkish civilization (although Christian boys were kidnapped, converted to Islam, and trained to become elite troops — the Janissaries). Instead they developed a *millet* system in which local communities were permitted considerable autonomy, including having their own non-Muslim leaders, as long as they paid their taxes and other obligations. The armed forces and the ruling classes of the Ottoman Empire systematically recruited from subjects who were neither Turks nor Muslims.

The Ottoman Empire held out a few centuries longer than the Roman, propped up by Europeans fearful its sudden collapse would transform the balance of power. Like Rome, the Ottomans overextended themselves relative to their resources and imperial will. Self-indulgence and counting on others to do the hard work left a leadership vacuum in which subject peoples, beginning with the Greeks and Egyptians, could win national self-determination.

Thus, the Ottomans, like the Romans, became too dependent on others to do the hard work of managing and defending their empire. Despite a somewhat tolerant approach to local communities, the Ottomans antagonized virtually all the non-Turkic peoples of their empire.

The Ottomans, like the Soviets, met the greatest resistance in East Central Europe. They were turned back at Vienna in 1683, the same place where Moscow began its retreat in 1955. Serbs and other Balkan peoples threw off Ottoman hegemony, as Tito did Stalin's claims in 1948.

Engrossed in Eastern Europe, the Ottomans lost touch with the Arabs in their domain. Despite their shared faith and other cultural traits, such as a common script, the Turks and Arabs lost any sense of common purpose. A similar fate befell Communist Russia's onetime alliance with China, undermined by Kremlin policies around the world.

Soviet leaders — certainly before 1985 — displayed a blind conservatism akin to that of the last sultans. They sought to resist change at all costs. For them, as for the Ottomans, seeking to hold on to empire skewed their attentions away from the basic needs of the Russian people and the Soviet state.

In the nineteenth century there was more economic dynamism in the outlying areas of the Ottoman Empire than at the center, a pattern occurring now in the erstwhile Soviet domain (especially if we include China). The Russians, like the Ottomans, find themselves making disproportionate sacrifices to maintain an imperial structure with little relevance to their basic needs.[14] If they follow the Turkish model, they will wait until the empire collapses and then follow a Kemal Ataturk to recreate a virtual nation-state without the trappings and distractions of a vast empire. As modern Turks can testify, it is difficult even to deal with Kurds and other local minorities without going further afield. A "Russian" nation-state would have its hands full just coping with Tatars and other encircled minorities.

Austria-Hungary

Along with Tsarist Russia, Austria-Hungary also hovered like a vulture over the "sick man of Europe," the Ottoman Empire. Had the truth been known, the dual monarchy was almost as ill as the sultanate. This descendant from the Holy Roman Empire also endured for many centuries, its Hapsburg dynasty ruling sometimes from Madrid and sometimes from Vienna. It exploited vast lands with rich resources, but its strength in the nineteenth century owed more to the weaknesses of its eastern and southeastern European neighbors than to any special skill or power in Vienna or Budapest. Unable to compete with Germany or France, Austria-Hungary could still divide and subdue its lesser neighbors. Allied with Germany it could even threaten Russia.

Austrian Germans and Magyars ruled over a large, increasingly resentful congeries of Czechs, Slovaks, Poles, Romanians, Croats, Slovenes, and Italians. Economic and social development gave rise to an articulate intelligentsia and middle class among the subject peoples. Some East European nationalists called for a dissolution of empire, but most called merely for a larger voice in its affairs — a broader electoral franchise, greater representation in regional assemblies, and laws putting their languages on an equal footing with German and Magyar. Zealous defense of the status quo by Vienna and Budapest only provoked further agitation.[15]

Unwilling to make concessions at Austrian or Hungarian expense or to permit reforms that might paralyze government, the Austro-Hungarian rulers avoided constitutional change and sought instead external action — more annexation of former Ottoman provinces. Challenged by Serbia, they plotted its destruction and incorporation, hoping this would terminate South Slav political aspirations. This policy collided with Russia's need, in the face of domestic weakness, to support its little Slavic brother. The result was a war that gave the coup de grace to many empires: Austro-Hungarian, Ottoman, Russian, and German.

Intrinsically weak, inefficient and unjust, the Austro-Hungarian empire quickly collapsed under the strains of World War I. Austria, like Turkey, sought to revive as a nation-state or, failing that, in a larger German Reich, without its onetime eastern satellites. Despite its many shortcomings, the Austro-Hungarian empire may have provided a better life for most of its peoples than they had in the decades that followed its demise. The idyllic memory of Austria-Hungary helped inspire a Pan-Europa movement in the interwar years. The imperial period recalls a time of relative peace, stability, cultural tolerance, and mutual trade.

The Austro-Hungarian example differed from and yet also resembled the USSR in 1990. Austria and Hungary were small relative to their subjects, unlike the giant Russian bear. Their subjects felt some respect for Austrians, unlike the Balts, Armenians, and other peoples of the tsarist empire who looked down on Russians. The peoples subject to Vienna and Budapest had not tasted much independence in recent memory. Few had been so alienated by Austrian or Hungarian actions as Poles and some other subjects of the Russian empire had been by St. Petersburg. The Russian state, however, remained a military superpower while Austria's might under Franz Josef was more myth than reality. One similarity hovered menacingly: Russians, no less than Austrians and Hungarians, were loath to renounce a hegemony that bolstered their imperial image as well as their material well-being. They too preferred a familiar status quo to unknown paths.

In the 1920s and 1930s Austrians suffered for various reasons, but not for loss of empire. After foreign occupiers left in 1955, Austrians built a life-style much more comfortable than that of Greeks, Turks, Russians, Hungarians, or other East Europeans.[16] They had no empire; belonged to no alliance; were forbidden to have guns that could shoot more than thirty kilometers; had few border problems with their neighbors; and enjoyed a late twentieth century form of *Gemütlichkeit*. In spite of being still at a crossroads between East and West, however, their cultural zip flagged. At Viennese cafe houses the quality newspapers came from Munich, Zurich, or Frankfurt. They produced no contemporary Mozart, Beethoven, Strauss, Mahler, or Freud. But since 1945 no Austrians have died for their country in foreign wars or in putting down nationalist insurrections.

Tsarist Russia

How did Gorbachev's USSR resemble or differ from the tsarist empire in the decades before 1917? The tsarist was more extensive, for it included Finland and most of Poland. Russia had spheres of influence in Iran and China recognized by the other great powers. It had a right to speak on the future of the Ottoman empire.

The tsarist state was more absolutist and unitary, at least on paper, than the Soviet ever became. Finland enjoyed considerable autonomy, and its people had rights unknown to Russians.[17] But neither Finland nor the other subject peoples of the tsar had the juridical status of the various autonomous and union republics that evolved under Soviet rule. Certainly they had no constitutional right to secede and no seat in international organizations. Nor did they enjoy the official respect accorded to local culture as under Stalin's slogan, "National in form, socialist in content." Even Finland was subjected to Russification at the end of the nineteenth century.

On the other hand, tsarist policy did not perpetrate genocide or ecocide. It did not strive so energetically or with such totalitarian ways to transform the content of its subject cultures, not only trying to Russify them but to extirpate traditional beliefs including religious. Only rarely, as in Aleutian seal hunting, did the pre-1917 economic apparatus and appetite radically despoil the environment as have those of Soviet Russia, destroying the base on which many indigenous cultures depended.

The Russian empire's border peoples did not defect to the other side in 1914 as many did in 1941. Some Poles, to be sure, flirted with Berlin or sat on the fence in 1914. And tsarist authorities removed thousands of Jews and Germans from western regions from fear of their disloyalty. Not unless revolution or war threatened the monarchy did the border peoples demand sovereignty and other rights as have their descendants since the 1980s. Still, the unpopularity of Russian rule was manifested in the fact that when the center faltered in 1917, the border lands grasped and fought for freedom and independence. Finland moved toward independence in spring 1917 and obtained Soviet recognition of Finnish sovereignty at year's end. Estonia moved more slowly, and did not proclaim its independence until February 1918 after prospects disappeared for autonomy within a Russian democratic federation. Eastern Slavs and the Transcaucasian peoples also broke from Moscow but were subjected again to centralized rule within a few years. Some Central Asians waged war against the Bolsheviks until the late 1920s. Finland, the Baltic states, and Poland maintained their independence until 1939-40.

Moscow's influence and popularity in the border lands in 1990 resembled that of St. Petersburg in 1917 or Stalin in 1941. Were the central regime to weaken or collapse for some reason, many—perhaps most—of the border lands would again bolt. Today's United Nations recognizes many ministates far smaller and more vulnerable than, say, Estonia or Armenia. And the neighbors of such border lands no longer threaten them as did the kaisers or sultans.

Lessons of Empire

Imperial dominion is difficult to maintain over prolonged periods. Systems based on exploitation of one people by another are unstable. Political organizations based on free association are not only more enduring but more effective, eliciting energies that can be directed toward common goals. Exploitative systems seek to extract values from the lesser or weaker party to benefit the more powerful. In the short run such systems may reap profits for one side; in the longer run, a system oriented toward creating values to be shared among partners is more likely to enhance the interests of the parties. Slavery offers the extreme case: It is less efficient, at least for modern economies, than free labor. The castrated stallion Gulsary can perform only the most elementary tasks for its master.[18]

Is it a rule that colonial systems tend to be replaced by hegemonic relationships as subject countries become more developed?[19] Thus, France no longer has colonies in sub-Saharan Africa but clients that depend on France economically and sometimes militarily. If the logic of material determinism prevailed, the Baltic countries would be neither colonies nor satellites of Russia, for their economies have long been the equal or superior to the metropole's. Balts were subjected to Moscow not by Russia's economic prowess, but by the bayonet or tank. The situation differed from the Americas, where Washington's influence derived primarily from U.S. economic clout and comparative advantage in trade.

The Baltic countries in the 1980s reached the same economic impasse as most of Eastern Europe. They had exhausted the resources that could be mobilized from domestic, Soviet, or Western sources under their Soviet-imposed economic and political system. They were locked into the USSR economy not just by central planning but by structural dependence. Hence, they faced not temporary but fundamental economic difficulties. This situation differed radically from that of Latin America, where constraints on development were less severe and stemmed more from internal than external factors.[20]

The situation between Russian metropole and periphery partially resembled the *dependencia* model favored by many Latin American and Third World economists in recent decades: All communications radiated to the republics from the hub, which tried to set the pace and content of all transactions. Reversing the Latin American model, however, the Russian hub supplied vital elements — energy and raw materials — to the periphery. Thus, the Balts and other border peoples depended heavily upon the center. The center also depended heavily upon the manufactured goods and food supplies provided by the periphery. The dependency, however, was not symmetrical. The Balts could not easily find other suppliers of fuel and materials at prices they could immediately pay. The Russians, if they sold their raw materials on world markets, could then buy most goods supplied from the Baltic. The Balts were more vulnerable than Russia to an economic blockade. In time, they might overcome it, but only with great difficulty.

The situation at the end of the 1980s, an Estonian political scientist argued, was that the USSR "retained the dependence of the province on the center, typical of tsarist Russia, with the role of the mother country being played by the central authorities in Moscow who identify the Soviet Union with Russia." What caused great damage was Moscow's unremitting emphasis on "the unity of the State and the people, which in effect displays the desire to carry on with imperialism and colonial policies." [21]

The Kremlin was caught in a no-win dilemma: If it refused to talk with the demandeurs and cracked down, all reforms could be aborted and "stagnation" turn into sure decline. But if Moscow surrendered to local demands, this would probably stimulate more demands from all claimants. A tough centralizing policy would generate resistance or internal migration by those whose energies the country desperately needed. Conciliation, on the other hand, risked being taken as a sign of weakness to be exploited.

Most Soviet citizens had experienced some improvement in living conditions in the 1970s, followed by a leveling off in the early 1980s. Gorbachev in 1985 promised them a better life, but the first years of perestroika yielded a perceptible worsening of living standards coupled with political chaos. Expectations had been raised but not fulfilled. As in France of 1789, so in Gorbachev's empire: Concessions from the center were likely to fuel ever greater demands. Here was a virtual recipe for revolution.

Alternative Futures for the Soviet Empire

Economic problems became entwined with nationality problems in the late 1980s. By 1990 many Russians as well as border peoples wanted to cut their ties with the Soviet system and liberate Russia of its imperial burdens.

Should the Soviet "center" and the republics move toward a tighter union? A federation? A confederation? Some looser association? Or dissolution of the imperial bonds between the Kremlin and at least some border lands? The answer hinged upon feasibility as well as desirability — from the standpoint of the center and the periphery.

Let us consider a range of alternative futures for the Kremlin in dealing with its erstwhile Union and Eastern Europe.

A Centralized Union

The Communists run China as a unitary state, but they confront national minorities amounting to less than 7 percent of the population, minorities whose material and communication capabilities are far weaker than the Han rulers'.

A unitary state exists in the United Kingdom where the English (81.4 percent of the population in 1988), over centuries, used sticks and carrots to induce the Scots, Welsh, and most Northern Irelanders to accept the British system and English language. The difficulty of maintaining a unitary system — even under comparatively favorable conditions — is seen in the Irish struggle for many centuries to escape London's diktat and discrimination, whatever the cost in blood.

Both tsar and commissar dreamed of making the Russian empire a unitary system, but could not overcome the vast cultural, social, and economic differences in their realms. The 1977 Brezhnev Constitution probably marked a last gasp in this direction. Kremlin policies such as collectivization, Russification, and deportation left deep wounds not healed by the sweet talk of perestroika. Ironically, the more unitary the Kremlin tries to make the USSR, the greater the incentives for the Balts and others to secede.[22]

A Russian Empire without Communism

Why not drop the irrationalities of Communist ideology and simply reassert Russian hegemony under the enlightened despotism of *kniaz'* Mikhail Sergeevich Gorbachev or some heroic marshal — a Russian Jaruzelski? If nothing else, this approach would inject some rationality into the system. One could chuck any dogmas that obstruct progress. The country would become more powerful as efficiency increased. Perhaps the regime "could also count on the support of the masses, who hate Europe because it was largely spared their own misfortune" and want it to be reduced to their level. The power élite could resume its imperialism with new vigor.[23]

The problem is that if the Communist regime sheds its ideological mantle, its legitimacy would fall and the whole edifice collapse. The Great Russians, only half the population, could not subjugate others so readily.

Throughout most of Eastern Europe and the USSR, the constitutional guarantee of Communist Party monopoly was eliminated in 1989-1990. Without some special claim to truth, Russians had no justification to dominate East Europeans or the various nations of Russia's inner empire. Some 114 million East Europeans cast off Russian hegemony in 1989-1990. Their anti-Russian, anti-Soviet sentiments add strength to the nearly 145 million non-Russians in the USSR.

In Russia itself there was little remaining imperial will. Gorbachev wanted to retain ties with former satellites and subject republics based mainly on consensus. But an element in the Russian national spirit wished to drop entirely the pretensions, costs, and duties of leading a multinational empire.

Federalism

Some Soviet analysts proposed another "treaty" like that of 1922 between the center and the republics spelling out their respective domains. Others worried that even the 1922 arrangement was a fiction for the unitary government sought by Stalin rather than the more democratic federation urged by Lenin. The 1977 USSR Constitution, they complained, was closer to Stalin's unitary vision than to Lenin's federal. Some urged that republics' rights be strengthened to approach those of "states" in the U.S. system.[24]

A federal system such as that of the United States, Canada, or Australia would be far more difficult to realize in the USSR for many reasons. First, both early and recent settlers *chose* to move to these countries. Second, the founders of their governments distrusted excessive central power and were dedicated to democratic processes. Third, the founders shared a common culture; newcomers *chose* to adopt it, most of them striving for assimilation. Fourth, cooperation and compromise were prompted in part by a sense of shared threats and opportunities. Fifth, local attachments have not been strong except in Quebec and the American South (an issue finally decided only by civil war).

The USSR has been and remains much more heterogeneous than the United States. Most of its minorities joined their Russian "brothers" after 1918 because they were coerced. Russian is little more than a lingua franca, now being eclipsed by English. Most minorities communicate among themselves in one or more local tongues. Centralized power in Moscow has heightened ethnic and religious self-consciousness more than it has cultivated broad acceptance of cultural diversity. Compromise and fair play are not part of the Russian ethos.

The possibility of a more democratic Soviet "federation" was strengthened in 1989 when the Congress of People's Deputies and its grand committee, the Supreme Soviet, were elected by procedures more democratic than had operated since 1918. The new bodies also acted more freely than their predecessors. Whatever their decisions on thorny national questions, they carried more legitimacy than those adopted by a handful of self-interested Politburo members. Still, each national minority — especially the non-Slavs — had only modest representation in the all-Union legislature. The minorities often felt that they confronted a steamroller. And whatever the legislature decides, strong-minded minorities may reject.

In theory a democratic federation might offer a rational solution to conflicting and yet overlapping interests of the present members of the Soviet Union. In the domain of interethnic feelings, however, one man's "reason" can be another's lunacy. Passions run high and lead generations of nationalists to assert their claims no matter the cost — witness Lebanon, Sri Lanka, Yugoslavia.

Prospects for a viable Soviet federation are diminished by the bad blood that has flowed and the demography that gives Russians and other Slavs an automatic upper hand.

Confederation

A less centralized solution would be a confederation in which the parts are more powerful than the center. Since the sovereignty of Union Republics fixed in the USSR Constitution has been more myth than reality, Soviet leaders and borderland nationalists have talked of creating a union (or alliance) of truly sovereign states based on a new Treaty of Union.[25] This treaty would specify the powers to be allocated to the center and the procedures for joining and leaving the Union. Although national defense and foreign policy are often thought of as central prerogatives, even these spheres would need careful debate and definition: It can be argued that "Estonia is sure to cope better with guarding its borders" than Moscow.[26]

Skeptics demanded: Show us the terms. Experience dictated caution: Both foreign affairs and defense were made joint responsibilities for the center and the Union Republics by the 1944 amendments to the Stalin Constitution, but these amendments were honored only in the breach. What would keep Moscow and Russians from continuing to run roughshod over the smaller border peoples?

Boris Yeltsin, elected president of the RSFSR, presented in summer 1990 a "500-day" program to transform Russia into a market economy. Reluctantly, Gorbachev endorsed this approach for the entire USSR. Some border republics welcomed these moves, hoping that they portended greater freedom. Most Balts, however, were reserved. They had already been promised the miracle of "self-financing" (*IME* in Estonian) in 1989, only to see it shredded by central banks and all-Union ministries in 1990. By year's end Gorbachev disavowed the 500-day cure.

Confederations are problematic. In today's world there is no classic confederation.[27] The United Arab Emirates may come closest to the model, but it is basically a federation (1971 constitution).

Experience suggests that confederations cannot cope with the demands put upon them. The newly liberated American states, having made common cause against England and sharing a common culture (especially by comparison with today's Soviet nations), found that their Articles of Confederation provided too weak a system of integration to be effective economically, militarily, or politically.

Canada, a loose federation, has long struggled with separatist tendencies that it has been unable to mollify or curtail — tendencies much less serious than those facing the Kremlin.

Switzerland since the mid-nineteenth century has edged away from confederation toward a more centralized federation.[28] The basic reason the Swiss cantons could collaborate for hundreds of years was their determination to combine against external foes such as the Hapsburgs. Other cantons — each small but proud of its distinctness—joined the *Bund*, aware that they had to respect the others' rights for the little community to repel large foes. Three languages were accepted as "national" in 1848; a fourth was recognized in 1938. Although nearly three-fourths of Swiss citizens have Swiss German as their first language in 1990, most Swiss can speak easily at least two tongues. Apprehension about foreign threats continues (if not from the east, perhaps from the north). Meanwhile, a common prosperity rewards Swiss for their cooperation. While religious wars once ripped apart Swiss unity, there is now a widespread Christian-secular consensus. Switzerland, unlike the USSR, has no foreign territorial ambitions and wishes to uphold its neutrality.

The republics of the USSR, in contrast to Switzerland, did not band together against external foes. They display much greater cultural diversity and much less tolerance. Also, some Soviet peoples believed that they could prosper better economically outside rather than within the Russian orbit.

As Stephen Kux has argued, transformation of the Soviet Union into a true federation or confederation would require more than modest adjustments of the constitutional framework developed since the early 1920s. It would require radical reforms such as granting substantive powers to the republics; meaningful representation for them at the all-Union level; decentralization of the many centralized administrative and legal structures; and the creation of mechanisms for the peaceful resolution of political and constitutional conflicts—an independent constitutional court.[29]

The spirit of compromise and tolerance, never strong between Moscow and the border peoples, would have to be nourished to make federalism or confederalism work. While this spirit was lacking, talk of new constitutional arrangements would spur centrifugal forces. The Yugoslav case suggests that a looser federal constitution could help tear a divided state further apart. In Kux's words, "A thin line divides federalism, i.e., freedom in alliance, from separatism, i.e., freedom from alliance." Many Baltic nationalists, for their part, see federalism simply as a step towards independence.

Molotov Plan Redux

Could there be an East-bloc economic community like the West's European Community? "We want to create a true Common Market within the socialist world," said a Soviet delegate to a Council of Mutual Economic Assistance (Comecon) meeting in 1989.[30] But this model had almost no appeal to Baltic nationalists. Independent Baltic republics would not relish an obligation to remain within the confines of a Soviet-dominated economic bloc. Since the late 1940s Comecon achieved rather little except to facilitate the exchange of Soviet raw materials for East European manufactures. Any country that tries to remain integrated with the Soviet economy must wrestle with meaningless prices, the whims of central planners, and a nonconvertible ruble. Some Gorbachev advisers wanted to eliminate these features of the Soviet economy, but such transformations could be slow and painful.

Even a special economic zone status within the USSR, as established in Guangdong and elsewhere in China, was unacceptable to most Baltic economic planners. They wanted fewer ties with the Soviet economy, not more, even if there were promises of a transformed relationship.

The East Europeans in 1989-1990 fled Comecon as if it were sinking ship. Gone was the erstwhile discipline of Communist solidarity and fealty to Moscow militating for integration and a common front. Instead, the East Europeans and even the Soviets were drawn as by a magnet westward, to the European Economic Community (EEC).[31] In theory the Eastern states might gain if they could approach the West together, negotiating from numerical strength. In practice, each journeyed alone, trying to work out the best deal it could for itself. A common approach could be taken only if the Comecon states first worked out a common market for themselves, but, as one Soviet analyst lamented, there was not even a true common market within the USSR![32] Not surprisingly, Foreign Minister Shevardnadze radiated glee when he concluded the USSR's first commercial accord with the EEC in December 1989.[33]

Hoping to integrate their economies with dynamic rather than backward neighbors, the Balts, like the East Europeans, looked west and north rather than east.

Cominform-Commonwealth Redux?

Might it be possible to revive in some new form the Cominform as a true Socialist Commonwealth? If no other intergovernmental framework were attainable, might there be a transnational association linking Communist regimes in the Baltic with those in Russia and other countries? If it resembled the Commonwealth left over from the British Empire, mutual obligations would be quite minimal. If membership in this organization were a condition for Baltic independence, there would be no deep obstacle to such an arrangement. The Soviets would probably try to dominate it, as in Cominform days, but the East Europeans and Balts could probably hold their own perhaps as well as Indians, Ugandans, and others in the erstwhile British Commonwealth.

The Republic of Ireland left the British Commonwealth soon after independence. The British Commonwealth in time became simply the Commonwealth. In the 1980s most of its members aligned against Great Britain on South Africa and other issues. Was the Commonwealth a face-saving device for London — a reminder of the good old days — or an expensive and exasperating nuisance?

For Moscow a Soviet Commonwealth could save face but would offer little substantial gain. Local Communists, at least in the Baltic, could probably win more votes by demonstrating their independence from Moscow. For them, any reaffirmation of ideological solidarity with the Kremlin could alienate local support, at the very time when they most needed it against extinction.

If Communists do not run Baltic governments, what ideology would hold Russia and its western neighbors together? Each would likely be motivated primarily by its own economic and geopolitical interests, which leaned not toward Leninism or the *mir* but toward the West.

A Pluralistic Warsaw Pact?

Could the Warsaw Treaty Organization (WTO) be maintained as an instrument of Soviet imperial control and security?

In 1989 all Warsaw Pact ministers agreed that the organization's 1968 intervention in Czechoslovakia had been illegal and unwise. Budapest's new political leaders in 1989 joined millions of Hungarian citizens in lamenting and denouncing the Soviet invasion of 1956 — another action that Moscow once justified under terms of the Warsaw Pact. How could an organization so condemned by its own members retain any role in their collective life? Hungary's Foreign Minister in 1990 suggested that his country join NATO.

What could be the Pact's role if most of its members shed their Communist institutions? All of Moscow's East European allies moved in 1989-1990 toward pluralistic economies and political structures. Some erstwhile "Communist" or "Workers'" parties changed their name and adopted a social democratic or other non-Leninist philosophy. Many East European Communists doubted there was any point in contending in the next elections, even under a different label. From Romania to Czechoslovakia, many East Europeans demanded that the Communist Party be outlawed.

Since 1955 the Pact was used mainly to enforce Soviet preferences and justify Soviet military interventions against member states that threatened to jettison communism. As pluralism replaced communism throughout Eastern Europe, the Soviet alliance became increasingly formal in character. Moscow might continue to exert its will on pact members by direct, physical coercion, but the internal controls previously exerted through willing Communist functionaries in each country would be lacking.[34]

The continued existence of the Warsaw Pact might provide a fig leaf to Soviet conservatives worried about the diminution of empire. Perhaps they might be more tolerant of Baltic independence if Vilnius, Tallinn, and Riga pledged to join the WTO. So long as NATO endured, Soviet leaders were loath to surrender its counterpart.

The traditional security concerns of both sides might be met if all parties adopted "defensive defense" postures. Each alliance agreed in 1990 to cut its tank forces to 20,000 and its combat aircraft to 6,800. But even these numbers would far exceed those of Europe in 1939.[35] A former U.S. negotiator called for 50 percent cuts in weapons and manpower on both sides, once the Pact reduced to NATO levels. He also advocated a zone free of offensive forces along the Central European front.[36] In winter 1990-91, however, arms control accords were put in doubt by Soviet military moves to evade 1990 obligations by moving equipment to Siberia and by reclassifying ground units as naval.

German reunification raised major questions for any European security. The two Germanies (minus East Prussia) reunited in 1990 with Moscow's permission for the entire country to belong to NATO, provided that Soviet troops could remain for some time in the former G.D.R.

With or without NATO, Soviet planners would probably prefer to retain forward defenses against possible German revanchism.

Moscow's "allies" in Prague, Warsaw, and Budapest, however, pressed the Kremlin in 1990 to withdraw all Soviet forces from their countries. If the Red Army departed these countries, Soviet forces in Germany would be isolated, leaving the Pact only a shade of its former presence and logistic network.

Soviet withdrawals from Eastern Europe combined with German unification raised the value to Moscow of its bases in the Baltic, Belorussia, and the

Ukraine, even if those republics became more autonomous. The naval base at Kaliningrad, formerly in East Prussia but now part of the RSFSR, became more isolated but also more precious. Lithuanian independence would sever Kaliningrad from the rest of the USSR and make overland supplies of oil and other goods hostage to Vilnius.

Thus, there were strong motives for the Kremlin to pressure its erstwhile satellites to remain members of the Warsaw Pact even though their pluralistic institutions gutted its élan. For similar reasons Moscow might want the Baltic republics to join the Pact if they became independent. Soviet "rental" payments for Baltic military bases, as demanded by some Balts, might be more thinkable if the Baltic republics belonged to a Soviet alliance.

Moscow in 1991 led in dissolving the Pact's military structure. It was futile and counterproductive to prop up an alliance that has lost its raison d'être. Russia in the 1990s had neither the will nor the means to compel the East Europeans to keep Soviet troops on their soil or to remain in a sham alliance. The German threat was not military but economic. The only way to cope with it was by rejuvenating Russia's economy and joining the West, perhaps "encircling" Germany with meaningful partners rather than adversaries.

If such new thinking prevailed, perhaps Moscow could also surrender military positions in the Baltic, falling back — if a military threat recurred — to the nuclear deterrent still wielded by a Fortress Russia.

Instead of trying to salvage the wreck of the Stalinist empire, Moscow and its erstwhile colonies and satellites would be better advised to explore new relationships that might help them to board the train of European integration rather than be left behind. In 1990 idealists talked of expanding the CSCE to subsume both alliances; history and realpolitik advised caution. NATO might still be useful to ensure that neither Russia nor Germany would again awake in ways that threatened their neighbors.

Country Models

System-wide solutions such as federalism offered little promise. What about the models provided by individual countries in the belt between Western Europe and Russia? All such models were abhorrent to Moscow because they implied at least the partial dissolution of the USSR and a diminution of Soviet territory and reach. But there were many considerations to mitigate or perhaps prevent a mass exit by other republics from Russian imperium.

If the Balts regained their independence, other republics — with no living memory of independence — might wait and watch.

Many-sided interdependence would remain between Russia and any independent republics. Geography would not change and existing trade ties could be mutually useful. Independence for Balts or others could be negotiated in bilateral or multilateral arrangements to safeguard Soviet interests.

Since politics remains the art of the possible, the Kremlin and its neighbors should at least ask whether these models might be preferable to other outcomes on the horizon. And such thought experiments could help guide all parties toward mutually beneficial solutions to present dilemmas.

The pre-1989 Hungarian Model: Liberal Communism

Some Balts in 1988 looked to Hungary as a case of economic and political liberalism and independence within the framework of a Moscow-dominated military alliance. The price to them looked small: They would have to kowtow to Moscow but they could be much freer in their internal life.

A chastened Kremlin might be pleased if the Baltic republics would settle for the pre-1989 Hungarian model. But once independence had been realized, what barriers would prevent the Balts from following the *post*-1989 Budapest line? In summer 1989 the Hungarian government pledged an irreversible shift toward a market economy and integration into the larger European economic order. In a memorandum to the twenty-four nations giving aid to Hungary and Poland it connected the "establishment of the institutional system of the market economy" with the replacement of the "monopoly of a single party...by pluralism" and the introduction of "institutional guarantees of the autonomy of the individual." Hungary asked the EEC to stop treating it as a "state-trading country" and to drop quantitative and sanitary restrictions on Hungarian exports.[37]

The president of the Hungarian parliament stated in October 1989 that Hungarian neutrality "could become a reality" even before NATO and the Warsaw Pact disappeared. He did not wish to create problems for Moscow and urged that Hungarian reforms be prepared "on the basis of mutual confidence with the Soviet Union." But "our society is ready to follow on the Austrian or

Finnish model." He urged reforms to make Hungary "democratic and free at the dawn of the 21st century." [38]

In short, the Hungarian model was open ended and led westward.

The "Levers of Power" Model

Another model emerged in August 1989 when Solidarity leaders took the helm of Poland's government but permitted Communists to retain control of the army, the police, and the secret police. Solidarity leader Lech Walesa insisted also that there could be no early withdrawal from the Warsaw Pact. The Polish approach aimed to preserve the "geopolitical" status quo while permitting ideological, political and, above all, economic change within the country. It reassured Moscow that ties with the USSR would not be severed, at least for the present.

This "levers of power" model could not placate Moscow planners worried about the inner empire and border lands. Communists once seized key ministries in Eastern Europe as a step toward total power. But their grip on these institutions in the 1990s could slip as history's reel did a fast rewind. There was no assurance that Communists would continue to control key ministries. Even if they did, the meaning of "Communist" had become uncertain, as most Communists came to put patriotism over "internationalism."

By 1990, Baltic nationalists were in no mood to keep Moscow-leaning Communists in charge of key ministries. Lithuanian prosecutors walked out when Soviet troops installed prosecutors from Moscow to enforce Soviet laws.

The levers of power approach held little appeal to Balts opposed to any curbs on their democracy or sovereignty. Anxious to shift toward free enterprise, they wanted to junk the whole ministerial structure inherited from Soviet rule. Bitter experience with Moscow's "salami tactics" in 1989-1990 only deepened their determination to have local patriots in charge of police, communications, banking, and other key ministries.

Finlandization

Finland served, like Sweden, as a dream for many Balts. For Estonians, Finns are special. The two peoples speak a mutually intelligible language. Estonia's epic hero, Kalevipoeg, swam back and forth to Finland looking for his mother, Linda. The myth-poem tells also how a giant oak fell to form a bridge from Estonia to Finland. The Finnish epic *Kalevala* helped inspire Estonia's *Kalevipoeg*.

Finland in 1990 was prosperous, just, clean, and independent. Estonians believe that they would live in that way were it not for their sovietization. Many Estonians go to Finland as guest workers, and Finns come to Estonia to explore the ground for joint ventures and to drink on weekends.

In 1990 Helsinki unilaterally abandoned clauses of the 1947 Traety of Paris limiting the size of its armed forces and restricting relations with Germany. But Finland's foreign policy, however, is limited by the 1948 Treaty of Friendship, Cooperation, and Mutual Assistance with the USSR. To be sure, the Finnish-Soviet treaty specifies mutual assistance only if Germany or its ally seeks to attack the USSR across Finnish territory. In the event of such attack, Soviet aid to Finland cannot be given automatically but is supposed to follow negotiations. Certainly such niceties could not be meaningful while Soviet troops remained at the Porkkala base (returned to Finland in January 1956). Even today, huge Soviet forces remain deployed from Vyborg to the Barents Sea, ready and able to move against Finland. If Germany or its NATO partners seemed to threaten the USSR, Moscow could invoke the 1948 pact. Such a recipe might suit Moscow, but not the Balts. The Finnish arrangement reminds them of similar pacts that their governments signed with Stalin, giving him a pretext to move in.

As the wind died behind Soviet sails, the threat implicit in the 1948 treaty became less meaningful. Acceptance of the treaty and compliance with it have served Finland not badly. While Finns denied that they knuckled under, however, their publishers long displayed a strange aversion to publishing Aleksandr Solzhenitsyn's *Gulag Archipelago*.

In the late 1980s some Estonians who yearned for a Hungarian model said that they could not aspire to Finnish-style independence. If they could obtain independence on the same conditions as Finland, their future options would be little curtailed.

Such a treaty would save face for Moscow and might be useful to the Kremlin under certain circumstances. It would, however, give a Stalinist overlay to Moscow's peace and friendship campaigns.

Nonaligned and Demilitarized—the Austrian Way

The USSR (along with Britain, France, and the United States) withdrew from Austria in 1955 on the understanding that the country would join no alliance and would possess only light arms.[39] This arrangement has suited the interests of all parties. Austria presents no threat to the USSR; its military vacuum adds to the protective buffer zone formed by the Warsaw Pact; it would also permit an easy march if Moscow decided to strike westward.[40] Austria is a hub for East-West trade and other contacts.[41] Its neutral status strengthened the appeal of nonalignment in Scandinavia, India, and other Third World countries that Moscow sought to pull from the Western orbit in the 1950s and later. Austria and Europe's other neutral democracies did not exacerbate and may have tempered East-West tensions in the decade before Gorbachev's ascendancy.[42]

For many years Moscow worried that Austria might join the EEC and thus jeopardize its neutrality.[43] In the late 1980s the Kremlin waffled on this possibility. At times Soviet spokesmen underscored Moscow's "understanding" of Austria's interest in joining the EEC, but they also emphasized their concern that this step could compromise Austrian neutrality in case the EEC someday became a political or political-military union.

Apart from foreign policy implications, Austria and Finland, along with Sweden and Switzerland, were among the small "law-governed" societies praised by Soviet liberals as models for the domestic development of their country.[44] And if Finland and Sweden looked especially attractive to Balts, Austria was Eden for Hungarians, East Germans, Czechs, and Slovaks.

Thus, there were many aspects to the Austrian model, but the crucial dimension for the Baltic was that Austria committed itself to a Swiss-style neutrality; that East and West pledged to respect this neutrality and to ensure that the country remains lightly armed.

An Austrian solution, then, would mean a measured risk for Soviet military security: The Baltic republics could not join the Warsaw Pact and Soviet forces would have to pull back their bases in those republics. Old thinking would call this madness, but new thinking for the nuclear-missile age might term it wisdom based on sufficiency.

East Central Europe and Global Interdependence

On balance, would Soviet interests gain or lose if the Baltic and some East European countries followed the Austrian model? Some strategists at Soviet think tanks averred in 1989 that the Kremlin could "tolerate" Hungarian and possibly even Baltic neutrality; they said also that reunification was for

Germans to decide — the prospect of a reunited Germany did not faze these analysts. Why? They argued that power and influence in today's world come primarily from having an efficient "information society", not from conventional or nuclear military weaponry. Old-style thinkers — especially those in Soviet military academies — doubtless saw a need to continue basing Soviet power on control of vast territory bristling with tanks and rockets. If liberal trends strengthened in Russia, however, old style power politics might lose favor and new thinking become more persuasive among Soviet decision makers.[45]

Russia's best chance to become integrated with what Gorbachev calls "our common European home" could be through a network of Austrian models from Central Europe to the RSFSR. Moscow might be well advised to bend with the thrust of history as the Baltic republics join Hungary, Poland, and other former satellites now asserting their determination to behave as free countries.

The Kremlin confronted an impossible problem in the Baltic as in all of East Central Europe. If Moscow gave these nations scope to sail into uncharted seas, they might travel further than Moscow wanted. Who can say to what extent Austria or Hungary may be sucked into a united Europe? If Moscow sought to block all motion, it might occur anyway, without the Kremlin's blessing and in anti-Soviet directions.[46]

Europe's future could follow a variety of paths. One scenario showed three rings of integration: (1) A core "United States of Europe" (USE); (2) a European Community — the core USE plus the United Kingdom, Ireland, Denmark, Norway, Austria, and Greece; (3) Associate Members of the European Community — Sweden, Finland, the Baltic Republics, most of Eastern Europe, Switzerland, and Turkey. Many variations on this theme were possible, for example, on the role of Austria and Norway. But if some such broad outline emerged, what would be the place of Russia? Not only did Russia have a different culture from Western and most of East Central Europe, but its sheer size would make it an Albatross for Europe. Its location if not its people was largely in Asia. And who could foretell which non-Russian areas would still accept Moscow's authority in the years ahead?

If Moscow acknowledged Baltic independence, would there be a domino effect throughout the realm? In 1990 most Union Republics — even the

RSFSR — as well as some autonomous republics and regions proclaimed their sovereignty. Were the Ukraine or Kazakhstan to break with the Union, this would have a more serious impact on Soviet power than if the small Baltic states regained their independence.

Because each nation within the erstwhile Union was so different, a single solution appropriate to all republics seemed unlikely. Thus, most politically active Armenians, Azeris, and Georgians in 1990 were quite anti-Soviet, but they were also unsure where to turn for support. An Austrian solution would not ease their intense fears of various neighbors. Georgia's Foreign Minister told me: "We learned the value of guarantees in 1921-1922." The republics of Central Asia were even more closed off from the West than those of the Caucasus.[47]

The withdrawal of Soviet combat forces from Afghanistan in 1988-1989 suggested that the Kremlin, in straitened circumstances, would leave at risk a Communist regime — especially if the West showed no desire to turn Moscow's erstwhile satellite into a base for operations against the USSR. A wiser Kremlin would have embraced an Austrian solution for Afghanistan as soon as it measured local opposition to Communist rule.

A Finnish solution for the Baltic might be more preferable to Moscow than an Austrian, because the Friendship Treaty with Helsinki gives the Kremlin a pretext for intervention in Finnish affairs.[48] Such treaties, however, are anachronistic; grate on local sensitivities; and are either meaningless or redundant.

The ultimate hope for Russia is not to be found in husbanding imperial prerogatives but in ushering in a new era of political and economic freedom. The Kremlin loses more trying to boss its border nations than it gains. The burdens of empire have mounted since the mid-1950s — the costs of lost opportunities as well as those spent occupying or subsidizing alien lands.[49]

As Estonian political maverick Tiit Made put it: "If Moscow were to stop and think, and forget for a moment its superpower ambitions, it would give Estonia its freedom. This could represent a significant economic and political gain" for Moscow as well as Estonia. "The Baltic countries still remain as the last vestige of a colonial system." The Kremlin should understand that a free Estonia could help deal with the USSR's deep economic crisis. If Estonians felt free, instead of being "robbed," they would "recover the desire to work."

Estonia would be able to produce more food and consumer goods and sell them to Russia.

"Estonia, Latvia and Lithuania could form an excellent buffer zone between East and West," Tiit Made asserted. "The Soviet Union is losing its middlemen in Finland, Austria, and Sweden who willingly bought goods in the West and sold them to the East. The Baltic states could take on this role....We have a European culture and are better equipped to establish contacts with people similar to ourselves in Sweden, Finland, Britain, and Canada. The Soviet Union...can only gain from giving the Baltic countries their freedom." [50]

History suggests the perils in trying to retain an empire in decay or which is rent by centrifugal forces. If Communist ideology is dead and the West does not menace Russia militarily, the Kremlin should seek a soft landing, such as a buffer on the Austrian model. A farsighted Kremlin would aim to release the energies of Russians and their neighbors, joining in a larger world that, as Gorbachev has often stated, is "contradictory yet integral and interdependent."

NOTES

1. N. Dolgopolova and A. Kokoshin, "Chemu uchat sud'by velikikh derzhav [What is the Lesson of the Fate of the Great Powers?]" *Kommunist*, 17 (November 1988), pp. 115-21, quote at p. 118. Kokoshin told me in 1989 that he regarded this as his most important essay in recent years.

2. Mikhail Kozhokin, "Vostochnaia Evropa: preodolenie krizisa," *Literaturnaia gazeta*, 50 (13 December 1989), p. 15.

3. See comments of Oleg T. Bogomolov, Viktor Belkin, Vladimir Tikhonov, and others attending an American Enterprise Institute conference in Washington: Robert Pear, "Soviet Experts Say Their Economy Is Worse Than U.S. Has Estimated," *The New York Times*, 24 April 1990, p. A14.

4. The inner and overseas domains are analyzed in Henry S. Rowen and Charles Wolf, Jr., eds., *The Future of the Soviet Empire* (New York: St. Martin's, 1987).

5. There is only passing reference here to overseas clients, increasingly compelled to fend for themselves.

6. For optimistic reports on how this principle could be implemented in the economic sphere, see Iu. D. Masliukov: "Strong Center — Strong Republics," *Pravda*, 23 March 1989, p. 2; and interview with A.I. Smirnov, chief of the USSR Council of Ministers, Administration of Affairs National Economy and Capital Construction Territorial Development Depart-

ment: "Toward Harmonization of Interests. Strong Center—Strong Regions," *Izvestiia*, 30 March 1989, p. 2.

7. See the roundtable, "To Listen to One Another," *Kommunist*, No. 6 (April 1989) pp. 62-80, cited point at p. 65.

8. Rein Taagepera, "Estonia's Road to Independence," *Problems of Communism*, 38, 6 (November-December 1989), pp. 11-26, at p. 13.

9. Ibid.

10. For these terms, see David A. Lax and James K. Sebenius, *The Manager as Negotiator: Bargaining for Cooperation and Competitive Gain* (New York: Free Press, 1986).

11. See the Mytilene debate in Thucydides, *The Peloponnesian War*, (Baltimore, Md: Penguin, 1956), III, 3, pp. 180-89.

12. Thucydides, V, 7, pp. 364-65.

13. See Walter C. Clemens, Jr., "Soviet Foreign Policy Since 1917: Achievements and Failures," *Survey*, 30, 4 (June 1989), pp. 87-112, at pp. 94, 100, 108.

14. Paul B. Henze, "The Spectre and Implications of Internal Nationalist Dissent," in S. Enders Wimbush, ed., *Soviet Nationalities in Strategic Perspective* (New York: St. Martin's Press, 1985), pp. 1-35, at pp. 30-35.

15. Richard Ned Lebow, "Dominant Powers and Subordinate Regions: 1914 and Today," in Jan F. Triska, ed., *Dominant Powers and Subordinate States: The United States in Latin America and the Soviet Union in Eastern Europe* (Durham, N.C.: Duke University Press, 1986), pp. 400-22, at pp. 404-5.

16. As a whole, Austria is also more affluent than unevenly developed Italy, erstwhile home to other empires.

17. See Eino Jutikkala with Kauko Pirinen, *A History of Finland* (New York: Dorset, 1988), pp. 161-64.

18. The castrated horse in *Farewell Gulsary!* by Chingiz Aitmatov, as suggested above in the Introduction, may be a metaphor for the Kirghiz and other Soviet nationalities.

19. James R. Kurth, "Economic Change and State Development," in Triska, *Dominant Powers and Subordinate States*, pp. 85-101, at p. 94.

20. Washington did not hold back but pressured Latin America to be more open to world trade and investment, to react to market shifts, and to upgrade its technology. North Americans paid Latins in a convertible currency that could be used anywhere. See Paul Marer and Kazimierz Z. Poznanski, "Costs of Domination, Benefits of Subordination," in Triska, *Dominant Powers*, pp. 371-99, at p. 372.

21. Tiit Käbin, "Treaty of the Union: The Estonian Solution?" *Homeland* (Tallinn), No. 3 (212), 18 January 1989, pp. 1-2.

22. This point is made also by Rein Taagepera, "How Empires End: Is the Soviet Union to Become a Commonwealth?" Estonian version published in *Looming*, March 1989, p. 8; English in *Homeland*, 12, 19, 26 July 1989.

23. See also Alain Besançon, "The Nationalities Issue in the USSR," *Survey*, 30, 4 (June 1989), pp. 113-30, at pp. 123-24.

24. See comments on federalism by Balts and other scholars in "To Listen to One Another," pp. 74-78.

25. Clear analysis is made more difficult by an ambiguity: The Russian word for "union" is the same as for "alliance," *soiuz*. "Allied" republics would seem to be virtually independent except for their alliance, probably specified in a treaty. "Union Republics," in Soviet practice, have been subordinate to Moscow.

26. Tiit Käbin in *Homeland*, 18 January 1989, p. 2.

27. A federation differs from a confederation in that the central power acts directly upon individuals as well upon states, thus creating the problem of dual allegiance. See *The New Columbia Encyclopedia* (New York: Columbia University Press, 1975), p. 931.

28. See *Die Schweiz vom Bau der Alpen bis zur Frage nach der Zukunft* (Lucerne and Zurich: Ex Libris Verlags AG, 1975), pp. 371ff.

29. Stephen Kux, "Soviet Federalism," *Problems of Communism*, 34, 2 (March-April 1990), pp. 1-20, at pp. 19-20.

30. Boris Koltsov, quoted in William Echikson, "Soviets Loosen Grip on East Bloc," *Christian Science Monitor*, 22 August 1989, p. 3.

31. When CMEA ministers met in Sofia early in 1990, Czechoslovakia, Poland, and Hungary made clear that they saw no function for the organization other than to provide the best conditions for its members to transform themselves into market economies. Major disputes centered around how to relate East European currencies to the ruble, how to pay for Soviet fuel supplies, and what aid to continue to Cuba, Outer Mongolia, and Vietnam. See John Lloyd, "Moscow and E. Europe in Row over the Future of Comecon," *Financial Times*, 15 January 1990, p. 18.

32. Kozhokin, "Vostochnaia Evropa."

33. Shevardnadze said that the ten-year agreement, calling for an end to most EEC quotas on Soviet products, "brings the construction of the economic foundation for a common European house one step closer." The accord stipulated cooperation in food processing, tourism, banking, insurance, oil and gas, and nuclear energy. *The New York Times*, 19 December 1989, p. D1.

34. For background on the Warsaw Pact, see J. F. Brown, *Eastern Europe and Communist Rule* (Durham, N.C.: Duke University Press, 1988), pp. 38-41.

35. William Colby and Daniel Plesch, "A New Aim: Not Cannons but Castles," *International Herald-Tribune*, 29 August 1989.

36. Jonathan Dean, *Meeting Gorbachev's Challenge: How to Build Down the NATO-Warsaw Pact Confrontation* (New York: St. Martin's, 1989); for obstacles to any reductions, see Robert D. Blackwill and F. Stephen Larrabee, eds., *Conventional Arms Control and East-West Security* (Durham, N.C.: Duke University Press, 1989).

37. John Lloyd, "Hungary Vows to Free Economy," *Financial Times*, 3 August 1989.

38. Matyas Szuros, president of the Hungarian parliament, quoted in *Financial Times*, 6 October 1989, p. 2.

39. The five-power state treaty of May 15, 1955, prohibited Austria from having atomic or other mass destruction weapons; any guided missile; guns with a range of more than thirty kilometers; stocks of poisons or bacteriological agents greater than needed for civil purposes. The Allies reserved the right to add prohibitions of any weapons evolved as a result of scientific development. But the treaty did not set ceilings on numbers of armed personnel, tanks, or aircraft. Text in *Department of State Bulletin*, June 6, 1955, p. 916. Austria's Constitution pledged Swiss-style neutrality and the country's perpetual neutrality was then recognized by notes from each of the four allies.

40. Walter C. Clemens, Jr., "An Austrian Solution for Eastern Europe," *The New York Times*, 10 July 1989, p. A18, discussed in "Öesterreich als Vorbild für Ost-Staaten," *Der Standard* (Vienna), 12 July 1989. The article was translated (with many inaccuracies) and critiqued in *Sovetskaia Estoniia*, 22 November 1989.

41. On an Austrian firm that has been successfully trading with the USSR since 1955, see Judy Dempsey, "Another Breed of Soviet Agent Thrives in Vienna," *Financial Times*, 3 August 1989, p. 3.

42. For case studies of Finland, Sweden, Ireland, Switzerland, and Austria since the mid-1970s, see Bengt Sundelius, ed., *The Neutral Democracies and the New Cold War* (Boulder, Colo.: Westview, 1987).

43. See Walter C. Clemens, Jr., "Maintaining the Status Quo in East Central Europe: The 1930s and 1960s," *World Affairs*, 133, 2 (September 1970), pp. 98-105.

44. Chinghiz Aitmatov, days after he proposed to the Congress of People's Deputies that Gorbachev be chairman of the Supreme Soviet, listed for the Congress these four states along with Norway, the Netherlands, Spain, and Canada (all NATO members) as "countries that do not call themselves socialist, but are none the worse for that." See *Izvestiia*, 4 June 1989, p. 2, cited by Archie Brown, "Political Change in the Soviet Union," *World Policy Journal*, 6, 3 (Summer 1989), pp. 469-501, at p. 474. Oleg Bogomolov, director of the Institute of Economics of the World Socialist System, when asked what he hoped the USSR would look like in twenty years, replied "Sweden or perhaps Austria." See Richard Parker, "Assessing Perestroika," *World Policy Journal*, 6, 2 (Spring 1989), p. 294.

45. Walter C. Clemens, Jr., "Inside Gorbachev's Think Tank," *World Monitor*, 2, 8 (August 1989), pp. 28-36.

46. Thus, when financial and legal pressures kept Austria from joining a customs union with Germany in 1931, this aggravated economic distress and helped bring on Hitler. See Walter C. Clemens, Jr., "Great and Small Power Collaboration to Enforce the Status Quo: France and Czechoslovakia Against the Vienna Protocol," *East European Quarterly*, 2, 4 (January 1969), pp. 385-412.

47. Perhaps the Kremlin should hold plebiscites to determine whether each people wants to continue its affiliation with Russia and, if so, in what format. The polls (if held under conditions that ensured a free choice) would confer some legitimacy on whatever arrangements proved most popular. But there are many problems in this approach. Would settlers be allowed to vote? Soldiers on temporary duty? What if the eastern Ukraine wanted to stay with Russia but the western wished to secede? What if Kishinev opted for union but the Moldavian countryside preferred to join Romania? Past plebiscites in Puerto Rico showed little support for independence but registered only slim majorities for "Commonwealth" over statehood.

48. Alternative Politburo member Nikolai Talyzin asserted during a 1989 visit to Helsinki that the "present level of Soviet-Finnish cooperation" is a "viable model of interstate relations, based on principles of equality and mutual respect." He looked forward to Gorbachev's visiting Finland and to the reconstruction of international relations on the basis of general human values. TASS in English, *FBIS-SOV*, 6 April 1989, pp. 22-23.

49. See Valerie Bunce, "The Empire Strikes Back: The Transformation of the Eastern Bloc from a Soviet Asset to a Soviet Liability," *International Organization*, 39, 1 (Winter 1985), pp. 1-46.

50. Tiit Made, "If Moscow Were to Give Estonia Its Freedom," *Svenska Dagbladet*, 22 March 1989, p. 2, *FBIS-SOV*, 30 March 1989, pp. 49-50.

*"Shall I weep if...an infant civilization be ruled
with rod or with knout?"*
Tennyson (1855)

15

Implications for the West:
How to Join Idealism
with Realism?

The fate of the Baltic peoples goes to the heart of idealistic as well as pragmatic concerns in the West. The two sets of impulses have often seemed to contradict one another, but enlightened self-interest could bring them together. The deepest interests of all concerned could be best served in arrangements that permitted the Baltic republics to exist as independent, nonaligned states helping to bridge Russia and the West.

This conclusion derives from historical experience in which idealism has often been sidetracked in favor of apparent realism. Let us review the past before assessing the future.

The right of national self-determination has been part of the American credo for over 200 years. President Woodrow Wilson pressed the world to make it an axiom of international organization and law. But this ideal runs against various practical considerations. Some "nations" may be too small to exist as independent states. Some — such as Navajos and Tatars — are surrounded by others. The fates of others have been so intertwined with larger, more powerful nations that independence seems infeasible.

Dilemmas such as these led Wilson to compromise his ideals as the World War I victors deliberated the fates of the many nations liberated from the German, Austro-Hungarian, Russian, and Ottoman empires. Slovaks and many Germans, for example, would have to coexist with a Czech majority in one Czecho-Slovak Republic. The League of Nations Council did not recognize the three Baltic republics until 1921; Washington put off their recognition until July 1922.

All history shows that the ability of any people to shape its own destiny is subject to a variety of internal and external factors. National self-determination for smaller peoples is often hostage to the great powers.

Spheres of Influence

Great powers are tempted to partition the realms between them into spheres of influence. Thus, Moscow and Berlin divided Eastern Europe in 1939-1940. Stalin and Winston Churchill also sought in October 1944 to partition the area in what the British Prime Minister conceded looked like an "offhand manner...fateful to millions of peoples." [1] While those accords were explicit, behavior can tacitly carry a similar message, for example: The USSR could moderate its support for leftists in Latin America in tandem with or in exchange for U.S. restraint in Eastern Europe or Russia's border lands.

Such policies could be labeled "value-creating," but they are really "value-claiming" because they extract gains at the expense of third parties. They may provide stability for a time, but in times of rapid change and global communications, they tend quickly to collapse and backfire. They readily lead not only to insurrections within one power's putative sphere but to head-on collisions between the great powers. Such "realism" can be unrealistic as well as morally bankrupt.

Pros and cons of spheres-of-interests accords were debated on the eve of the Peloponnesian War. [2] That confrontation differed greatly from today's East-West relations, but the Greek debates stated the issues in classic form. Just as Gorbachev asked the West not to interfere in the Baltic in 1989-1990, Corinth told Athens not to exploit its temporary weakness by siding with Corcyra (Corfu), a Corinthian colony revolting against its mother polis. Corinth warned Athens not to "establish a precedent by which a power may receive into its alliance the revolted subjects of another power." Corinth recalled that Athenian leaders had themselves argued that "every power should have the right to control [and punish] its own allies." Corinth suggested that "an act of kindness done at the right moment"—refraining from aiding Corcyra—"has a power to dispel old grievances quite out of proportion to the act itself," an idea that more than two thousand years later sometimes stirred hope in Washington. The Corinthians added: "The power that deals fairly with its equals finds a truer security than the one which is hurried into snatching some apparent but dangerous advantage."

Just as Balts later looked to the West, so Corcyrans appealed to Athens for support. They explained that they were in revolt because Corinth had treated them badly, like slaves. Corcyra had proposed arbitration of disputes, but Corinth prosecuted its claims by force. Athens, Corcyrans warned, should not be lured into "deceitful traps or listening to what may appear to be [Corinth's] straightforward demands. When one makes concessions to one's enemies, one regrets it afterwards."

Corcyrans asked Athens not to reject them in their hour of peril. Corcyra argued that Athens would not breach its treaty with Sparta by taking Corcyra into its alliance, because Corcyra was neutral. To turn away Corcyra would be to build up the strength of the Corinth-Sparta axis.[3]

Atlantic Charter and/or Grand Alliance?

The Cold War started not over Poland or Iran but the Baltic—even as Churchill, Stalin, and Roosevelt sought to weld a grand coalition against the Axis. Each party buttressed its position by a variation on the classic Greek arguments uttered more than two millennia before. Thus Stalin told Britain's Anthony Eden on December 16, 1941 that an Anglo-Soviet alliance should include explicit recognition of Soviet frontiers as they existed just before the German attack in June 1941. The Kremlin wanted Britain to recognize Soviet absorption of the Baltic republics and parts of Finland, Romania, and Poland. Moscow also sought bases in Romania and Finland and considered extension of Soviet borders into East Prussia. Eden refused to make such commitments, citing London's pledge to Washington not to enter any secret accords on territorial revisions during the course of the war. The Americans held that acceptance of such requests would violate the principles of the Atlantic Charter signed August 14, 1941, by Churchill and Roosevelt.[4]

In March 1942 Churchill wavered and informed Roosevelt: "The increasing gravity of the war has led me to feel that the principles of the Atlantic Charter ought not to be construed so as to deny Russia the frontiers she occupied when Germany attacked her. This was the basis on which Russia acceded to the Charter [along with more than twenty other countries on January 1, 1942], and

I expect that a severe process of liquidating hostile elements in the Baltic States, etc., was employed by the Russians when they took these regions at the beginning of the war. I hope therefore that you will be able to give us a free hand to sign the treaty which Stalin desires as soon as possible." Churchill predicted an immense renewal of the German invasion of Russia soon and said "there is very little we can do to help the only country that is heavily engaged with the German armies." He implied that since the West could do little else to aid Russia, Stalin should be thrown the bone of little peoples, of whom, as Neville Chamberlain once said, "we know nothing." [5]

Eden and other British representatives told Washington that recognition of the boundaries Stalin claimed was a small price to pay for Soviet cooperation in the war, even if this meant consigning the Baltic peoples forever to Russian overlordship. A readiness to yield on the frontier issue had become the acid test of Britain's new relationship with Moscow.[6]

The Kremlin for three months demanded recognition not just of its gains in Finland and the Baltic but in Poland and Romania. Churchill and Stalin wanted Washington to go along, but the State Department was obdurate. The British told Washington they were ready to act unilaterally, Secretary of State Cordell Hull warned that Washington might denounce the territorial clauses and disavow the whole business.

This stiffened Eden, who suggested to Molotov in May 1942 that their treaty omit any territorial clauses. Against Churchill's expectations — and to the surprise of the Soviet ambassador to London — the Kremlin relented. Having consulted with Stalin, Molotov accepted a twenty-year treaty of alliance with Britain that omitted all reference to frontiers. "This was a great relief to me," Churchill noted, "and a far better solution than I had dared to hope." Although he and Eden had been ready to give in, Churchill attributed the outcome to Anglo-American solidarity and Eden's skillful timing! American envoy W. Averell Harriman noted that, having conceded the territorial issue, Molotov had a stronger claim on the West to open a second front.[7]

Roosevelt had approved Hull's resistance to a territorial deal, but in 1943 he decided to negotiate these matters with Stalin personally. He hoped to dissuade Stalin from unilateral action by explaining to him the many benefits for the USSR that would flow from "decent behavior" as contrasted to the "violent antagonism" Moscow would encounter if it just seized certain territories. The benefits would include equal seating among the Great Powers at council tables; U.S. support for measures to strengthen Russia's security such as internationalization of access to the Baltic; and postwar economic assistance. He wanted plebiscites in the Baltic, Harriman observed, not realizing that once the Russians occupied a territory, the vote would almost certainly go their way.[8]

What seemed to be a matter of principle in 1941-1942 was explained to Stalin as vote-getting expediency when Roosevelt met him at Tehran in 1943. Perhaps this was not Roosevelt's intention, but it comes across this way in the Russian minutes of their meeting, sandwiched between more formal tripartite meetings.[9]

Roosevelt asked Stalin to see him — without Churchill present — on a matter of internal American politics, the 1944 elections. As a self-styled "practical man," he could not ignore the six to seven million Americans voters of Polish extraction. Roosevelt did not personally object to reconstituting the Polish government and moving Poland's boundaries to the Oder River, but he could not publicly approve such changes until after next year's elections.

Roosevelt said that there were also Americans of Lithuanian, Latvian, and Estonian origin. Public opinion in the United States and the world might in the future demand that the Baltic peoples, after reoccupation by Soviet forces, be able to express their own opinion in a referendum. Stalin replied that these nations did not have "autonomy" in tsarist Russia. When the tsar allied with the United States and England, no one raised the issue of Baltic exit from Russia. Why raise this issue now?

Roosevelt explained that "public opinion does not know history." Stalin answered that they should be informed and some propaganda work done. But perhaps neither Roosevelt nor Stalin knew history, because Washington never allied with tsardom although it associated itself with Russia's Provisional Government after April 1917. Compounding the historical mixup, Roosevelt assured Stalin: "I know that Lithuania, Latvia, and Estonia in the past and even recently were a part of the Soviet Union [*sic*]."

Smiling (according to Harriman), Roosevelt added that he did not intend to go to war with the USSR "when Russian troops again enter the [Baltic] republics....But public opinion will demand a plebiscite there."

Stalin assured him that "in our setup [*u nas*] there will be not infrequent occasions to give to the peoples of these republics an opportunity to express their will."

Gratified by such ambiguity, Roosevelt replied: "That will be useful to me."

Weakening his commitment still further, Stalin clarified: "This, of course, does not mean, that a plebiscite in these republics must take place under any kind of international inspection [*kontrol'*]."

Roosevelt replied, "Of course not." adding that it would be useful to announce at an appropriate time that elections would some day take place in these republics.

Stalin: "Certainly, it will be possible to do this."

At Tehran Roosevelt did not promise to recognize Soviet annexation of the Baltic, but he implied that if Stalin arranged at least a show election, Washington would go along. Roosevelt also sided with Stalin on Finnish issues, and proposed replacing the "pro-Nazi" government in Finland. Churchill argued against forcing Finland to pay reparations to the USSR, because it was so poor.

The fate of East Prussia was also decided that afternoon. Churchill agreed to position a new Poland between the Curzon Line and the Oder River, provided Poland got part of East Prussia. Churchill gave the rest of East Prussia to Stalin, including Königsberg and Memel (soon, Kaliningrad and Klaipeda), to satisfy his need for warm water Baltic ports.[10]

In February 1945 the U.S. president again talked cynically about Polish voters and asked Stalin to "save face" for all concerned with Poland — in no way preparing Stalin for the strong Western reaction to sovietization of Eastern Europe.[11] Roosevelt was also quite cavalier in awarding Russia huge parts of the Far East. His generous initiatives — without stipulating conditions — seemed to touch Stalin.[12]

In 1944 the Soviet Constitution was changed to give each Union Republic its own foreign and defense ministries. The Soviets then demanded a seat for each republic at the United Nations. In February 1945, however, Molotov asked for only two or three UN seats besides that of the USSR — for the Ukraine, Belorussia, and Lithuania. Roosevelt and Churchill turned down the bait to give Lithuania a seat, a move that would have implied recognition of Baltic annexation.[13]

Despite the spirit of Yalta, the State Department in March 1945 reiterated that "the United States Government has not formally recognized any territorial changes brought about by the present war in Europe." Hence the United States refused to force refugees from the Baltic or eastern Poland to return to Soviet jurisdiction. This policy was reinforced by orders from the Supreme Commander of the Allied Expeditionary Force, General Dwight D. Eisenhower, on June 2, 1945.[14]

"Captive Nations" versus Detente?

Soviet-Western relations deteriorated quickly after the defeat of Germany, with Moscow tightening the screws in the Baltic and other parts of its empire. The Cold War eased a bit in July 1955 and September 1959 when Eisenhower, now the U.S. president, met with Khrushchev in Geneva and Washington. While many Americans welcomed detente with Moscow, many did not forget the peoples subject to Communist tyranny. The U.S. Congress by joint resolution approved July 17, 1959, authorized and requested the President to designate the third week of July each year as Captive Nations Week.

For decades to come the United States commemorated Captive Nations Week — often at the very time that it sought understandings on arms control and other East-West differences.

President Gerald Ford signed the Helsinki Final Act in 1975, making clear that Washington did not recognize as legal any occupation or acquisition of territory in violation of international law. He reiterated that Washington's "official policy of nonrecognition" of Soviet incorporation of the three Baltic states was "not affected by the results of the European Security Conference.[15]

The Helsinki documents affirmed that Europe's borders were inviolable and should not be changed by force, but they also pledged all signatories to respect and promote human rights — which increased Moscow's vulnerability to criticism for its policies in the Baltic and elsewhere.

The Reagan administration sustained Washington's critical stance toward Soviet occupation of the Baltic. On November 18, 1983, the president announced the establishment of a new Baltic States Service Division at Radio Liberty, saying that the new service would "reinforce the distinct identities of the Baltic States and separate them from the rest of the Soviet Union."

The State Department's *Country Reports on Human Rights Practices* initiated separate ledgers on the Baltic republics. Ambassador Max Kampelman detailed Soviet abuses of human rights in the Baltic — the cases of Juris Bumeisters, Algirdas Statkevicius, and Juri Kukk — at the Madrid Conference of the CSCE. Ambassador Richard Schiftler complained to the UN Human Rights Commission in March 1984 about imprisonment of Latvian human rights activists.[16]

Baltic Independence versus Perestroika?

Even after Reagan's relations with Gorbachev's Kremlin improved, Washington did not relax the pressure. American officials reaffirmed the nonrecognition policy at a conference held at Jurmala, Latvia, September 15-19, 1986. They also criticized Moscow's Baltic policies. Telling Latvians that they were not forgotten, U.S. representatives probably lifted Baltic spirits, heightened expectations for a reevaluation of Latvia's status within the USSR, and added impetus to the national revival. Some 40,000 copies of the conference proceedings were printed in Latvian by a Riga publishing house.[17]

U.S. government maps continued to underscore Washington's nonrecognition of Baltic annexation. The United States refused to talk to the heads of the Baltic governments, because they had not been democratically elected since 1940. But Washington also refused to deal with representatives of the independent governments that were crushed in 1940. American diplomats in the Leningrad consulate, however, maintained contacts with Baltic political groups on many levels.

Congress by joint resolution designated June 14, 1989, Baltic Freedom Day and asked President George Bush to issue a proclamation. The president's proclamation detailed political, religious, and cultural repression in the Baltic and environmental degradation there. He noted that the Baltic peoples "demand and deserve lasting guarantees of their fundamental rights." He reaffirmed that Washington "does not and will not recognize the unilateral incorporation by force of arms of the Baltic States into the Soviet Union." [18]

Despite this declaration, President Bush and his top advisers seemed to distance themselves from the Baltic independence movement in 1989. A paradox emerged: The United States had long affirmed the Balts' right to self-determination. As prospects for Baltic independence soared, Washington seemed to pull back its support or at least remain silent. Bush and Secretary of State James Baker—at least in public—treated the Baltic as an internal problem of the USSR, to be resolved by peaceful dialogue.

Since the "dialogue" was between parties of such radically different strengths, it was not a contest between equals. Bush often reiterated that the United States had never recognized Soviet annexation of the Baltic, but he said almost nothing to underscore a moral preference for national self-determination and did almost nothing to ease the isolation of the Balts.

The Kremlin offered little thanks for Washington's measured behavior and sharply rebuked any semblance of U.S. interference in Soviet "domestic affairs." *Pravda* on September 1, 1989, noted that Bush had called on Gorbachev to display restraint in response to Baltic demands for greater independence. Bush's statement came after he met with Senate minority leader Robert Dole, who had just returned from visiting the USSR and Poland. Having described Moscow's attitude as one of great understanding, Bush expressed a hope that Soviet policy would continue in this way as fast-moving changes continued their advance in Poland and in other countries.

Pravda correspondent V. Gan asked: "Who in Moscow needs the U.S. president's advice? We need no compliments, either. Everything we do is for ourselves and for our own sake, actually guided by universal considerations and values."

Bush probably wanted the best of both worlds: constructive East-West relations *plus* greater freedom for the nations of the USSR. If pressured to choose, however, he placed the former goal well above the latter.

Whereas the Reagan administration had met often with Baltic Americans, Bush and his advisers sidestepped any such encounter for more than a year. On April 11, 1990, however, Bush and other ranking officials sat down with fourteen representatives of Baltic-American organizations.[19] The president allowed that this was a "time of hope and yet of frustration." He supported freedom but his agenda included "many items important to the world." He gave Gorbachev "credit that Eastern Europe enjoys a chance to permanentize and solidify democracy." He had discussed the Baltic with Gorbachev since their 1989 meeting in Malta, stressing "our commitment to self-determination."

Bush resented portraits of himself as a "cold-hearted elitist" who did not "care about human rights." But he wanted to avoid "a whole reversal inside the USSR" and feared a "catastrophe" if Gorbachev were replaced.

Secretary of State Baker, also present, took note of suggestions by Baltic Americans: that Bush send a letter of congratulations to Landsbergis on his election; that Washington establish a liaison office in Vilnius; that Baltic independence be a condition for most-favored-nation treatment of the USSR.

Baker asserted that the Soviet leadership understood the inevitability of change in the Baltic and was trying to develop a legal procedure for it. Washington approved this approach but insisted it not be "onerous or a subterfuge" such as the new Soviet law on secession.

Little Bark, No Bite: Unrealpolitik

Meanwhile, tensions mounted between Moscow and Vilnius throughout April 1990. When Gorbachev demanded that Lithuania retract its declaration of independence, Bush called again for peaceful dialogue. When Moscow stepped up the pressure, the White House warned that if the Kremlin went too far, Washington would not give most-favored-nation treatment to the USSR and would thwart plans to ease the Soviets' path to a more active role in world commerce. The Americans promised to select measures that would hurt the USSR far more than the United States, while keeping arms control and other accords of mutual interest on track. Economic and cultural sanctions, they said, would not derail the Bush-Gorbachev summit planned for Washington in late May.

But when the Kremlin cut off oil, gas, and other supplies to Lithuania, the White House backed down on April 24, 1990. Bush said he feared doing something "imprudent" that caused the USSR "to take action that would set back the cause of freedom around the world." U.S. spokesmen hinted to the press that Lithuania had been unreasonable and could not expect Western help for such a poorly planned scheme. The summit was still on and Washington would delay any possible sanctions against the USSR. It would wait and see how things developed in the Baltic. The State Department even refused in April 1990 to give a visa to Lithuania's Prime Minister except for a private visit. When President Bush finally received her, White House guards did not permit the Prime Minister's brother and others in her delegation to enter the building. Meanwhile, U.S. trade negotiators wrapped up a deal with their Soviet counterparts, which Congress — divided on Baltic issues — could scuttle.

Bush's wait-and-watch policy in effect sided with Gorbachev and did nothing to ease mounting strains upon Lithuania. President Landsbergis likened the American posture to the sellout of Czechoslovakia at Munich.

Washington's approach, however, seemed to win favor in Paris, London, and Bonn — all concerned with trade and detente. A poll showed that 61 percent of U.S. voters also put improved relations with the USSR above efforts to promote Lithuanian independence. This helped Bush reply to Landsbergis that he worked for the American people and that they approved of his course.

Like Roosevelt during World War II, Bush evidently took no deep interest in national self-determination for the Baltic peoples. His major concerns were approval ratings from American voters and improved Soviet-U.S. relations. Like British diplomats in 1942, Bush probably thought that consigning Balts to Soviet overlordship was a small price to pay for Moscow's cooperation in other matters. He thought, as Roosevelt did, that the current Soviet leader was unique and that personal diplomacy with him could work wonders. Bush, no less than Roosevelt, somehow thought that the United States needed to cajole a country that was almost flat on its back and desperate for assistance.

The Bush team rejected any major priority for human rights. The president did not let himself be swayed by sympathy for oppressed peoples trying to break from the yoke of dictators and imperialist metropoles. His preference for "realism" over sentiment was demonstrated in 1989 when he immediately dispatched National Security Assistant Brent Scowcroft to kowtow in Beijing after China's rulers butchered young people crying for democracy at Tiananmen Square. Bush's words and deeds indicated that he saw the struggle for self-determination in the Baltic and elsewhere as internal problems for Moscow and Beijing.

Perhaps the president worried that Moscow and Beijing would reject expanded trade and technology transfers if Washington failed to endorse their repressive moves. Unless the United States expressed "understanding" of Soviet and Chinese firmness with dissidents, perhaps one or both Communist giants would crank up the arms race and scuttle arms control.

The Bush administration, like others, seemed to exaggerate the strength and perhaps the expansionist intentions of the Communist states. Did the White House not see that Communism everywhere — even in Beijing and Moscow — was on the run? No Communist regime was in a position to demand approval for its barbaric ways.

The president's flipflop of traditional American values harmed not only the democrats and national minorities of the USSR and China: It pushed the United

States toward a shortsighted, greedy egotism contrary to its best interests as well as its deepest ideals. When the president ate crow, it made the entire country look wimpish. Even American democracy suffered, because Scowcroft's two visits to Beijing in 1989 were hushed up and contradicted Bush's declared policy of breaking off high-level contacts after Tiananmen. The Scowcroft-Tiananmen two-step signified that Washington's bark had no bite. Washington trembled lest any U.S. words or deeds be seen as interference in Chinese or Soviet internal affairs.

Rushing in where angels would fear to tread, the White House expressed its understanding for Soviet military action against Azerbaijan. Preventing racial violence, remarked James Baker, is different from repressing peaceful dissidents. To be sure, Moscow *said* that it wanted only to halt massacres of Armenians, but Defense Minister D. T. Yazov admitted on January 26, 1990, that Soviet forces sought to destroy Azerbaijan's Popular Front. Whatever the motive, such operations could become a precedent for armed repression of peaceful Baltic separatists. Any coercive acts by Soviet forces should have engendered alarm, not complacency.[20]

Trying to save face for dictators in Moscow and Beijing, the U.S. president diminished his own and his country's image. Why threaten economic penalties and then back off? Why jeopardize the moral and legal power accumulated by half a century of support for nonrecognition of Soviet annexation of the Baltic?

The president endeavored to combine a form of realpolitik with heavy reliance on personal relations with foreign leaders, seeking to build good will with Deng Xiaoping, Gorbachev, and others. Bush seemed to believe that realism required him to resist moral judgments on world affairs — the Tiananmen massacre, the blockade of Lithuania, even Iraq's threat to resume chemical warfare.[21]

What Bush achieved was an unrealpolitik, actions that evaded principle and substituted personal diplomacy for the hard-nosed, steadfast polices required by real realism. Here was a double mistake: no clear policies and no clear principles. Bush's investment in the fate of selected foreign autocrats compromised American support for democracy when the market for it was at a record high.

Perhaps the president, like ancient Corinth, wanted to work out a sphere-of-interests arrangement for the great powers. "Let Washington,

Moscow, and Beijing each police its internal affairs and backyard" seemed to be Bush's motto, no matter how far the "backyard" reached. Indeed, there were even reports that Bush blessed the idea of Soviet intervention in Romania in 1989. If U.S. forces could invade Panama and police the seas and jungles of Latin America, why not the Red Army in Bucharest?

Such attitudes were morally weak, legally dubious, failure-prone, and unnecessary. The West was in a strong position to support self-determination in the Baltic in the 1990s. Instead of hinting "understanding" when Beijing repressed Tibet and Han liberationists, and when Moscow sent troops to subdue unruly nationalists, Washington should have affirmed its solidarity with all captive nations — certainly those oppressed by Communist dictatorships.[22] The West, far more than Moscow or Beijing, possessed an array of sticks and carrots to support its values and interests abroad.

There was no excuse in 1990 to repeat the hypocrisy of 1956 or the shortsightedness of 1968. In the mid-1950s America hinted it would help East Europeans "roll back" the Iron Curtain, but then stood inert as Soviet tanks crushed Hungarians. In 1968 Secretary of State Dean Rusk made clear beforehand that America would not act if the Kremlin halted Czechoslovakia's liberalization.

"All or nothing at all" seems to have been America's guiding light in 1956, 1968, and 1990 — Armageddon or utter passivity. Bush repeatedly told Baltic Americans on April 11, 1990, that he wanted to avoid the kind of "humiliation" that America experienced over Hungary. But a creative foreign policy can be conducted on dozens of planes short of nuclear war or utter passivity.

The U.S. Congress resolution in 1990 declaring June 14 to be Baltic Freedom Day used stronger language than the previous year. It requested the president to "submit to the Congress within sixty days a statement" listing U.S. actions to support "restoration" of Baltic independence and "encourage Soviet support for a peaceful transition to independence...in the Baltic States." The Joint Baltic American National Committee and the Baltic American Freedom League lobbied hard for the resolution.

In late July 1990 Latvia's Prime Minister, Ivars Godmanis, and his Foreign Minister, Janis Jurkans, met President Bush, Secretary of State Baker, National Security assistant Brent Scowcroft and over a dozen U.S. Senators in Washington. Meetings at this level between Latvian and U.S. officials were unprecedented. Not even during the interwar years had Latvian officials ever visited the White House or met with a U.S. president. Godmanis later told reporters that Bush had encouraged their quest for a gradual transition to independence from the USSR. Reporter Amity Shlaes of the *Wall Street Journal* called the visit evidence of "creeping recognition" of Baltic governments by Washington. But Foreign Minister Jurkans urged the United States to go further and develop a "transition recognition policy" that encouraged Latvian independence. Scandinavian governments, he noted, were setting up offices in Riga that could later become consulates. Dr. Anatols Dinbergs, chargé d'affaires of the Washington-based legation of Latvia, was also present during meetings between Jurkans and Baker. The legation had not established formal ties with the new government in Riga but worked closely with its new leaders, as did their hosts—the American Latvian Association and its National Strategic Task Force of business leaders. The State of Delaware agreed to set up a Latvian trade center in Wilmington and planned to open its own office in Riga.

Iraq's attempted takeover of Kuwait in August 1990 had contradictory implications for the Baltic. On the one hand, it brought the USSR (as well as many Arab countries) closer to Washington's foreign policy preferences. Moscow shifted gears on Iraq and approved UN collective security measures. On the other hand, Gorbachev's line on Kuwait was an implicit rebuke of Stalin's Baltic policy. The USSR tried to eliminate Baltic independence in 1940 just as Iraq did Kuwait's fifty years later. Responding to the Persian Gulf situation, Latvia's parliamentary leadership in September called for the withdrawal of some fifty Iraqi naval technicians training near Riga under a long-standing treaty between Moscow and Baghdad.

Long-range Planning: Worst Case and Best Case

To develop a clearer picture of the policy implications the Baltic presents to the West, let us sketch a worst and best case that might develop in the 1990s.

Worst-case Scenario

Pushed against the wall by ethnic strife within the USSR and the loss of Eastern Europe, a coalition of ideological hardliners, military, and KGB leaders manages a coup d'état against Gorbachev's perestroika/glasnost team. Confronted with determined secession in the Baltic, hardliners seize upon

Gorbachev's absence — has he had a heart attack or is he writing another book in the Crimea? — to take power in the name of the CPSU Central Committee. The coup is supported by growing numbers of ordinary Russians who see their jobs threatened by a market economy, their honor insulted by ungrateful minorities, and the USSR's superpower status evaporating in disarmament and ideological submission to the West.

The new regime asserts its determination to repulse any separatist moves within the USSR. Armored columns fill Baltic streets; low-flying planes buzz separatist demonstrators in the parks of Tallinn, Riga, and Vilnius; KGB moles within the independence parties spread confusion. Some local "moderates" — their deepest affiliations obscure — urge capitulation to Soviet power. Some *Spetsnaz* commando teams assassinate independence leaders; others take over television and radio stations; others set up roadblocks and controls at railroad stations and airports. The Kremlin warns that vital Soviet interests are at risk. Any interference from the West could be a casus belli.

Georgia and other republics have considered following the Baltic example, but the Kremlin interposes overwhelming force to cow most parties; remaining dissidents are disposed of brutally, as Romanian troops did at Timisoara in 1989.

The crackdown crushes overt challenges but solves no fundamental Soviet problems. True-to-Moscow Communists are discredited in the Baltic and other border lands, but they rule as satraps of the distant metropole. Nationalists go underground, promising to be less moderate "next time."

Some Westerners urge a sympathetic understanding of Moscow's problems. One former U.S. security adviser sagely declares that no great power could tolerate the secession of its constituent parts. He notes that Communists do not share Western moral scruples and calls for a resumption of commercial activity with the USSR after a decent interval. His consulting firm floats loans to help the Soviet system recover from internal confusion.

Other Western leaders urge the permanent quarantine of the USSR by the civilized world. Instead of arms cuts the West looks toward a system of deterrence and perhaps of defense based upon radical innovations in technology.

The Balts and other minority peoples of the Russian empire languish as an iron curtain descends. Kalevipoeg remains, legless, guarding the gate of Hades with one fist welded to the wall.

Best-case Scenario

European integration manages to bring Europeans together without alienating North America or Russia. Indeed, America's economic ties with Europe strengthen and become more meaningful. The European Community creates various categories of associate status to make room for other European states including Czechoslovakia, Hungary, and Poland. Alternative ways to associate even Russia with this process are actively considered.

A reunited Germany lives in harmony with its neighbors. Europes's old alliance systems lose their importance as old sources of insecurity are supplanted by transforming processes of integration. The role of the CSCE system increases, focusing on mutual security assurances. U.S. troops remain in Europe, but their size and arsenals are vastly reduced. The United States and the USSR maintain medium-sized nuclear umbrellas. The Soviet deterrent, like the American, is increasingly based at sea.

Perestroika and *demokratizatsii*a continue in the USSR, gradually increasing the scope of economic and political freedom. Living standards improve slowly.

All Baltic Communist parties break with the CPSU, although small factions remain faithful to Moscow. All major Baltic parties support independence. The major vote-getters are liberals and social democrats, but winning coalitions are shaped by agrarian, Christian, Green, and "international" parties. Most "international" settlers support independence, having been assured that minority rights will be respected.

The Kremlin acknowledges the independence of each Baltic republic. Noting the coercion used in 1940 to obtain accession of these states to the USSR, Moscow declares the Baltic situation a special case not pertinent to other Soviet republics. Each Baltic republic pledges not to join any military alliance. Each adopts a constitution, like Austria's, stipulating perpetual neutrality — even if it associates with the European Community. All CSCE participants guarantee Baltic neutrality.

Sweden and Finland take the lead in investing in joint ventures in the Baltic. Other Western governments and banks provide substantial sums for a four-year Baltic Development Plan. Funds go to emergency relief, training, and investment in needed projects too risky for private capital.

Russia chooses not to penalize the Baltic economically. It continues to supply oil, but demands either goods or payment in hard currency. Moscow tries to benefit from economic advance in the Baltic. Russia commences reforms needed to join the realms of international finance and commerce.

Some other Soviet republics move toward independence; still others work out a new treaty relationship with Russia that is part confederation, part federation.

We reach the "end of history" in Europe about the year 2000 as liberal capitalism sweeps eastward. This sets an inspiring but too-challenging example for most other parts of the world, where dictatorships, mafias, and ethnic strife still rule.

Promoting Baltic Independence

Today and tomorrow, as in the past, the Baltic links East and West. How can the concerned parties act so as to make the worst-case scenario recede and the best-case prevail?

East and West must first take full account of the biological and cultural imperatives driving Baltic politics. Estonians, Latvians, and Lithuanians felt at the cusp of the 1990s that it was now or never for them to regain their independence. Their physical and cultural survival depended upon halting Russification. They did not wish to secede from a "Union" they had never joined voluntarily. They wanted to reestablish the independent republics suppressed by Stalin in 1939-1940. Perhaps Lithuania had been rash to declare its independence, but so were those who signed a similar document on July 4, 1776. America's founders would not have repealed their declaration just because it would cause them many years of hardship, discomfit King George, and promote instability and rebellion worldwide.

How could Baltic independence be meshed with the security and economic needs of Russia? And how could the West promote such arrangements?

An optimal solution cannot be found in unilateral value-claiming by any party. The best approach will probably come from strategies that create values, making the most from the interdependence that links Russia, the Baltic, all of Europe, and North America. Interdependence portends both dangerous vulnerability and opportunity. It derives from a closeness and dependency in which all parties can help or hurt one another. Russia has become accustomed to extracting values from this relationship on its own terms, but one-sided diktat has become infeasible and counterproductive. It must be replaced by a new relationship in which Russia deals with its Baltic neighbors on the basis of legal equality and comparative advantage.

Beset with multiple crises, Kremlin leaders may relapse into "old thinking" and old ways in the Baltic and elsewhere. The West should therefore underscore the potential gains of new ways and the costs of heavy-handed imperialism. This requires a creative blend of firmness and flexibility. For a start, the West should continue and deepen its moral and legal support for Baltic independence. It should also drop sophist distinctions between Soviet use of force against peaceful dissidents and violent racists, because Moscow can find a pretext to tar even the Baltic's "singing revolutionaries" as fomenters of ethnic unrest.

Strategic Military Considerations

The Baltic offers a potential springboard for Russia to menace the West. For centuries, however, it has usually been a carpet over which Western armies have advanced into Russia. If neither NATO nor Soviet forces wish to attack the other side, demilitarization and neutralization of the Baltic region could serve the interests of all parties.

The disadvantage to NATO planners of Baltic demilitarization is that it could sharpen antinuclear, antimilitary sentiments in the West—in Sweden and Finland as well as NATO countries such as Denmark and Germany. Such feelings could end up disarming the West before the Bear has been thoroughly tamed.

Strategically, however, the Baltic republics play a very subordinate role compared to their larger neighbors. Developments in East Central Europe will shape the pace of regional denuclearization and demilitarization far more than events in the Baltic.

The Baltic lands have served as forward extensions of Russian power for more than fifty years. If the Soviet armies retreat, the result is a net gain for the West. Such a withdrawal can also benefit Kremlin objectives by cutting costs and reducing friction between Soviet forces and the Baltic populations.

For the USSR to withdraw militarily from the Baltic countries would weaken Russia's forward defense line and diminish Moscow's threat to Europe. Still, *if* the Baltic were demilitarized and nonaligned, it could form part of a protective glacis for Russia. Fiercely nationalistic, the Balts could be counted on—even with some arms limitations—to defend their lands if

Germany ever considered another push to the East. They could create their own version of "defensive defense" using a blend of cadre troops and territorial militia. Such forces could slow a German advance without being a threat to Russia.

The West should reassure the Kremlin that it is willing to treat the Baltic republics as nonaligned countries, their arms limited by international treaty on the 1955 Austrian model. That approach has satisfied all parties. It assured that Austria could be free internally but nonaligned internationally. It would not follow West Germany into NATO. Austria has itself become prosperous, and has served as a meeting ground for arms control negotiators and as a funnel for commerce between East and West. Austria wishes in the 1990s to join the European Community, conditioned on guarantees for its neutrality.

Unlike neutral Switzerland and Sweden, Austria does not possess powerful armed forces. It is banned from having weapons that can shoot more than thirty kilometers. It lies in a plain that leaves it quite vulnerable to attack from the east. Its condition resembles that of the Baltic republics: small and unprotected geographically.

To be sure, the Kremlin is unlikely to send its foreign minister to Washington begging assurances that independent Baltic republics not be swept into an expanded NATO. But Western diplomacy could help Gorbachev to save face and confront hardliners complaining that he has given away the store.[23]

Soviet diplomats in 1920 pushed for demilitarized zones between Russia, the Baltic republics, and Finland. The 1920 Tartu Treaty provided that if "Estonia's neutrality be internationally guaranteed, Russia undertakes to respect such neutrality and to join in guaranteeing it." If the Gulf of Finland were neutralized, Soviet Russia and Estonia agreed to take part.

Russia's weaknesses and the changing nature of global politics may make such arrangements more meaningful than in the 1920s. Some leading Soviet international relations specialists argued in 1989-1990 that power and prosperity come from mastery of the "scientific-technological revolution," not from coercive military power. Germany, they said, needs trading partners — not subjects, allies, or *Lebensraum*. With a military threat from the West barely thinkable, the Soviet analysts believed that the USSR's internal weaknesses could compel the Kremlin to accept neutrality in the Baltic as well as in East Central Europe.[24]

Political Objectives

NATO for decades has sought to contain if not roll back Soviet expansion. Whatever the motes in Western eyes, the United States and its allies have generally championed the causes of national self-determination and individual human rights. To the extent that the Baltic peoples control their own fates, to the extent that individual human rights flourish in the region, Western objectives are fulfilled.

The downside to Baltic independence is that it could increase political instability in Eastern Europe as well as in other Soviet border republics. Large strides toward Baltic independence could be a sort of last straw for the opponents of perestroika. As in 1968, when the Kremlin disagreed for months about how do deal with the Czechoslovak liberals, so in the 1990s: the Soviet leadership is likely to split over Baltic demands for independence. In these circumstances the West needs both carrots and sticks to bolster those Soviets who oppose armed intervention in the Baltic.

Russia will ultimately gain from granting a free choice to its border peoples. To be the master is almost as bad as being the slave. Slaves are restrained physically but are free to think. Slave-masters cannot hope to secure the primacy of all-human values that have become the avowed principle of Gorbachev's reforms. So long as the Kremlin must bully its subjects, rationalize and deceive — itself as well as others — Russians cannot be free. Unburdened by rebellious and ungrateful colonies, Russians can better approach their own ideals. They will be in a better position to claim admittance to a common European home.

Unburdened by empire, Russia can concentrate on its internal development and be a more fit partner in a community of civilized peoples. East and West can then better cooperate in approaching common problems with the environment and the profound security and other problems of the South.

If Moscow is recalcitrant, the West could wield the weapon of diplomatic recognition. Never having accepted Soviet annexation of the Baltic, Washington and its allies could extend formal recognition to the new governments that emerge there in free elections.[25]

The West could also counter Soviet demands that the UN Secretariat cut off all contacts with leaders of Baltic independence movements. Are the Baltic movements less legitimate or worthy than the Palestinian Liberation Organization, a group that Moscow has long supported?

Until the Baltic republics enjoy complete independence, Western governments should strive to ease cultural exchanges and discourage harassment of such exchanges by Soviet authorities. Two dozen delegates from Latvia's Popular Front who visited Latvian communities in North America in April 1989 were strip- searched when they returned to Moscow.[26] The West should press for conditions in which Baltic citizens can learn freely about alternative concepts of politics, economics, and human rights.

The West should also underline the measures taken by the Baltic governments to protect minority rights, for example, the Estonian Supreme Soviet's pledge on March 30, 1990, to work out during the transition to independence "legal guarantees for all residents, regardless of ethnic origin." While anti-Russian sentiments remained strong in some circles, the Baltic independence movements were committed to opening citizenship to all residents. On this point Western radio broadcasts could commend the farsightedness of the new regimes and undercut agitators inflaming Russian chauvinism and ethnic fears.

Economic and Environmental Policy

Westerners no less than Balts and Russians need the Baltic region to be prosperous, salubrious, and clean. The poverty and environmental difficulties of the USSR also impoverish the West. But conditions in the Baltic republics have a direct impact on their economic and environmental well-being. How can they clean the water and air of the region while trying to develop trade based on comparative advantage?

One of the most promising approaches to Baltic problems is for Europe to become more integrated and prosperous, with a potential to associate Russia in its ranks. To the extent that Europe becomes a functioning community, regional security threats should be less worrisome. If Russians feel that they can participate in a larger process with opportunities for their economic advance, the total picture could be transformed, riveting Moscow's attentions on Brussels or Strasbourg rather than on Vilnius or Tallinn. Europeans could ease the way for ruble convertibility.

The West should condition economic cooperation upon Baltic independence. How could the West even contemplate observer status for the USSR in GATT or relax barriers to high-technology transfers if, as in April 1990, the Kremlin turns loose paratroopers in Vilnius just weeks after promising to avoid coercive measures in Lithuania?

Pribaltika is the most likely conduit for linking the Western economies with those of Eastern Europe and Russia. This raises the economic stakes for all parties. The Baltic could be a lifeline for the struggling Russians. It could be a vehicle for Western investors to approach the vast Russian market. If economic freedom raises living standards and hopes in the Baltic, this will resonate in Eastern Europe and Russia. If free enterprise fails in the Baltic, prospects in neighboring regions will be dimmer.

It should be easier to make the Baltic a showplace of free enterprise than in larger countries with weaker entrepreneurial traditions. A Marshall Plan for the Baltic would be more feasible and probably more successful than in larger countries nearby. Aid to the Baltic is more likely to be well used, because a work ethic and work skills there are more developed. An economic rebirth of the Baltic would not guarantee similar results in Russia, but it would surely produce a positive spillover.

If chaos dominates the Baltic, outsider investors will hold back or retreat. Perhaps governments can risk billions for good causes, but individual firms cannot. To dispel investors' fears should be a high priority in the Baltic and in the West.

Even with good will and ample funding, the economic and environmental problems of the Baltic will pose severe challenges to economic and political decision makers. For decades Baltic manufacturers have found broad markets in Russia but not in the West. If Russians have to pay hard currency for Baltic goods, they may prefer West European products, unless there is a significant price differential. Russians may prefer to sell oil or gold for dollars rather than subsidize the Baltic. Baltic factories need to be modernized and made ecologically acceptable, but needed funds are in short supply.

In short, economic opportunities in the Baltic are bountiful, but so are the challenges.

Legal Interests

It is in the West's interest that the rule of law prevail worldwide. Rule by force, tyranny, deceit, caprice are contrary to the interests of peace, predictability, and commerce. The United States and most Western governments have refused to recognize the annexation of the Baltic by Moscow in 1940. The West has acquiesced in other changes effected by the Red Army. It pledges no effort to change Europe's boundaries by force. The other Western governments press

Germany to renounce any interest in reclaiming territories lost to Poland or Russia.

Having kept alive the principle that conquest does not justify de jure recognition, the West stands on the threshold of a great victory for international law. Soviet rights in the Baltic have been diminished by many factors: the Kremlin's recognition of many Stalinist crimes; Moscow's declaration that the Molotov-Ribbentrop pact was immoral and illegal; Gorbachev's support for noninterference in the exercise of national self-determination in Eastern Europe. The fact that the West has never accepted Baltic absorption into the USSR has denied legitimacy to the Soviet presence in the Baltic and strengthened the Stimson Doctrine in international law.[27]

Soviet legal institutions would also benefit from shedding the Baltic albatross, the least defensible of Soviet annexations. If the Kremlin wishes to establish a "law-abiding" state, it must disgorge any conquests that compel hypocrisy, deception, and coercion. As Secretary of State Baker has put it, the Soviet secession law should not be onerous or a subterfuge.

In the Baltic republics, legal processes require the removal of any pressure from a Russian Big Brother. The republics should be free to adapt their own traditions with whatever they find useful in the West or elsewhere.

Morality dictates freedom of choice, for peoples as well as individuals. To the extent that any people is repressed, these principles suffer. In the 1980s there was a massive movement toward real self-government in much of Latin America and Eastern Europe. In the 1990s it should extend to the Baltic.

The Real World of Shared Interests

To transcend zero-sum politics and create values in the Baltic requires understanding and reciprocity by all concerned. If one actor alone seeks joint gains, another party may exploit the situation for its narrow objectives. Lenin's *kto kovo?* outlook led several generations of his successors to conduct a no-holds-barred quest to get whatever they wanted at home and abroad. In the late 1980s, however, the Kremlin averred its willingness to put "all-human" considerations above every other — class, national, race, religious.

At the onset of the 1990s there were signs that Moscow and the West were ready to seek their objectives through value-creating. With many shared interests at stake, each party could afford to give in some domains if it gained in others. This condition could make it easier for the Kremlin to acquiesce in independence for at least some border republics.

Karl Marx noted as early as 1848 that capitalism had made the world "interdependent." In the words of the *Communist Manifesto*: "In place of the old local and national seclusion and self-sufficiency, we have intercourse in every direction, universal interdependence of nations....National one-sidedness and narrow-mindedness become more and more impossible." [28]

Today, interdependence means mutual vulnerability.[29] It means linkages sufficiently close to help — or hurt — one another. The USSR and United States share a mutual strategic interdependence, because each can destroy the other. In other domains their relations are less symmetrical, because the United States and its partners lead in most fields of economic, scientific, and political activity.

A common threat, Soviet Communism, helped pull France and West Germany together in the 1950s. Several shared threats militate for cooperation between Russia and the West in the 1990s: environmental degradation and the security problems arising from weapons proliferation, rogue governments, and resource depletion everywhere. These challenges are much more pressing and much more difficult to cope with than any residual revanchism in Germany or chauvinism elsewhere in East Central Europe.

The best strategy for the West is to encourage evolution within the erstwhile Russian empire, rewarding positive change. Baltic independence will be most readily achieved — and maintained — in a broader movement toward complex interdependence linking Russia, Europe, and North America.[30]

NOTES

1. Winston S. Churchill, *The Second World War: Triumph and Tragedy* (New York: Bantam, 1962), pp. 196-97.
2. Thucydides, *The Peloponnesian War* (Baltimore: Penguin, 1954), I, 3, pp. 31-38.
3. Thinking that war with Corinth was inevitable, Athens opted to ally with Corcyra and do what it could to weaken its future adversaries Corinth and Sparta. This act helped catalyze the Peloponnesian war. Today's White House could cite this case as an argument for

appeasing Moscow. But the particulars of the Peloponnesian confrontation do not fit today's Baltic-East-West relationship. Corcyra was one of three major naval powers. Its weight added to that of Athens sharply altered the balance of power. War was indeed imminent. The Baltic republics are tiny compared to other actors in world affairs. If they became independent, they would necessarily not join a Western alliance.

4. This and the following paragraphs are based on Winston S. Churchill, *The Second World War: The Hinge of Fate* (New York: Bantam, 1962), pp. 285-86, and W. Averell Harriman and Elie Abel, *Special Envoy to Churchill and Stalin, 1941-1946* (New York: Random House, 1975), pp. 110, 125, 135-36. Harriman stressed Eden's desire to erase "certain suspicions" from Stalin's mind, while Secretary of State Cordell Hull, an old Wilsonian, led the fight against secret accords. Harriman saw some use in negotiating territorial issues before the Red Army turned the tide.

5. Churchill, *Hinge of Fate*, p. 285.

6. Harriman, *Special Envoy*, p. 135.

7. Churchill, *Hinge of Fate*, p. 292; Harriman, *Special Envoy*, pp. 135-36; Ivan Maisky, *Memoirs of a Soviet Ambassador. The War: 1939-43* (New York: Charles Scribner's Sons, 1967), p. 267.

8. Harriman, *Special Envoy*, p. 227.

9. Harriman's paraphrase and Chip Bohlen's are nearly the same as the Russian in substance, but make Roosevelt look less cynical and more knowledgeable. The Russian text consists of direct quotes, not a paraphrase. But the preface to the Soviet Russian edition says that the Russian has been "corrected" on the basis of American notes (Bohlen's) and British archives. For the Russian account, see *Sovetskii Soiuz na mezhdunarodnykh konferentsiiakh perioda Velikoi Otechestvennoi voiny 1941-1945 gg. Tegeranskaia konferentsiia rukovoditelei trëkh soiuznykh derzhav—SSSR, SShA i Velikobritanii (28 noiabria-1 dekabria 1943 g.)*, 6 vols. (Moscow: Polizdat, 1978-80), II, 168-69. For Harriman's report, see *Special Envoy*, p. 279; for Bohlen's, see *Foreign Relations of the United States: The Conferences at Cairo and Tehran 1943* (Washington, D.C.: Government Printing Office, 1961), p. 594.

10. Discussions of Finland are recorded in *Tegeranskaia konferentsiia*, pp. 160-61; on Poland and East Prussia, at p. 167.

11. Diane Shaver Clemens, *Yalta* (New York: Oxford University Press, 1970), p. 179.

12. See Anatolii A. Gromyko, *Pamiatnoe*, 2 vols. (Moscow: Politizdat, 1988), 2, pp. 188-91.

13. The U.S. Secretary of State implied that giving the Soviets even two extra votes was the result of a private deal between Roosevelt and Eden behind the backs of other U.S. delegates. See Edward R. Stettinius, Jr., *Roosevelt and the Russians: The Yalta Conference* (New York: Doubleday, 1949), pp. 173-74, 191-93, 196.

14. See background documents in *Foreign Relations of the United States: The Conference of Berlin, 1945*, 2 vols. (Washington, D.C.: Government Printing Office, 1960), 1, pp. 794-801, esp. pp. 799, 800.

15. Statement issued on 25 July 1975, Office of the White House Press Secretary.

16. See also Elliott Abrams, Assistant Secretary of State for Human Rights and Humanitarian Affairs: "The Baltic States' Struggle for Freedom," address to Third Annual Human Rights Conference of the Baltic American Freedom League, Los Angeles, 17 March 1984.

17. The U.S.-Soviet conference was sponsored by the Chatauqua Institution, the Eisenhower World Affairs Institute, and the USSR-USA Society. See Juris Dreifelds, "Latvian National Rebirth," *Problems of Communism*, 38, 4 (July-August 1989), pp. 77-94, at p. 81.

18. Presidential Documents, "Baltic Freedom Day, 1989," *Federal Register*, 84, 115, 16 June 1989.

19. The meeting was planned for thirty minutes but took more than sixty. Fourteen representatives of Baltic American organizations met in the Roosevelt Room of the White House with Bush, Secretary of State James Baker, White House Chief of Staff John Sununu, press secretary Marlin Fitzwater, Robert Gates and Robert Hutchings, both on the National Security Council, Curtis Kamman, Deputy Assistant Secretary of State for Europe, and Sichan Siv, White House liaison office. Notes were taken by Mari-Ann Rikken of the Estonian American National Council. A day or two after the meeting all fourteen Baltic Americans got phone calls from the White House telling them how impressed the president was with their reasoned positions. Rikken interpreted this to connote: "There, there; be quiet, nice little Baltics."

20. There were many sources of Mr. Bush's "realism." One contributing factor was the president's aristocratic background. As James David Barber argued in *The New York Times* (Op-ed, 27 January 1990), one could read his lips but his actions were another thing: More fox than lamb, he worked to advance the rich and powerful while confusing the masses. Barber concluded that Americans needed "a President who will advance real democracy — not class greed and the lust for power — at home and abroad."

21. See Elliott Abrams, "Bush's Unrealpolitik," *The New York Times*, 30 April 1990, p. A17.

22. Whether to support national liberation movements in friendly countries such as the United Kingdom, Canada, and Spain is a more complicated question that need not be analyzed here.

23. "Would it help if the West proposed an Austrian solution for the Baltic?" I asked Dr. Toivo Kuldsepp, Estonia's Deputy Foreign Minister, on 12 March 1990. "By all means," he replied. "You can be sure that the Soviets won't propose it."

    The Estonian Communist newspaper *Sovetskaia Estoniia* reprinted an article by me on 22 November 1989 urging an Austrian model for the Baltic. The editors criticized what they saw as the anti-Soviet tone but not the essence of the idea.

24. See Walter C. Clemens, Jr., *Can Russia Change? The USSR Confronts Global Interdependence* (Boston: Unwin Hyman, 1990), pp. 346-51.

25. The West could find itself in a quandary if a Baltic or other Soviet republic chose to remain in the USSR but gained sufficient autonomy to demand membership in UNESCO or even the United Nations, recognition of its sovereignty, and reopening of its embassies abroad. Would any kind of autonomy short of full separation from the USSR be seen as sufficient cause to grant renewed de jure recognition of a Soviet republic? See Juris Dreifelds, "Latvian National Rebirth," *Problems of Communism*, 38, 4 (July-August 1989), pp. 77-94, at p. 95.

26. See Dreifelds, "Latvian National Rebirth," p. 92.

27. For background, see William J. H. Hough, III, "The Annexation of the Baltic States and Its Effect on the Development of Law Prohibiting Forcible Seizure of Territory," *New York Law School Journal of International and Comparative Law*, 6, 2 (Winter 1985), entire issue.

28. The German for interdependence read: *eine allseitige Abhängigkeit der Nationen voneinander*, "an all-sided dependency of the nations upon one another."

29. On "interdependence" and the model of "complex interdependence," see Robert O. Keohane and Joseph S. Nye, Jr., *Power and Interdependence*, 2d ed. (Glenview, Ill.: Scott, Foresman, 1989).

30. Such a movement will be facilitated if joined by Japan, China, and many Third World countries. For Baltic interdependence, however, the sine qua non is Russian cooperation with Europe and North America.

16
The Hard Road to Independence

The Son of Kalev, with Latvia's Bear Slayer and spirit of Lithuania, were forged to the rocks at the Gate to Hades for half a century. They tried for decades to pull away but, in vain. Still, their wills were not broken. Eventually, the walls cracked and flames of hope broke out, cutting loose their hands. The spirits of Estonia, Latvia, and Lithuania were not immediately freed, but greater prospects of liberation brought a kind of happiness to the Baltic peoples. The Sorcerer stumbled backward, his spells broken—at least for the moment.

Mythology can be a surer guide to reality than newspapers, statistical handbooks, or Party programs. Proverbs also have their own deep wisdom. In May 1990 President Vytautas Landsbergis recalled a Lithuanian saying: "Water falling drop by drop can split even large stones." He added: "There are lots of stones in Moscow and our joint drop of water will be very important."

Freedom came to the Baltic in the late 1980s from various sources. Its embers had never died in the souls of the Baltic peoples; these embers were blown by new winds churning throughout the Soviet empire; they were part of a Zeitgeist that fostered economic and political freedom globally—from South America to the Philippines to South Africa. Balts took heart particularly from winds of change in Poland and Hungary; Balts gave heart to other "Soviet" nations—from the Caucasus to Russia itself.

But passing new laws and electing new assemblies was not equivalent to independence. Sovereignty could be claimed and still remain a mirage.[1]

The new realities presented deep dilemmas for all concerned — the erstwhile hegemons in Moscow, the peoples of the Baltic, and their neighbors in the West. The new realities raised questions about free will versus determinism. Could reformers in Moscow and in the Baltic republics control the destinies of their peoples? Could outsiders be more than bystanders?

Kremlin Dilemmas

The Kremlin in the early 1990s looked out on four alternatives. First, it could try to reintegrate the disparate nationalities of the USSR and form an improved union from their myriad cultures and diverse strengths. Second, the hegemon could muddle through, partially paralyzed by the nationalities' conflicts with each other and with the center. Third, it could allow all or some of the subject nations to become independent, leaving the shell of a shrunken Union. Fourth, it could try to rule with an iron hand.

Voluntary Integration

The first alternative would be difficult to achieve even if Gorbachev had with full awareness and determination set out to pursue it in 1985. To overcome the accumulated pain and inefficiency promoted by generations of Soviet imperium would not be easy. Unfortunately for Gorbachev, he seemed not to perceive the seriousness of the nationality problem until at least two years after taking power. Thus, in January 1987 he conceded that "not a single major issue can be solved...without taking into account the fact that we live in a multinational country." But in February 1987 he was so tactless as to praise — while in Latvia! — the "Russian soldier-liberator who helps the Baltic farmer and fisherman to defend their native land against desecration and servitude, to protect it against the foreign aggressor." [2] In April 1987 Gorbachev exposed the state of his knowledge by proposing "autonomous areas" for blacks, Puerto Ricans, Poles, and other minorities in the United States. [3] By January 1988, however, he acknowledged that the Communist Party had lagged behind the processes taking place in society. [4] On May 30, 1989 he admitted that at the beginning of perestroika, the Party leadership had "not fully appreciated the necessity of reviewing nationalities policy" and that this had led to a "delay in solving a number of urgent matters." Even so, he still denied the depth of nationality issues, instead castigating "certain elements" who made economic and social problems worse by "speculating on general difficulties." On several occasions he urged Soviet scholars to take a harder look at the national question.

Gorbachev's early support for perestroika aimed at promoting an imperial nationalism. Perestroika sought to modernize the Soviet economy as an instrument of superpower politics. The Kremlin leader gave little or no thought to the chance that his policies might strengthen non-Soviet or anti-Soviet nationalism. But the companions to perestroika — glasnost and democratization — unleashed expressions of two other kinds of nationalism: (1) anomic nationalism — in response to Russification, militant atheism, and the dysfunctions of forced industrialization-modernization; and (2) ideological demands for national self-determination — escalating from self-management to sovereignty to independence.

Even though some of his advisers were conversant in Western social science, Gorbachev ignored warnings that an increase in political participation — especially in ethnically pluralistic societies where minorities had long felt deprived — risks great instability. Perestroika and glasnost led to de-institutionalization at a much faster pace than the hapless process of re-institutionalization. Glasnost did more for local nationalism than for economic reform.[5]

Too little and too late, Gorbachev slowly moved to form a more perfect union. In late 1990 he eliminated his Presidential Council and upgraded the Federal Council (the USSR president and the heads of state from each Union Republic) from an advisory to a decision-making body — on paper, the Union's highest executive organ. But the way that this was done — and the total context — only underscored the great powers being accumulated by Gorbachev. Even the Council of Ministers was subordinated to him rather than, as earlier, to the Supreme Soviet.

Meanwhile, Gorbachev was still crippled by the dilemma that in order to integrate the subject nations of their own volition, the center would have to give them unprecedented freedoms in a federation, confederation, or commonwealth. Party bureaucrats and all-Union ministries in Moscow and of Russian workers in the provinces opposed national self-determination for Balts and other border peoples. Even if Russian chauvinists reconciled themselves to diluting their authority and privilege, the subject nations might not be satisfied. Baltic memories and desires for independence were too strong for them to trust their fates to still another Soviet constitution.

Muddling Through

The second alternative, muddling through, did not appear a promising course for Moscow. By 1988-1989 the Balts and other subject nations were taking power into their own hands. They ignored Kremlin decrees and gradually prepared to make independence a reality — "drop by drop." Only if the West somehow propped up the USSR, as it once did the decrepit Ottoman Empire, could the Leviathan endure.

Disintegration

In the millennium's last decade it seemed likely that the center would lose control over some, if not all, of its subject nations. If Gorbachev could recognize this reality as a necessity, he might accommodate it — as Britain did the loss of India and Ceylon. But military, KGB, and other entrenched forces within Soviet society wanted to maintain central control over the subject nations — by force if need be. As Edward Shevardnadze warned in December 1990, resigning as foreign minister, there was rising support within the USSR for another "dictatorship."

The caged lions let loose by Gorbachev gained favor not only in the non-Russian republics but in Russia itself. Many Russians were fed up with imperium — whether Soviet or Russian. Many suffered from profound anomie and wanted to rejuvenate Russian traditions.[6] Many felt it was time to assert Russian sovereignty — even, independence from the USSR. If they withdrew their allegiance and placed it with Mother Russia, what moral foundation would remain for the Soviet state? Still, talk might prove cheap. In 1990 RSFSR President Boris Yeltsin acted as the benefactor and supporter of sovereignty for the border republics, but many Balts doubted that — if push came to shove — he would passively observe the disintegration of Russia's empire.

The Iron Hand

The Kremlin faced a double dilemma: If it cracked down on those who challenged Gorbachev's ever changing line, this would undermine the innovative spirit believed necessary to rejuvenate the Soviet economy. Repression would also jeopardize Western approval, credit, and relaxed trade that Gorbachev wanted to help rebuild the USSR and move the country from the Second (or Third) to the First World.

Challenged in Russia as well as in the other republics, Gorbachev probably thought, like some political scientists, that order is a prerequisite for economic progress and for freedom. He may even have believed, like Dostoevsky's Grand Inquisitor, that the masses prefer bread and security to freedom, and could be bemused by a spectacle of "miracle, mystery, and authority" as celebrated in glasnost and Soviet-U.S. summitry.[7] Gorbachev may have hoped, after restoration of order, to control the organs of repression. But he might have been paving the way for a military coup, if only there were a Soviet version of General Jaruzelski in the wings. As has been the case in some less developed countries, the final solution might be military rule with promises of "free elections" when order was restored.

For countries such as China and the USSR, however, significant rejuvenation required a fusion of order *with* freedom. Order by itself — repressive order without freedom — would be nothing but the old sterility. And while the Han masses of China displayed considerable fealty to central authority, the many peoples of the USSR felt no reason to trust or respect Moscow. This made freedom a sine qua non for all else in the erstwhile Soviet empire. Freedom first, order later — perhaps. Order, if it came, would probably require a new framework, one so different that it would transcend historical wounds and structures of tyranny.

Thus, Soviet defenders of old ways were probably fighting a losing cause. Throughout the Baltic and even in Russia, KGB operations against "anti-Soviet" elements increased in late 1990-early 1991. Radio and TV transmitters were set up on Soviet military bases in Baltic countries as an instrument of thought control in case of a crackdown. They could dominate the air waves, but hardly the thought waves of Baltic peoples. The crisis of legitimacy gradually overtook even the agencies of law and order. "Whom do you represent" — Baltic nationalists asked KGB officials — "our government or Moscow?" Secret police functionaries denied there was any contradiction, but many defenders of empire gradually lost their will and self-confidence. In November 1990 a Soviet procurator noted for his role in political trials, Erich Vallimäe, returned from three years in Murmansk to work again in Tallinn, but immediately faced demands from the Council of Estonia that he himself be tried for criminal activity.[8]

Russia's deepest interests ran contrary to dictatorial imperialism. The reason was implicit in the question often posed by Tunne Kelam, elected head of the Congress of Estonia in 1990: "Would Russia be better off with four Finlands on its border or with just one Finland and three rebellious provinces?"

It is debilitating for any country to rule others against their will. If Gorbachev wanted to build a "law-abiding state," he dared not act as though "might makes right." Not just the Balts but *all* Soviet border peoples were compelled to join the USSR by force. It was unfair — and incendiary — to demand that, to leave the union, republics had to run the mine field laid out in the 1990 amendment on secession, really a law *against* secession.

The Soviet state had became too big for its own good. Perestroika would be more manageable if Moscow did not try to set rules for more than a hundred different peoples spread over eleven time zones.

The Russian republic is — or could be — one of the most self-sufficient countries in the world. What it lacks could easily be obtained by trading with neighbors or more distant countries.

Russia and its neighbors have long needed Adam Smith's "invisible hand." If these peoples could live and produce as they chose, the results would surely be more beneficial — *mutually* — than obeying the whims of Moscow planners.

Soviet efficiency — economic and otherwise — was undermined by ethnic diversity and turmoil, which — after the cork was unplugged in the late 1980s — could not be long repressed by coercive power.

For the Kremlin to wage economic warfare with its subject peoples would be unwise. For starters, the Soviet regime owed them a great deal for deportations, collectivization, genocide, and ecological damage. If the Kremlin denied reparations, at least Moscow should not play economic hardball with peoples it had exploited for decades.

Economic warfare boomerangs. If Moscow punished the Balts, they could block their ports or charge exorbitant rates for Russia's shipments through Tallinn, Riga, and Klaipeda. Even in 1918 Soviet diplomats sought guarantees that Russian goods could cross Germany-occupied Estonia without interference. The Bolsheviks wanted similar assurances in their 1920 peace treaty with Estonia. Even in 1920 the Bolsheviks recognized that northwestern Russia needed Estonian electric power.

Baltic Dilemmas

Centrifugal forces, unleashed, are hard to rein. The Soviet peoples long groaned under Stalinism. Allowed greater freedoms in spurts since 1953, they wanted still more. Gorbachev's concessions of the mid- and late-1980s whetted appetites for change far more radical than he envisioned.

Natives of Estonia, Latvia, and Lithuania opted for independence in the late 1980s-early 1990s, but was it practical? Bread or freedom? Balts were not slavish like the masses described by the Grand Inquisitor, but did not relish economic blockades resulting in half-day queues to keep autos running. *Part* of the Balts' rebellion was anger at the contrast between their living standards and those of Finland and Sweden. They did not want to sink even further into a long period of even greater poverty.

Some Western and Soviet economists predicted that, given a choice, most border peoples would voluntarily stay in Russian fold. Rather than pay hard currency and world prices for Russian oil, they would toe the line. But this prediction proved wrong — at least in the Baltic in 1990. Not by bread alone. Indeed, Finnish businessmen complained that Estonians rejected any joint ventures that might compromise their republic's economic independence.

Balts blamed the Kremlin — and Russians — for their economic backwardness. Despite subsidies, Soviet border lands gained little from ties with Russia. The Kremlin treated them as colonies, looting resources and diluting their cultures. Unlike Balts, some nations lost even their writing systems — Arabic and Latin — to please the Cyrillic Russians.

But how could Balts enter a new life while tied to the old? Not only did they depend on cheap Soviet oil, but on Soviet buyers for their food and industrial products. Tied to the East, how could the Balts shift west? Soviet central banks had trustees in Western banks; Baltic banks in 1990 did not. The simplest credit transactions were complicated by the lack of established banking machinery.

Some Balts trusted in reason: Russia needed the oil refinery in Lithuania for its own purposes and for export. Indeed, Russia needed the main Baltic ports for import and export trade with the West. Russia needed Baltic food — even, electricity. Independent states could still trade. Russian cross-country skiers could still train summer and winter in Estonia's rolling hills — for a reasonable price. The danger was that, passions uncoiled, material self-interest would be ignored in favor of a bear-like squeeze.

Balts wanted self-rule and pluralism, but they were not trained in democracy. A half century of totalitarian rule did not foster tolerance for differing approaches to politics. Some Balts criticized even Moscow's *Literaturnaia gazeta* because, in the late 1980s, it presented no single line. "We cannot afford a diversity of opinion" said one Estonian "democrat." Such attitudes were muffled in spring 1990 as new parties were formed throughout the Baltic, but when the going got tough, old suspicions and recriminations surfaced again. At least three views toward an independent foreign policy emerged among Estonian politicians in 1990.[9] Lithuania's Prime Minister and her cabinet resigned in January 1991 — just as Moscow increased coercive pressures — when Lithuania's parliament canceled food price increases aimed at jolting the country toward a market economy. This followed months of tension between the pragmatic Prime Minister Prunskiene, and the idealistic President Landsbergis.

Balts who spent years in prison or house arrest distrusted late-in-life reformers who had occupied privileged positions in the Brezhnev-Andropov-Chernenko years. Thus, Tunne Kelam and others in the Estonian National Independence Party opposed the government of Popular Front founder Edgar Savisaar. Arguing that Prime Minister Savisaar's government enjoyed only a bare majority in parliament, Kelam in November 1990 proposed a "government of national unity" formed by the ENIP and the Free Estonia group of old time Communists. This idea cost Kelam support among those who had valued his refusal to compromise any principle. Social Democrat Marju Lauristin warned the factions against creating a political vacuum that outsiders could exploit.

Despite such problems, Balts also managed nearly unprecedented cooperation with each other. Thus, a joint session of parliaments from the Baltic republics was held in Vilnius in December 1990. Delegations from each republic approved documents calling for withdrawal of Soviet troops from their territories, recognition of Baltic independence by the West, and a start of negotiations with the USSR on Baltic independence.

Another Baltic dilemma concerned the aliens in their midst — Russians and others who did not speak their language, practice their faith, or sing their songs.[10] Could Balts extend to them the same privileges that they demanded for themselves? If they did, this would water down the national culture. If they did not, they would be inconsistent and risk civil unrest. Balts firmly opposed secession movements from their existing territories, but avoided the open clashes with minorities that took place in Georgia and other Soviet republics.

An even larger question loomed: Was it appropriate for a modernizing nation to nourish a culture that dated from an earlier age? Was it right or wise to stress possibly anachronistic traditions when the First World increasingly depended upon English, Microsoft, and WordPerfect? A few European countries—above all, Switzerland with its four languages and multiple cultures—showed that nations could balance their own traditions and modernity, but such examples would not be easy to follow in the Baltic or other formerly Communist lands.

Many Balts would have preferred to turn their backs on Russia, writing it off as a bad dream. But this would be naive. If the prosperity and peace of Western Europe depended in part on that of East Central Europe, did not that of the Baltic require a modicum of stability and well being in Russia? No nation—especially a small, vulnerable one—could aspire to be an island.

Should Balts go slow or fast? A slow approach would conceivably give Moscow time to draft a reasonable Union Treaty and show that perestroika was working. In 1990, however, accumulating experience showed the bankruptcy of attempts to save the Union. Furthermore, the passage of time increased chances that Moscow's attentions would be diverted to larger problems—the Ukraine, Kazakhstan, Russia—limiting the attention it could give to the Baltic.

Surely the Balts would avoid the mistake the American South made in 1861: a frontal attack on a Union base. Seven states seceded in 1860-early 1861 and adopted a Confederate Constitution on February 4, 1861. Inaugurated as president March 4, Abraham Lincoln warned against rash actions. On April 6 he notified the governor of South Carolina that he was sending "provisions only" to Fort Sumter, in Charleston's harbor—not "men, arms, or ammunition" unless the union fort were attacked. On April 12, as the relief expedition approach Charleston, Confederate batteries began to shell Fort Sumter, compelling its surrender the next day. The Civil War began, resulting in huge casualties for both sides and the destruction of the Confederacy.

Since the Balts were almost unarmed in the early 1990s, it was more likely that the "union forts" on their islands and in their midst would attack them. Having been savaged in an earlier guerrilla war, Balts showed no desire to prod Soviet forces into action.[11] But even the most patient of peoples would likely respond to violence with violence if sufficiently provoked. Soviet military takeovers of buildings and searches for draft-resisters risked crossing that threshold.

Interdependence is a reality of modern times. But it entails danger as well as opportunity. Interdependence means mutual vulnerability — rooted in relationships so close that their twists and turns can hurt or benefit both parties. The Baltic lands help to bridge East and West. But they are caught in between. Misfortune to either side inarguably affects Balts as well.

Western Dilemmas

For decades the West put principles of national self-determination on the back burner. So long as the cold war raged, avoidance of war became the overriding concern of foreign policy. As East-West tensions relaxed, and as captive nations demanded freedom, the West was compelled to think again about human and national rights in the Soviet realm.

Morality found common cause with legality in that most Western nations had never recognized Soviet annexation of the Baltic. But morality and legality collided with realpolitik, because Western governments liked Gorbachev's promises of stability, peace, and enhanced East-West trade. Even survival issues intruded. If Moscow lost control of weapons — including nuclear arms — deployed in the border republics, world security would be at risk.

Other large land empires had been kept alive for centuries, partly because more vigorous powers feared their dissolution. No Western government coveted the border lands of Russia's empire. In that sense, the balance of power among competing nations would not be disrupted by the demise of Soviet imperium. Still, a pandora's box of ethnic strife and border conflict could follow dissolution of Russian hegemony.

To be sure, the Baltic republics were so small — and so peaceful in their approach — that they might separate from the USSR without destroying Gorbachev's realm. But life itself showed that the other captive nations were inclined to follow the Baltic example — without their dedication to non-violence.

President Bush seemed grateful that Gorbachev did not obstruct U.S.-United Nations efforts to deal with Iraq and Kuwait in late 1990-early 1991. The Persian Gulf crisis added to the pragmatic considerations moving Western governments to bolster the Gorbachev regime, even sending in care packages in winter 1990-1991. National Security Council member Condoleezza Rice told Baltic Americans on December 15, 1990, that the suspension of Jackson-Vanik restrictions on aid to the USSR was meant to "create a set of circumstances in which the outcome we want is likely to happen."

Baltic Americans, however, were not persuaded. They recalled that just three days before — December 12 — KGB chairman Vladimir Kriuchkov pledged that the secret services would wage battle "with all means at their disposal" against "anti-Communist" forces that threaten the authority of Soviet central power whether from within the USSR or from abroad. Kriuchkov's threat was another step "to intimidate Baltic leaders into signing the new Union treaty," said Sandra Aistars of the Joint Baltic American National Committee. "Just a word of warning from President Bush to Shevardnadze [visiting the White House that same day] would make all the difference." Other critics asked why the United States fought to drive Iraq from Kuwait but responded so lamely to Soviet occupation and attempted resubjugation of the Baltic.

Could the West just move in and bail out the entire Soviet system? This was infeasible. As Rice noted, there was "very little money in the package." Western means would not suffice, for the task was much larger than that undertaken in the Marshall Plan years — and without the favorable preconditions existing then in Europe. More importantly, a spirit of hard work and enterprise cannot be imposed from without, especially where the ruling ideology (like that of the Grand Inquisitor) has long preached the security of egalitarian poverty. From this perspective, it was a disservice to the Soviet economy as well as to the captive nations to prop up the central government with economic aid.

Western policy could more easily hurt than help the Soviet economy. The West could underscore that Moscow's self-interest required a free choice for its captive nations. If Moscow reverted to the knout instead of the plebiscite, the West could prevent easy access for the Soviet state into global commerce. Instead, in winter 1990-1991 the Western governments supported a Kremlin that was moving away from liberalization in every sphere — from nationality policy to market economics.

Whereas aid to the Kremlin would soon be swallowed up by the immense Leviathan, Western support for the fledgling free enterprise of the Baltic could have multiple effects there. The scale was manageable; the intangible preconditions were more favorable than for the USSR as a whole. Shifting course in early 1991, Washington authorized U.S. shipments of medical supplies directly to the three Baltic republics and the Ukraine. And while the CSCE had refused even observer status to the Baltics and the Ukraine, Iceland offered to recognize Lithuania.

Must the Past Be the Future?

The Gorbachev era ushered in high hopes for East-West accord and for liberal reform within the USSR. Many commentators asserted flatly that the Cold War had ended and that dictatorship could never return to the Soviet Union. Against these hopes, however, was a dogged pattern of Soviet history: an oscillation between a hard and moderate line in foreign policy. Since 1917 the Kremlin has alternated between a "left" and "right" syndrome, usually lasting between four and six years. A right or moderate syndrome began in 1985 and—if the past were also future—would run its course by the early 1990s.

What factors produced these cycles of hard and moderate inflections in Soviet policy? Ideological zeal and desperation impelled the "War Communism" of 1917-1921. Exhaustion triggered the "New Economic Policy" from 1921-1927. Stalin's ascendancy and drive to industrialize pushed Soviet policies left from 1928 through 1933, when Hitler drove the Kremlin to reverse gears and seek collective security at the League.

Zigs and zags continued: Attempted condominium with Hitler in 1939; grand alliance with the West, 1941-1946; intense cold war, 1947-1953; Khrushchev's "peaceful coexistence," 1954-1958; frontal pressures on Berlin and Cuba, 1958-1962; the "Spirit of Moscow" and Glassboro, 1963-67; the Czech crackdown and tensions in Europe, 1968-71; the Nixon-Brezhnev detente of the early 1970s, followed by a Soviet forward strategy in the Third World in the late 1970s-early 1980s. Domestic policy usually moved in sync with foreign, but sometimes they moved in opposite directions.

The underlying problem was the Kremlin's devotion to Lenin's orientation of *kto kovo?* Intent on destroying their foes, the Bolsheviks gave and expected no quarter. This orientation softened after Stalin, and was *officially* replaced under Gorbachev by the view that "all-human" principles are more important than class, nationality, race, or religion. But Gorbachev's New Thinking could not obliterate the distrust that Soviet leaders have felt toward all rivals and even their own subjects, whom they deemed vulnerable to foreign troublemakers and sentiments of nationality or material gain. In the early 1990s some Communists still believed that truth was on their side, but most had simply become accustomed to privilege and power, and were loath to give them up without a struggle.

Cooperation and understanding between Communist regimes and Western democracies have always been fragile, owing to different world views, habits, and perceived interests. The Grand Alliance collapsed after 1945 as Stalin reached for Eastern Europe and spurned international controls of atomic energy; "peaceful coexistence" got derailed in 1958 as Khrushchev sought to exploit the leverage of the world's first ICBM and again in 1968 as Soviet troops occupied Czechoslovakia; "detente" broke in the late 1970s over Africa and Afghanistan. Western governments have also acted so as to confirm the darkest suspicions of Communist leaders.

In 1990-1991 Presidents Bush and Gorbachev, backed up by their counterparts in Western Europe and Japan, seemed to want continued peace, cooperation, and trade between the First and Second Worlds. But they had to deal with Kremlin interests that were much more explosive than many that cut short previous periods of detente — for example, Ethiopia.

Now the Communist regime and the core Soviet empire were at stake. Gorbachev had hoped to restructure the USSR economy — a sort of Soviet "New Deal" — while preserving Communist rule and a centralized empire. But halfway measures had proven ineffective while vested interests and popular fears resisted a sweeping switchover to market economics. Economic and social chaos increased, multiplied by unrest and outright resistance among the many subject peoples of the Soviet empire.

Gorbachev went far toward curtailing the Soviet military-industrial complex. For example, he halted nuclear testing for eighteen months while the Reagan Administration continued to test. But when personal perks are threatened, even the faithful military machine may resist. In 1990 Russian settlers and uniformed Soviet officers in the Baltic unfurled banners proclaiming "The Army and People Are One" (supplanting earlier claims that "The Party and People Are One"). A Soviet nuclear test at Novaya Zemlya toward the end of 1990 seemed to catch the central political authorities by surprise. And Foreign Minister Shevardnadze expressed anger that the Soviet military withdrew tanks and other equipment behind the Urals in 1990, defying the spirit of the Conventional Forces in Europe disarmament agreement that he negotiated.[12]

The Balts had pursued a "singing revolution," seeking to avoid violent encounters with Russians. They had declared their independence, but had not gotten rid of the Soviet military bases and all-Union factories in their midst. In November 1990 the Latvian Supreme Council instructed municipalities to stop providing supplies and social services to Soviet Armed Forces in Latvia. On December 19 the commander of the Baltic Military District warned Latvians against pushing the army "to extreme measures." Over a million Latvians signed a petition in December 1990 opposing Latvian participation in new Union treaty. The Balts would not initiate a civil war, as Confederate President Jefferson Davis did by ordering the shelling of Fort Sumter. The Estonian parliament on December 18, 1990, called for civil disobedience in the event of a Soviet military crackdown. But even the Balts' patience could break if sufficiently provoked.

The Kremlin in January 1991 ordered in paratroopers to round up draft resisters in the breakaway republics. Lithuania's regional defense force consisted of unarmed volunteers patrolling its borders and trained for civil defense or relief work.[13] Latvia and Estonia had alternative service programs in place and urged draft age recruits to lie low. Georgia, however, had created its own national guard as well as alternative service options. Soviet arsenals had been raided in many parts of the Caucasus.

Military service had become an issue of *kto kovo?* — a criterion for deciding who was in charge, to what regime loyalty was due. Such issues were far more incendiary than economic blockade. Human life — not just material hardship — was at stake. The situation was more inflammatory than in the American South just before the Civil War, because of organized pro-Union fronts in the Baltic, the Ukraine, Moldova (formerly Moldavia), and some other republics.

In early 1991 Gorbachev and others aligned with him opted for the "iron hand." Having accumulated more powers (in March, September, and December 1990) than Brezhnev or even Stalin, Gorbachev had some warrant — on paper — to rule by presidential decree. Like Nicholas II in January 1917, he risked losing his throne and his empire. To avoid this, he acted out Shevardnadze's prediction: presidential dictatorship, backed by the army and the KGB.

Rump Communist organizations still faithful to Moscow became more active in the Baltic in December 1990. In January 1991 they formed Committees of National Salvation, the nuclei of puppet governments as in 1940. The spokesman for Lithuania's Committee of National Salvation asserted that a revolution was under way to regain power from the nationalist, fascist anti-Soviets who had usurped authority in 1990. Soviet troops took over buildings; they maimed or killed peaceful demonstrators; and they tried to intimidate not just the Balts but all captive nations.

The *kto kovo* instinct had not disappeared from the Kremlin. Having announced in a fifteen minute television address that he was giving his Nobel Peace Prize money to charity, Gorbachev reached into a Bolshevik repertory of dirty tricks and naked force. War Communism lived again, proroguing the freely elected Constituent Assembly in January 1918; Lenin's efforts to disclaim responsibility for murdering the Romanovs; his outlawing of fractionalism in 1921. The worst excesses of Stalin were avoided, but Gorbachev used deceptions like those of 1956 against Imre Nagy and of 1968 against Alexander Dubcek. On Gorbachev's watch armed might had already been used against Kazakhs in 1986; Georgians and Uzbeks in 1989; Azeris in 1990. Lithuanians had a foretaste of armed repression in 1990, but in 1991 they and others would get more. Gorbachev tried to disavow responsibility for the blood spilled, but said that the troublemakers received what they deserved. The Lithuanian Committee for National Salvation even warned Boris Yeltsin not to visit Vilnius because the Committee would not be responsible for his safety. Yeltsin, however, signed a mutual assistance protocol with the Baltic republics and asked Russian soldiers not to fire on civilians. He sought a treaty aligning Russia with the Ukraine, Kazakhstan, and Belorussia.

The hardline pointed toward generalized repression or civil war or both. In early 1991 Gorbachev could hope that, as in 1956 or 1968, the West would be too focused on conflicts in the Third World to object mightily to black berets and paratroopers enforcing Soviet imperium. The Kremlin had already won tremendous leverage from its mere acquiescence in UN resolutions against Iraq. Putting up nothing substantial — no men, no money, no matériel — Gorbachev aligned the USSR with the "United Nations" and the United States.

If the Kremlin drew more blood to deny national self-determination to its own peoples, American patience could wear thin. Perhaps President Bush might put up with a Tiananmen Square writ large in the Soviet republics, but Congress would not.

All the ingredients were present for a swing back toward confrontation between the Kremlin and the West. Care packages would not dissuade hardliners in Moscow from asserting their vested interests. It was probably a time for Western policy to demonstrate more firmness than flexibility toward Moscow's ruling circles.

Joint Dilemmas

Sometimes things must get worse before they get better. Europe's unity did not emerge until after two devastating wars and the emergence of a new threat, Stalinism. Soviet-U.S. relations did not improve until Moscow and Washington were sobered by the threat of nuclear war and the high cost of "regional conflict." Perhaps most of the formerly Communist societies of the East will be tempted to experiment with halfway reforms before they grasp the need for more fundamental change. Perhaps civil war will be needed before Moscow and the Kremlin's subject peoples accept the necessity of noninterference in each others' lives and, later, of mutual aid.

But history also allows for more hopeful conclusions. Individuals and groups do not have to wait passively for the wheels of fate to grind them down and then reformat them for another incarnation. Sometimes a paradigm shift or enlightened leadership clears the way for truly new thinking and acting.

Husbanding and enriching our habit — the tasks of ecology and economics — could spark such a paradigm shift. Baltic waters and air have become badly polluted. This is part of a global problem, but one that has become especially acute in East Central Europe and other parts of the former Soviet domain.

Environmental problems helped to spark the anti-Moscow revolutions in the Baltic and other parts of the USSR. Environmental solutions might provide part of the answer to the dilemmas that have unfolded. But there are no simple cures. Economic breakthroughs will be short-lived and incomplete without comprehensive, long-term programs to restore environmental quality. Erstwhile Communist countries have not the means to affect such change without help from the West.

Nor is this an issue only for economists and ecologists. Military installations — factories and bases — are among the leading sources of environmental degradation. They also consume human and material resources that could better be used for less destructive, more productive ends. But to regulate or reduce these military operations requires political action—in Moscow, in the Baltic, and probably in the West. A model for such action—and for what individuals can do to change history—was provided by Kazakh poet Olzhas Suleimenov. In 1989-1990 he formed a "Nevada-Semipalatinsk" movement, backed by International Physicians for Prevention of Nuclear War, to halt all nuclear tests (with their environmental degradation)—not just in the USSR but worldwide. This case showed how local nationalism (the survival of Kazakhs, Polynesians, American Indians, and others) could intertwine with economics, politics, militarism, and racism—locally and globally.[14]

To preserve and foster life, cooperation is needed among all sides, all peoples. Perhaps a widening concern for public health will promote greater awareness of public goods such as clean air and security. Still, it is unrealistic to assume that public goods will suddenly take priority over sectarian and private aspirations. Rather, we must look for ways to make the private and public, the national and transnational more congruent.

The optimal way to promote national and transnational interests lies not in value-claiming but in value-creating strategies, adopted by all concerned parties. Russian/Soviet imperialists, however, continue to demand the familiar values to which they have become accustomed. Intransigent, they defend the status quo. Focusing on their own claims, they are blind to those of others. Environmental issues and the promise of a new world order play second- or even tenth-fiddle to their most urgent concerns.

While Shevardnadze in December 1990 predicted a dictatorship, he also asserted that it would not succeed and that "the future lies with democracy and freedom." History is not ending in the Baltic lands, even though Marxism-Leninism has fallen. To survive and flourish, Balts and their neighbors must create a new beginning. If they are enlightened, diligent, and fortunate, they can develop a history more auspicious than their past. But the Sorcerer still stands at the Gate. The way to Hell remains open.

NOTES

1. Tracing the links between goals and means, a number of valuable works appeared in 1990: Lubomyr Hajda and Mark Beissinger, eds., *The Nationalities Factor in Soviet Politics and Society* (Boulder: Westview); Alexander J. Motyl, *Sovietology, Rationality, Nationality* (New York: Columbia University Press); Uri Ra'anan, ed., *The Soviet Empire: The Challenge of National and Democratic Movements* (Lexington: Lexington Books); Bohdan Nahaylo and Victor Swoboda, eds., *Soviet Disunion: A History of the Nationalities Problem in the USSR* (New York: Free Press); Alfred E. Senn, *Lithuania Awakening—1988* (Berkeley: University of California Press). A new journal appeared in 1990 — *Journal of Soviet Nationalities* — adding to the ongoing analysis published in *Report on the USSR*, *Nationality Papers*, *Journal of Baltic Studies*, and *Problems of Communism*. For the wider context, *Canadian Review of Studies in Nationalism* continued to provide scholarly analyses of developments in all parts of the world include the USSR.

2. Radio Moscow, 19 February 1987, cited in Nahaylo and Swoboda, *Soviet Disunion*, p. 262.

3. *The New York Times*, 18 April 1987.

4. *Pravda*, 13 January 1988.

5. See the last chapters of Beissinger and Hajda, *The Nationalities Factor*, and Motyl, *Sovietology*, and works by Myron Weiner, Samuel P. Huntington, Ted Robert Gurr, Chalmers Johnson, Charles Tilly, and Theda Skocpol cited there.

6. Even in *Kommunist*, a wide variety of Soviet writers sought to restore the authority of Russian "cosmicism," a paean to the traditions of Pan-Slavism and the Russian soul. See Walter C. Clemens, Jr., *Can Russia Change? The USSR Confronts Global Interdependence* (Boston: Unwin Hyman, 1990), pp. 184-97.

7. Feodor Dostoevsky, *Brothers Karamazov*, Bk. 5, chap. 5.

8. Vallimäe had prosecuted two Estonian dissidents who later died in prison—Jüri Kukk and Johannes Hint. Some reports indicated that Vallimae would be employed at the procurator's office in the Dvigatel defense plant, also a center for Intermovement activity. The procurator's office within the defense plant operated independently of the Estonian government and Estonian procurator's office. Officially part of the Soviet Armed Forces, it was called procurator's office no. 9362.

9. See Riina Kionka, "The Lack of Consensus in Estonian Foreign Policy," *Report on the USSR*, 2, 42 (19 October 1990), pp. 30-31.

10. A play on this theme staged in a Vilnius church drew large crowds in 1990. The actors, young people of different nationalities, were sometimes required to role play their opposite numbers.

11. Red Army losses in the Baltic, the Ukraine, Turkestan, and Daghestan after World War II far exceeded those of the partisans, but local resisters could not compete with the manpower reserves of the Union. See Motyl, *Sovietology*, p. 125.

12. See Quentin Peel, "Gorbachev put to the test by an army flexing its muscles" and Leyla Boulton, "Baltics draft evasion reflects general unease" in *Financial Times*, 9 January 1991, p. 5. To round out a picture of a day in the life of the Soviet Union, see also the front page where Peel reported on a Gorbachev deal with the republics to avert a deadlock on spending and Boulton's story that Lithuania's cabinet had resigned over a parliamentary vote against price hikes. The editorial page outlined the limits of Western support for the Gorbachev regime.

13. In Lithuania only 1,000 of 11,000 draft-age men heeded an end-of-1990 deadline for the call-up by the Soviet Armed Forces.

14. Walter C. Clemens, Jr., "Can a Poet Stop Nuclear Testing?" *Christian Science Monitor*, 26 December 1990, p. 19.

INDEX